Slow Cooker: The Best Cookbook Ever

Slow Cooker:

THE BEST COOKBOOK EVER

With More Than 400 Easy-to-Make Recipes

Diane Phillips

PHOTOGRAPHS BY James Baigrie

CHRONICLE BOOKS

SAN FRANCISCO

Library of Congress Cataloging-in-Publication Data available.

ISBN 978-0-8118-6657-6

Manufactured in China

Design and illustration by Rachel Pedersen, LyonStreet Design
Prop styling by Sara Slavin
Food styling by Randy Mon

10 9 8 7 6 5 4 3 2 1

Chronicle Books LLC
680 Second Street
San Francisco, California 94107

www.chroniclebooks.com

To Nancy Deason Boeninghausen; my profile in courage.

TABLE OF CONTENTS

Introduction

Whenever I look at my slow cooker, I think of the lyrics to that old Sinatra standard, "I'm not much to look at, nothing to see," but upon closer inspection the slow cooker is like the girl in high school who everyone said had a nice personality. This decidedly simple piece of equipment isn't the most attractive item ever to grace your kitchen counter but can it cook!

Slow cookers are the answer to that age-old question, "What's for dinner?" You can smile and say, "It's in the slow cooker." Slow cookers do all the work. You simply prep a few ingredients and let the cooker work its magic over the hours. Slow cookers are made for busy people who would love to have dinner made when they come home, but short of having a personal chef or eating take out, that doesn't happen. By prepping a few ingredients in the morning or the night before and then tossing them in the slow cooker when you leave for the day, you can return to a slow-cooked, deeply-flavored dinner ready to serve. The only job left is to prep a side dish or two and wait for the compliments.

Another advantage of the slow cooker is the aroma. This gives you an edge because when you open the door to your home, you are greeted with the aromas of slow-cooked goodness. Just smelling the food as you enter will make the work of the day a distant memory.

Many of my students have complained about the slow-cooker books on the market. There are either too many preparation steps, so that the dish is almost cooked before it goes into the cooker, or the flavors are washed out and bland and the dishes all taste the same. This book is dedicated to finding the balance between streamlined prep and full flavor, using fresh ingredients and a palate of flavors from around the world. So come along for the ride. Take the lid off that slow cooker, and let's find out what that appliance with the great personality really has to offer!

{Getting Started}

WHAT DOES IT DO?

Slow cookers operate on the principle of low and slow heat. The "low" setting on a slow cooker keeps food at 180°F and the "high" setting at 300°F. So think of "high" as a low and slow oven for braises, and "low" as a setting for longer and slower braises. Recipes for the low setting will cook at least 8 hours, about the time most of us would spend outside the home while at work or play. The beauty of the high setting is that a meal can be put into the machine and be ready in about 4 hours, about the time it takes to go to soccer, dance, and music lessons after school. Either way, you've got it made—a delicious meal that cooks itself.

WHY DO I NEED ONE?

CONVENIENCE Slow cookers produce one-pot meals with minimal prep and easy cleanup, and the slow cooker will keep an entrée or side dish warm at the table. Instead of turning on the oven in the heat of summer, you can use the slow cooker as the oven and turn out great dishes.

SAVES TIME Slow cookers offer minimal preparation times and no fussing over the food once it's in the cooker. You can literally set it and forget it.

SAVES MONEY Slow cookers use less electricity than a stovetop or oven, or about as much as a 75-watt lightbulb. Also, a slow cooker can produce delicious, meltingly-tender meals out of less expensive cuts of meat.

NUTRITIONAL BENEFIT Because slow cookers should always remain covered, nutrients that might be lost in an oven or uncovered pot are retained.

WHAT SIZE SHOULD I GET?

If you bought this book, you either have a slow cooker that you aren't using or are tempted to buy one. My advice is to buy what you will need, not what is on sale. There are lots of slow cookers to choose from, and they come in sizes from a 1½-quart pot used to keep dips warm to a 7-quart cooker that will feed an army of hungry soldiers.

If yours is a two-person household but you love to cook and freeze your leftovers, then a 5- to 7-quart cooker would be my recommendation. If you are a two-person household but only want a meal and maybe a lunch leftover that week, then something in the 4- to 5-quart size is probably your best choice.

For families of four or more, I'd recommend anything in the 5- to 7-quart range. Try a few of the recipes in the book, and you may decide you like this type of cooking so much you might get a an additional smaller or larger size. Remember that the slow cooker is a great tool when entertaining because it keeps dishes warm as well as cooks them.

CARE AND FEEDING OF THE SLOW COOKER

Food safety is always important, regardless of the equipment you are using. Make sure to wash your slow cooker insert thoroughly with hot soapy water, rinse it thoroughly, and dry it completely after washing. Keeping the outside clean is also important. The exterior of a slow cooker tends to get spotted with food stains, but cleaning those stains after cooling the slow cooker is a snap. Make sure to read the manufacturer's directions on safe usage, cleaning, and storage of your slow cooker. Make sure to follow these simple rules for food safety:

Cool hot ingredients before adding them to cold ingredients.

Wash cutting boards thoroughly after each use and run them through the dishwasher if possible.

Use separate cutting boards for meats and vegetables.

Wash your hands thoroughly with soap and water before undertaking any type of prep work.

Recently slow-cooker liners have become available. Made of heatproof plastic, these liners are a lifesaver when you are making a dish that is guaranteed to stick to your pan. I also like to line the slow cooker when I am making a casserole. I will partially freeze the insert with the casserole until the casserole will hold its shape, then I remove the liner with the partially frozen casserole, wrap it in plastic wrap or in a zipper-top plastic bag, seal it airtight, and freeze it. When ready to cook, I then defrost the frozen casserole overnight in the refrigerator before putting it into the slow cooker the next morning. See individual recipes for instructions.

Some slow cookers come with a rack, which can be used to keep dishes like custard cups and ramekins from touching the bottom. Racks also help steam food at a constant temperature and are an added feature I find useful.

CONVERTING YOUR RECIPES TO THE SLOW COOKER: If you have a dish that is braised on the stovetop or in the oven that you would like to convert to the slow cooker, follow these general guidelines.

CONVENTIONAL OVEN OR STOVETOP	SLOW COOKER
½ hr	1½ hrs high/3 hrs low
1 hr	3½ hrs high/6 to 7 hrs low
2 hrs	4½ hrs high/9 to 10 hrs low
3 hrs	5½ hrs high/10 to 11 hrs low

Never fill your slow cooker more than two-thirds full. When foods give up their moisture over the long cooking process, you may find your cooker filled to the brim with liquid by the time you are ready to serve. Also make sure that the ingredients fill the slow cooker at least halfway, to ensure even cooking. If you don't have enough ingredients to fill the cooker halfway, your timing will be off.

TIPS AND TECHNIQUES FOR GETTING THE MOST FLAVOR

Chef Jose Andres, one of the world's most renowned chefs, said that his father told him that "every step in cooking is important." Andres expanded his father's advice by saying "every inglorious" step helps you prepare dishes that are flavorful and memorable. So if you think that browning the meat before it goes into the cooker isn't important, remember that every step is important. I have tried where appropriate to streamline the prep so that it is minimal, but if I instruct you to brown, or stir, or lift the top off the cooker, it's because the finished dish benefited from that step.

There are lots of tricks to use with slow cooking. Because the foods themselves give off moisture in the form of liquid, you will need to back off on the amount of liquid that you add to the pot (this is especially true if you are converting a conventional recipe for a slow cooker), and this will concentrate the flavors in the dish. Even beyond that simple rule, there are other tricks that will help coax the maximum flavor from your dishes.

Brown meats, poultry, and other proteins before adding them to the slow cooker. The *fond* (French for "base") are the browned bits left in the bottom of the pan after sautéing, and you can use their essence to heighten the flavor of your slow-cooker meal. Think of browning as the base to build the flavor of your dish and add other ingredients to this pan to extract the most flavor.

Sautéing onions, garlic, dried herbs, and spices before adding them into the cooker gives you a balanced flavor. In many instances, if you add these ingredients to the pot without first sautéing them all you will smell after cooking is raw garlic and onion rather than the sweet perfume that develops when they release their oils during sautéing.

Use dried rather than fresh herbs when slow cooking. I go by the 30-minute rule: if it simmers more than 30 minutes, use a dry herb. One exception to this rule is rosemary, which is woody and stands up to long cooking times. If at the end of the cooking time you wish to refresh a flavor of the finished dish, then certainly add some fresh herbs to it. This actually adds a bit of color, as well as flavor and freshness.

Using soup bases and double-strength broths (such as Campbell's) helps you boost flavors.

Dried mushrooms and dried fruits boost flavors when added to the pot.

Sometimes your slow-cooked meal will have a sauce that tastes bland after hours of simmering with the lid on. Try a few of the following tricks to liven up your dish:

Stir in grated lemon or orange zest; stir in chopped fresh herbs; heat a few tablespoons of olive oil on the stove and sauté a few cloves of chopped garlic until they are softened; but not browned, and add them to the sauce; stir in 2 or 3 dried mushrooms and simmer for another 20 minutes. If all else fails, drain the sauce into a small saucepan and boil the sauce until it is reduced by half. This usually will concentrate the flavor and give you a delicious pan sauce for your meal.

Depending upon your dish, these flavors will give it a boost without too much trouble:

Soy sauce, Asian fish sauce, sun-dried tomatoes, capers, olives, peanut butter, ham, prosciutto, bacon, and the rind from Parmigiano-Reggiano (chop it into pieces and add to soups, stews, and sauces).

Last, remember that this is not (an exact) science. Just as your home oven may cook a bit hotter or colder than the stated temperature in a recipe, so may your slow cooker. The cooking times in this book are approximations. To gauge how your slow cooker will cook, check the instruction manual that came with it, look at recipes similar to the ones in this book, and see what times they suggest. This will give you a good idea of how your slow cooker cooks. Remember that an instant-read thermometer is invaluable for determining if your food is cooked through.

A BAKER'S DOZEN SLOW-COOKER TIPS

1. As a general rule, dishes cooked on low can be cooked safely on high for half the time.

2. Keep a lid on it. Slow cookers can lose 20 to 30 minutes of cooking time when the lid is removed.

3. Don't place frozen foods in a slow cooker; make sure foods are totally defrosted.

4. Never fill a slow cooker more than two-thirds full, and no less than halfway, for optimum performance.

5. Use dried herbs and spices for long, slow simmers. At the end of the cooking time, add fresh herbs to refresh the flavor of the cooked sauce.

6. For best results, remove excess fat from meats and the skin from poultry before putting it into a slow cooker.

7. Always brown ground meats before adding them to a slow cooker.

8. Layer ingredients so those that are the most dense and take the longest to cook (think potatoes) are on the bottom.

9. Cut all the ingredients into uniform pieces so they will cook evenly.

10. Buy a slow cooker for your needs. If there are only two of you at home, the 7-quart model that's on sale will give you beef stew into the next millennium. (A 7-quart model would be terrific for entertaining though, so don't rule it out altogether.) Buy the one you'll need for everyday cooking first.

4-quart serves 2 to 3
5- to 6-quart serves 4 to 6
6- to 7-quart serves 6 to 8

11. Separate pre-prepped meats and veggies into zipper-top plastic bags and refrigerate before using.

12. Browning meats and poultry before adding them to a slow cooker will give a deeper flavor to the finished dish.

13. Don't forget to use your slow cooker as a warmer for gravy, mashed potatoes, or other side dishes on a buffet table for entertaining or holiday meals.

THE LINGO

There are a few terms that will help you when using this book, and I think it's important to read through this section so you know what I'm talking about.

UNTIL TENDER

When something is tender, the tip of a knife inserted into it will go through easily without any resistance.

UNTIL FORK TENDER

Fork tender means that a fork can shred the meat when inserted into the meat.

FIRM TO THE TOUCH

When you push a finger into the meat, it doesn't feel squishy or wobbly.

DOUBLE-STRENGTH BROTH

Also called "condensed," this broth is usually diluted with an equal amount of water. For stronger flavors, don't dilute it.

CHOPPING

One medium onion yields about ½ cup chopped. One large onion yields about ¾ to 1 cup chopped.

FINELY CHOPPED

¼- to ½-inch pieces

COARSELY CHOPPED

1- to 2-inch pieces (the veggies will either retain their shape or be puréed later into a smooth soup or sauce)

WINE

White wines used in cooking should be crisp and dry without a lot of oak flavor; therefore, I don't recommend Chardonnay because the oak flavor will overwhelm any dish. Try for a Pinot Grigio, Pinot Gris, or Sauvignon Blanc. If you are out of white wine, dry vermouth makes an adequate substitute and keeps in your pantry for months.

For most braises, a medium- or full-bodied red wine is what is needed to draw out the flavor of the ingredients. Medium-bodied wines would be Chianti, Pinot Noir, and some wines from the Burgundy region. Full-bodied wines would include Merlot, Syrah (or Shiraz), Zinfandel, Bordeaux (older vintages), Cabernet Sauvignon, and Barolo.

Many people would prefer not to add wine to their braises, and for them I would recommend adding an equal amount of broth to the braise in place of the wine called for in the recipe.

YOU SAY "SLOW COOKER," I SAY "CROCK-POT"

"Crock-Pot" is a trademark owned by the Rival Corporation, who introduced the cooking vessel to America in 1971. If you buy a Rival-brand pot, it's truly a Crock-Pot; but if you buy a different brand, it's a "slow cooker." Either way, they do essentially the same thing: low and slow cooking.

{What's in a Slow-Cooker Pantry?}

REFRIGERATOR AND FREEZER

Unsalted butter

Heavy cream

Cheeses: your favorites here, but Parmigiano-Reggiano, Cheddar, Monterey Jack, and Swiss or Gruyère are staples in my home.

Whole milk

Frozen veggies: keep an assortment, including, white and yellow corn, frozen chopped spinach, petite peas, and artichoke hearts.

Fruits: fresh or frozen berries, mango, and rhubarb.

Fresh citrus: lemons, limes, and oranges. You can't get zest from that plastic lemon at the supermarket.

DRY PANTRY

Vegetable oil: use it to start dishes when you want the sautéed ingredients to have the starring role. Vegetable oils offer a flat palate and are used when you want a neutral base for starting a sauté or braise. Canola and safflower oils are my choices; corn oil can sometimes have too strong a flavor, and peanut oil has a very strong flavor.

Extra-virgin olive oil: if a recipe specifies extra-virgin olive oil, it is to flavor the dish. Extra-virgin olive oil has a strong taste, so use it when its flavor won't overpower the other flavors in a dish. It is also used as a base flavoring, as when sautéing vegetables before adding them to a slow cooker.

Olive oil: I am referring to golden olive oil, which is refined and has a less pronounced flavor than extra-virgin olive oil. It's a good starting point when you don't want the stronger flavor of extra-virgin olive oil.

Canned and dried beans

Canned tomatoes: The Andy Rooney effect, as I call it, has happened to standard cans of tomatoes. (Andy is always complaining

BUYING FROZEN VEGGIES

When you put your hand in the freezer case at the supermarket, make sure that the veggies you buy aren't frozen in a block. They should be somewhat loose in the bag. If they are frozen solid, that means at some point they have defrosted a bit (in transit) and may have some freezer burn. Also make sure to thoroughly defrost vegetables before adding them to the slow cooker, because frozen vegetables will lower the temperature of the cooker, adding to the cooking time and adding extra moisture as well.

when manufacturers change the weight of the can of coffee and other items that he uses.) The range of size in tomato cans is 15 to 18 ounces for small and 28 to 32 ounces for large. Just when you think the manufacturers have it standardized, it changes—again. Since slow cooking is casual in terms of ingredients, I've stated in each recipe the range of ounces for the cans that should be used.

Tomato paste in a tube

Broths: chicken, beef, and vegetable. I'm fond of College Inn and Swanson's, as well as Superior Touch "Better than Bouillon" soup bases that can be reconstituted.

Pastas: assorted small sizes. I prefer imported Italian pastas; they are made from hard Durham wheat and hold up well in the low and slow cooking. Barrilla is a favorite at our house.

Rice: white, wild, jasmine, arborio, and basmati.

Balsamic vinegar

Soy sauce

Sesame oil, toasted Asian

Miso paste

Fish sauce

Rice vinegar

Rice wine (mirin)

Hoisin sauce

Mustards: Dijon, ballpark yellow, and whole grain

Tabasco sauce

Chipotle chiles in adobo

Canned roasted green chiles

Prepared salsa

Dried fruits, such as apricots, figs, golden raisins, and plums.

SPICE PANTRY

Allspice (both whole and ground)

Basil

Bay leaves (Bay leaves can be dangerous when left in a dish for serving because they are stiff and one can choke on them unwittingly. Make sure to remove any bay leaves before serving.)

Cayenne pepper

Celery seeds

Chile powders (ancho, chipotle, and all-purpose chili mix)

Chinese five-spice powder

Cinnamon (ground and whole sticks)

Cloves (whole and ground)

Coriander (ground)

Cumin (ground)

Curry powder

Dill weed

Fennel seeds

Garam masala

Herbes de Provence

Jerk seasoning

Marjoram

Mustard seeds and powdered mustard

Nutmeg (whole for grating fresh)

Oregano (Greek and Mexican—if you can only get one, Greek is my favorite)

Paprika

Peppercorns (black, white, and assorted)

Rosemary

Saffron

Sage

Thyme

Turmeric

Chapter 1
Souper Bowls—Soups and Chilies

The slow cooker is made for slow-cooked soups and chilies. A bowl of comfort can be prepped and then tossed into the slow cooker for a day of slow simmering. Warming bowls of soup can be the balm that soothes your family after a hectic day. Serve the soups in hollowed-out bread bowls or with biscuits, crusty breads, or cornbread, and you'll have your family singing the hallelujah chorus. The best part is that you put the ingredients in the slow cooker in the morning, and at the end of the day you will come home to a pot of delicious homemade soup.

Chilies are also terrific to make in the slow cooker. Sauté the ingredients ahead of time to allow the dried spices to bloom, then stir it all together in the slow cooker to simmer for hours. You'll come home to a pot full of spicy goodness to soothe and satisfy after a long day.

Totally Awesome Veggie Stock

Vegetable stock, rich in flavor, can be frozen for use in soups, stews, or vegetarian chilies. A slow cooker takes the mundane task of making stock and makes it simple by allowing you to pile everything into the cooker and let it slowly simmer for hours. You just need to strain the goodness into refrigerator or freezer containers for later use.

¼ cup olive oil

2 large sweet onions, such as Vidalia, coarsely chopped

4 large carrots, cut into 1-inch chunks

4 stalks celery with leaves, cut into 2-inch pieces

4 medium parsnips, cut into 1-inch chunks

8 ounces cremini mushrooms, quartered

2 tablespoons tomato paste

1 bunch Swiss chard, cut into 1-inch pieces (about 3 cups)

2 teaspoons dried thyme

1 bay leaf

2 teaspoons salt

½ teaspoon whole black peppercorns

2 cups water

put all the ingredients into the insert of a 5- to 7-quart slow cooker and toss to combine. Cover and cook on high for 5 hours or on low for 8 to 10 hours.

remove the cover and take out the large pieces of vegetables with a slotted spoon. Strain the stock through a fine-mesh sieve and discard the solids.

skim off any fat from the top of the stock. Refrigerate for up to 5 days or freeze for up to 6 months.

makes about **8** cups

Chicken Stock, the Slow-Cooker Method

Meaty chicken thighs make a terrific chicken stock, and this stock is gold in your freezer for making sauces, soups, or casseroles. Forget that can or box of broth, even though they can save you in a pinch. This is homemade goodness you can't buy and it's so simple to make. The best news is that you don't have to watch it all day!

3 pounds chicken, skin removed

2 teaspoons salt

1 teaspoon freshly ground black pepper

3 tablespoons olive oil

2 large sweet onions, such as Vidalia, coarsely chopped

½ cup dry white wine

3 cups water

4 large carrots, peeled and cut into 2-inch chunks

4 stalks celery with some leaves, cut into 2-inch lengths

2 teaspoons dried thyme

1 teaspoon dried sage, crumbled

sprinkle the chicken evenly with the salt and pepper. Heat the oil in a large skillet over high heat. Add the chicken and brown evenly on all sides.

transfer the chicken to the insert of a 5- to 7-quart slow cooker. Add the onions to the same skillet over medium-high heat and sauté until they begin to soften, about 3 minutes.

transfer the onions to the slow-cooker insert. Deglaze the pan with the wine and bring the mixture to a boil. Add the water and scrape up any browned bits from the bottom of the pan.

transfer the contents of the skillet to the slow-cooker insert. Add the carrots, celery, thyme, and sage to the insert. Cover and cook on high for 4 to 5 hours or on low for 8 to 10 hours.

remove the chicken from the slow-cooker insert (it should be falling off the bone) with a slotted spoon and transfer to a plate or cutting board. Strain the stock through a fine-mesh sieve and discard any solids. Skim off any fat from the stock and store in refrigerator or freezer containers.

remove the chicken meat from the bones, discarding the bones and any gristle or tendons. The meat can be used in soups, casseroles, or salads. Store the meat in the refrigerator for up to 2 days or in the freezer for up to 1 month.

makes about **6** cups

slow-cooker savvy
Skin off please! When cooking chicken in the slow cooker, the skin acts as a tourniquet and buckles around the meat. It is also very unappetizing and adds to the fat that you need to skim off any stock or broth. It is best to remove chicken skin before cooking.

Crocked Beef Stock

Many students ask about the difference between stock and broth. The easiest way to differentiate between stock and broth is that stock is made from browning the elements before simmering them for a long period of time to reduce and concentrate the flavors. Broth is made by simmering the elements for a shorter period of time, without browning the ingredients before adding the liquid. The resulting broth is not as deeply colored or as full-flavored as stock. Beef stock in the slow cooker is a two-step process. First, the bones and vegetables are slathered with a paste, then browned in a hot oven. The contents of the roasting pan is then added to the slow cooker along with more vegetables, herbs, and liquid to simmer all day. Once strained, this deeply colored and flavorful beef stock can be used in any preparation, from reduction sauces to old-fashioned soups. Once again, the slow cooker saves you the hassle of watching and stirring. Just set it and forget it.

¼ cup tomato paste

2 teaspoons sugar

2 teaspoons salt

1 teaspoon freshly ground black pepper

4 cloves garlic, minced

2 teaspoons dried thyme

1 teaspoon dried sage

3 large sweet onions, coarsely chopped

4 large carrots, coarsely chopped

1½ pounds beef stew meat, cut into 1-inch pieces

2 pounds meaty beef bones, sawed in a few pieces (your butcher can do this for you)

4 cups water

preheat the oven to 425°F. Line a baking sheet with a silicone baking liner or aluminum foil.

stir together the tomato paste, sugar, salt, pepper, garlic, thyme, and sage in a large mixing bowl. Put the vegetables, meat, and bones in the bowl and rub the paste over them until they are coated.

spread the mixture out on the baking sheet and bake for 30 minutes, turning the pieces once during the cooking process. Transfer the mixture with any liquid to the insert of a 5- to 7-quart slow cooker. Add the water and stir to blend.

cover and cook on high for 4 to 5 hours or on low for 8 to 10 hours. Remove the solids from the stock, then strain the stock through a fine-mesh sieve into a bowl. Allow the stock to cool, and skim off the fat from the surface.

refrigerate the stock for 3 days or freeze for up to 8 weeks. The meat from the stock may be frozen separately and used in soups, stews, or chilies.

makes about **6** cups

Turkey Carcass Broth

I teach a lot of Thanksgiving classes. At the end of each class, after the students have tasted the Thanksgiving dinner and we are looking at the naked turkey carcass, I tell my pupils that if they can't stand to make turkey soup after the Thanksgiving meal, to put the carcass in a two-gallon zipper-top plastic bag and freeze it. When they are ready to make turkey soup, they can just defrost it overnight in the refrigerator and put it in the slow cooker the next day. Once you have turkey stock in the freezer, you can make soup, casseroles, and all manner of sauces. This same formula can be used for chicken as well, but if you are only using one chicken, cut the ingredients in half.

1 turkey carcass, broken up into pieces

2 medium onions, coarsely chopped

3 medium carrots, coarsely chopped

3 medium stalks celery with leaves, coarsely chopped

8 cups chicken stock

2 teaspoons dried thyme

1 teaspoon dried sage leaves

1 bay leaf

4 whole black peppercorns

Salt

put all the ingredients except the salt in the insert of a 5- to 7-quart slow cooker. Cover and cook on high for 4 to 5 hours or on low for 8 to 10 hours.

season with salt. Strain the broth through a colander to remove the large solids, then strain again through a fine-mesh sieve.

cool the stock to room temperature, then store in airtight containers in the refrigerator for up to 5 days or in the freezer for up to 6 months.

makes about **8** cups

slow-cooker savvy
I generally don't save the meat from this stock. It doesn't freeze well, and since it's now been cooked twice, it's pretty soft and not very appetizing.

Minestrone with Parmigiano-Reggiano

The word *minestrone* in Italian means "without stock," so it is essentially a vegetarian soup that uses the juices of the vegetables as its stock. This soup is terrific in the slow cooker. Even though there doesn't seem to be enough liquid for the soup at first glance, the vegetables will add a lot of liquid to the pot as they cook. For a strictly vegan soup, omit the cheese rind.

2 tablespoons extra-virgin olive oil

3 cloves garlic, minced

1 cup coarsely chopped sweet onion

1 cup coarsely chopped carrots

1 cup coarsely chopped celery

1 tablespoon finely chopped fresh rosemary

One 14- to 15-ounce can plum tomatoes, with their juice

¼ cup dry white wine

2 medium zucchini, cut into ½ inch rounds

One 14- to 15-ounce can small white beans, drained and rinsed

1 head escarole or Savoy cabbage, cut into small pieces

8 ounces green beans, ends snipped, cut into 1-inch pieces

1 medium head cauliflower, cut into florets

Rind from Parmigiano-Reggiano cheese, cut into ½-inch pieces, plus ½ to 1 cup finely grated Parmigiano-Reggiano cheese for garnishing

2 cups vegetable broth

1 teaspoon salt

½ teaspoon freshly ground black pepper

8 ounces cooked small pasta (shells, ditalini, or other short tubular pasta)

heat the oil in a large skillet over medium-high heat. Add the garlic, onion, carrots, celery, and rosemary and sauté until the vegetables begin to soften, 4 to 5 minutes.

add the tomatoes and wine and allow some of the liquid to evaporate in the pan.

transfer the contents of the skillet to the insert of a 5- to 7-quart slow cooker. Add the zucchini, white beans, cabbage, green beans, cauliflower, Parmigiano-Reggiano rind, broth, salt, and pepper.

cover the slow cooker and cook on high for 3 to 4 hours or on low for 6 to 8 hours.

stir in the cooked pasta at the end of the cooking time, cover, and set on warm until ready to serve.

serve the soup garnished with the grated Parmigiano-Reggiano.

serves **8**

Shiitake Mushroom Miso Soup

Miso soup is not only good for you but also terrific for a warm-up on a cold day. This soup is enriched with bok choy and shiitake mushrooms, making it a hearty vegetable soup to serve anytime.

2 tablespoons vegetable oil

1 clove garlic, minced

1 teaspoon freshly grated ginger

8 ounces shiitake mushrooms, stems removed, caps sliced

4 small baby bok choy, stem ends removed and chopped into ½-inch pieces (see savvy)

¼ cup light miso paste (see savvy)

6 cups vegetable or chicken broth

2 teaspoons soy sauce

6 green onions, finely chopped using the white and tender green parts

1 pound firm tofu, drained and cut into ½-inch cubes

heat the oil in a medium skillet over medium-high heat.

add the garlic and ginger and sauté, about 1 minute until fragrant. Add the mushrooms and toss to combine.

transfer the contents of the skillet to the insert of a 5-quart slow cooker and add the bok choy. Stir in the miso paste, broth, and soy sauce.

cover the slow cooker and cook on high for 2½ to 3 hours.

remove the cover and stir in the green onions and tofu.

serve the soup from the slow cooker.

Serves **6–8**

bok choy savvy
If bok choy is very expensive, as it can be, chopped napa cabbage may be substituted. You should have about 2 cups.

miso savvy
Miso is found in the Asian section of your supermarket.

Triple Mushroom Soup

Three different types of mushrooms slow cook in a bacon-and-sage broth to deliver a delicious soup to serve as a main course or starter. Make sure to check the expiration date on your dried mushrooms; if they are old, chances are they will take away from the flavor of the soup.

8 strips bacon, cut into ½-inch dice

1 large onion, finely chopped

1 teaspoon dried sage leaves, crushed in the palm of your hand

1 pound cremini mushrooms, sliced

1 pound shiitake mushrooms, stems removed, caps sliced

1 ounce dried porcini mushrooms

¼ cup soy sauce

3 cups chicken broth

1 cup heavy cream

½ cup snipped fresh chives for garnishing

sauté the bacon in a large skillet over medium heat until crisp and remove it from the pan to drain.

add the onion and sage to the pan and sauté until the onion is softened. Add the cremini and shiitake mushrooms and toss until the mixture is combined.

transfer the contents of the skillet to the insert of a 5- to 7-quart slow cooker. Add the porcini mushrooms, soy sauce, broth, and bacon.

cover and cook on high for 3 hours or on low for 5 to 6 hours. At the end of the cooking time, add the cream and stir to combine.

serve the soup garnished with the chives.

serves **8**

slow-cooker savvy
If you would like a smooth soup, purée with an immersion blender.

Creamy Onion Soup

When I was a teenager, I watched Julia Child prepare French onion soup on her TV program, and I was never the same. Although I grew up in an Italian home where there was never store-bought bread or canned soup, Julia brought French food into my life and I have been hooked ever since. Chances are the French onion soup you have had is a poor imitation of the real McCoy. This slow-cooker method delivers a creamier soup with lots of onions that melt during the cooking process. I recommend using a soup base or demi-glace to get full flavor, but you can still use beef broth if you prefer.

½ cup (1 stick) unsalted butter

2 tablespoons olive oil

5 large sweet onions, such as Vidalia, thinly sliced

2 tablespoons sugar

1 tablespoons dried thyme

1 teaspoon salt

½ teaspoon freshly ground black pepper

1 bay leaf

¼ cup white wine (see savvy)

5 cups beef stock (see savvy)

1½ cups finely shredded Gruyère cheese for garnishing

turn a 5- to 7-quart slow cooker on high, add the butter and oil to the insert, cover until the butter is melted.

remove the cover and add the onions, sugar, thyme, salt, pepper, and bay leaf. Stir the onions until they are coated with the butter and seasonings.

cover and cook on high for 7 to 8 hours, until they are caramelized to a deep golden brown.

remove the cover and add the wine and beef stock. Cover and cook the soup on high for an additional 30 minutes or on low for an additional 1 hour.

remove the bay leaf before serving and garnish each serving with a sprinkling of Gruyère cheese.

serves **8**

white wine savvy
One of Julia's tricks was to use white vermouth if you don't have any leftover white wine. It makes a good substitute and keeps in the pantry for months.

beef stock savvy
I recommend Superior Touch "Better than Bouillon" brand soup base (available in supermarkets or at www.superiortouch.com) or reconstituted "More than Gourmet" brand Glace de Viande Gold, which is a classic reduced brown stock (available in gourmet stores or at www.morethangourmet.com.)

Butternut Squash Soup

Butternut squash, that rather shapely but not-too-attractive squash, becomes the star of the slow cooker in this delicious soup. The slow cooker takes the rock-hard squash and cooks it to almost a purée. If you would like a smoother soup, a run around the cooker with your immersion blender is all that it takes. Try garnishing this soup with one of your favorites: lump crabmeat, crumbled goat cheese, or croutons. It can be served immediately, or cooled and refrigerated for up to 4 days, or frozen for up to 6 weeks.

4 tablespoons (½ stick) unsalted butter

1 cup finely chopped sweet onion

½ cup finely chopped carrot

½ cup finely chopped celery

2 teaspoons dried thyme

8 cups 1-inch pieces peeled and seeded butternut squash

4 cups chicken or vegetable broth

Salt and freshly ground black pepper

melt the butter in a large skillet over medium-high heat. Add the onion, carrot, celery, and thyme and sauté until the vegetables are softened, 3 to 4 minutes.

transfer the contents of the skillet to the insert of a 5- to 7-quart slow cooker. Add the squash and broth, and season with salt and pepper.

cover the slow cooker and cook on high for 3 hours or on low for 6 hours. At the end of the cooking time, stir the soup and season with salt and pepper. If you would like to purée the soup, use an immersion blender, or cool the soup and purée it in a blender.

serve warm from the cooker.

serves **8**

Ginger Pear Pumpkin Soup

Pumpkin isn't just for Halloween and shouldn't be reserved for pies. This delicious soup spiked with ground ginger will be a welcome warm-up on a cool evening when served with some crusty bread. The soup can be frozen for up to two months.

4 tablespoons (½ stick) unsalted butter

½ cup finely chopped sweet onion

½ cup finely chopped celery

½ cup finely chopped carrot

2 medium red pears, peeled, cored, and finely chopped

½ teaspoon ground ginger

Two 15-ounce cans pumpkin purée (see savvy)

3 cups chicken broth

Salt and freshly ground black pepper

1 cup heavy cream

melt the butter in a medium skillet over medium-high heat. Add the onion, celery, carrot, pears, and ginger and sauté until the vegetables begin to soften, about 3 minutes. Transfer the contents of the skillet to the insert of a 5- to 7-quart slow cooker.

stir in the pumpkin and broth. Cover and cook on high for 3 hours or on low for 5 to 6 hours.

season with salt and pepper. Stir in the cream, cover, and leave on warm for 30 minutes before serving.

serves **8**

pumpkin savvy
Pumpkin purée sold in cans is terrific for any preparation that calls for pumpkin. Cooking your own pumpkin can be a messy and frustrating process that sometimes ends with a watery mess. Make sure to buy pumpkin purée and not pumpkin pie filling.

Roasted Tomato Soup with Spinach Pesto

Roasting tomatoes in the slow cooker intensifies their flavor and gives them a whole new personality. Flavored with aromatic herbs and garlic and simmered with chicken broth, ricotta, and Parmigiano cheese, this soup is sure to please even the fussiest eaters. If that isn't enough, a dollop of garlicky spinach pesto tops it all off! This soup is another candidate for that grown-up grilled cheese sandwich, the panini, or accompanied with bruschetta.

SOUP

Two 28-ounce cans peeled whole tomatoes, drained

½ cup extra-virgin olive oil

2 teaspoons dried basil

1 teaspoon dried marjoram

½ cup chopped red onion

6 cloves garlic, coarsely chopped

1½ teaspoons salt

Pinch red pepper flakes

½ cup vegetable or chicken broth

1 cup whole-milk ricotta cheese

1½ cups heavy cream

½ cup freshly grated Parmigiano-Reggiano

Spinach Pesto (recipe follows)

SPINACH PESTO

Two 10-ounce packages baby spinach

½ cup pine nuts

2 cloves garlic, peeled

Grated zest of 1 lemon

½ cup packed fresh basil leaves

½ cup freshly grated Parmesan cheese

⅔ cup olive oil

Salt and freshly ground black pepper

combine the tomatoes, olive oil, basil, marjoram, onion, garlic, salt, pepper flakes, and broth in the insert of a 5- to 7-quart slow cooker.

cover the slow cooker and cook on low for 6 hours, until the tomatoes and onion are softened. Using an immersion blender, purée the soup, or cool the soup and purée it in a blender or food processor. Whisk in the ricotta, cream, and Parmigiano-Reggiano.

cover the cooker and turn it to warm. Allow the soup to come to serving temperature (the retained heat in the cooker will heat the cheese and cream, without it separating).

serve the soup garnished with the spinach pesto.

serves **8**

Spinach pesto retains its bright green color and adds zip and color to roasted tomato soup, but it can also be tossed with pasta or as a sauce for pasta or potato salad.

put the spinach, pine nuts, garlic, lemon zest, basil, and Parmesan cheese in the work bowl of a food processor or a blender. Pulse the food processor on and off until the leaves are chopped and the mixture is chunky. With the machine running, slowly pour in the oil and process until the mixture comes together.

season with salt and pepper. Store the pesto, covered, in the refrigerator for up to 1 week or in the freezer for up to 6 weeks.

makes about **3** cups

Creamy Broccoli Soup

This beautifully colored soup is open to a lot of variations, and the secret to keeping the broccoli bright green is the addition of baking soda to the pot. Try all the variations; they are a great way to serve your family vegetables.

2 tablespoons unsalted butter

1 medium onion, finely chopped

3 medium carrots, cut into ½-inch dice

2 bunches broccoli (about 1½ pounds), stems trimmed, cut into florets

1 teaspoon baking soda

3 cups chicken or vegetable broth

Salt and freshly ground black pepper

1 cup heavy cream (to lower the fat, use whole milk, or add more broth)

turn a 5- to 7-quart slow cooker on high, add the butter to the insert, and cover until the butter is melted. Add the onion, carrots, and broccoli and toss the vegetables in the butter. Dissolve the baking soda in the broth and add to the vegetables.

cook on high for 2½ to 3 hours or on low for 5 to 6 hours. Season with salt and pepper and stir in the cream. Turn off the slow cooker and let the soup rest for 15 minutes to come to serving temperature.

serves **6–8**

CURRIED BROCCOLI SOUP

add 2 teaspoons curry powder to the vegetables and butter before adding the broth. Proceed as directed.

CHEESY BROCCOLI SOUP

with the heavy cream, add 2 cups finely shredded sharp or mild Cheddar cheese.

BROCCOFLOWER SOUP

use 2 medium heads broccoflower in place of the broccoli.

Creamy Loaded Baked-Potato Soup

Whenever I order baked-potato soup in a restaurant, I am invariably disappointed. Usually it tastes of flour and has no real flavor—just a bland soup base mixed with some sorry potatoes. This smooth soup is made flavorful by cooking the potatoes in chicken broth, then embellishing it with green onions, bacon, and sharp Cheddar. This soup is a whole meal and can be the centerpiece for a casual weekend dinner with friends. Make sure to serve extra cheese, bacon, onions, and sour cream on the side.

4 tablespoons (½ stick) unsalted butter

2 medium leeks, finely chopped, using the white and some of the tender green parts

4 large russet potatoes, peeled and cut into ½-inch dice (see savvy)

4 cups chicken broth

1 cup whole milk

2 cups finely shredded sharp Cheddar cheese

6 green onions, finely chopped, using the white and some of the tender green parts

8 strips bacon, cooked crisp, drained, and crumbled

Salt and freshly ground black pepper

1 cup sour cream for garnishing

heat the butter in a large skillet over medium-high heat. Add the leeks and sauté until softened, 2 to 3 minutes. Transfer the leeks to the insert of a 5- to 7-quart slow cooker and add the potatoes and broth. Cover the slow cooker and cook on high for 3 hours or on low for 5 to 6 hours, until the potatoes are tender. Using an immersion blender, purée the soup, or cool the soup and purée it in a blender.

reduce the heat to low and add the milk, cheese, green onions, and bacon. Cover the slow cooker and cook for an additional 1 hour. Season with salt and pepper.

serve the soup garnished with a dollop of sour cream.

serves **8–10**

potato savvy
I use russet (baking) potatoes because they will be puréed at the end of the cooking time, giving a rich creamy texture to the soup. If you prefer a chunky soup, use 6 medium red or Yukon gold potatoes.

cooking savvy
Always cool mixtures before puréeing in a food processor or blender, so that if they erupt all over you, you won't get burned.

serving savvy
Serving soup in hollowed-out bread bowls is a nice way to serve a crowd. Cut the top off a bread round and hollow out the inside, using a serrated knife, leaving about ¾-inch all the way around the inside. I usually brush the inside with butter or olive oil and bake the bread at 350°F for about 10 minutes. This helps to crisp up the bread.

Julia's Potato and Leek Soup

This riff on Julia Child's traditional vichyssoise, a cold potato and leek soup, is so simple to make in the slow cooker, and the best news is, it can be made and then chilled, kept waiting for your next soirée. If you prefer to serve the soup warm, it's terrific topped with crème fraîche and lump crabmeat.

4 tablespoons (½ stick) unsalted butter

4 leeks, finely chopped, using the white and a bit of the tender green parts

4 large russet potatoes, peeled and cut into 1-inch chunks

3 cups chicken broth

Salt and freshly ground black pepper

1 cup heavy cream

½ cup snipped fresh chives for garnishing

turn a 5- to 7-quart slow cooker on high, add the butter to the insert, and cover until the butter is melted. Add the leeks and toss with the butter. Add the potatoes and broth. Cover the slow cooker and cook the soup on high for 3 hours or on low for 5 to 6 hours, until the potatoes are tender.

purée the soup with an immersion blender, or mash with a potato masher. Season with salt and pepper. Stir in the cream and turn off the slow cooker. Cool the soup, then refrigerate until chilled.

serve the soup in chilled bowls and garnish with the chives.

serves 8–10

VARIATION

instead of chives, finely chopped smoked salmon makes a lovely garnish, as does lump crabmeat or finely chopped cooked shrimp or lobster.

White Bean and Rosemary Soup

Creamy, tender white beans, chunks of spicy Capicola or other ham, and rosemary combine for a hearty soup that is terrific to serve for lunch or as part of a soup-and-sandwich supper. Try serving this soup with grown-up grilled cheese—panini made with fontina, provolone, and fresh mozzarella topped with pesto. Now that's a great meal!

3 tablespoons extra-virgin olive oil

4 ounces of spicy Italian ham or Capicola, cut into ½-inch dice

1 medium onion, finely chopped

2 cloves garlic, minced

3 stalks celery with leaves, finely chopped

3 medium carrots, finely chopped

2 teaspoons finely minced fresh rosemary

One 14- to 15-ounce can plum tomatoes, crushed and drained

2 cups dried beans, picked over for stones, soaked (see quick-soak method, page 36), or two 14- to 15-ounce cans small white beans, drained and rinsed

6 cups chicken or vegetable broth

Salt and freshly ground black pepper

heat the oil in a skillet over medium-high heat.

add the ham and sauté until it begins to get crisp, about 3 minutes. Add the onion, garlic, celery, carrots, and rosemary and sauté until the vegetables begin to soften, about 3 minutes. Add the tomatoes and stir to combine.

transfer the contents of the skillet to the insert of a 5- to 7-quart slow cooker. Stir in the beans and the broth.

cover the slow cooker and cook on low for 8 to 9 hours, until the beans are tender. Season with salt and pepper before serving.

serves **8**

Nona's Umbrian Lentil Soup

I remember this soup from childhood, with its warm inviting aroma and stick-to-your-ribs quality. One bowl of this soup and I could return to playing with my friends filled with energy! I like to use brown lentils in this soup because they are easy to find and make a very nice soup. My grandmother's roots in Umbria account for the large amount of celery in this dish. In Umbria, they grow a lot of celery, and the most prized is the *sedano nero*, or black celery. It's not black at all but has a milky white base from being covered while growing, and very dark, almost black, green leaves and stalks. The celery in this dish not only adds flavor but also texture to our soup. *Buon appetito!*

3 tablespoons extra-virgin olive oil

1 large onion, coarsely chopped

2 cloves garlic, minced

3 medium carrots, coarsely chopped

6 stalks celery with leaves, coarsely chopped

2 teaspoons dried whole sage leaves or 2 whole fresh sage leaves, finely chopped

One 14- to 15-ounce can chopped plum tomatoes, drained

2 cups brown lentils

6 cups vegetable broth

Salt and freshly ground black pepper

heat the oil in a large skillet over medium-high heat. Add the onion, garlic, carrots, celery, and sage leaves and sauté until the garlic and onion are fragrant, 3 to 4 minutes.

add the tomatoes and cook for 2 to 3 minutes to evaporate some of the juices. Transfer the contents of the skillet to the insert of a 5- to 7-quart slow cooker.

stir in the lentils and broth. Cover the cooker and cook on high for 4 hours or on low for 7 to 8 hours, until the lentils are tender. Check the soup at around 3 or 6 hours to make sure there is enough broth and the soup isn't sticking to the pan; add more broth if it is sticking.

season with salt and pepper before serving.

serves 6—8

Grandma's Che Che Bean Soup

My Italian *nona*, Aleandra, used to make this soup with garbanzo beans. As a kid I found it warm, filling, and a delight to the senses. The aroma of its inviting flavors of rosemary, garlic, and tomato mingled with garbanzo beans, vegetables, and pasta were more than I could resist. The slow cooker does a great job with this soup and will keep it warm for those who come in from the cold at different times. The vegetables can go directly into the slow cooker, but sautéing them first gives the soup a much richer flavor.

3 tablespoons olive oil

1 large sweet onion, such as Vidalia, finely chopped

3 stalks celery, finely chopped

2 carrots, finely chopped

3 cloves garlic, finely chopped

2 tablespoons finely chopped fresh rosemary

One 14- to 15-ounce can crushed tomatoes, with their juice

4 cups vegetable broth

Two 14- to 15-ounce cans garbanzo beans, drained and rinsed

2 cups cooked small pasta, such as ditalini or tubetti

½ cup freshly grated Pecorino-Romano cheese for garnishing

heat the oil in a skillet over medium-high heat. Add the onion, celery, carrots, garlic, and rosemary and sauté until the vegetables begin to soften and are fragrant, 3 to 4 minutes.

add the tomatoes and sauté for another minute to incorporate. Transfer the contents of the skillet to the insert of a 5- to 7-quart slow cooker and add the broth and garbanzo beans.

cover and cook on low for 6 hours or on high for 3 hours. Remove the cover, stir in the pasta, and cook for an additional 20 minutes on low or 10 minutes on high.

serve the soup garnished with the cheese.

serves **8**

cheese savvy
If you have rind from Parmigiano-Reggiano cheese, add it to this soup to simmer all day; it becomes soft and chewy and rounds out the flavor of your soup.

Caribbean Black Bean Soup

A soup with tropical influences that will warm you with its spicy flavors, serving black bean soup is also a terrific way to get your family to eat legumes. We like to serve this soup over steamed rice with cornbread on the side.

Quick-soak method for beans: Dried beans are typically soaked overnight in cold water, but you can jump-start them by quick soaking. This method works well if you want to use any type of dried beans in your preparations. Cover dried beans with cold water in a large saucepan. Bring to a boil and cook, uncovered, over medium heat for 2 minutes. Remove from the heat, cover the pan, and let the beans soak for 1 hour. Drain the beans and use in any preparation. The beans may be kept refrigerated in an airtight container for up to 3 days. Freeze the cooked beans for up to 2 months.

2 tablespoons vegetable oil

2 large white onions, finely chopped

4 cloves garlic, minced

2 jalapeño peppers, seeded and finely chopped

½ teaspoon ground allspice

1 teaspoon ground cumin

4 cups presoaked black beans (see savvy)

1 bay leaf

4 cups vegetable or chicken broth

Salt and freshly ground black pepper

heat the oil in large skillet over medium-high heat.

add the onions, garlic, jalapeños, allspice, and cumin and sauté until the onion are softened.

transfer the contents of the skillet to the insert of a 5-to 7-quart slow cooker and add the beans, bay leaf, and broth.

cover the slow cooker and cook on high for 3 hours or on low for 6 hours. Season with salt and pepper. Remove the bay leaf before serving.

Serves **8–10**

bean savvy
Although I prefer to soak the beans overnight for this soup, you may substitute four 14- to 15-ounce cans black beans (drained and rinsed), and cook on low for 4 hours instead of the 6 called for.

Monterey Bay Bean Soup

This is a favorite soup with my students. It goes together in 5 minutes, and at the end of the day you have a hearty vegetarian main course. Don't let the chiles scare you away; they are there for flavor and not heat!

⅓ cup vegetable oil

1 large onion, finely chopped

1 clove garlic, minced

4 Anaheim chiles, seeded and chopped

1½ teaspoons chili powder

One 14- to 15-ounce can chopped tomatoes, drained

Two 14- to 15-ounce cans pinto beans, drained and rinsed

6 cups chicken broth

2 cups cooked chorizo sausage, crumbled (optional)

Salt and freshly ground black pepper

2 cups broken fried tortilla strips

½ cup shredded mild Cheddar or Monterey Jack cheese

½ cup sour cream for garnishing

4 green onions, chopped, using the white and tender green parts for garnishing

½ cup finely minced fresh cilantro for garnishing

heat the oil in a large skillet over medium heat. Add the onion, garlic, and chiles and sauté until the vegetables are softened, about 5 minutes. Stir in the chili powder and cook, stirring, for about 1 minute, until fragrant.

transfer the contents of the skillet to the insert of a 5- to 7-quart slow cooker. Add the tomatoes, beans, broth, and sausage (if using).

cover the slow cooker and cook the soup on high for 3 to 4 hours or on low for 7 to 8 hours.

season with salt and pepper. Add the tortilla strips to the soup, cover, and let stand for 10 minutes, until the strips just begin to soften.

divide the cheese among 8 bowls and ladle the soup over. Garnish each serving with a dollop of sour cream, chopped green onion, and minced cilantro.

serves **8**

Greens 'n' Beans Soup

This simple vegetable soup gets its rich flavor from escarole, creamy white beans, and the rind from Parmigiano-Reggiano cheese. Although you can put everything directly into the slow cooker, I recommend the sauté at the beginning to develop the flavors of the onion and garlic.

2 tablespoons extra-virgin olive oil

1 large sweet onion, coarsely chopped

3 stalks celery, coarsely chopped

2 carrots, coarsely chopped

2 cloves garlic, minced

2 heads escarole, tough outer leaves removed, cut into 1-inch pieces (see savvy)

2 cups small white beans, picked over for stones, soaked (see quick-soak method, page 36), or two 15-ounce cans small white beans, drained and rinsed (see savvy)

4 cups vegetable or chicken broth

¼ cup chopped rind from Parmigiano-Reggiano, plus ½ cup freshly grated Parmigiano-Reggiano cheese for garnishing (optional)

Freshly ground black pepper

Salt

heat the oil in a skillet over medium-high heat. Add the onion, celery, and carrots and sauté until the onion begins to soften. Add the garlic and continue to cook for about 2 minutes, until the vegetables are fragrant but not soft.

transfer the contents of the skillet to the insert of a 5- to 7-quart slow cooker. Top the vegetables with the escarole, stir in the beans, and pour the broth over the escarole. Add the cheese rind (if using) and ½ teaspoon of pepper and stir to combine.

cover the slow cooker and cook on low for 4 hours or on high for 2 hours. Remove the cover and season with salt and pepper.

serve the soup garnished with freshly grated Parmigiano-Reggiano, if desired.

serves 8

bean savvy
If you are in a hurry and don't have time to soak the beans overnight, canned beans will work. Make sure to rinse and drain them in a sieve before adding them to the cooker.

escarole savvy
If escarole is pricey or not available, Swiss chard or Savoy cabbage are nice replacements. Chop the chard, including the stems, which will become tender during the long cooking process.

slow-cooker addition
Add 2 cups cooked chicken with the other ingredients and proceed as directed.

Many Bean Soup

This hearty soup requires soaking the beans overnight and then putting everything in the slow cooker for the day. It's a colorful, flavorful, and healthful choice for dinner, and your slow cooker makes it a no-brainer for a day when you want to come home to a bowl of comfort food. A loaf of crusty bread or freshly baked cornbread makes the perfect accompaniment.

The choice of beans is up to you; it's really more about color, texture, and the beans that you like. (You can double up on one type if that appeals.) I like to buy my beans at health food stores where they have bulk-food bins, so that I only buy what I need. Many markets sell a blend of beans for this soup, so you can keep a bag of beans in your pantry just in case of a soup emergency!

¼ cup dried red beans

¼ cup dried small white beans

¼ cup dried pinto beans

¼ cup dried kidney beans

¼ cup dried cranberry beans

¼ cup dried baby lima beans

¼ cup dried black-eyed peas

¼ cup dried green split peas

¼ cup dried yellow split peas

¼ cup dried red lentils

¼ cup dried brown lentils

1 large onion, finely chopped

3 medium carrots, chopped

3 stalks celery, finely chopped

2 teaspoons dried thyme

1 bay leaf

One 15-ounce can chopped plum tomatoes, with their juice

1 smoked ham hock or ham bone

8 cups chicken or vegetable broth

Salt and freshly ground black pepper

soak the red, white, pinto, kidney, cranberry, lima beans, and black-eyed peas overnight in water to cover. Drain and rinse thoroughly.

add the soaked beans, split peas, and lentils to the insert of a 5- to 7-quart slow cooker. Add the remaining ingredients up through the broth and stir to combine.

cook on low for 8 to 10 hours, until the beans are tender and the ham is falling off the bone.

remove the ham hock or bone from the soup, chop any meat, removing the fat, and return the meat to the slow-cooker.

season with salt and pepper. Remove the bay leaf before serving.

serves 8–10

slow-cooker savvy
When I have ham for a holiday dinner, I will generally freeze the bone after we have cleaned off most of the meat. Then when I want to make soup, I'll defrost it and place it in the slow cooker with the other ingredients. Ham hocks and smoked hams tend to be salty, so I recommend not salting the soup until close to the end of the cooking time.

Vegetarian Confetti Split Pea Soup

Split pea soup is a favorite at my house, but it usually has a base of smoked sausage or a ham bone to give it flavor and punch. When I decided to try a vegetarian version, I added yellow split peas and red lentils to give the soup beautiful color and flavor.

2 tablespoons olive oil

1 large onion, chopped

4 medium carrots, diced

4 stalks celery, diced

2 teaspoons dried thyme

1 bay leaf

2 cups dried green split peas

1 cup dried yellow split peas

½ cup dried red lentils

8 cups vegetable broth

Salt and freshly ground black pepper

heat the oil in a skillet over medium-high heat. Add the onion, carrots, celery, thyme, and bay leaf and sauté until the vegetables begin to soften, 4 to 5 minutes.

transfer the contents of the skillet to the insert of a 5- to 7-quart slow cooker and add the split peas, lentils, and broth, and stir to combine.

cover the slow cooker and cook on high for 4 hours or on low for 8 hours; check the soup at 3 or 7 hours to make sure that it isn't sticking to the pot. If it appears too thick, add more broth.

season with salt and pepper before serving.

serves **8**

Confetti Split Pea and Smoked Sausage Soup

Split pea soup is one of my family's favorites. I'm not sure if the thyme or the smoked sausage flavors the thick soup more—either way, it's nice for lunch or dinner, and leftovers freeze well. I like to use yellow and green split peas as well as red lentils, but it's also fine to only use green split peas.

1½ pounds smoked sausage, cut into ½-inch rounds

1 large onion, finely chopped

3 medium carrots, finely chopped

3 stalks celery with leaves, finely chopped

2 teaspoons dried thyme

1½ cups dried green split peas

½ cup dried yellow split peas

¼ cup dried red lentils

8 cups chicken or vegetable broth (see savvy)

Salt and freshly ground black pepper

cook the sausage in a large skillet over high heat. Render the fat and remove all but 2 tablespoons from the skillet.

add the onion, carrots, celery, and thyme and sauté until the vegetables are softened, about 3 minutes.

transfer the contents of the skillet to the insert of a 5- to 7-quart slow cooker. Add the remaining ingredients, except salt and pepper, and stir to combine.

cover and cook on high for 4 to 5 or on low for 8 to 10 hours, until the peas have split and the soup is thick. Check the soup several times during cooking to make sure there is enough broth and the soup isn't sticking to the pan.

season with salt and pepper before serving.

serves **8**

 slow-cooker liquid savvy
As I said in the introduction, all slow cookers are different and their temperatures vary a bit. The cooking time and amount of liquid that evaporates may vary. Just to be on the safe side, check the soup during the day to make sure that it's not sticking to the pan and that there is enough liquid.

Creamy Chicken and Wild Rice Soup

Comfort food doesn't get much better than this creamy soup brimming with chunks of moist chicken (or turkey), vegetables, and crunchy wild rice. If you have leftover chicken or turkey, this is a great way to use it. Wild rice is actually a grain and takes quite a while to cook, which is where your slow cooker comes in—you literally set it and forget it.

4 tablespoons (½ stick) unsalted butter

1 medium onion, finely chopped

4 medium carrots, finely chopped

4 medium stalks celery with leaves, finely chopped

1 pound cremini mushrooms, cut into ½-inch slices

1 teaspoon dried thyme

1 teaspoon dried sage, crushed in the palm of your hand

1½ teaspoons salt

1 teaspoon freshly ground black pepper

8 cups chicken broth

3 cups bite-size pieces cooked chicken or turkey, either shredded or diced

2 cups wild rice, rinsed several times with cold water

1 cup heavy cream

¼ cup finely chopped fresh Italian parsley (optional)

heat the butter in a large skillet over medium-high heat.

add the onion, carrots, and celery and sauté until the vegetables are softened, about 3 minutes. Add the mushrooms, thyme, and sage to the pan and season with the salt and pepper.

transfer the contents of the skillet to the insert of a 5- to 7-quart slow cooker. Stir in the chicken broth, chicken, and wild rice.

cover the slow cooker and cook on low for 4 to 5 hours, until the wild rice is tender and the soup is thickened.

stir in the cream and parsley (if using), turn the cooker to warm, and serve the soup.

serves **6–8**

slow-cooker savvy
Vegetarian wild rice soup? Omit the chicken or turkey and substitute vegetable or mushroom broth for the chicken broth.

STARTING THE POT

Many cuisines have a basic mixture of vegetables that starts a variety of dishes. In France, a *mirepoix* is a mixture of onion, celery, and carrot; New Orleans has its trinity—onion, bell pepper, and celery; Italy has *battuto*—onion, garlic, celery, carrot, and tomato; and Spain has its *sofrito*, which is generally olive oil, garlic, onions, and tomatoes.

Chicken and Spinach Soup

Vibrantly colored spinach gives this beautiful soup its color, while garlic and ginger add to its personality. This soup is terrific as a starter before a meal, but it's also nice served in mugs for a warm-up after playing in the snow.

3 tablespoons vegetable oil

2 cloves garlic, minced

2 teaspoons freshly grated ginger

3 chicken breast halves, skin and bones removed, cut into ½-inch dice (see savvy)

¼ cup soy sauce

6 cups chicken broth

Three 10-ounce packages baby spinach

Toasted sesame oil for garnishing

Chopped green onions for garnishing

heat the oil in a large skillet or wok over medium-high heat. Add the garlic and ginger and sauté until fragrant, about 30 seconds.

add the chicken and sauté until the chicken is white on the outside. Add the soy sauce and cook until the soy sauce is almost evaporated.

pour some of the chicken broth into the skillet and transfer the mixture to the insert of a 5- to 7-quart slow cooker, scraping any browned bits from the bottom of the skillet. Add the remaining broth and the spinach to the cooker. Cover and cook on low for 4 to 5 hours.

serve the soup in bowls garnished with a dot of sesame oil and a few pieces of green onion.

serves **8**

chicken savvy
If you would like to use leftover cooked chicken, toss the chicken with the garlic and ginger, add the soy sauce as directed, and proceed with the recipe.

Mom's Chicken Noodle Goodness

Mom's comfort food, this noodle soup is filled with veggies and chunks of chicken to make even the worst day seem bearable. Pair this with Cheddar cheese biscuits or scones.

2 tablespoons olive oil

1 cup finely chopped onion

2 cups finely chopped celery

2 cups finely chopped carrot

2 small zucchini, finely chopped

1 teaspoon dried thyme

12 cups chicken broth

4 cups bite-size pieces cooked chicken

Two 10-ounce packages fresh baby spinach

Salt and freshly ground black pepper

8 ounces medium-width egg noodles, cooked al dente

heat the oil in a large skillet over medium-high heat. Add the onion, celery, carrot, zucchini, and thyme and sauté until the vegetables are softened, about 7 minutes.

transfer the contents of the skillet to the insert of a 5- to 7-quart slow cooker. Stir in the broth, chicken, and spinach.

cover and cook on high for 4 hours or on low for 8 hours.

season with salt and pepper. Add the noodles to the soup, stir, cover, and let stand for 5 minutes before serving.

serves 8–10

Chicken, Mushroom, and Barley Soup

Barley is a natural thickener for soups, and it becomes creamy in a slow cooker. This soup is thick with chicken, chewy barley, and meaty cremini mushrooms; the added infusion of sherry and dried porcini mushrooms give it personality. It is also a great way to use the leftovers from that rotisserie chicken you bought earlier in the week. If you don't have leftover cooked chicken, it's easy enough to sauté chicken before adding it to the pot.

3 tablespoons olive oil

2 leeks, chopped, using the white and some of the tender green parts

3 stalks celery with leaves, chopped

3 medium carrots, chopped

1 pound cremini mushrooms, sliced

1 teaspoon dried thyme

1 bay leaf

1 cup pearl barley

6 cups chicken broth

¼ cup dried porcini mushrooms

¼ cup dry sherry

2 cups bite-size pieces cooked chicken

heat the oil in a large skillet over medium-high heat. Add the leeks, celery, carrots, cremini mushrooms, thyme, and bay leaf and sauté until the vegetables are softened, about 3 minutes. Transfer the contents of the skillet to the insert of a 5- to 7-quart slow cooker and stir in the barley, broth, dried mushrooms, sherry, and chicken.

cover the slow cooker and cook on low for 6 to 7 hours, until the barley is tender.

remove the bay leaf before serving.

serves **8**

Chicken Tortilla Soup

A bit of Southwestern spice flavors this warm and hearty soup. Make sure to serve some condiments on the side for everyone to make their own special bowl.

2 tablespoons vegetable oil

1 red bell pepper, seeded and coarsely chopped

1 green bell pepper, seeded and coarsely chopped

1 yellow bell pepper, seeded and coarsely chopped

2 medium sweet onions, such as Vidalia, thinly sliced

4 cloves garlic, chopped

2 tablespoons chili powder

2 teaspoons ground cumin

¼ cup gold tequila (optional)

One 14- to 15-ounce can chopped tomatoes, drained

4 cups chicken broth

3 cups shredded cooked chicken

Salt and freshly ground black pepper

Fried corn tortilla strips

Grated Colby or Monterey Jack cheese for garnishing

1 bunch cilantro, stems removed, leaves chopped for garnishing

Avocado Garnish (recipe follows)

heat the oil in a large skillet over medium-high heat. Add the bell peppers and onions and sauté for about 2 minutes, until softened.

add the garlic, chili powder, and cumin and cook for another 2 minutes. Add the tequila (if using) to the pan and cook until it is almost evaporated.

transfer the contents of the skillet to the insert of a 5- to 7-quart slow cooker. Add the tomatoes, broth, and chicken.

cover the slow cooker and cook on high for 3 to 4 hours or on low for 7 to 8 hours. Season with salt and pepper.

place the tortilla strips in bowls, ladle in the soup, and top with the cheese, cilantro, and the avocado garnish.

serves **8**

AVOCADO GARNISH

1 ripe Hass avocado, peeled, seeded, and chopped

½ cup fresh corn kernels or defrosted frozen corn

¼ cup chopped green onions

2 tablespoons fresh lime juice

2 tablespoons chopped fresh cilantro

combine all the ingredients in a small bowl. Cover with plastic wrap and refrigerate for up to 4 hours or serve immediately.

makes **1** cup

Take-Me-to-the-Kasbah
Chicken Vegetable Soup with Couscous

I have always been fascinated by the foods of Morocco. Using a diverse palate of flavors, the food is spicy with a hint of sweetness that comes from using dried fruits and spices like cinnamon and clove. This soup is reminiscent of one that I enjoyed with my daughter on a rainy night in Paris at a delightful restaurant called Table de Fes.

2 tablespoons olive oil

1 medium onion, finely chopped

1 teaspoon ground cumin

1 teaspoon sweet paprika

¼ teaspoon ground cinnamon

Pinch of cayenne pepper

2 medium zucchini, diced

2 medium yellow squash, diced

One 14- to 15-ounce can diced tomatoes, with their juice

6 cups chicken broth

3 cups shredded cooked chicken

½ cup golden raisins

3 cups cooked couscous

heat the oil in a large skillet over medium-high heat.

add the onion, cumin, paprika, cinnamon, and cayenne and sauté until the onion begins to soften, about 3 minutes. Add the zucchini, squash, and tomatoes and toss to coat with the spices and onion.

transfer the contents of the skillet to the insert of a 5- to 7-quart slow cooker. Stir in the broth, chicken, and raisins.

cover and cook on low for 6 hours, until the chicken and vegetables are tender.

serve the soup over couscous in individual bowls.

serves **8**

Raj Chicken Vegetable Soup

Fragrant with curry and filled with vegetables and a hint of apple, this chicken soup makes a delicious change of pace for lunch or dinner. Serve the soup over rice, if you are looking for a heartier presentation.

¼ cup vegetable oil

1 medium onion, coarsely chopped

2 stalks celery, coarsely chopped

4 medium carrots, coarsely chopped

1 large Granny Smith apple, peeled, cored, and coarsely chopped

1 teaspoon sweet curry powder (see savvy)

2 tablespoons all-purpose flour

8 cups chicken broth

2 tablespoons honey

2 cups shredded cooked chicken or turkey

2 cups diced small new potatoes or Yukon gold potatoes

Salt and freshly ground black pepper

1 cup sliced almonds, toasted, for garnishing

heat the oil in a large skillet over medium-high heat. Add the onion, celery, carrots, apple, curry powder, and flour; sauté until the vegetables are softened, 5 to 7 minutes.

transfer the mixture to the insert of a 5- to 7-quart slow cooker. Stir in the chicken broth, honey, chicken, and potatoes, stirring to distribute the ingredients.

cover the slow cooker and cook on high for 3 hours or on low for 5½ to 6 hours. Season with salt and pepper.

serve the soup garnished with the toasted almonds.

serves **8**

curry savvy
If you prefer your soup with a bit more spice, add ½ teaspoon hot curry powder along with the sweet curry powder. This will give you about a 7 on a 10-point heat meter.

more curry savvy
Curry powder should smell fresh. If yours doesn't have an aroma or smells flat, toss it and buy new. Penzey's Spices carries a variety of curry powders and they are terrific, but you can find curry powder in your grocery store, too.

Saigon Chicken Rice Soup

This simple soup with a complex character is inspired by a favorite of mine at a local San Diego area restaurant called Le Bambou. Flavored with ginger and chili garlic sauce, it is filled with shredded chicken, rice, and delicate ribbons of carrot, green onion, and Napa cabbage.

8 cups chicken broth

4 chicken breast halves, skin and bones removed

3 dime-size thin slices fresh ginger

1 tablespoon soy sauce

1 teaspoon Asian fish sauce

1 teaspoon chili garlic sauce

½ cup grated carrot

1 cup thinly sliced Napa cabbage

6 green onions, thinly sliced on a diagonal

2 cups cooked jasmine rice

pour the broth into the insert of a 5- to 7-quart slow cooker.

place the chicken in the bottom of the slow-cooker insert with the broth and add the ginger, soy sauce, fish sauce, and chili sauce. Cover the cooker and cook on high for 4 hours.

strain the broth through a fine-mesh sieve into a bowl, at the end of the 4 hours, and shred the chicken.

return the chicken and broth to the slow-cooker insert and add the carrot, cabbage, green onions, and rice. Keep warm on low for up to 2 hours before serving. If the soup thickens, add more broth.

serves **8**

Cajun Chicken Gumbo

Gumbo makes me smile—it's simple to prepare and reminds me of New Orleans, a city with a rich culinary heritage. I make it to soothe our souls during the winter. Gumbo is one of those recipes that you can tinker with and it always turns out delicious. Try using other meats or seafood, and garnish it with green onions and, of course, filé powder (crushed sassafras), which is de rigueur in the South. This gumbo begins with a roux, which you can make the night before putting your gumbo into the slow cooker. Although the roux is not hard to make, it does require some attention, so leave yourself some time to make it.

½ cup vegetable oil

½ cup all-purpose flour

1½ cups chopped onions

1½ cups chopped celery

1½ cups chopped green bell peppers

4 cloves garlic, minced

1 tablespoon Old Bay or Creole seasoning

1 pound andouille or other smoked sausage, cut into ½-inch dice

4 cups chicken broth

3 cups bite-size pieces cooked chicken

1 bay leaf

3 cups cooked long-grain rice

6 green onions, chopped, using the white and tender green part, for garnishing

Gumbo filé powder for serving

Assorted hot sauces for serving

heat the oil in a large skillet over medium-high heat. Add the flour and whisk to combine. Reduce the heat to medium and whisk the roux until it is a dark golden-brown, 15 to 20 minutes.

add the onions, celery, bell peppers, garlic, and seasoning and sauté until the vegetables are softened, about 5 minutes. (At this point, the mixture can be refrigerated for up to 24 hours. Rewarm the roux before adding it to the slow cooker.)

transfer the contents of the skillet to the insert of a 5- to 7-quart slow cooker and stir in the sausage, broth, chicken, and bay leaf. Cook on high for 4 to 5 hours or on low for 8 to 10 hours. Remove the bay leaf from the gumbo.

serve the gumbo over the rice and garnish with the green onions. Serve with the filé powder and assorted hot sauces on the side.

serves **8–10**

okra savvy
If you love okra, you can add it to this recipe, but don't add it till the last hour of cooking. Two cups sliced (¼ inch) fresh okra works well here. Frozen or canned okra becomes stringy and is unappetizing.

Pacific Rim Pork and Noodle Soup

This soup is one of my favorites with its ginger-flavored broth, red cooked pork, noodles, and vegetables. Basically a stir-fry-soup, you can swap leftover chicken, seafood, or beef, for the pork.

½ cup soy sauce

¼ cup hoisin sauce

¼ cup rice wine (mirin)

Pinch five-spice powder

2 tablespoons toasted sesame oil

1 pork tenderloin 1¼ to 1½ pounds, silver skin removed, cut into ½-inch slices

2 tablespoons vegetable oil

2 teaspoons freshly grated ginger

2 cloves garlic, minced

1 medium onion, coarsely chopped

1 bunch bok choy, cut into 1-inch pieces

2 medium carrots, cut into julienne strips

8 cups beef broth

8 ounces fresh soba noodles, or 12 ounces dried

4 green onions, finely chopped, using the white and tender green parts

¼ cup toasted sesame seeds for garnishing

whisk together the soy sauce, hoisin, rice wine, five-spice powder, and sesame oil in a large glass bowl. Add the pork, cover, and refrigerate for at least 1 hour and up to 8 hours.

heat the vegetable oil in a large skillet or wok over high heat. Remove the pork from the marinade and add to the skillet. Stir-fry, a few pieces at a time, until the pork begins to color, 3 to 4 minutes.

transfer the pork to the insert of a 5- to 7-quart slow cooker. Add the ginger and garlic to the same skillet and stir-fry for 1 minute, until fragrant. Add the onion, bok choy, and carrots and stir-fry until the vegetables are softened, 3 to 4 minutes. Deglaze the skillet with 1 cup of the broth, scraping up any browned bits from the bottom of the pan.

transfer the contents of the skillet to the slow-cooker insert. Add the remaining 7 cups broth to the slow-cooker insert. Cover and cook on low for 4 to 5 hours, until the pork and vegetables are tender. Add the noodles and green onions. Cover and cook for an additional 45 minutes.

serve the soup garnished with the toasted sesame seeds.

serves **8**

Turkey Minestrone

This soothing slow-cooked meal-in-a-bowl is a terrific way to use up leftover turkey from a holiday meal. Brimming with vegetables, turkey, and cheese tortellini, it is sure to please on a cold fall or winter evening. The rind from Parmigiano-Reggiano cheese flavors the soup, and although it's optional, it gives the soup a great depth of flavor. Save rinds in zipper-top plastic bags in the freezer for adding to soups and sauces.

3 tablespoons extra-virgin olive oil

1 cup chopped sweet onion

2 cups chopped carrots

2 cups chopped celery

2 teaspoons chopped fresh rosemary

½ cup dry white wine

One 14- to 15-ounce can chopped tomatoes, with their juice

5 cups chicken broth

Rind from Parmigiano-Reggiano cheese, cut into ½-inch pieces (optional)

3 medium zucchini, diced (about 1½ cups)

1 cup 1-inch pieces green beans (about 5 ounces)

4 cups bite-size pieces cooked turkey or chicken

One 15-ounce can small white beans or garbanzo beans, drained and rinsed

1 head escarole, tough leaves removed, cut into 1-inch pieces, or two 10-ounce bags baby spinach

1 teaspoon salt (you will need more if you don't use the cheese rind)

1 teaspoon freshly ground black pepper

12 ounces fresh cheese tortellini, cooked according to package directions and drained

1 cup freshly grated Parmigiano-Reggiano cheese for garnishing

heat the oil in a large skillet over medium-high heat.

add the onion, carrots, celery, and rosemary and sauté until the vegetables begin to soften, about 6 minutes. Add the wine and allow it to boil for 2 minutes, stirring. Add the tomatoes and cook for 4 minutes, until some of the liquid evaporates.

transfer the contents of the skillet to the insert of a 5- to 7-quart slow cooker. Add the broth and cheese rind (if using). Add the zucchini, green beans, turkey, white beans and escarole and stir to combine.

cover and cook on high for 4 hours or on low for 8 to 10 hours.

season with the salt and pepper. Stir in the cooked tortellini. Cover and cook on high for another 30 minutes or on low for 1 hour.

garnish with the Parmigiano-Reggiano cheese before serving.

serves **10–12**

starchy savvy
Whenever you add pasta, rice, or other starches to a soup, make sure to cook it separately first and then add it to the soup. It will still absorb some of the liquid but will not suck up so much that there is no broth left.

Italian Wedding Soup with Turkey Meatballs

This whole-meal soup is a real crowd pleaser. Filled with tiny meatballs and vegetables in a hearty chicken broth, it will warm up even the coldest day. I find this soup to be very kid friendly—meatballs floating in broth can be much like bobbing for apples for some children. If you don't have time to make your own meatballs, buy prepared frozen mini meatballs, but make sure to defrost them before adding to the soup.

SOUP

8 cups chicken broth

4 cups coarsely chopped escarole or Swiss chard (about 1 pound)

One 15-ounce can small white beans, drained and rinsed

TURKEY MEATBALLS
(Makes about 16–20 one-inch meatballs)

2 slices soft-crusted Italian bread

¼ cup milk

1 pound ground turkey

1 medium shallot, finely chopped

⅛ teaspoon freshly grated nutmeg

1 teaspoon salt

½ teaspoon freshly ground black pepper

⅓ cup grated Parmigiano-Reggiano cheese, plus freshly grated Parmigiano-Reggiano cheese for garnishing

2 tablespoons finely chopped fresh Italian parsley

1 large egg, beaten

put the broth, escarole, and beans in the insert of a 5- to 7-quart slow cooker. Cover and cook on low while preparing the meatballs.

put the bread a large mixing bowl, pour the milk over it, and allow it to soak in.

add the turkey, shallot, nutmeg, salt, pepper, ⅓ cup cheese, parsley, and egg, and stir until the mixture is combined, being careful not to compact it. Using a small scoop, form the mixture into 1-inch balls.

drop the meatballs into the slow-cooker insert. Cover and cook the soup on low for 5 hours, until the meatballs float on the surface.

skim off any foam that may have formed from the top of the soup.

serve the soup garnished with the freshly grated cheese.

serves **8**

Alphabet Beef Vegetable Soup

All of us had an alphabet soup that we ate for lunch as children. It was always fun to find the letters and maybe play a game of "soup Scrabble" with your siblings. This slow-cooker version of alphabet soup is filled with beef, vegetables, and, of course, lots of alphabet noodles in a tomato-based beef broth. So sharpen up your vocabulary skills because this soup will have you playing with your food!

1½ pounds beef sirloin, cut into ½-inch pieces

1½ teaspoons salt

½ teaspoon freshly ground black pepper

2 tablespoons vegetable oil

1 medium onion, finely chopped

3 medium carrots, finely chopped

One 15-ounce can tomato sauce

3 cups beef broth

2 cups chicken broth (see savvy)

4 ounces green beans, ends snipped, cut into 1-inch lengths

2 cups frozen petite peas, defrosted

2 cups frozen corn, defrosted

2 cups cooked alphabet noodles or other small pasta shapes

sprinkle the beef with the salt and pepper. Heat the oil in a large skillet over high heat. Add the beef a few pieces at a time and brown on all sides. Transfer the browned beef to the insert of a 5- to 7-quart slow cooker. Add the onion and carrots to the same skillet and sauté until the onion is softened, about 3 minutes.

transfer the contents of the skillet to the slow-cooker insert and add the tomato sauce, beef broth, chicken broth, and green beans. Cover and cook on low for 5 to 6 hours. Remove the cover and add the peas, corn, and noodles.

cover and cook for an additional 45 minutes before serving.

serves **6–8**

broth savvy
For this soup I wanted a lighter broth with a beef flavor, so I added chicken broth along with the beef broth. Vegetable broth may also be used in place of the chicken broth.

Old-Fashioned Beef and Barley Soup

Barley thickens this hearty soup, and the aromas of the thyme, red wine, and meaty broth are a nice welcome-home after a long day. Serving this soup in hollowed-out bread bowls is a great idea for serving a crowd—there is minimal cleanup because you eat the bowl!

2½ to 3 pounds beef chuck, sirloin, or flap meat, cut into ½-inch pieces

Salt and freshly ground black pepper

2 tablespoons extra-virgin olive oil

2 cloves garlic, minced

2 medium onions, coarsely chopped

8 ounces cremini mushrooms, quartered

1½ teaspoons dried thyme

4 medium carrots, coarsely chopped

3 stalks celery with leaves, coarsely chopped

3 tablespoons tomato paste

1 cup medium- to full-bodied red wine, such as Merlot, Chianti, Barolo, or Cabernet

6 cups beef broth

½ cup pearl barley

sprinkle the beef evenly with the 2 teaspoons salt and 1 teaspoon pepper. Heat the oil in a large skillet over high heat. Add the meat a few pieces at a time and brown on all sides. Transfer the browned meat to the insert of a 5- to 7-quart slow cooker.

add the garlic, onions, mushrooms, and thyme to the same skillet over medium-high heat and sauté until the liquid from the mushrooms is evaporated.

transfer the contents of the skillet to the slow-cooker insert. Add the carrots and celery to the cooker and stir to combine. Deglaze the skillet with the tomato paste and wine and allow the wine to reduce by about ¼ cup, stirring up any browned bits from the bottom of the pan.

transfer the tomato mixture to the slow-cooker insert and add the broth and barley. Cover the slow cooker and cook on low for 6 to 7 hours, until the beef and barley are tender.

season with salt and pepper before serving.

serves **8**

Steak and Ale Soup

Pub grub has gotten a bad rap for years for being tasteless and boring, but this hearty soup with root veggies simmering in a rich ale-infused beef broth is anything but. The ale adds a sweet note to the rich beefy flavor of the broth.

2 tablespoons olive oil

¼ cup all-purpose flour

Salt and freshly ground black pepper

2 pounds beef chuck or short ribs, fat trimmed and cut into 1-inch pieces

2 medium onions, coarsely chopped

3 cloves garlic, sliced

1 teaspoon dried thyme

One 12-ounce bottle dark ale

3 cups beef broth

4 cups baby carrots

4 medium parsnips, cut into 1-inch lengths

2 cups red, Yukon gold, or new white potatoes

heat the oil in a large skillet over high heat. Combine the flour, 1½ teaspoons salt and ½ teaspoon pepper in a zipper-top plastic bag. Toss the meat in the flour, a few pieces at a time.

add the meat, a few pieces at a time, to the oil and brown on all sides. Transfer the browned meat to the insert of a 5- to 7-quart slow cooker.

when all the beef is browned, add the onions, garlic, and thyme to the same skillet over medium-high heat and sauté until the onions begin to soften and become translucent. Add the ale to the pan and scrape up any browned bits from the bottom of the pan.

transfer the contents of the skillet to the slow-cooker insert and add the broth, carrots, parsnips, and potatoes.

cover the slow cooker and cook on high for 4 to 5 hours or low for 8 to 10 hours, until the vegetables are tender and the beef is fork tender.

season with salt and pepper before serving.

serves **8**

Steak and Mushroom Soup

When I grill steaks at home, the side dish I most often make to accompany the steak is sautéed or grilled mushrooms. I love the combination of beefy flavor and earthy mushrooms, and this creamy soup is a great way to get both, in a soup fragrant with sherry and thyme. Wild or cultivated "wild" mushrooms are a great choice for this soup, adding complexity and flavor, but you can always stick to a mixture of cremini and white buttons if other types are not available.

4 tablespoons (½ stick) unsalted butter

1 cup finely chopped shallots (about 6 medium)

1½ pounds assorted mushrooms, tougher stems removed, cut into ½-inch-thick slices

2½ teaspoons salt

1 teaspoon freshly ground black pepper

1½ teaspoons dried thyme leaves

2½ to 3 pounds beef top sirloin, cut into ½-inch pieces

¼ cup cream sherry (see savvy)

4 cups beef broth

2 tablespoons cornstarch mixed with ¼ cup water or broth

1 cup heavy cream

½ cup finely chopped fresh Italian parsley

melt 2 tablespoons of the butter in a large skillet over medium-high heat. Add the shallots and mushrooms and sprinkle them with ½ teaspoon of the salt, ½ teaspoon of the pepper, and the thyme. Sauté until the mushrooms start to color, 10 to 15 minutes.

transfer the mushrooms to the insert of a 5- to 7-quart slow cooker. Sprinkle the meat with the remaining 2 teaspoons salt and ½ teaspoon pepper.

melt the remaining 2 tablespoons butter in the skillet over high heat. Add the meat a few pieces at a time and brown on all sides.

transfer the browned meat to the slow-cooker insert. Deglaze the pan with the sherry and scrape up any browned bits from the bottom of the skillet.

transfer the sherry to the insert and stir in the broth. Cover and cook the soup on low for 5 to 6 hours, until the meat is tender.

add the cornstarch mixture and the cream to the soup and stir to combine. Cook for an additional 30 minutes, until the soup is thickened.

stir in the parsley before serving.

serves 6—8

sherry savvy
Dry or cream sherries are fortified wines, and my choice of cream sherry for this soup is purely personal. I like the nutty flavor that it imparts to the dish, but if you prefer dry sherry, then certainly use that, or omit all together.

Kansas City Steak Soup

Every Junior League or church cookbook has some version of this soup, which is supposed to have originated at the Plaza III Steakhouse in Kansas City. I've changed the original that included ground beef, Spice Islands beef soup base, and frozen peas and carrots and updated it with sirloin, beef broth, and some fresh vegetables.

2 pounds sirloin, cut into ½-inch pieces

1½ teaspoons salt

½ teaspoon freshly ground black pepper

4 tablespoons (½ stick) unsalted butter

2 medium yellow onions, finely chopped

4 medium carrots, finely chopped

4 stalks celery with leaves, finely chopped

3 tablespoons all-purpose flour

6 cups beef broth

One 16-ounce package frozen corn, defrosted

2 cups frozen petite peas, defrosted

sprinkle the sirloin evenly with the salt and pepper. Heat 1 tablespoon of the butter in a large skillet over medium-high heat. Add the meat a few pieces at a time and brown on all sides. Transfer the browned meat to the insert of a 5- to 7-quart slow cooker.

melt the remaining 3 tablespoons butter over medium-high heat in the same skillet. Add the onions, carrots, and celery and sauté until the onions are fragrant and the vegetables begin to soften, about 5 minutes.

stir in the flour and cook the vegetables for another 2 to 3 minutes. Gradually stir in the broth and heat, stirring until the mixture comes to a boil. Transfer the contents of the skillet to the slow-cooker insert.

cover and cook on low for 4 to 5 hours, until the meat is tender. Remove the cover and stir in the corn and peas.

cover and cook for an additional 45 minutes to 1 hour before serving.

serves 6–8

Curried Meatball Soup

In this soup, spicy meatballs flavored with curry and sweet chutney float in a rich beef broth. Simmered with bok choy and snow peas and topped with fresh bean sprouts, it is sure to win raves from your family. The meatballs can be made beforehand and stored in the refrigerator overnight or in the freezer for up to one month. Make sure to thaw frozen meatballs before adding to the soup. The meatballs also make a nice appetizer when served with a chutney sauce.

MEATBALLS
(makes 12–14 one-inch meatballs)

1 cup cooked long-grain rice

1½ pounds 85-percent lean ground beef

1 teaspoon sweet curry powder

2 tablespoons soy sauce

4 green onions, finely chopped, using the white and tender green parts

1 tablespoon Major Grey's chutney or other mild chutney

1 large egg, beaten

SOUP

7 cups beef broth

½ cup soy sauce

1 bunch bok choy, cut into 1-inch pieces (about 2 cups)

1 cup snow peas, ends trimmed and strings removed

2 cups fresh bean sprouts or other sprouts such as radish or broccoli for garnishing

put all the meatball ingredients in a large bowl and stir to combine. Using a small scoop, form the meat into 1-inch balls.

add the broth and soy sauce to the insert of a 5- to 7-quart slow cooker.

add the meatballs, cover, and cook on high for 3 hours, until the meatballs float to the top. Skim off any foam that may have formed from the top of the broth.

add the bok choy and snow peas to the cooker and cook on low for an additional 1 hour, until the bok choy is tender.

serve the soup garnished with the fresh bean sprouts.

serves **8**

Portuguese Kale and Sausage Soup

My friend Lora Brody's terrific book *The Cape Cod Table* also has a lovely version of this soup, which is popular in my hometown San Diego's large Portuguese community. Spicy smoked sausage, kale, potatoes, and broth combine to make a substantial lunch or dinner.

2 tablespoons olive oil

1 pound smoked linguiça, chorizo, or andouille sausage, cut into ½-inch rounds

2 medium onions, finely chopped

4 medium carrots, finely chopped

1 pound kale, chopped into 1-inch pieces

5 medium red potatoes, peeled (or unpeeled) and cut into ½-inch pieces

6 cups chicken broth

2 bay leaves

¼ cup finely chopped fresh cilantro

heat the oil in a large skillet over high heat. Add the sausage, onions, and carrots and sauté until the onions are translucent.

transfer the contents of the skillet to the insert of a 5- to 7-quart slow cooker. Add the kale, potatoes, broth, and bay leaves to the cooker and stir to combine. Cover and cook on low for 5 to 6 hours, until the potatoes are tender.

remove the bay leaves and stir in the cilantro before serving.

serves **8**

Sopranos-Style Sausage Minestrone

Another hearty soup for a winter's day. I picture Tony Soprano and his gang eating this soup, which is filled with Italian sausage, vegetables, and orzo in a hearty beef broth, while discussing who they will "whack" next! You can put any of your favorite vegetables in minestrone, so if you have some leftovers from last night's dinner, feel free to add them to the soup.

1½ pounds sweet Italian sausage, bulk or removed from casing

2 tablespoons extra-virgin olive oil

4 slices prosciutto, cut into julienne strips

2 medium onions, coarsely chopped

4 medium carrots, coarsely chopped

4 stalks celery with leaves, coarsely chopped

2 teaspoons finely chopped fresh rosemary

½ cup medium- to full-bodied red wine

One 15-ounce can crushed plum tomatoes, with their juice

4 medium red potatoes, cut into ½-inch dice

4 ounces green beans, ends snipped, cut into 1-inch lengths

2 medium zucchini, cut into ½-inch half rounds

1 cup dried brown lentils or split peas, (see quick-soak method, page 36)

1 head escarole or Swiss chard, cut into 1-inch pieces

Rind from Parmigiano-Reggiano cheese, cut into ½-inch pieces (optional)

8 cups beef broth

2 cups cooked orzo

cook the sausage in a large skillet over high heat, breaking up any large pieces, until it is no longer pink.

transfer the sausage to the insert of a 5- to 7-quart slow cooker. Remove all but 2 tablespoons of fat from the pan and add the olive oil. Add the prosciutto and sauté for 2 minutes, until it begins to get crisp.

add the onions, carrots, celery, and rosemary and sauté until the onions begin to soften, about 5 minutes. Deglaze the pan with the wine and boil until the wine is reduced by half, about 3 minutes. Add the tomatoes and cook for 2 minutes.

transfer the contents of the skillet to the slow-cooker insert and stir in the potatoes, beans, zucchini, lentils, escarole, cheese rind (if using), and broth. Cover and cook on low for 8 to 10 hours, until the soup is thickened and the lentils are softened.

stir in the orzo and serve.

serves **8**

slow-cooker seasoning savvy
Where's the salt and pepper? Italian sausage is usually highly seasoned with salt and pepper. The cheese rind, prosciutto, and beef broth will also provide seasoning for the soup.

Five-Alarm Hill-o'-Beans Chili

This vegetarian chili is a terrific entrée to serve to your friends. Thick with beans and vegetables, it's got a great kick from the addition of ancho chile powder and jalapeño peppers. Serve this with warmed flour or corn tortillas and condiments on the side.

2 tablespoons olive oil

2 medium onions, coarsely chopped

2 cloves garlic, minced

2 jalapeño peppers, seeded and finely chopped

2 teaspoons ancho chile powder

1 teaspoon ground cumin

1 teaspoon dried oregano

2 medium red bell peppers, seeded and coarsely chopped

1 pound cremini mushrooms, quartered

2 cups dried red beans, soaked (see quick-soak method, page 36), or two 14- to 15-ounce cans red beans, drained and rinsed

2 cups dried small white beans, soaked (see quick-soak method, page 36), or two 14- to 15-ounce cans white beans, drained and rinsed

2 cups dried pinto beans, soaked (see quick-soak method, page 36), or two 14- to 15-ounce cans pinto beans

One 14- to 15-ounce can tomato purée

3 cups vegetable, chicken, or beef broth

One 16-ounce package frozen corn, defrosted and drained

Salt and freshly ground black pepper

½ cup finely chopped fresh cilantro

Finely shredded Monterey Jack and Colby cheeses for garnishing

Sour cream for garnishing

heat the oil in a large skillet over medium-high heat. Add the onions, garlic, jalapeños, chile powder, cumin, and oregano and cook until the onions are softened and the spices are fragrant, about 3 minutes.

transfer the contents of the skillet to the insert of a 5- to 7-quart slow cooker. Add the bell peppers, mushrooms, beans, tomato purée, broth, and corn, and stir to distribute the ingredients in the slow cooker.

cook on low for 8 to 10 hours.

season with salt and pepper. Stir in the cilantro.

serve the chili garnished with the Monterey Jack cheese and a dollop of sour cream.

serves 8–10

White Chicken Chili

Flavored with chipotle chiles, this unique chili filled with vegetables, white beans, and chicken is a delightful change of pace from traditional meat-lovers chili. Corn tortillas thicken the chili and add a delicious flavor.

3 tablespoons olive oil

2 medium onions, finely chopped

1 medium red bell pepper, seeded and finely chopped

1 medium green bell pepper, seeded and finely chopped

4 chipotle chiles in adobo, finely chopped (see savvy)

1 teaspoon ground cumin

1 teaspoon dried oregano

8 cups chicken broth

Four 6-inch corn tortillas, torn into small pieces

Two 14- to 15-ounce cans small white beans, drained and rinsed

3 cups cooked chicken or turkey

One 16-ounce package frozen corn, defrosted

½ cup finely chopped fresh cilantro

2 cups finely shredded mild Cheddar or Monterey Jack cheese for garnishing

2 cups sour cream for garnishing

heat the oil in a large skillet over medium-high heat. Add the onions, bell peppers, chiles, cumin, and oregano and sauté until the vegetables are softened, 5 to 7 minutes.

transfer the contents of the skillet to the insert of a 5- to 7-quart slow cooker. Add the broth, tortillas, beans, chicken, and corn.

cover the slow cooker and cook on low for 8 to 10 hours, until the chili is thick and the beans and vegetables are tender. Stir in the cilantro.

serve each bowl garnished with cheese and sour cream.

serves **8**

chipotle savvy
Chipotle chiles are smoked jalapeños. They add more smoke than heat, but it's important to sauté the chiles to allow them to develop their flavor. Chipotles come canned in a sauce called adobo. You will have chiles left over. Mound individual chiles with a bit of the adobo sauce on a piece of aluminum foil on a cookie sheet. Freeze the chiles until firm, then transfer them to a zipper-top plastic bag, label, and freeze.

Turkey, Corn, and Black Bean Chili

This chili offers a great way of transforming Thanksgiving leftovers into a stick-to-your-ribs lunch or dinner for the weekend. Sweet corn, ancho chile powder, moist turkey, and black beans combine for a delicious meal in a bowl.

2 tablespoons olive oil

1 medium onion, chopped

2 cloves garlic, minced

1½ teaspoons dried oregano

2 teaspoons ancho chile powder

½ teaspoon ground cumin

2 Anaheim chiles, seeded and finely chopped

1 medium red bell pepper, seeded and chopped

1½ teaspoons salt

2 teaspoons cornmeal

6 cups chicken or turkey broth

One 16-ounce package frozen corn, defrosted

Two 14- to 15-ounce cans black beans, rinsed and drained

3 cups shredded cooked turkey or chicken

¼ cup chopped fresh cilantro

heat the oil in a large skillet over medium-high heat. Add the onion, garlic, oregano, chile powder, and cumin and sauté until the spices are fragrant. Add the chiles, bell pepper, and salt and sauté until the vegetables are softened.

transfer the contents of the skillet to the insert of a 5- to 7-quart slow cooker. Stir in the cornmeal, broth, corn, beans, and turkey.

cover the slow cooker and cook on low for 8 to 10 hours, until the chili is thickened and the vegetables are tender.

stir in the cilantro before serving.

serves **8**

Super Bowl Sunday Chili

I could probably write a book just on slow-cooker chilies, there are so many of them. This one features beef short ribs that become tender and flavorful as the chili bubbles away in the slow cooker. I've added pinto beans and just the right amount of cilantro at the end. The next time it's your turn to host the Super Bowl Party, this can be your go-to dish. Make sure to have a condiment bar so your guests can load up on cheese, sour cream, onions, pickled jalapeños, and an assortment of hot sauces. Any leftover chili can be refrigerated for up to 3 days or frozen for up to 6 weeks.

3 tablespoons vegetable oil

2 medium onions, finely chopped

1 jalapeño pepper, seeded and finely chopped

1 teaspoon ancho chile powder

½ teaspoon dried oregano

2 pounds boneless beef short ribs or chuck, cut into ½-inch pieces

3 cups beef broth

One 28- to 32-ounce can crushed tomatoes, with their juice

Two 14- to 15-ounce cans pinto beans, drained and rinsed

heat 2 tablespoons of the oil in a large skillet over medium-high heat. Add the onions, jalapeño, chile powder, and oregano and sauté until the onions become soft, about 3 minutes.

transfer the contents of the skillet to the insert of a 5- to 7-quart slow cooker. Heat the remaining 1 tablespoon of oil in the same skillet over high heat.

add the meat, a few pieces at a time, and brown on all sides. Transfer the browned meat to the slow-cooker insert. Add the broth, tomatoes, and beans to the slow-cooker insert.

cover and cook on low for 8 to 10 hours or on high for 4 to 5 hours, until the beef is tender and the sauce is thickened.

serve the chili from the cooker set on warm.

serves 8—10

Ryan's Chili

My son, the sports blogger, loves to eat chili while watching games. His chili is just meat in a thick sauce—no beans to complicate things—and enough spice to make it interesting. This is a simple chili, but it's always a crowd pleaser, and it's terrific over baked potatoes, burgers, or dogs at a barbecue. Don't forget the shredded Cheddar cheese and chopped red onion for garnish!

2 tablespoons vegetable oil

2 pounds 15-percent lean ground beef

2 teaspoons ancho chile powder

1 teaspoon dried oregano

½ teaspoon ground cumin

Salt

Pinch of cayenne pepper

2 teaspoons cornmeal

2 cups beef broth

4 cups tomato sauce

Freshly ground black pepper

Tortilla chips for garnishing

Shredded Cheddar cheese for garnishing

Chopped red onion for garnishing

heat the oil in a large skillet over high heat. Add the beef and brown, breaking up any large pieces.

transfer the meat to the insert of a 5- to 7-quart slow cooker. Add the chile powder, oregano, cumin, 2 teaspoons salt, and the cayenne to the same skillet and cook until the spices are fragrant, 30 to 45 seconds.

add the cornmeal to the pan and stir until the mixture thickens. Add the broth and whisk until smooth. Transfer the contents of the skillet to the slow-cooker insert and stir in the tomato sauce.

cover and cook on low for 6 to 7 hours, until the chili is thickened. Season with salt and pepper.

serve the chili in bowls and garnish with tortilla chips, shredded Cheddar cheese, and chopped red onion.

serves **8**

Lone Star Sirloin Chili

Because this Tex-Mex favorite will serve an army, you can make a batch and freeze for up to six weeks. Real Texas chili, according to my Texan friends, doesn't include beans or tomatoes. Since I'm not a real Texan, I've adapted this recipe to make it a crowd pleaser using Lone Star beer and chunks of sirloin and black beans. When you serve it, provide a condiment bar with tortilla chips, grated cheese, sour cream, chopped onions, and chopped pickled jalapeños for your guests to add as they please.

2½ pounds beef sirloin, cut into ½-inch pieces

2 teaspoons salt

Pinch of cayenne pepper (optional)

4 tablespoons olive oil

2 large sweet onions, such as Vidalia, coarsely chopped

2 cloves garlic, minced

2 tablespoons finely chopped jalapeño

2 teaspoons ancho chile powder (see savvy)

½ teaspoon ground cumin

½ teaspoon dried oregano

¼ cup cornmeal

2 cups beef broth

One 12-ounce bottle Lone Star or other beer

One 14- to 15-ounce can tomato purée

Two 14- to 15-ounce cans black beans, drained and rinsed

½ cup chopped fresh cilantro

sprinkle the beef evenly with the salt and cayenne (if using). Heat 2 tablespoons of the oil in a large skillet over medium-high heat. Add the beef in batches and brown on all sides.

transfer the meat to the insert of a 5- to 7-quart slow cooker.

lower the heat to medium-low and heat the remaining 2 tablespoons oil. Add the onions, garlic, jalapeño, chile powder, cumin, and oregano and sauté until the onions are softened, about 5 minutes, being careful to stir the mixture so the chile powder doesn't burn. Add the cornmeal and stir until blended with the other ingredients, and cook for 1 minute. Stir in the broth, whisking, and bring to a boil.

transfer the contents of the skillet to the slow-cooker insert. Add the beer, tomato purée, and beans. Cover and cook on high for 4 to 5 hours or on low for 8 to 10 hours, until the meat is tender and the sauce is thickened.

skim off any fat from the top of the chili and stir in the cilantro before serving.

serves **8–10**

chile savvy
Ancho chile powder can be found in the Hispanic section of your grocery store and sometimes in the spice section. If you would prefer to use an all-purpose chili powder, Gephardt's is a good brand, or try mail ordering from Penzey's Spices (www.penzeys.com).

more savvy
Always sauté dried herbs and spices to release their oils, otherwise the finished dish will not have a balanced flavor. This is especially true of chili powders, which need to "bloom" in fat to reduce their harshness.

Back Bay Corn Chowder

Smoky, creamy, and sweet, this delicious warm-up filled with sweet corn, bacon, and potatoes is terrific to serve in mugs on a cold winter day. Cream and whole milk are my choices for this chowder; add them at the end of the cooking time to prevent separating.

8 strips bacon, cut into ½-inch dice (see savvy)

1 cup finely chopped onion

3 stalks celery, finely chopped

1½ teaspoons dried thyme leaves

½ cup all-purpose flour

4 cups chicken or vegetable broth

Tabasco sauce

4 cups diced red potatoes (see savvy)

One 16-ounce package frozen petite white corn, defrosted

1 cup heavy cream

Salt

cook the bacon in a large skillet over medium heat until crisp. Add the onion, celery, and thyme and cook over medium-high heat until the onion begins to soften. Add the flour and cook, stirring, over medium heat for 3 minutes. Gradually add the broth and 8 drops of Tabasco, whisking until smooth, and bring the mixture to a boil.

transfer the contents of the skillet to the insert of a 5- to 7-quart slow cooker. Add the potatoes and corn. Cover the slow cooker and cook on high for 3 hours or on low for 6 to 7 hours.

at the end of the cooking time, stir in the cream, cover the slow cooker, and cook on low for an additional 30 minutes. Season with salt and Tabasco.

serve the chowder hot.

serves **8**

bacon sauté savvy
When sautéing bacon with other ingredients, make sure to render the fat, and cook the bacon until it is just crisp. The addition of vegetables like onions to the sauté will add some water and prevent the bacon from becoming crisp, so make sure it is crisp before adding the vegetables. I usually cook a whole pound of bacon and use the extra for garnish because we all know everything tastes better with bacon!

potato savvy
I will leave the skins on potatoes if they are unblemished and don't have a greenish tinge. If they do look a bit green, it is from exposure to light and the green tinge should be peeled off because it is a toxin and can give you a tummy ache. Choices for potatoes in this soup would be the waxy varieties: red, Yukon gold, fingerling, or white creamers. Baking potatoes aren't recommended because they have a tendency to fall apart in soup.

New England Fish Chowder

Filled with potatoes, onion, celery, bacon, and fresh fish, creamy seafood chowders are a staple not only in New England but across America. This fish chowder is a basic slow-cooker recipe for any type of creamy chowder—it's a matter of substituting more than changing the cooking technique. Fish chowder should be made with a thick-fleshed fish that will not disintegrate in the cooker, such as halibut, sea bass, or cod. Make sure the fish is fresh, not frozen. Frozen fish tends to disintegrate when cooked low and slow. Fish stock can easily be made on your stovetop, but if you don't have any, a mixture of chicken broth and clam juice also works well. Superior Touch Better Than Bouillon has a clam base as well as a delicious lobster stock that you could certainly use.

8 strips thick-cut bacon, cut into
½-inch pieces

1 large onion, finely chopped

4 stalks celery, finely chopped

1 teaspoon dried thyme

3 tablespoons all-purpose flour

3 cups chicken broth

Two 8-ounce bottles clam juice

5 medium red or Yukon gold potatoes,
cut into ½-inch chunks

1 bay leaf

1½ pounds thick-fleshed fish, such as sea
bass, halibut, haddock, or cod, cut into
2-inch cubes

1½ cups heavy cream

¼ cup finely chopped fresh Italian parsley
for garnishing

¼ cup finely chopped fresh chives
for garnishing

cook the bacon in a large skillet over medium-high heat until crisp and remove it to paper towels to drain. Remove all but ¼ cup of the bacon drippings from the skillet.

add the onion, celery, and thyme and sauté until the onion is translucent, 5 to 7 minutes. Stir in the flour and cook for 3 minutes, whisking the roux constantly (see savvy). Gradually stir in the broth and clam juice and bring to a boil.

transfer the contents of the skillet to the insert of a 5- to 7-quart slow cooker. Add the potatoes and bay leaf. Cover and cook on high for 2½ to 3 hours, until the potatoes are tender.

stir in the bacon, fish, and cream. Cover and cook for an additional 45 minutes to 1 hour, until the fish is cooked through.

remove the bay leaf and serve the chowder garnished with the parsley and chives.

serves **8**

roux savvy
When whisking a roux with vegetables, I use a flat whisk because the veggies don't get stuck in it. Also, after adding the liquid to the roux, always bring it to a boil, otherwise it won't thicken properly.

Clam Chowder

Although it's most often called "New England clam chowder," each state in the Northeast has its own chowder. This recipe is based on what is served in Massachusetts, where I spent time growing up. The original recipes call for salt pork, but I like the flavor that thick-cut bacon brings to this hearty soup.

8 strips thick-cut bacon, cut into ½-inch pieces

1 large onion, finely chopped

4 stalks celery, finely chopped

1 teaspoon dried thyme

3 tablespoons all-purpose flour

1½ cups chicken broth

Two 8-ounce bottles clam juice

5 medium red or Yukon gold potatoes, cut into ½-inch chunks

Three 10-ounce cans chopped or minced clams, with their juice

1 bay leaf

2 cups milk

cook the bacon in a large skillet over medium-high heat until crisp and remove it to paper towels to drain. Remove all but ¼ cup of the bacon drippings from the skillet.

add the onion, celery, and thyme and sauté until the onion is translucent, 5 to 7 minutes. Stir in the flour and cook for 3 minutes, whisking the roux constantly (see savvy, page 69). Gradually stir in the broth and clam juice and bring to a boil.

transfer the contents of the skillet to the insert of a 5- to 7-quart slow cooker. Add the potatoes, clams, and bay leaf. Cover and cook on high for 2½ to 3 hours, until the potatoes are tender.

stir in the bacon and milk. Cover and cook for an additional 45 minutes to 1 hour, until the soup is heated through.

remove the bay leaf before serving.

serves **8**

Spicy Manhattan-Style Clam Chowder

As a child I loved this chowder because it was so different from its creamy New England cousins. Thyme, tomato, clams, and vegetables flavor the soup, giving it great character. Tomato-based chowders started appearing the mid-1800s when Italian and Portuguese fishermen started adding tomatoes to chowder rather than cream or milk. Some say this was originally called "Fulton Market Clam Chowder," but whatever you call it, it is a satisfying meal any day of the week.

8 strips bacon, cut into ½-inch slices

2 medium onions, finely chopped

4 stalks celery, finely chopped

2 teaspoons dried thyme

½ cup dry white wine or vermouth

One 14- to 15-ounce can tomato purée

Two 10-ounce cans chopped or minced clams, with their juice

One 8-ounce bottle clam juice

1 bay leaf

5 medium Yukon gold or red potatoes, cut into ½-inch dice

Salt and freshly ground black pepper

cook the bacon in a large skillet over medium heat until crisp and remove it to paper towels to drain. Remove all but 3 tablespoons of the drippings.

add the onions, celery, and thyme and sauté until the vegetables begin to soften, 3 to 4 minutes.

deglaze the pan with the wine, scraping up any browned bits from the bottom of the pan. Transfer the contents of the skillet to the insert of a 5- to 7-quart slow cooker.

stir in the remaining ingredients, except the salt and pepper. Cover and cook on low for 6 hours, until the potatoes are tender. Season with salt and pepper.

remove the bay leaf before serving.

serves **8**

Shrimp Chowder

Plump shrimp, spicy Old Bay seasoning, and smoky bacon give this chowder lots of personality and pizzazz. Serve this in hollowed-out sourdough bread bowls for a great casual meal.

8 strips thick-cut bacon, cut into ½-inch pieces

1 large onion, finely chopped

4 stalks celery, finely chopped

1 teaspoon dried thyme

2 teaspoons Old Bay seasoning

3 tablespoons all-purpose flour

3 cups chicken broth

Two 8-ounce bottles clam juice

5 medium red or Yukon gold potatoes, cut into ½-inch chunks

1 bay leaf

1½ pounds medium shrimp, peeled and deveined

1½ cups heavy cream

¼ cup finely chopped fresh Italian parsley for garnishing

¼ cup finely chopped fresh chives for garnishing

cook the bacon in a large skillet over medium-high heat until crisp and remove it to paper towels to drain. Remove all but ¼ cup of the bacon drippings from the skillet.

add the onion, celery, thyme, and seasoning and sauté until the onion is translucent, 5 to 7 minutes. Stir in the flour and cook for 3 minutes, whisking the roux constantly (see savvy, page 69). Gradually stir in the broth and clam juice and bring to a boil.

transfer the contents of the skillet to the insert of a 5- to 7-quart slow cooker. Stir in the potatoes and bay leaf. Cover and cook on high for 2½ to 3 hours, until the potatoes are tender. Stir in the bacon, shrimp, and cream.

cover and cook for an additional 45 minutes to 1 hour, until the shrimp is cooked through.

remove the bay leaf and serve garnished with parsley and chives.

serves **8**

Mixed Shellfish Chowder

This velvety chowder filled with lobster, crab, and scallops is a whole meal in a bowl. Make sure to use lobster stock for this chowder because it gives the soup the necessary richness it needs alongside the luxurious seafood.

4 tablespoons (½ stick) unsalted butter

1 medium onion, finely chopped

3 stalks celery, finely chopped

1 teaspoon sweet paprika

½ teaspoon dried thyme

3 tablespoons all-purpose flour

6 cups lobster stock (see savvy, page 74)

2 tablespoons brandy

½ pound cooked lobster meat, picked over for shells and cartilage

½ pound lump crabmeat, picked over for shells and cartilage

¼ pound bay or sea scallops, cut into quarters

1 cup heavy cream

¼ cup finely chopped fresh chives for garnishing

melt the butter in a saucepan over medium-high heat. Add the onion, celery, paprika, and thyme and sauté until the vegetables begin to soften, about 3 minutes. Stir in the flour and cook for 2 to 3 minutes, whisking the roux constantly (see savvy, page 69). Stir in the stock and brandy and bring to a boil.

transfer the contents of the skillet to the insert of a 5- to 7-quart slow cooker. Cover and cook for 4 hours on low. Add the lobster, crab, scallops, and cream and cook on low for an additional 1 hour.

serve the soup garnished with chives.

serves **8**

Cajun Corn and Crab Soup

This delicious soup begins with a roux, which flavors the soup with Creole seasoning and gives it a spicy quality that balances well with the sweet corn and crabmeat. You can certainly substitute shrimp for the crab, or for those allergic to shellfish, many of my students love this soup with leftover chicken or turkey. Anyway you make it, it's a winner when served with some crusty bread.

½ cup (1 stick) unsalted butter

2 medium sweet onions, such as Vidalia, finely chopped

4 stalks celery, finely chopped

½ teaspoon sweet paprika

¼ teaspoon freshly ground black pepper

⅛ teaspoon cayenne pepper

½ teaspoon dried thyme

3 tablespoons all-purpose flour

5 cups seafood stock (see savvy)

One 16-ounce package frozen white corn, defrosted

1 pound lump crabmeat, picked over for cartilage and shells

1 cup cream

Salt and freshly ground black pepper

½ cup finely chopped fresh chives

melt the butter in a saucepan over medium-high heat.

add the onions, celery, paprika, black and cayenne peppers, and thyme and sauté until the vegetables are softened, 3 to 5 minutes. Stir in the flour and cook for 3 minutes, whisking the roux constantly (see savvy, page 69). Stir in the stock and bring the mixture to a boil.

transfer the contents of the skillet to the insert of a 5- to 7-quart slow cooker. Add the corn, cover, and cook on high for 2 hours. Stir in the crabmeat and cream and cook on low for an additional 30 minutes.

season with salt and pepper. Garnish each serving with chives.

serves **8**

seafood-stock savvy
Your local grocer or gourmet retailer may sell seafood stock. My preferences are More Than Gourmet seafood stock or Better Than Bouillon lobster stock. Another way to approximate seafood stock to is mix equal parts clam juice and chicken broth.

Mediterranean Shrimp and Rice Soup

Simmered with garlic, oregano, tomato, and lemon zest, this soup will have you dreaming of Greek islands and the blue coastal waters of the Mediterranean. This soup can also be made with fish, such as halibut or sea bass, cut into one-inch chunks.

3 tablespoons extra-virgin olive oil

2 cloves garlic, minced

1 medium onion, finely chopped

2 teaspoons dried oregano

1 teaspoon dried basil

Grated zest of 1 lemon

1 cup dry white wine or vermouth

One 14- to 15-ounce can chopped tomatoes, with their juice

4 cups chicken or vegetable broth

1 cup raw converted rice

1½ pounds medium shrimp, peeled and deveined

½ cup finely chopped fresh Italian parsley for garnishing

1 cup crumbled feta cheese for garnishing

heat the oil in a large sauté pan over medium-high heat. Add the garlic, onion, oregano, basil, and lemon zest and sauté until the onion is softened, about 3 minutes.

deglaze the pan with the wine, scraping up any browned bits from the bottom of the pan, and transfer the contents of the sauté pan to the insert of a 5- to 7-quart slow cooker.

stir in the tomatoes, broth, and rice. cover and cook on high for 2 hours or on low for 4 hours, until the rice is tender. Stir in the shrimp, cover, and cook for an additional 20 minutes, until the shrimp is cooked through.

serve garnished with the parsley and feta.

serves 8

Veracruz-Style Fish Soup

Another example of fishermen making the most of everything they catch, this simple soup combines zesty south-of-the-border flavors and seafood to make a terrific one-pot meal for a casual fiesta or weeknight dinner.

Four 6-inch corn tortillas, cut into thin strips

2 tablespoons vegetable oil

1 medium onion, finely chopped

2 cloves garlic, minced

1 jalapeño pepper, seeded and finely chopped

2 medium red bell peppers, finely chopped

1 teaspoon ground cumin

1 teaspoon dried oregano

One 12-ounce bottle Corona or other light Mexican beer

One 28- to 32-ounce can chopped tomatoes, with their juice

One 8-ounce bottle clam juice

1 pound sea bass, halibut, or red snapper fillets, cut into 1-inch chunks

2 cups cooked long-grain rice

½ cup finely chopped fresh cilantro

Salt and freshly ground black pepper

place the tortillas in the bottom of the insert of a 5- to 7-quart slow cooker.

heat the oil in a large skillet over medium-high heat. Add the onion, garlic, jalapeño, bell peppers, cumin, and oregano and sauté until the vegetables are softened, about 5 minutes.

deglaze the pan with the beer, scraping up any browned bits from the bottom of the skillet. Transfer the contents of the skillet to the slow-cooker insert and stir to combine with the tortillas. Stir in the tomatoes and clam juice.

cover and cook on low for 4 to 5 hours. Stir in the fish, rice, and cilantro and cook for an additional 1 hour, until the fish is cooked through.

season with salt and pepper before serving.

serves **8**

Miso Soup with Tofu, Shiitakes, and Shrimp

Miso soup, like mom's chicken soup, is good for what ails you. A recent television show in Japan had contestants do a blind taste test of miso soups and all of them identified their mom's soup on the first try! Early use of miso soup as a restorative dates back to the 7th century, when it was served to Samurais to heal their bodies and minds. Miso is generally started with a dried sardine-based stock called *dashi*, but vegetable stock works as well. In this soup, the miso and shiitakes simmer to produce a delicious broth that infuses flavor into the shrimp and tofu.

2 tablespoons vegetable oil

1 clove garlic, minced

1 teaspoon freshly grated ginger

8 ounces shiitake mushrooms, stems removed, caps sliced

¼ cup light miso paste

6 cups vegetable or chicken broth

2 teaspoons soy sauce

1 pound firm tofu, cut into ½-inch cubes

1 pound medium shrimp, peeled and deveined, tails removed

6 green onions, finely chopped

Toasted sesame oil for drizzling

Toasted sesame seeds for garnishing

heat the vegetable oil in a large skillet over high heat. Add the garlic and ginger and sauté until they are fragrant, about 1 minute. Add the mushrooms and toss with the garlic and ginger.

transfer the contents of the skillet to the insert of a 5- to 7-quart slow cooker. Stir in the miso, broth, and soy sauce.

cover and cook on high for 2½ to 3 hours. Add the tofu and shrimp, cover, turn the cooker to low, and cook until the shrimp are pink and cooked through, about 30 minutes.

add the green onions to the soup and serve drizzled with the sesame oil and garnished with sesame seeds.

serves 8

Sailors' Shellfish Stew

Cioppino is a regional dish from the San Francisco Bay Area. In the days when fishing fleets plied the cold waters off San Francisco, fishermen would return and use the scraps from their hauls to make a delicious stew, which they called cioppino. A quick check with any fishing community will tell you they all have some kind of soup or stew made with bits and leftovers. This one shows its Italian influences in the garlic, tomato, basil, and oregano. In San Francisco they serve this with crusty sourdough bread, which you can purchase in most areas of the country. If you can't find sourdough, a crusty French or Italian loaf sops up the flavorful juices just as well.

¼ cup extra-virgin olive oil

1 medium onion, finely chopped

3 cloves garlic, minced

1 medium green bell pepper, seeded and finely chopped

1½ teaspoons dried oregano

1½ teaspoons dried basil

⅛ teaspoon red pepper flakes

1½ cups white wine

One 28- to 32-ounce can plum tomatoes, drained and chopped

3 tablespoons tomato paste

One 8-ounce bottle clam juice

1 bay leaf

½ teaspoon freshly ground black pepper

1 large Dungeness crab or 4 large king crab legs, cracked and cut into bite-size pieces (see savvy)

2 lobster tails, split and cut into 1-inch chunks

1 pound sea bass, cut into 1-inch chunks

¾ pound medium shrimp, peeled and deveined

24 littleneck clams, shells scrubbed

½ cup finely chopped fresh Italian parsley for garnishing

heat the oil in a large skillet over medium-high heat. Add the onion, garlic, bell pepper, oregano, basil, and red pepper flakes and sauté until the onion is softened, about 3 minutes. Deglaze the pan with the wine, scraping up any browned bits from the bottom of the pan, and bring to a boil. Reduce by half.

transfer the contents of the skillet to the insert of a 5- to 7-quart slow cooker. Stir in the tomatoes, tomato paste, clam juice, bay leaf, and pepper. Cover and cook on low for 5 hours. Add the crab, lobster, sea bass, shrimp, and clams.

cover and cook on low for 1 hour, until the shrimp are pink and the clams have opened. Discard the bay leaf and any clams that have not opened. Carefully stir the stew, being careful not to break up the sea bass chunks.

serve the stew garnished with the parsley.

serves **8**

seafood savvy
The shells from the seafood add flavor, and I recommend that you cut them with kitchen shears so that they are easier to dig into when served.

Seafood Jambalaya

Jambalaya is a Cajun rice dish that is the perfect one-pot meal. It's not so much a soup as an explosion of rice, vegetables, spices, seafood, and spicy sausage. I love to serve this to a crowd—it's simple to get the base ready to go, add the rest of the ingredients, and let the slow cooker work its magic. Serve the jambalaya directly from the slow cooker with an assortment of hot sauces on the side.

1 pound andouille sausage or polish kielbasa, cut into ½-inch rounds

1 large onion, finely chopped

2 medium green bell peppers, finely chopped

4 stalks celery, finely chopped

3 cloves garlic, minced

1 teaspoon dried thyme

1 bay leaf

1 teaspoon dried oregano

1 teaspoon dried basil

½ teaspoon freshly ground black pepper

¼ teaspoon cayenne pepper

One 14- to 15-ounce can chopped tomatoes, with their juice

10 cups chicken broth

1½ cups raw converted rice

2 pounds cleaned mixed shellfish such as shrimp, oysters, clams, crab, and crawfish

6 green onions, finely chopped for garnishing

Assorted hot sauces for serving

cook the sausage in a large skillet over high heat until it renders some fat and begins to color.

transfer the sausage to the insert of a 5- to 7-quart slow cooker. Add the onion, bell peppers, celery, garlic, thyme, bay leaf, oregano, basil, and black and cayenne peppers to the same skillet and sauté until the onion is beginning to turn golden, 5 to 7 minutes.

add the tomatoes and cook until some of the liquid evaporates, 3 to 4 minutes. Transfer the contents of the skillet to the slow-cooker insert and stir in the broth and rice. Cover and cook on high for 2 hours or on low for 4 hours.

remove the cover and add the shellfish and cook on high for 20 minutes, until the rice is tender and the shellfish is cooked. Remove the bay leaf.

garnish with green onions and serve directly from the slow cooker with an assortment of hot sauces.

serves 8–10

Chapter 2
Is That a Casserole in There?

This chapter contains all those wonderful casseroles that you love to make but want to leave in the pot so you won't have to think about them. Lasagna, tuna noodle casserole, mac and cheese, and all their cousins shine in this chapter. I love casseroles because they recycle your leftovers and become a completely different meal. Casseroles also stretch your food dollar, using starches like potatoes, pastas, and rice to bulk up the proteins in the dish. Since cooking noodles and rice from their dry state with other ingredients in the slow cooker can be a bit tricky, I recommend planning ahead by cooking extra pasta and rice and freezing them in zipper-top plastic bags. With a zap in the microwave to defrost them, you are on your way to assembling your slow-cooker casserole.

For these casseroles, I'd recommend either spraying the inside of the ceramic insert with nonstick cooking spray or using a slow-cooker liner (see Care and Feeding of the Slow Cooker, page 10) to prevent sticking and make cleaning up easier.

Noodles

Even though it's just me and my husband at home, I still cook a pound of pasta when making it for the two of us—old habits die hard. I've learned to freeze the leftover plain pasta to use it later for casseroles and soups made in the slow cooker. Fresh pasta doesn't need to be cooked before it goes into the slow cooker, but if you are adapting a favorite recipe to use fresh pasta, add extra sauce, as the pasta will absorb quite a bit while it's cooking. Also, make sure not to cook the dry pasta too long before adding it to the slow cooker. It should be just short of al dente, or about 2 to 4 minutes short of your average cooking time, so that it won't become mushy when it cooks again. Casseroles can be made ahead of time in slow-cooker liners and then refrigerated, or in some cases frozen, until you are ready to cook them. Your favorite chicken and noodles, mac and cheese, and lasagna will be ready when you are.

Not-Your-Mother's Tuna Noodle Casserole

In my classes I tell a story about how, as a child, I would beg my mother to let me go to my friends' homes on Friday nights so I could eat tuna noodle casserole. My mom didn't have a single can of soup in her pantry and was horrified that I thought these foods were exotic and homey! When we first were married, my husband loved tuna noodle casserole. The one time I made it for him, however, the man who would eat anything asked if we could go out to dinner! I've come a long way since then; this tuna noodle casserole is an elegant comfort food filled with sautéed mushrooms and a delicious cream sauce. It's a great party dish and, of course, you can substitute chicken for the tuna if you'd like.

½ pound wide egg noodles, cooked just short of al dente

Two 6-ounce cans solid white albacore tuna packed in oil, drained and broken into chunks (see savvy)

4 tablespoons (½ stick) unsalted butter

1 small onion, finely chopped (about ¼ cup)

2 stalks celery, finely chopped

8 ounces button mushrooms, sliced

¼ cup all-purpose flour

3 cups milk

4 drops Tabasco sauce

½ teaspoon salt

½ cup finely crushed potato chips

coat the insert of a 5- to 7-quart slow cooker with nonstick cooking spray or line it with a slow-cooker liner according to the manufacturer's directions.

put the noodles and tuna in the slow-cooker insert and stir to combine. Melt the butter in a large skillet over high heat. Add the onion, celery, and mushrooms and sauté until the liquid in the pan begins to evaporate (you should still have some fat in the pan).

stir in the flour and cook for 3 minutes, stirring constantly. Gradually add the milk and bring to a boil, stirring constantly. Stir in the Tabasco and salt. Transfer the contents of the skillet to the slow-cooker insert.

cover and cook on low for 4 to 5 hours. Remove the cover, sprinkle the chips over the casserole, re-cover, and cook for an additional 30 minutes.

serve from the slow cooker set on warm.

serves **6—8**

tuna savvy
I find that water-packed tuna is bland, and although it may have a bit less fat, it doesn't have much flavor. Buy the oil-packed solid albacore—you'll be glad you did.

Lasagna alla Bolognese

Lasagna can seem like a big production, but it's really just a few components made ahead of time and then assembled. This lasagna can be put together and frozen in the slow-cooker insert until firm and then stored in a zipper-top plastic bag in the freezer for up to three months.

The Bolognese sauce can be homemade in the slow cooker or on the stovetop. This lasagna isn't the traditional all-American version with ricotta cheese; it's a lighter version that has creamy béchamel sauce and fresh mozzarella layered between delicate no-boil lasagna noodles.

4 tablespoons (½ stick) unsalted butter

¼ cup all-purpose flour

1½ cups chicken broth

1½ cups milk

2½ cups freshly grated Parmigiano-Reggiano cheese

6 cups Bolognese Sauce (page 399) or Mom's Sunday Sauce (page 401)

One 9-ounce box no-boil lasagna noodles

1 pound fresh mozzarella, cut into ½-inch slices

coat the insert of a 5- to 7-quart slow cooker with nonstick cooking spray or line it with a slow-cooker liner according to the manufacturer's directions.

melt the butter in a medium saucepan over medium-high heat. Stir in the flour and cook for 3 minutes, whisking constantly. Gradually add the broth and milk and bring to a boil, whisking constantly to make a béchamel sauce.

remove from the heat and stir in 1½ cups of the Parmigiano. Spoon some of the bolognese sauce on the bottom of the slow cooker, covering the bottom of the pan. Top with a layer of noodles (depending on the cooker, you may have to cut the noodles down to size). Spoon a layer of the béchamel sauce over the noodles and top with some of the mozzarella. Continue layering the bolognese sauce, noodles, béchamel sauce, and mozzarella in this order, ending with the bolognese sauce.

sprinkle the remaining 1 cup Parmigiano over the lasagna. Cover and cook on low for 4 to 5 hours, until the lasagna is bubbling. Remove the cover and cook for an additional 45 minutes.

serve from the cooker set on warm.

serves **8**

Pecorino Romano Lasagna

Pecorino romano is a sheep's milk cheese that is sometimes studded with peppercorns or truffles. The peppercorn variety works well in this white lasagna flavored with mushrooms, spinach, and ham.

½ cup (1 stick) unsalted butter

¼ cup finely chopped onion

2 cloves garlic, minced

One 16-ounce package frozen chopped spinach, defrosted and squeezed dry

1 pound cremini or white mushrooms, sliced

1½ teaspoons salt

½ teaspoon freshly ground black pepper

¼ cup all-purpose flour

2½ cups milk

¼ cup dry white wine or vermouth

3 cups finely grated pecorino romano cheese, plus 1 cup crumbled into pea-sized pieces

One 9-ounce box no-boil lasagna noodles

4 ounces black forest ham, cut into julienne strips

coat the insert of a 5- to 7-quart slow cooker with nonstick cooking spray or line it with a slow-cooker liner according to the manufacturer's directions.

melt half the butter in a large skillet over high heat. Add the onion and garlic and sauté until the onion is softened, about 3 minutes. Add the spinach, mushrooms, salt, and pepper and sauté until the mushrooms begin to turn golden and the spinach is dry, 5 to 7 minutes.

remove from the heat and set aside to cool. Melt the remaining butter in a saucepan over medium-high heat. Stir in the flour and cook for 3 minutes, whisking constantly. Add the milk and bring the sauce to a boil. Remove the sauce from the heat and stir in the wine and finely grated pecorino.

spoon one-quarter of the sauce on the bottom of the slow-cooker insert. Top with a layer of noodles, cutting them to fit. Spread half the vegetables and half the ham over the noodles. Spread one-quarter of the sauce over the vegetables and ham. Sprinkle with ⅓ cup of the crumbled pecorino. Arrange a layer of noodles over the vegetables and ham, then spread the remaining vegetables, ham, one-quarter of the sauce, and ⅓ cup of the crumbled pecorino on top. Top with another layer of noodles, and spread the remaining sauce and ⅓ cup pecorino over the noodles.

cover and cook on low for 4 to 5 hours, until the lasagna is cooked through and bubbling. Remove the cover and cook for an additional 30 minutes.

serve from the cooker set on warm.

serves **8**

Penne Lasagna

This decadent lasagna is similar to a "Timpano," the extravagant layered dish that was featured in the Stanley Tucci classic film *Big Night*. Although a timpano is usually encased in dough, this entrée has layers of pasta, meatballs, cheese, hard-boiled eggs, mushrooms, and sausage in a creamy red-pepper-and-vodka tomato sauce. In Calabria, cooks empty their refrigerators and pantries of food they won't be able to eat during Lent and pile them into layered pasta dishes such as this one.

5 cups Vodka Cream Sauce (recipe follows)

1 pound penne, cooked 2 minutes short of al dente

4 cooked meatballs, quartered (facing page)

4 hard-cooked eggs, sliced ½ inch thick (facing page)

½ cup jarred roasted red peppers, cut into strips

4 links cooked Italian sweet sausage (see facing page), cut into ½-inch rounds

8 ounces button mushrooms, sautéed (see facing page) until the liquid in the pan evaporates

½ pound fresh mozzarella, cut into ½-inch cubes

1 cup freshly grated pecorino romano cheese

coat the insert of a 5- to 7-quart slow cooker with nonstick cooking spray or line it with a slow-cooker liner according to the manufacturer's directions.

put 1½ cups of the vodka cream sauce and the penne in a large bowl and stir to coat.

spread one-third of the pasta on the bottom of the slow-cooker insert. Top the pasta with a layer of the meatballs, hard-cooked eggs, and roasted peppers. Top with half of the remaining pasta, followed by a layer of the remaining sausage, the mushrooms, and mozzarella. Top with the remaining pasta.

spoon the remaining sauce evenly over the top of the lasagna and top with the grated cheese.

cover the cooker and cook on low heat for 4 to 5 hours, until the lasagna is bubbling and is cooked through.

remove the cover and cook for an additional 30 minutes.

serve the lasagna from the cooker set on warm.

serves **12**

VODKA CREAM SAUCE

1 teaspoon red pepper flakes

1 cup vodka

½ cup (1 stick) unsalted butter

One 28- to 32-ounce can crushed tomatoes

1 cup heavy cream

¼ cup finely chopped fresh Italian parsley

¼ cup finely chopped fresh basil

soak the pepper flakes in the vodka for 1 hour.

strain the vodka through a fine-mesh sieve into a medium saucepan, discarding the pepper flakes. Over high heat, bring the vodka to a boil and reduce to ¼ cup.

add the butter, tomatoes, cream, parsley, and basil. Bring the sauce to a boil, stirring to combine.

makes about **5** cups

MEATBALLS

1¼ pounds ground beef

½ cup finely chopped onion

1 clove garlic, minced

Grated zest of 1 lemon

1 teaspoon salt

1 teaspoon freshly ground
black pepper

2 tablespoons chopped
fresh parsley

½ cup soft bread crumbs

1 large egg, beaten

Olive oil for frying

combine the beef, onion, garlic, lemon zest, salt, pepper, parsley, bread crumbs, and egg in a large bowl until blended. Form the mixture into small balls and set on a plate or baking sheet. At this point, you can cover and refrigerate the meatballs for up to 2 days.

heat ½ inch of oil in a large skillet until a piece of bread dropped in it begins to float and bubble. Add the meatballs a few at a time, being careful not to crowd them, and fry until browned on all sides and cooked through. Using a slotted spoon or tongs, remove the meatballs from the pan and drain on paper towels.

repeat with the remaining meatballs until they are all cooked. Cooked meatballs may be cooled and refrigerated for up to 2 days, or frozen for up to 2 months.

makes **6** meatballs

PERFECTLY HARD-COOKED EGGS

6 large eggs

place the eggs in a 3-quart saucepan and cover with water. Bring the water in the pan to a boil, and remove the pan from the heat.

cover the pan, and allow to sit for 12 minutes. At the end of 12 minutes, plunge the eggs into ice water, to stop the cooking process. Use the eggs immediately or refrigerate for up to 1 week.

TO COOK SAUSAGE

1 to 2 pounds sausage (this instruction is for uncooked sausages such as Italian, bratwurst, or country pork sausages)

½ cup water, wine, or broth

place the sausages in a skillet, add the water, prick the sausages with the tip of a sharp knife, cover, and bring to a boil. Simmer the sausages for 10 minutes, remove the cover, and sauté until the liquid has evaporated and the sausages have browned.

TO SAUTE MUSHROOMS

2 tablespoons olive oil

1 pound sliced mushrooms

Salt and freshly ground pepper

heat the oil in a skillet, and sauté the mushrooms until they begin to color, seasoning with salt and pepper.

Salmon, Artichoke, and Noodle Casserole

This is a gorgeous casserole with delicate pink salmon and light green artichoke hearts in a creamy dill-flavored sauce. It will be a hit at your next potluck dinner or family meal. Use leftover grilled salmon or poached salmon from the slow cooker (see page 152) for this special seafood dinner. I like to use wide egg noodles for this casserole but leftover fettuccine or spaghetti, cut into two-inch lengths, will also work. This casserole is also delicious using medium cooked shrimp, cooked chicken or turkey, or leftover firm-fleshed fish such as sea bass or halibut.

½ pound wide egg noodles, cooked just short of al dente

1 pound salmon fillet, poached, skin and any bones removed, and flaked (2½ to 3 cups, see savvy)

One 16-ounce package frozen artichoke hearts (see savvy), defrosted, drained, and cut in half

4 tablespoons (½ stick) unsalted butter

1 small onion, finely chopped (about ½ cup)

3 tablespoons all-purpose flour

3 cups milk

¼ cup finely chopped fresh dill

1½ teaspoons salt

½ teaspoon freshly ground black pepper

½ cup crushed buttery crackers, such as Ritz or Pepperidge Farm Golden Butter Crackers

coat the insert of a 5- to 7-quart slow cooker with nonstick cooking spray or line it with a slow-cooker liner according to the manufacturer's directions.

put the noodles, salmon, and artichoke hearts in the slow cooker and stir to combine.

melt the butter in a medium saucepan over medium-high heat. Add the onion and sauté until the onion is softened, about 3 minutes. Stir in the flour, and cook for 3 additional minutes.

gradually add the milk and bring the sauce to a boil, whisking constantly. Add the dill, salt, and pepper. Pour the sauce over the ingredients in the slow-cooker insert, stirring to coat the ingredients.

cover and cook on low for 4 to 5 hours. Remove the cover, sprinkle the crackers over the casserole, and cook for an additional 30 minutes.

serve from the cooker set on warm.

serves **6—8**

salmon savvy
Although canned salmon may seem convenient, it is not an option for me; it has a strong flavor and will overwhelm the other ingredients in this casserole.

artichoke savvy
If you cannot find frozen artichoke hearts, use two 14- to 15-ounce cans artichoke hearts, drained, and quartered.

Sun-Dried Tomato Pesto and Tortellini Casserole

This casserole is a terrific meatless entrée or side dish. It's beautifully colored, with spinach tortellini peeking through the creamy pink sun-dried tomato sauce. Since this is a rich dish, I lightened up the sauce by using chicken broth and milk instead of milk and heavy cream.

1½ cups sun-dried tomatoes packed in oil, drained

2 cups packed basil leaves

2½ cups freshly grated Parmigiano-Reggiano cheese

6 garlic cloves, peeled

½ cup raw pine nuts

½ teaspoon freshly ground black pepper

2 tablespoons balsamic vinegar

½ cup (1 stick) unsalted butter, at room temperature

3 tablespoons flour

1½ cups chicken broth

1½ cups milk

1½ pounds fresh spinach and cheese or other tortellini

coat the insert of a 5- to 7-quart slow cooker with nonstick cooking spray or line it with a slow-cooker liner according to the manufacturer's directions.

put the tomatoes, basil, 1½ cups of the Parmigiano, the garlic, pine nuts, pepper, and balsamic vinegar in the bowl of a food processor. Pulse on and off to break up the tomatoes, garlic, and pine nuts. Add the butter and flour, and pulse on and off until the mixture is incorporated, about 30 seconds.

transfer the mixture to a large skillet over high heat. Add the broth and bring the sauce to a boil, whisking until thickened. Add the milk and bring the sauce back to a boil. Remove from the heat and set aside.

spread half the tortellini in the slow cooker. Top with half the sauce and half the remaining 1 cup cheese.

top with layers of the remaining tortellini, sauce, and cheese. Cover and cook on low for 4 to 5 hours, until the pasta is tender and the casserole is bubbling. Remove the cover and cook for an additional 30 minutes.

serve from the cooker set on warm.

serves **6**

Old-Fashioned Mac and Cheese

Macaroni and cheese is the ultimate comfort food. In a slow cooker, chunks of cheese can be laced between the layers of noodles, allowing the cheese to melt slowly during the cooking process, giving you more of its cheesy, oozy goodness. The template for macaroni and cheese is simple: a creamy white sauce, plenty of cheese, and any small pasta, such as shells or tiny rigatoni, if you don't have elbow macaroni on hand. Variations happen when you substitute cheese and add other ingredients that your family enjoys—so have fun with this one. If your children absolutely won't eat a mac and cheese that doesn't have that Day-Glo orange color, the King Arthur Flour Web site sells powdered cheese for just that effect! The entire casserole can be assembled in a slow-cooker liner and then refrigerated or frozen for later use. Before cooking, defrost the frozen casserole over-night in the refrigerator, bringing it up to room temperature for 45 minutes, and you will be on your way to slow-cooked comfort.

4 tablespoons (½ stick) unsalted butter

1 small onion or shallot, finely chopped (about ¼ cup, see savvy)

3 tablespoons all-purpose flour

1½ cups chicken broth

1½ cups milk

4 drops Tabasco sauce

5 cups finely shredded mild yellow and sharp white Cheddar cheese, plus extra to top

6 cups elbow macaroni, cooked just short of al dente (see savvy)

½ cup crushed buttery crackers such as Ritz or Pepperidge Farm Golden Butter Crackers

coat the insert of a 5- to 7-quart slow cooker with nonstick cooking spray or line it with a slow-cooker liner according to the manufacturer's directions.

melt the butter in a saucepan over medium-high heat. Add the onion and sauté until the onion is softened, about 2 minutes. Stir in the flour, and cook for 2 to 3 minutes, whisking constantly. Gradually add the broth and milk and bring the sauce to a boil, whisking constantly.

add the Tabasco and remove the sauce from the heat. Add 3 cups of the cheese to the sauce and stir to melt. Spread half the macaroni in the slow-cooker insert and pour half the sauce over the macaroni.

sprinkle 1 cup of the cheese over the layer. Repeat with the remaining macaroni and sauce and 1 cup of the cheese. Cover and cook for on low for 4 to 5 hours, until the mac and cheese is bubbling and cooked through.

sprinkle a little more cheese and the crackers over the top of the mac and cheese. Remove the cover and cook for an additional 30 minutes. Allow the mac and cheese to rest about 10 minutes.

serve in the cooker set on warm.

serves 6–8

BLUE CHEESE MAC AND CHEESE

follow the directions for the Old-Fashioned Mac and Cheese.

add 2 teaspoons Worcestershire sauce with the Tabasco.

substitute crumbled blue cheese for 3 cups of the Cheddar. Use half the blue cheese in the sauce and the rest between the layers and sprinkled on top. Proceed as directed.

SMOKY GOUDA MAC AND CHEESE

follow the directions for the Old-Fashioned Mac and Cheese.

substitute 3 cups finely shredded smoked Gouda and 2 cups finely shredded Monterey Jack cheese for the Cheddar.

combine the cheeses in a bowl and use them equally as directed in the sauce, between the layers, and on top. Proceed as directed.

MAC AND FOUR-CHEESE ITALIANO

follow the directions for the Old-Fashioned Mac and Cheese.

substitute 1¼ cups each finely grated Parmigiano-Reggiano and pecorino romano, 1¼ cups fresh mozzarella, and 1¼ cup crumbled Gorgonzola for the Cheddar cheeses.

use the Parmigiano and pecorino in the sauce and layer the mozzarella and Gorgonzola in between the layers and sprinkled on top. Proceed as directed.

APPLEWOOD SMOKED BACON, CARAMEL-IZED ONION, AND WHITE CHEDDAR MAC AND CHEESE

cook 8 strips of applewood smoked bacon in a large skillet over medium heat until crisp, remove it from the pan to drain, and crumble.

caramelize 4 large sweet onions (see page 360) in a sauté pan with ½ cup (1 stick) unsalted butter, 2 tablespoons olive oil, 1 tablespoon sugar, 1 teaspoon salt, and ½ teaspoon dried thyme until onions are golden, about 15 to 20 minutes.

use all sharp white Cheddar for the cheese. Distribute the bacon and onions between the layers and proceed as directed.

onion savvy
Onion-phobic children may not like the onion in here. In that case leave it out, and just cook the butter-and-flour roux as directed.

macaroni savvy
Since the macaroni will cook again in the slow cooker, don't cook it any longer than al dente, or the resulting mac and cheese will be mushy and the noodles will fall apart. To avoid this, undercook the noodles by 2 to 4 minutes, until they are soft but still chewy.

Rice

Rice casseroles are a terrific supplement to a weeknight dinner or a gala occasion. Plan ahead by cooking extra rice and freezing it in 1- or 2-cup portions in zipper-top plastic bags. Although brown rice might seem like a healthier option, I don't recommend it. It is too coarse and the texture fights with the other ingredients in the casseroles. For all the rice dishes in this chapter we used converted rice, like Uncle Ben's, because it is reliable in the slow cooker. Other rice tends to absorb too much liquid, or not enough. I discourage the use of short-grain or scented rice, like jasmine rice. Short-grain rice doesn't absorb sauce well and becomes gummy, and jasmine rice will take over the flavor of the casserole.

Porcini and Sage Rice

Terrific as a side dish, this casserole is filled with dried porcini and sage-scented cremini mushrooms and is a winner any night of the week. I love to serve it alongside grilled meat, chicken, or seafood.

2½ cups beef broth

4 ounces dried porcini mushrooms, crumbled

½ cup (1 stick) unsalted butter

1 pound cremini mushrooms, quartered

6 fresh sage leaves, finely sliced

1 teaspoon dried sage

1½ teaspoons salt

½ teaspoon freshly ground black pepper

¼ cup full-bodied red wine

4 cups cooked white rice

coat the insert of a 5- to 7-quart slow cooker with nonstick cooking spray or line it with a slow-cooker liner according to the manufacturer's directions.

add the broth and the porcini to a large bowl and allow the porcini to reconstitute while you prepare the other ingredients.

melt the butter in a large skillet over high heat. Add the cremini, fresh and dried sage, salt, and pepper and sauté until the mushrooms have begun to color, 5 to 7 minutes. Add the wine and cook for another 2 minutes, stirring up any bits that may have stuck to the bottom of the pan.

remove from the heat and set aside to cool. Put the rice and the sautéed mushrooms in a large bowl and stir to combine. Strain the broth and porcini through a fine-mesh sieve into the rice and transfer the mixture to the slow-cooker insert.

cover and cook on high for 2 hours. Remove the cover and cook an additional 30 to 45 minutes, until the liquid has been absorbed.

serve from the cooker set on warm.

serves **8**

Chicken, Artichoke, and Mushroom Rice Casserole

Filled with chicken, artichoke hearts, and mushrooms in a creamy sherry-and-cheese-flavored sauce, this swell rice casserole offers a terrific way to use up leftover chicken or turkey. You could also use medium cooked shrimp or cooked salmon for a seafood option. Serve this with a green salad with fruit and a sweet vinaigrette.

½ cup (1 stick) unsalted butter

1 medium onion, finely chopped

1 pound white button mushrooms, sliced

⅓ cup all-purpose flour

¼ cup cream sherry

4 cups milk

⅛ teaspoon freshly grated nutmeg

1½ teaspoons salt

½ teaspoon freshly ground black pepper

2½ cups finely grated Parmigiano-Reggiano cheese

4 cup cooked white rice (see savvy)

One 16-ounce package frozen artichoke hearts, defrosted and drained

3 cups bite-size pieces cooked chicken or turkey

coat the insert of a 5- to 7-quart slow cooker with nonstick cooking spray or line it with a slow-cooker liner according to the manufacturer's directions.

melt the butter in a large skillet over medium-high heat. Add the onion and sauté until it has softened, about 3 minutes. Add the mushrooms and cook until they are colored, 8 to 10 minutes.

add the flour and cook for 3 minutes, stirring constantly. Add the sherry and milk and bring the mixture to a boil. Add the nutmeg, salt, and pepper. Remove from the heat and add 1½ cups of the cheese, stirring until it is melted.

put 2 cups of the sauce and the rice in a large bowl and stir to combine. Put the artichokes, chicken, and the remaining sauce in another bowl, stirring to blend. Add half the rice mixture to the slow-cooker insert. Top with half the artichoke mixture and ½ cup of the cheese. Repeat with the remaining ingredients.

cover and cook on low for 4 to 5 hours, until the casserole is bubbling and is cooked through. Remove the cover and cook for an additional 30 minutes.

serve from the cooker set on warm.

serves **8**

rice savvy
A mixture of white and wild rice works well in this casserole, taking it out of the everyday and turning it into a party dish.

Green Chile and Sour Cream Rice Casserole

A perfect side dish for your next fiesta, this rice is mixed with sour cream, cheese, and vegetables to add color and texture. This dish tastes best alongside grilled entrées.

½ cup (1 stick) unsalted butter

1 medium onion, finely chopped

1 Anaheim chile, seeded and finely chopped

1 medium red bell pepper, seeded and finely chopped

1 medium yellow or orange bell pepper, seeded and finely chopped

2 cups corn kernels, fresh off the cob or frozen and defrosted

1 teaspoon ground cumin

½ teaspoon ancho chile powder

1 cup milk

3 cups sour cream

4 cups cooked white rice

1½ cups finely shredded mild Cheddar cheese

1 cup finely shredded Monterey Jack cheese

coat the insert of a 5- to 7-quart slow cooker with nonstick cooking spray or line it with a slow-cooker liner according to the manufacturer's directions.

heat the butter in a large skillet over medium-high heat. Add the onion, chile, bell peppers, corn, cumin, and chile powder and sauté until the vegetables are softened, 5 to 7 minutes.

remove from the heat and transfer the mixture to a large mixing bowl to cool. Once the vegetables are cool, stir in the milk and sour cream, rice, 1 cup of the Cheddar, and ½ cup of the Monterey Jack cheese and stir to combine.

transfer the mixture to the slow-cooker insert and sprinkle the remaining cheese over the top of the casserole. Cover and cook on low for 4 to 5 hours, until the casserole is cooked through and is bubbling. Remove the cover and cook for an additional 30 minutes.

serve from the cooker set on warm.

serves 6–8

Chicken and Triple Mushroom Casserole

Different from your usual chicken-and-rice casserole, this dish uses three different types of mushrooms, lemon zest, wild rice, dried apricots, and Marsala wine, and makes a terrific one-pot meal.

½ cup (1 stick) unsalted butter

1 medium onion, finely chopped

1½ pounds assorted mushrooms, such as button, cremini, shiitake, trumpet, and oyster, coarsely chopped

1 teaspoon dried thyme

1½ teaspoons salt

½ teaspoon freshly ground black pepper

¼ cup Marsala wine

Grated zest of 1 lemon

½ cup finely chopped dried apricots (about 5)

3 cups cooked chicken, cut into bite-sized pieces or shredded

4 cups cooked wild rice

1½ cups chicken broth

coat the insert of a 5- to 7-quart slow cooker with nonstick cooking spray or line it with a slow-cooker liner according to the manufacturer's directions.

melt the butter in a large skillet over medium-high heat. Add the onion, mushrooms, thyme, salt, and pepper and sauté until the mushrooms begin to turn golden, 5 to 7 minutes. Stir in the Marsala, remove from the heat, and set aside to cool.

put the remaining ingredients in the slow-cooker insert. Add the cooled mushrooms and stir to combine. Cover and cook on high for 2 to 3 hours, until the casserole is cooked through. Remove the cover and cook until the liquid is absorbed, an additional 30 to 45 minutes.

serve from the cooker set on warm.

serves **6–8**

Arancini Casserole

A classic southern Italian dish from Palermo, *arancini* are tiny balls of leftover rice. Stuffed with goodies such as gooey cheese, mushrooms, eggplant, and sun-dried tomatoes, the arancini are deep-fried and served with a tomato sauce for a light lunch or as antipasti. In larger towns, tiny shops sell up to a dozen varieties, all using leftovers as a base. Instead of deep-frying balls of rice, this dish layers rice and Italian ingredients and makes a stellar side dish or main course along with an accompanying salad.

4 cups cooked white rice

2 cups mascarpone cheese

1 cup chicken broth

2 cups finely grated pecorino romano cheese

6 ounces fresh mozzarella, cut into eight ½-inch-thick slices

6 slices Genoa salami or sopressata, cut into julienne strips

3 cloves garlic, minced

¼ cup finely chopped fresh Italian parsley

¼ cup extra-virgin olive oil

coat the insert of a 5- to 7-quart slow cooker with nonstick cooking spray or line it with a slow-cooker liner according to the manufacturer's directions.

put the rice, mascarpone, broth, and 1 cup of the pecorino in a large bowl and stir to combine. Put half the rice mixture in the slow-cooker insert. Layer half the mozzarella and all the salami over the rice.

put the garlic, parsley, oil, and the remaining 1 cup pecorino in another small bowl and stir to combine. Spread half the garlic mixture over the salami. Layer with the remaining rice mixture, the mozzarella, and the remaining garlic mixture.

cover and cook on low for 3 to 4 hours, until the casserole is heated through.

remove the cover and cook until the liquid in the casserole has been absorbed, an additional 30 to 45 minutes.

serve from the cooker set on warm.

serves 6–8

Tortillas

Tortilla casseroles are terrific to make in the slow cooker. The cooker doesn't dry them out, and you will have a lovely south-of-the-border feast ready for your family on a busy day. Accompany with salad or fresh fruit, and dinner is all set. I recommend you use either white or yellow corn tortillas because flour tortillas tend to become gummy in a slow cooker. Blue corn tortillas turn everything an ugly shade of purple, so I don't recommend them either. Enchiladas are traditionally made by wrapping tortillas around a filling. Since all slow cookers are shaped differently, it's much easier to layer strips of tortillas rather than whole tortillas—I find this distributes the ingredients better than the traditional wrapping method.

Enchiladas Verde

A simple comfort food, enchiladas verde are covered with a green tomatillo sauce, rather than a red chile-flavored sauce. In this casserole, a light-green sauce peeks out from under a blanket of bubbling Monterey Jack and mild Cheddar cheeses and tortillas enfold sour cream and *queso fresco*, blending together to make a terrific meatless main dish to serve anytime.

2 tablespoons vegetable oil

1 medium onion, finely chopped

1 Anaheim chile pepper, seeded and finely chopped

4 tablespoons finely chopped fresh cilantro

3 cups tomatillo salsa (see savvy)

½ cup chicken broth

2½ cups finely shredded mild Cheddar cheese

2 cups finely shredded Monterey Jack or pepper Jack cheese

2 cups crumbled queso fresco (see savvy)

2 cups sour cream

Twelve 6-inch round white or yellow corn tortillas, cut in strips or roughly torn

coat the insert of a 5- to 7-quart slow cooker with nonstick cooking spray or line it with a slow-cooker liner according to the manufacturer's directions.

heat the oil in a medium saucepan over medium-high heat. Add the onion and chile and sauté until they are softened and fragrant, 3 to 5 minutes.

add 2 tablespoons of the cilantro, the salsa, and broth and simmer for 30 minutes, until the sauce is reduced and thickened a bit. Remove from the heat and set aside to cool slightly. Put the Cheddar and Monterey Jack cheese in a mixing bowl and stir to combine.

put the *queso fresco*, the remaining 2 tablespoons cilantro, and the sour cream in another bowl and stir to combine. Spoon a thin layer of the sauce on the bottom of the slow-cooker insert. Layer one-third of the tortillas evenly on the bottom of the slow cooker.

spread half the *queso fresco* mixture over the tortillas and top with one-third of the shredded cheese. Repeat, layering the tortillas, sauce, *queso fresco*, and shredded cheese. Finish layering the remaining tortillas, sauce, and shredded cheese. Cover and cook on low for 3 to 4 hours, until the casserole is cooked through and the cheese is bubbling. Remove the cover and cook for an additional 30 to 45 minutes.

serve from the cooker set on warm.

serves 6–8

salsa savvy
Tomatillo salsa, or salsa verde, can be found in the Hispanic section of your supermarket. I'm partial to La Victoria's thick and chunky variety.

queso fresco savvy
Queso fresco is a found in the fresh cheese section of the grocery store. Generally sold in rounds, it crumbles easily but doesn't have the melting qualities that Monterey Jack or Cheddar have. If you cannot find *queso fresco*, feta is a good substitute, but make sure to rinse it thoroughly, as it can be much saltier than *queso fresco*.

Chicken Enchiladas with Ranchero Sauce

In this casserole, mildly-spiced ranchero sauce, filled with bell peppers and onions, soaks into layers of tortillas, chicken, cheese, corn, and onion. Flavored with cilantro, this dish makes a delicious dinner any night of the week.

RANCHERO SAUCE

3 tablespoons olive oil

2 large sweet onions, coarsely chopped

2 medium yellow bell peppers, seeded and coarsely chopped

2 medium red bell peppers, seeded and coarsely chopped

2 medium green bell peppers, seeded and coarsely chopped

1 teaspoon ground cumin

¼ teaspoon ancho chile powder

½ cup gold tequila (optional)

Two 28- to 32-ounce cans tomato purée

2 tablespoons olive oil

4 chicken breast halves, bones and skin removed and cut into bite-size pieces, or 3 cups diced or shredded cooked chicken

1 medium onion, finely chopped

¼ cup finely chopped fresh cilantro

2 cups corn kernels, fresh off the cob or frozen and defrosted

2½ cups finely shredded mild Cheddar cheese

1½ cups finely shredded Monterey Jack cheese

Twelve 6-inch tortillas, roughly torn or cut in strips

heat the 3 tablespoons oil in a large skillet over medium-high heat. Add the onions, bell peppers, cumin, and chile powder and sauté until the onions begin to soften, 5 to 7 minutes.

add the tequila (if using) and swirl in the pan. Add the tomato purée and simmer the sauce for 30 minutes. Remove from the heat and allow to cool before proceeding.

heat the 2 tablespoons oil in a large skillet over high heat. Add the chicken and sauté until it is cooked through, 5 to 8 minutes. Add the onion and sauté until the onion is softened, another 2 minutes. Transfer the mixture to a bowl and stir in the cilantro and corn. Set aside and allow the mixture to cool.

combine the Cheddar and Monterey Jack cheeses in another bowl, sprinkle 3 cups of the cheese over the cooled chicken mixture.

coat the insert of a 5- to 7-quart slow cooker with nonstick cooking spray or line it with a slow-cooker liner according to the manufacturer's directions.

spoon one-quarter of the sauce in the slow cooker and top with one-third of the tortillas. Spread half of the chicken mixture over the tortillas and top with another layer of the sauce.

top with another layer of the tortillas, the remaining chicken mixture, and sauce. Top with the last layer of tortillas and the remaining sauce. Sprinkle the casserole with the remaining cheese. Cover and cook on low for 3 to 4 hours, until the casserole is cooked through and bubbling. Remove the cover and cook for an additional 30 to 45 minutes.

serve the casserole from the cooker set on warm.

serves **6–8**

Beef Enchiladas with Chipotle Sauce

A smoky sauce of chipotle chiles mingles with shredded beef, layers of tortillas, *queso fresco*, and Cheddar in this special casserole. A terrific vehicle for recycling leftover roast beef, this is a great casserole to serve to couch potatoes while they watch football on the weekend.

CHIPOTLE SAUCE

2 tablespoons vegetable oil

1 medium onion, finely chopped

4 chipotle chiles in adobo, minced

½ teaspoon ground cumin

Two 28- to 32-ounce cans tomato purée

4 cups shredded or diced cooked roast beef

¼ cup finely chopped fresh cilantro

1 cup crumbled queso fresco

Twelve 6-inch yellow or white corn tortillas, roughly torn or cut in strips

2 cups finely shredded mild Cheddar cheese

heat the oil in a medium saucepan over medium-high heat. Add the onion, chipotles, and cumin and sauté for 3 to 4 minutes, until the onion is softened. Add the tomato purée and simmer the sauce for 30 minutes.

set aside to cool before proceeding.

coat the insert of a 5- to 7-quart slow cooker with nonstick cooking spray or line it with a slow-cooker liner according to the manufacturer's directions.

combine the beef, cilantro, and *queso fresco* in a medium bowl and toss to combine. Set aside. Pour some of the sauce in the bottom of the slow cooker. Top with a layer of tortillas, half the beef mixture, one-third of the cheese, another layer of tortillas, and some sauce. Continue with layers of the tortillas, the remaining beef mixture, and half the remaining cheese.

finish assembly with layers of the remaining tortillas, remaining sauce, and remaining cheese. Cover and cook on low for 3 to 4 hours, until the casserole is cooked through and is bubbling. Remove the cover and cook an additional 30 to 45 minutes.

serve the casserole from the cooker set on warm.

serves 6–8

King Ranch Casserole

King Ranch Casserole has been a staple at potlucks, church suppers, and celebrations for years in my family. It's a terrific buffet dish and is filled with chicken, turkey, or seafood (see savvy) in a creamy, green chile–flavored sauce. You can make the sauce spicy or mild, depending upon your preferences. I like it in the milder range, but you can certainly add more chile powder if you prefer it spicier.

4 tablespoons (½ stick) unsalted butter

2 medium onions, finely chopped

2 cloves garlic, minced

One 4-ounce can diced green chiles, rinsed and drained

½ teaspoon chili powder

¼ cup all-purpose flour

2 cups chicken broth

2 cups milk

Salt and freshly ground black pepper

¼ cup finely chopped fresh cilantro

4 cups bite-size pieces cooked chicken

2 cups sour cream

2 cups finely shredded mild Cheddar cheese

2 cups finely shredded Monterey Jack cheese

Twelve 6-inch yellow or white corn tortillas, cut in strips or roughly torn

coat the insert of a 5- to 7-quart slow cooker with nonstick cooking spray or line it with a slow-cooker liner according to the manufacturer's directions.

melt the butter in a large skillet over medium-high heat. Add the onions, garlic, chiles, and chili powder and sauté until the onions are softened and beginning to look translucent, 4 to 5 minutes.

transfer ¼ cup of the mixture from skillet to a bowl and set aside. Add the flour to the skillet and cook for 3 minutes, whisking constantly. Gradually add the broth and milk, and bring the sauce to a boil. Season the sauce with salt and pepper.

add 2 tablespoons of the cilantro to the sauce and set aside to cool. Put the chicken, sour cream, remaining cilantro, and 1 cup of each cheese in the bowl containing the reserved onion-chile mixture and stir to combine.

spread some of the sauce on the bottom of the slow cooker. Top with one-third of the tortillas, half of the chicken mixture, and one-third of the sauce. Continue to layer the tortillas, the remaining chicken mixture, and some of the sauce. Finish assembly with layers of the remaining tortillas, sauce, and cheese.

cover and cook on low for 3 to 4 hours, until the casserole is bubbling and is cooked through. Remove the cover and cook for an additional 30 to 45 minutes.

serve from the cooker set on warm.

serves **6–8**

slow-cooker savvy
Substitute cooked turkey for the chicken or use a mixture of turkey and chicken for a delicious variation. You can also substitute cooked shrimp, crab, or halibut for the chicken and proceed as directed.

Tamale Pie

In the 1950s, cafeterias around the country served ghastly versions of tamale pie, and what a shame. When done right, it's absolutely delicious and is a nice introduction to the glories of Mexican food. Tamales are usually savory mixes that are wrapped in a cornmeal paste, and then tucked into a corn husk and steamed. They tend to be labor intensive but have their devotees. This pie has a savory filling of pork and vegetables that simmers under a cornmeal crust, and it makes a delicious and hearty dinner any night of the week. I recommend a fruit salad for a refreshing side dish.

1 teaspoon salt

½ teaspoon chili powder

2 pounds pork shoulder, fat trimmed, cut into 1-inch pieces

1 tablespoon olive oil

2 garlic cloves, minced

1 medium onion, finely chopped

1 Anaheim chile, seeded and finely chopped

½ teaspoon ground cumin

One 28- to 32-ounce can crushed tomatoes

One 16-ounce package frozen corn, defrosted, or 3½ cups fresh corn, cut off the cob

1 cup yellow cornmeal

2 tablespoons sugar

1 cup all-purpose flour

1 tablespoon baking powder

2 tablespoons unsalted butter, melted

¾ cup milk

2 large eggs

1 cup finely shredded Cheddar cheese

6 shakes Tabasco

sprinkle the salt and chili powder over the pork. Heat the oil in a large skillet over high heat.

add the pork and brown on all sides. Transfer the meat to the insert of a 5- to 7-quart slow cooker. Add the garlic, onion, chile, and cumin to the same skillet and sauté until the onion is softened, 5 to 7 minutes.

add the tomatoes and cook until soft, scraping up any browned bits from the bottom of the pan. Put the sauce, browned pork, and corn in the slow cooker and stir to combine. Cover the slow cooker and cook on high for 4 hours, until the meat is tender. When the meat is cooked through and tender, make the crust.

combine the cornmeal, sugar, flour, and baking powder in a mixing bowl and stir to combine, whisking to aerate the flour. In another bowl, add the butter, milk, and eggs and lightly beat.

add the wet ingredients to the dry and stir until the batter is smooth. Fold in the cheese and Tabasco. Skim off any fat from the casserole and spread the cornmeal mixture over the meat.

cover and cook on high for an additional 1 hour, until the cornbread is cooked through or when a skewer inserted into the center comes out clean, without any crumbs. Remove the cover and cook for an additional 30 to 45 minutes.

serve from the cooker set on warm.

serves 6–8

Chapter 3
A Chicken or Turkey in Every Pot

Chicken is on American tables three to four nights a week; chicken and turkey make terrific choices for the slow cooker. For dinner, boneless cuts are my first choice because they can be served directly from the slow cooker. Poultry on the bone, after cooking for such a long time, falls off and becomes a nuisance when serving. Dark meat absorbs liquid and becomes tender and succulent when simmered for hours. Flavors from around the globe turn bland and dry chicken breasts, with the addition of aromatic vegetables and herbs, into main courses that will become family favorites. Turkey is also terrific in the slow cooker, absorbing flavors and becoming succulent and juicy. With turkey parts widely available, turkey can slow cook many nights of the week. In many recipes I instruct you to remove the skin from the chicken—this is because the skin adds extra fat to the dish, and it also acts as a tourniquet, making the chicken buckle during cooking. Use a pair of kitchen scissors to snip off the skin and discard it.

Chicken Balsamico with Yukon Gold Potatoes

Known as "Grandma's Chicken" in my house, this chicken dish is flavored with bacon, rosemary, and balsamic vinegar, and incorporates Yukon gold potatoes for a one-pot dish that will have everyone hanging around the slow cooker waiting for it to be done. I've chosen meaty chicken thighs for this dish, but you can use a cut-up whole chicken, if you would prefer—just make sure to remove most of the skin.

6 medium Yukon gold potatoes, quartered

8 strips bacon, cut into ½-inch pieces

8 chicken thighs, skin removed

Salt and freshly ground black pepper

2 tablespoons finely chopped fresh rosemary

8 cloves garlic, quartered

1 cup balsamic vinegar

½ cup chicken broth

Salt and freshly ground black pepper

put the potatoes in the insert of a 5- to 7-quart slow cooker. Cook the bacon in a large skillet over medium heat until crisp and remove it to paper towels to drain, leaving the drippings in the pan.

sprinkle the chicken evenly with 1½ teaspoons salt and ½ teaspoon pepper and add to the bacon drippings.

brown the chicken on all sides, 12 to 15 minutes. Add the rosemary and garlic and sauté for 1 to 2 minutes. Deglaze the skillet with the vinegar, scraping any browned bits from the bottom, and transfer the contents of the skillet to the slow-cooker insert.

add the broth. Cover and cook on high for 3 hours or on low for 5 to 6 hours, until the chicken and potatoes are tender. Season with salt and pepper.

sprinkle the reserved bacon over the top of the chicken and potatoes before serving.

serves **6–8**

Bistro Chicken Thighs

The flavors of Provence combine in this delicious slow-cooker entrée, which turns your kitchen into a French bistro for the night. The thighs soak up the garlic, red wine, and thyme-flavored tomato sauce that is delicious served over potatoes, pasta, or rice.

10 chicken thighs, skin removed

1½ teaspoons salt

½ teaspoon freshly ground black pepper

2 tablespoons extra-virgin olive oil

2 tablespoons unsalted butter

2 medium onions, coarsely chopped

3 cloves garlic, minced

2 teaspoons dried thyme

1 cup red wine

One 14- to 15-ounce can crushed tomatoes, with their juice

½ cup finely chopped fresh Italian parsley

sprinkle the chicken evenly with the salt and pepper. Heat the oil in a large skillet over medium heat. Add the chicken and brown on all sides.

transfer the browned meat to the insert of a 5- to 7-quart slow cooker. Melt the butter in the same skillet. Add the onions, garlic, and thyme and sauté until the onion is softened, about 5 minutes.

add the wine and tomatoes and scrape up any browned bits from the bottom of the skillet. Transfer the contents of the pan to the slow-cooker insert. Cover and cook on low for 6 to 8 hours, until the chicken is cooked through and tender, falling off the bone. Skim off any fat from the top of the sauce.

stir in the parsley and serve from the cooker set on warm.

serves 6–8

Smoked-Paprika Chicken Thighs

Smoky bacon, fragrant smoked paprika, and confetti-colored bell peppers make this chicken dish a great change of pace during the week. I like it served over buttered noodles.

6 strips thick-cut bacon, cut into 1-inch pieces

10 chicken thighs, skin removed

1½ teaspoons salt

½ teaspoon freshly ground black pepper

2 tablespoons olive oil

2 medium onions, cut into half rounds

2 medium red bell peppers, seeded and cut into ½-inch-thick slices

1 medium yellow bell pepper, seeded and cut into ½-inch-thick slices

1 medium orange bell pepper, seeded and cut into ½-inch-thick slices

2 cloves garlic, minced

1½ teaspoons smoked paprika

One 14- to 15-ounce can double-strength chicken broth (not diluted)

One 14- to 15-ounce can chopped tomatoes, drained

½ cup finely chopped fresh Italian parsley

cook the bacon in a large skillet over medium heat until crisp and remove it to paper towels to drain, leaving the drippings in the pan.

sprinkle the chicken evenly with the salt and pepper and add to the bacon drippings. Brown the chicken on all sides, about 7 to 10 minutes.

transfer the browned chicken pieces to the insert of a 5- to 7-quart slow cooker. Heat the oil in the same skillet over medium-high heat. Add the onions, bell peppers, and garlic and sauté until the vegetables begin to soften, 4 to 6 minutes. Add the paprika and sauté for 2 minutes. Add the broth and scrape up any browned bits from the bottom of the skillet.

transfer the contents of the skillet to the slow-cooker insert. Add the tomatoes and stir to combine. Cover and cook on low for 6 to 8 hours, until the chicken is cooked through and tender. Skim off any fat from the top of the sauce.

stir in the reserved bacon and the parsley and serve from the cooker set on warm.

serves **6–8**

Chicken Cacciatore with Porcini and Cremini Mushrooms

Chicken cacciatore, or hunter's-style chicken, varies region to region in Italy, where it originates. This is a recipe given to me by a friend from Naples, where tomatoes and oregano are staples of regional cooking.

4 tablespoons extra-virgin olive oil

1 pound cremini mushrooms, quartered

2 teaspoons salt

Pinch red pepper flakes

1 teaspoon dried oregano

3 cloves garlic, minced

¼ cup dried porcini mushrooms, crumbled

¼ cup red wine

One 28- to 32-ounce can crushed tomatoes, with their juice

10 chicken thighs, skin and bones removed

heat 2 tablespoons of the oil in a large skillet over high heat. Add the mushrooms, 1 teaspoon of the salt, red pepper flakes, oregano, and garlic and sauté until the liquid in the pan has evaporated, about 7 to 10 minutes.

add the porcinis and the wine to a small bowl and allow the porcinis to soften. Add the wine mixture and the tomatoes to the skillet.

transfer the contents of the pan to the insert of a 5- to 7-quart slow cooker.

sprinkle the chicken evenly with the remaining 1 teaspoon salt. Heat the remaining 2 tablespoons oil in the same skillet over high heat. Add the chicken to the skillet and brown on all sides, 15 to 20 minutes.

transfer the browned meat to the slow-cooker insert, submerging it in the sauce. Cover and cook on low for 4 to 5 hours, until the chicken is tender and cooked through. Skim off any fat from the top of the sauce.

serve from the cooker set on warm.

serves 6–8

Barbecued Chicken Legs

In this dish, meaty chicken legs absorb a sugar-and-spice barbecue sauce and slow-cook to tender perfection. They are messy to eat but well worth licking every finger! If you don't want to make your own barbecue sauce, you can substitute your favorite one.

10 chicken legs, skin removed

1 teaspoon salt

½ teaspoon freshly ground black pepper

2 tablespoons unsalted butter

1 medium onion, finely chopped

1 clove garlic, minced

1 tablespoon Dijon mustard

1 tablespoon Worcestershire sauce

1½ cups ketchup

½ cup chicken broth

½ cup firmly packed light brown sugar

¼ cup molasses

½ teaspoon hot sauce

spray the insert of a 5- to 7-quart slow cooker with nonstick cooking spray, or line it with a slow-cooker liner according to the manufacturer's directions.

sprinkle the chicken legs evenly with the salt and pepper and transfer to the slow-cooker insert.

melt the butter in a large saucepan over medium-high heat. Add the onion and garlic and sauté until the onion is softened, about 3 minutes.

add the remaining ingredients and stir to combine. Pour the sauce over the chicken. Cook on low for 8 hours, until the chicken is tender and cooked through. Remove the cover from the slow cooker and skim off any fat.

serve the chicken from the cooker set on warm.

serves **8**

Braised Chicken with Niçoise Olives

Robustly flavored with Niçoise olives, wine, and lemon, serving this chicken dish is a nice way to turn your dinner table into a Mediterranean bistro. Serve this dish with lots of crusty bread to soak up the flavorful sauce.

½ cup all-purpose flour

Salt (see savvy) and freshly ground black pepper

8 chicken thighs, skin and bones removed

¼ cup extra-virgin olive oil

4 garlic cloves, sliced

¾ cup dry white wine or vermouth

1½ cup chicken broth

1 cup pitted Niçoise olives

1 lemon, cut into ½-inch-thick slices (see savvy)

1 bay leaf

combine the flour, ½ teaspoon salt, and ½ teaspoon pepper in a large plastic bag. Add the chicken to the bag and shake to coat. Heat the oil in a large skillet over high heat.

add the chicken and brown on all sides, 7 to 10 minutes.

transfer the browned chicken to the insert of a 5- to 7-quart slow cooker. Add the garlic to the same skillet and cook until it is fragrant, about 30 seconds.

add the wine and deglaze the skillet, scraping up any browned bits from the bottom. Transfer the contents of the skillet to the slow-cooker insert. Add the remaining ingredients and stir to combine. Cover the slow cooker and cook on low for 4 to 5 hours, until the chicken is tender.

season with salt and pepper before serving.

serves **6**

salt savvy
Since olives are naturally salty, I advise you to go easy on the salt until the dish is finished cooking, and then season.

lemon savvy
Most citrus and other fruits are waxed when they are shipped to your local market. Make sure that you remove any wax from the fruit that you add to your pot, or the wax will make your dish have an off-flavor. Scrubbing the fruit with a plastic wire brush before washing does the trick.

Chicken Dijonaise

This chicken dish is one of my favorites. The chicken is infused with the flavor of Dijon mustard and surrounded with button mushrooms, artichoke hearts, and cippolini onions. Serve with steamed rice, or it's equally delicious with crispy roasted potatoes.

3 to 4 pounds chicken parts (breasts, thighs, legs, or any combination), skin removed (see savvy)

Salt and freshly ground black pepper

3 tablespoons extra-virgin olive oil

4 cloves garlic, minced

8 ounces cippolini onions

1 pound button mushrooms, cut in half if large

One 16-ounce package frozen artichoke hearts, defrosted and quartered (see savvy)

½ cup dry white wine or vermouth

1½ cups chicken broth

⅔ cup Dijon mustard

1 bay leaf

sprinkle the chicken evenly with 1½ teaspoons salt and ½ teaspoon pepper. Heat the oil in a large skillet over high heat. Add the chicken a few pieces at a time and brown on all sides.

transfer the browned chicken to the insert of a 5- to 7-quart slow cooker. Add the garlic and onions to the same skillet and sauté until the onions begin to color, about 4 minutes. Add the mushrooms and sauté until the liquid in the pan begins to evaporate, 3 to 4 minutes.

add the artichoke hearts to the pan and sauté for another 3 to 4 minutes, to color the artichoke hearts.

deglaze the pan with the wine, stirring up any browned bits from the bottom. Transfer the contents of the pan to the slow-cooker insert. Put the broth and mustard in a small bowl and whisk to combine.

add the broth mixture to the slow-cooker insert and add the bay leaf, stirring to combine. Cover and cook on low for 4 to 5 hours, until the chicken is tender.

season with salt and pepper before serving.

serves **8**

chicken savvy
Removing the skin before slow cooking helps cut down on the fat in the dish and helps the chicken cook evenly. Use a pair of kitchen shears to cut through the skin, and then pull it off and discard.

artichoke-heart savvy
Fresh baby artichoke hearts work well in this braise, but they aren't always available and can be pricey. If you can find them, trim the tough outer leaves, cut about ¾ inch off the top, and cut the artichokes in half before adding to the cooker. They may require a little more cooking time, around 15 to 30 minutes. If frozen artichoke hearts aren't available, two 15-ounce cans of artichoke hearts will also work. I'd advise adding those 2 hours into the cooking time because they are quite soft and may disintegrate after the long cooking time.

Tandoori Chicken

A *tandoor* is a wood-fired clay oven that is used in India for cooking. Although a slow cooker will give you more of a tandoori stew than a traditional tandoori, it's still delicious. The flavors of yogurt, Indian spices, (see savvy) and chicken mingle to make this a great dish to serve with steamed rice. Don't forget the traditional accompaniments of raita, a cooling cucumber-yogurt sauce, and naan or flat bread for dipping.

1½ cups plain yogurt

2 teaspoons fresh lemon juice

1 teaspoon ground coriander

½ teaspoon ground cumin

½ teaspoon ground cardamom

½ teaspoon turmeric

1 teaspoon sweet paprika

2 cloves garlic, minced

1 teaspoon freshly grated ginger

One 3 to 4 pound chicken, cut into 8 pieces and skin removed

combine the yogurt, lemon juice, coriander, cumin, cardamom, turmeric, paprika, garlic, and ginger in a 1-gallon zipper-top plastic bag.

add the chicken in the bag and marinate for at least 8 hours and up to 24 hours. Put the chicken and the marinade in the insert of a 5- to 7-quart slow cooker.

cover and cook on high for 4 hours, until the chicken is cooked through (170°F on an instant-read meat thermometer).

remove the chicken from the pot and serve warm or at room temperature.

serves **6**

tandoori savvy
If you prefer to buy a tandoori seasoning instead of making your own, there are several good ones on the market, which you can find at gourmet retailers or at Penzey's Spices (www.penzeys.com).

Fruited Chicken Tagine

The word *tagine* refers not only to a dish but also to the vessel in which it is cooked. Originally from North Africa, cooking tagines have a flat dish that holds ingredients, and a conical lid with a vent. Tagines also can be made successfully in a slow cooker with excellent results. This tagine slowly simmers chicken thighs, dried apricots, and dried plums together to make a sweet and savory dish that is terrific with steamed rice or couscous.

8 chicken thighs, skin and bones removed

1½ teaspoons salt

⅛ teaspoon cayenne

¼ cup olive oil

1 medium onion, coarsely chopped

1 teaspoon ground turmeric

2 cloves garlic, minced

½ teaspoon ground cumin

½ teaspoon ground ginger

1 tablespoon brown sugar

½ cup dried apricots, cut into quarters (see savvy)

½ cup dried plums (see savvy)

½ cup orange juice

Grated zest of one orange

1½ cups chicken broth

¼ cup water mixed with 2 tablespoons cornstarch

3 cups cooked couscous

sprinkle the chicken with the salt and cayenne. Heat the oil in a large skillet over high heat. Add the chicken a few pieces at a time and brown on all sides.

transfer the browned chicken to the insert of a 5- to 7-quart slow cooker. Add the onion, turmeric, garlic, cumin, ginger, and brown sugar to the skillet and sauté until the onion begin to soften, about 4 minutes.

transfer the contents of the skillet to the slow-cooker insert. Add the apricots, plums, orange juice, orange zest, and broth to the cooker. Cover and cook on high for 4½ to 5½ hours, until the chicken is tender and the fruit is plump.

stir in the cornstarch mixture and cook for an additional 30 to 45 minutes, until the sauce is thickened.

serve the chicken, fruit, and sauce over a bed of the couscous.

serves **6**

apricot savvy
To prevent the apricots from sticking to your knife while cutting, spray the knife with nonstick cooking spray.

plum savvy
Dried plums are really prunes. Marketers decided that prunes had gotten a bad rap so now they're called dried plums!

Braised Chicken in Stout

Guinness stout is a favorite in the United Kingdom and is a delicious addition to your slow-cooker dishes. This chicken is braised in Guinness, with added Asian flavors, and turns out as a delicious stew to serve over steamed rice or noodles.

1 whole chicken (about 4 pounds), cut into 8 pieces, or 8 pieces of your favorite chicken parts, skin removed

1 teaspoon salt

½ teaspoon freshly ground black pepper

3 tablespoons vegetable oil

2 medium onions, coarsely chopped

2 teaspoons freshly grated ginger

2 cloves garlic, minced

¼ cup soy sauce

2 cups baby carrots (see savvy)

One 12-ounce can Guinness stout

1 cup chicken broth

½ pound shiitake mushrooms, stems removed and caps sliced in half

2 tablespoons cornstarch mixed with ¼ cup water

Chopped green onion for garnishing

sprinkle the chicken evenly with the salt and pepper. Heat the oil in a large skillet over high heat. Add the chicken and brown on all sides.

transfer the browned chicken to the insert of a 5- to 7-quart slow cooker. Add the onions, ginger, and garlic to the skillet and sauté until the onions are softened, 3 to 4 minutes. Add the soy sauce and scrape up any browned bits from the bottom of the skillet.

transfer the contents of the skillet to the slow-cooker insert. Add the carrots, Guinness, broth, and mushrooms to the cooker. Cover and cook on low for 6 hours.

remove the cover and stir in the cornstarch mixture. Cover and cook for an additional 30 to 45 minutes, until the stew is thickened and the chicken is tender.

serve the stew garnished with the green onions.

serves **6–8**

carrot savvy
The baby carrots you see in bags in the supermarket aren't really "baby" carrots at all! They are large carrots that have been put through a machine and turned into little nuggets of carrot.

Southern Brunswick Stew

Until I did a bit of research, I did not realize there are two different states that claim Brunswick Stew as their own. Many maintain that Brunswick, Georgia, is the home to Brunswick Stew, where it is made with meat rather than chicken. Others insist that Brunswick County, Virginia, is the true home of Brunswick Stew, where it is made with chicken. One thing that all agree on is that the original was probably a hunter's stew made with game, such as squirrel or other small animals. The other ingredients have remained the same for years: corn, lima beans, tomatoes, onion, and okra; additions to the stew are determined by the cook. We will use meaty chicken thighs and ham to flavor this all-American stew. Serve the stew with spoon bread or cornbread.

½ cup all-purpose flour

Salt

¼ teaspoon sweet paprika

Pinch of cayenne pepper

8 chicken thighs, skin removed

3 tablespoons olive oil

One 1-pound ham steak, cut into 1-inch pieces

1 medium onion, coarsely chopped

1 medium red bell pepper, seeded and coarsely chopped

1 teaspoon dried thyme

One 15-ounce can chopped tomatoes

1 tablespoon Worcestershire sauce

1 cup chicken broth

6 medium red potatoes, quartered

One 10-ounce package frozen lima beans, defrosted

One 16-ounce package frozen corn, defrosted

2 cups fresh okra, cut into ½-inch slices

6 drops hot sauce (see savvy)

Freshly ground black pepper

put the flour, 1½ teaspoons salt, the paprika, and cayenne in a large plastic bag. Add the chicken to the bag and toss to coat. Remove the chicken from the bag and shake off any excess flour.

heat the oil in a large skillet over high heat. Add the chicken a few pieces at a time and brown on all sides. Transfer the browned pieces to the insert of a 5- to 7-quart slow cooker.

add the ham to the same skillet and sauté for 3 minutes, until it begins to color. Transfer to the slow cooker. Add the onion, bell pepper, and thyme to the skillet and sauté until the vegetables begin to soften, about 3 minutes. Add the tomatoes and Worcestershire, stirring up any browned bits from the bottom of the pan.

transfer the mixture to the slow-cooker insert. Add the broth, potatoes, lima beans, and corn to the cooker and stir to combine. Cover and cook the stew on low for 6 hours.

remove the cover and add the okra and hot sauce. Cover and cook an additional 1 hour, until the potatoes and chicken are tender.

season with salt and pepper before serving.

serves **6–8**

 hot-sauce savvy
We all have favorite hot sauces, whether it's Tabasco, Cholula, Crystal, or Frank's, so I leave it up to you. My favorites are Tabasco, which has more of a vinegar flavor and is traditionally Southern, and Frank's, which has a more pronounced pepper flavor.

Braised Basque Chicken

The Basque region is in the western Pyrenees, which run along the border between France and Spain. Its cuisine varies from place to place, but this chicken dish can be found on many restaurant menus in the region. Chicken with sausage, bell peppers, onions, and paprika is braised until the chicken is falling off the bone, and a sauce coats the chicken and vegetables. It's delicious served with crusty bread and a green salad with avocados and oranges.

¼ cup extra-virgin olive oil

10 chicken thighs, skin removed

1½ teaspoons salt

½ teaspoon freshly ground black pepper

2 medium onions, cut into half rounds

2 cloves garlic, minced

2 medium red bell peppers, seeded and cut into ½-inch-thick slices

1 medium yellow bell pepper, seeded and cut into ½-inch-thick slices

1 teaspoon sweet paprika

1 teaspoon dried thyme

2 tablespoons sherry vinegar

1 cup chicken broth

4 ounces Spanish chorizo or sopressata (see savvy), cut into ½-inch dice

heat the oil in a large skillet over medium-high heat. Sprinkle the chicken evenly with the salt and pepper.

add the chicken to the skillet and brown on all sides. Transfer the browned meat to the insert of a 5- to 7-quart slow cooker. Add the onions, garlic, bell peppers, paprika, and thyme to the skillet and sauté until the vegetables are softened, 7 to 8 minutes.

deglaze the pan with the vinegar and broth, scraping up any browned bits from the bottom of the skillet. Transfer the contents of the skillet to the slow-cooker insert. Add the chorizo and stir to combine. Cover and cook on low for 7 to 8 hours, until the chicken is tender and cooked through.

skim off any fat from the top of the sauce and serve the stew from the cooker set on warm.

serves **8**

salami savvy
Spanish chorizo may be difficult to find in your area, but sopressata, a salami that is cured with wine, makes a nice substitute.

Spicy Asian Braised Napa Cabbage Wraps

I love lettuce wraps at Asian restaurants—the cooling lettuce against the warm and spicy chopped chicken and vegetables is great combination. This wrap pairs the spicy chicken with Napa cabbage, and braises the cabbage like traditional stuffed cabbage rolls. These wraps make a delicious dinner, served over stir-fried noodles.

1 head Napa cabbage

2 cups chicken broth

½ cup soy sauce

4 slices fresh ginger

2 tablespoons vegetable oil

2 cloves garlic, minced

1 teaspoon freshly grated ginger

6 canned water chestnuts, finely chopped

2 chicken breast halves, skin and bones removed, finely chopped

4 green onions, finely chopped, using the white and tender green parts

2 tablespoons hoisin sauce

1 tablespoon cornstarch mixed with 2 tablespoons water

core the cabbage and separate the leaves, being careful not to tear them. Put the broth, soy sauce, and ginger in a large stockpot and bring to a boil.

blanch the cabbage leaves, one at a time, for 30 seconds until limp. Drain the leaves and set aside. Add the broth mixture to the insert of a 5- to 7-quart slow cooker. Cover and set on warm while preparing the filling.

heat the oil in a sauté pan over high heat. Add the garlic, ginger, and water chestnuts and sauté for 30 seconds. Add the chicken and cook until the chicken turns white, 3 to 5 minutes.

transfer the contents of the pan to a bowl and stir in the green onions and hoisin sauce. Place 2 to 3 tablespoons of filling at the stem end of a cabbage leaf and roll up, tucking in the sides of the leaf as you go. Place the cabbage wraps on a rack in the slow cooker.

cover and cook on high for 1½ to 2 hours, until the chicken is cooked through. Remove the wraps and set aside. Strain the broth through a fine-mesh sieve into a saucepan and bring to a boil. Add the cornstarch mixture and bring back to a boil.

serve the wraps with the sauce on the side.

serves **8**

Basic Poached Chicken Breasts

If you need a lot of chicken meat for a salad luncheons or casseroles, then this is your recipe. Load up the cooker with boneless chicken breasts and then let the cooker do its work. In five hours, you can have enough chicken to shred and store in your freezer for months to come.

2 cups chicken broth

3 whole black peppercorns

½ teaspoon dried thyme

12 chicken breast halves, skin and bones removed

mix together the broth, peppercorns, and thyme in the insert of a 5- to 7-quart slow cooker. Place the chicken breasts in the slow cooker, stacking them in an even layer.

cover and cook on low for 4 to 5 hours, until the chicken is cooked through and tender. Let the chicken cool and remove it from the slow cooker. Refrigerate for 2 days or freeze for up to 10 weeks.

serves 8

Chicken with Miso and Broccoli

This is a simple supper that is not only delicious, but also good for you! Miso broth poaches the chicken and steams the broccoli that rests on top of it, preventing it from being overcooked. The chicken can be served in shallow bowls on udon or soba noodles with some of the broth and broccoli.

2 cups chicken broth

¼ cup white miso paste

1 clove garlic, sliced

2 thin slices fresh ginger

6 chicken breast halves,
skin and bones removed

1 pound broccoli, stalks trimmed
and peeled and cut into florets

pour the broth into the insert of a 5- to 7-quart slow cooker. Add the miso, garlic, and ginger and stir to combine.

place the chicken in the broth and place the broccoli on top of the chicken. Cover and cook on high for 1½ to 2 hours, until the chicken is cooked through and the broccoli is tender.

remove the chicken from the broth and arrange it on a serving platter, surrounded by the broccoli. Strain the broth through a fine-mesh sieve and serve in bowls. The chicken can also be served in bowls.

serves **6**

Boursin and Spinach–Stuffed Chicken Breasts

Though they require a bit more work than most chicken dishes, these stuffed chicken breasts will garner rave reviews from your family and friends. The tasty spinach-and-Boursin combination bursts from the interior when the breasts are sliced, and the white wine sauce, finished off with a bit of cream, takes it over the top.

6 chicken breast halves, skin and bones removed

2½ teaspoons salt

1½ teaspoons freshly ground black pepper

2 tablespoons olive oil

¼ cup finely chopped shallot

One 16-ounce package frozen chopped spinach, defrosted and squeezed dry (see savvy)

⅛ teaspoon freshly grated nutmeg

One 2-ounce package Boursin cheese

½ cup dry white wine or vermouth

1½ cups chicken broth

1 cup heavy cream

¼ cup finely chopped fresh chives

place the chicken breasts between sheets of plastic wrap and pound until the chicken is a uniform thickness. Sprinkle the chicken evenly with some of the salt and pepper.

heat the oil in a medium skillet over medium-high heat. Add the shallots and sauté until they are fragrant, about 2 minutes. Add the spinach and sauté until it is wilted and dry. Season with the remaining salt and pepper, add the nutmeg, and stir to blend. Let the filling cool, then add the Boursin and stir to blend.

spread the stuffing over the chicken breasts and roll up each one from the top of the breast, tucking in the sides to enclose the filling. (I find that if you roll these and then lay them into the cooker seam-side down, without stirring them, there is no need to secure them: they remain rolled during the cooking. If you would like to secure them, use 4-inch skewers and lace the skewer through the meat on the underside of the roll, or use kitchen string or silicone loops.)

place the stuffed breasts in the insert of a 5- to 7-quart slow cooker, wedging them in to fit. Pour the wine and chicken broth into the slow cooker.

cover and cook on high for 2½ to 3 hours, until the chicken is cooked through (170°F on an instant-read thermometer). Carefully remove the chicken from the cooker and cover with aluminum foil. Pour the sauce into a saucepan and boil until reduced by half. Reduce the heat, stir in the cream, and bring it to serving temperature. Stir in the chives. Remove the skewers, kitchen string, or loops before using a serrated knife to cut each chicken breast crosswise into 4 pieces.

serve the chicken in a pool of the sauce and nap with additional sauce.

serves **6**

spinach savvy
Another use for your potato ricer is for squeezing spinach dry. If you don't have a potato ricer, put the spinach in a colander and press the extra moisture out with your hands.

Chicken with Figs and Balsamic Vinegar

Sweet balsamic vinegar flavors this fruit-and-chicken dish, which I think embodies all the attributes I love in dishes. A balance of sweet and tart, mild and tangy, each bite has a different texture and flavor. The sweet figs infuse the chicken with a honey-like flavor, and the vinegar cuts the sweetness without overpowering it. This is delicious served over a bed of wild rice pilaf, especially once the sauce and rice have mingled.

2 tablespoons vegetable oil

8 chicken breast halves, skin and bones removed

1½ teaspoons salt

½ teaspoon freshly ground black pepper

½ cup balsamic vinegar

½ cup Ruby Port

½ cup chicken broth

1 teaspoon dried thyme

16 dried figs, cut in half

heat the oil in a large skillet over medium-high heat. Sprinkle the chicken evenly with the salt and pepper.

add the chicken to the skillet and brown on all sides.

transfer the chicken to the insert of a 5- to 7-quart slow cooker. Deglaze the pan with the vinegar and port, scraping up any browned bits from the bottom of the pan. Add the broth and transfer the contents of the skillet to the slow cooker.

add the thyme and figs and stir to combine. Cover and cook on high for 2 hours, until the chicken is cooked through and the sauce is syrupy.

serve the chicken from the cooker set on warm.

serves **6–8**

Tarragon Chicken

The slow-cooker treatment of this French bistro classic will get a four-star rating from your family and friends. The creamy sauce, fragrant with tarragon and Dijon mustard, envelops the chicken and makes it perfect to pair with rice, pasta, or potatoes.

2 tablespoons extra-virgin olive oil

8 chicken breast halves, skin and bones removed

Salt and freshly ground black pepper

1 clove garlic, minced

1 medium onion, finely chopped

1 pound white button mushrooms, halved or quartered if large

1 teaspoon dried tarragon

¼ cup dry white wine or vermouth

1½ cups chicken broth

¼ cup Dijon mustard

½ cup heavy cream

2 teaspoons cornstarch

2 tablespoons finely chopped fresh tarragon, plus additional for garnish (see savvy)

heat the oil in a large skillet over high heat. Sprinkle the chicken evenly with 1 teaspoon salt and ½ teaspoon pepper. Add the chicken to the skillet and brown on all sides. Transfer the chicken to the insert of a 5- to 7-quart slow cooker.

add the garlic, onion, mushrooms, and dried tarragon to the skillet and sauté until the onion is softened and the mushroom liquid has evaporated, 7 to 10 minutes. Deglaze the skillet with the wine, scraping up any browned bits from the bottom.

transfer the contents of the skillet to the slow-cooker insert. Add the broth and mustard to the cooker and stir to combine. Cover the slow cooker and cook on high for 2½ hours or on low for 4 to 5 hours.

add cream, cornstarch, and two tablespoons fresh tarragon to the slow cooker and stir to combine. Cover and cook for an additional 15 minutes on high or 30 minutes on low, until the sauce is thickened. Season with salt and pepper.

serve the chicken garnished with the additional fresh tarragon.

serves **6**

fresh herb savvy
My 30-minute rule applies here: cooking the chicken in dried tarragon for over 30 minutes, then refreshing the flavor of the sauce with fresh tarragon right before the dish is finished cooking. This gives you a sauce with a deep tarragon flavor enhanced by the addition of the fresh herb.

Boneless Buffalo Chicken for Sandwiches

Similar to pulled chicken but flavored with a buttery hot sauce, these chicken breasts can be stacked in the slow cooker and cooked until they are fall-apart tender. Serve the pulled meat and sauce on soft rolls with butter lettuce and blue cheese dressing for an authentic buffalo-wings taste!

1 cup (2 sticks) unsalted butter, melted

½ cup vegetable oil

1 cup Frank's Red Hot Hot Cayenne Pepper Sauce

10 chicken breast halves, skin and bones removed

add the butter, oil, and hot sauce to the insert of a 5- to 7-quart slow cooker and stir to combine. Add the chicken to the sauce and turn to coat, stacking the chicken in even layers.

cover and cook on low for 4 to 5 hours, turning the chicken in the sauce a few times during the cooking time. Remove the chicken from the sauce and pull the meat apart using two forks. Return the chicken to the sauce and stir to coat.

serve from the cooker set on warm.

serves **8**

Chicken Braised in Cider with Apples and Bacon

When my husband and I visited Normandy, we fell in love with the countryside and the people. Our biggest surprise was that there were no vineyards—just apple orchards producing cider in many varieties. This dish is similar to one we had for dinner in Normandy. Cooked in cider with apples and finished with a bit of cream, it is delicious served over buttered noodles.

4 tablespoons (½ stick) unsalted butter

5 large cooking apples, peeled and cored, cut into 8 wedges each

2 medium onions, cut into half rounds

2 teaspoons dried thyme

2 tablespoons Dijon mustard

¼ cup firmly packed light brown sugar

1½ cups apple cider

2 chicken bouillon cubes

8 strips thick-cut Applewood smoked bacon, cut into 1-inch pieces

8 chicken breast halves, skin and bones removed

½ teaspoon freshly ground black pepper

½ cup heavy cream

½ cup finely chopped fresh Italian parsley

melt the butter in a large skillet over medium-high heat. Add the apples, onions, and thyme and sauté until the onions begin to soften, 5 to 7 minutes.

add the mustard, sugar, and cider and stir to combine, melting the sugar. Transfer to the insert of a 5- to 7-quart slow cooker. Add the bouillon cubes to the cooker, crushing them to dissolve. Set the cooker on warm while you sauté the chicken.

wipe out the skillet, cook the bacon until crisp, and remove it to paper towels to drain. Sprinkle the chicken with the pepper. Add the chicken to the bacon drippings in the skillet and brown on all sides.

transfer the chicken to the slow-cooker insert. Cover and cook on low for 3 to 4 hours, until the chicken is cooked though and the apples are tender. Add the cream and parsley and stir to combine.

serve from the cooker set on warm.

serves 8

Curried Chicken Divan

Chicken Divan is a classic chicken-and-broccoli dish from the 1950s that is terrific in the slow cooker, with a few minor adjustments. Broccoli in the slow cooker tends to disintegrate and turn gray, so my advice is to serve the broccoli on the side. Cook the chicken in the slow cooker—it will be tender and juicy cooking under its curry-and-Cheddar-cheese sauce. For this slow-cooker meal you just need to prepare the sauce and then load in the chicken—no browning required.

4 tablespoons (½ stick) unsalted butter

1½ teaspoons curry powder

¼ cup all-purpose flour

2 cups chicken broth

1 cup evaporated milk

8 chicken breast halves, skin and bones removed

1½ cups finely shredded sharp Cheddar cheese

melt the butter in a saucepan over medium-high heat. Add the curry powder and sauté for 30 seconds.

add the flour and cook for 3 minutes, whisking constantly. Add the broth and bring to the mixture to a boil. Add the milk and remove the sauce from the heat and allow to cool.

place the chicken in the insert of a 5- to 7-quart slow cooker, stacking evenly. Pour the cooled sauce over the chicken. Cover and cook on high for 3 hours.

sprinkle the cheese over the chicken, cover, and cook for an additional 1 hour, until the chicken is cooked through.

serve the chicken from the cooker set on warm.

serves **6**

Old-Fashioned Chicken Pot Pie

Although we can't put a flaky crust on this pot pie, there are several other options for crusts that work well in the slow cooker. Mashed potatoes (see savvy) and noodle dumplings are certainly appropriate, or you can bake biscuits and serve them split, covered with pot-pie filling. This dish is a winner any night of the week, and it's a great way to recycle leftover chicken.

3 cups chicken broth

1 teaspoon dried thyme

4 medium Yukon gold potatoes, cut into ½-inch cubes

2 cups baby carrots

4 cups cooked chicken, cut into bite-size pieces or shredded

1½ cups frozen petite peas, defrosted

1 cup frozen white corn, defrosted

2 tablespoons unsalted butter, at room temperature

2 tablespoons all-purpose flour

pour the broth in the insert of a 5- to 7-quart slow cooker. Add the thyme, potatoes, and carrots, and stir to combine. Cover and cook on high for 3 to 4 hours, until the potatoes are tender.

add the chicken, peas and corn and stir to combine. In a small bowl, stir the butter and flour and make a paste. Add the paste to the slow cooker and stir to combine. Cover and cook for an additional 45 minutes to 1 hour, until the sauce is thickened.

serve from the cooker set on warm.

serves 6–8

pot pie savvy
To cover your pot pie with mashed potatoes (see page 195), spread them over the pot pie filling 3 to 4 hours into the cooking time.

Chicken Meatballs in Chunky Tomato Sauce

These light delicious chicken meatballs make a great filling for submarine sandwiches, are a terrific snack at a grazing party, or are nice for dinner, served with pasta.

QUICK MARINARA

2 tablespoons extra-virgin olive oil

1 medium onion, finely chopped

2 cloves garlic, minced

Pinch red pepper flakes (optional)

1 teaspoon dried basil

Two 28- to 32-ounce cans crushed tomatoes, with their juice

1½ teaspoons salt

1 teaspoon freshly ground black pepper

½ cups finely chopped fresh Italian parsley

CHICKEN MEATBALLS

¼ cup milk

1 cup fresh bread crumbs

½ cup freshly grated Parmesan cheese

2 tablespoons finely chopped fresh Italian parsley

½ cup finely chopped onion

1 clove garlic, minced

1½ teaspoons salt

½ teaspoon freshly ground black pepper

2 pounds ground chicken or turkey

1 large egg, beaten

heat the oil in a small sauté pan over medium-high heat. Add the onion, garlic, red pepper flakes (if using), and basil and sauté until the onion is softened and begins to turn translucent, about 5 minutes.

transfer the mixture to the insert of a 5- to 7-quart slow cooker. Add the tomatoes, salt, pepper, and parsley to the cooker and stir to combine.

cover and cook on low for 2 to 4 hours while making the meatballs.

put the milk and the bread crumbs in a large mixing bowl and stir to combine. Add the remaining ingredients and stir until well combined.

form the mixture into 2-inch balls and transfer them to the slow-cooker insert. Spoon some of the sauce over the meatballs.

cover and cook on high for 3 hours, until the meatballs are cooked through and register 175°F on an instant-read thermometer. Skim off any fat from the top of the sauce.

serve the meatballs from the cooker set on warm.

serves 6–8

Jamaican Chicken

This spicy, smoky, and sweet chicken gets a kick from jerk seasoning and a sweetness from a glaze made from fruit nectar. This is a nice dish to serve with rice and black beans, or bring it along for a picnic.

2 teaspoons jerk seasoning

1½ cups mango nectar

½ cup firmly packed light brown sugar

2 tablespoons dark corn syrup

2 tablespoons rice vinegar

8 chicken breast halves, skin and bones removed

add the jerk seasoning, nectar, sugar, corn syrup, and rice vinegar to the insert of a 5- to 7-quart slow cooker and stir to combine.

add the chicken breasts and turn to coat in the sauce. Cover and cook on high for 2½ to 3 hours, until the chicken is cooked through.

serve the chicken hot, warm, or at room temperature.

serves **8**

Barbecued Turkey

Winter can be depressing in some places, with snow still falling in April and those gray days hanging around for too long. When you have a hankering for a picnic on the patio in the middle of winter, this is your go-to dish. The turkey breast becomes succulent and juicy in the tangy barbecue sauce, and all you need to complete this dinner is slaw or potato salad. Serve the turkey sliced on rolls and topped with some of the pan sauce.

3 large onions, coarsely chopped

2 red bell peppers, seeded and coarsely chopped

One 4-pound bone-in turkey breast, skin removed

1 cup ketchup

1 cup tomato sauce

½ cup Dijon mustard

¼ cup firmly packed light brown sugar

2 tablespoons Worcestershire sauce

½ teaspoon Tabasco sauce

put the onions and bell peppers in the bottom of an insert of a 5- to 7-quart slow cooker. Put the turkey breast on top of the vegetables. Stir the ketchup, tomato sauce, mustard, sugar, Worcestershire, and Tabasco in a small mixing bowl to combine.

brush some of the barbecue sauce on the turkey breast, then pour the rest in the slow-cooker insert. Cover and cook on high for 3 to 4 hours, until the turkey is cooked and registers 175°F on an instant-read thermometer.

carefully remove the turkey from the slow cooker, cover with aluminum foil, and allow to rest for 20 minutes before carving.

strain the sauce through a fine-mesh sieve into a bowl, discarding the solids. Return the sauce to the slow cooker.

carve the turkey and serve with the sauce or return the turkey to the slow cooker with the sauce and serve from the cooker set on warm.

serves 6

Turkey Braised in Tomato Sauce

A meaty, cremini mushroom–and-bacon sauce flavors turkey thighs in this dish. Rustic and full of flavor, the turkey can be pulled off the bone, returned to the sauce, and served over polenta or pasta.

6 strips thick-cut bacon, cut into ½-inch pieces

1 medium onion, finely chopped

1 teaspoon dried basil

1 pound cremini mushrooms, quartered

1½ teaspoons salt

½ teaspoon freshly ground black pepper

One 28- to 32-ounce can crushed tomatoes

½ cup finely chopped fresh Italian parsley

4 turkey thighs (about 3½ pounds), skin removed

cook the bacon in a sauté pan over medium heat until it renders some fat and is beginning to turn crisp. Add the onion and basil and sauté until the onion is softened, about 3 minutes.

add the mushrooms, salt, and pepper and sauté until the mushrooms begin to color, 7 to 10 minutes. Transfer the mixture to the insert of a 5- to 7-quart slow cooker. Add the tomatoes and parsley and stir to combine. Add the thighs in the sauce.

cover and cook on high for 3 hours, until the thighs are cooked through and register 175°F on an instant-read thermometer. Skim off any fat from the top of the sauce. Remove the thighs from the sauce and discard the bones.

cut the meat into serving-sized pieces and return to the sauce.

serve from the cooker set on warm.

serves 8

Garlicky Lemon and Thyme Turkey

A paste of of garlic, lemon zest, and thyme is rubbed on turkey legs, which cook low and slow until they fall off the bone. The pan sauce (see savvy) is a delicious accompaniment to the turkey served over rice or mashed potatoes.

8 cloves garlic, peeled

Grated zest of 4 lemons

2 teaspoons fresh thyme leaves

Salt and freshly ground black pepper

¼ cup extra-virgin olive oil

6 turkey legs, skin removed

½ cup dry white wine

1 cup chicken broth

put the garlic, zest, thyme, 1½ teaspoons salt, ½ teaspoon pepper, and oil in a food processor or blender and blend to a paste. Rub the paste on the turkey and put the turkey in the slow cooker.

pour the wine and chicken broth in the insert of a 5- to 7-quart slow cooker.

cover and cook on low for 6 to 8 hours, until the turkey is cooked through and registers 175°F on an instant-read thermometer.

remove the legs from the sauce and cover with aluminum foil. Strain the sauce through a fine-mesh sieve into a sauce-pan and bring to a boil.

season with salt and pepper before serving.

serves **6**

saucy savvy
If you would like to thicken the sauce, blend 2 tablespoons unsalted butter and 2 tablespoons all-purpose flour in a small bowl and stir to combine. Add the paste to the sauce, stir to combine, and bring the sauce back to a boil. Stir in ½ cup finely chopped fresh Italian parsley. Carve the meat off the turkey legs and serve with the sauce.

Teriyaki Turkey Thighs

In this dish, ginger, garlic, and soy sauce flavor meaty thighs, which are terrific served with salads, steamed rice, and vegetable stir-frys. It is best to marinate the turkey overnight before cooking.

½ cup soy sauce

2 tablespoons hoisin sauce

2 cloves garlic, minced

1 teaspoon freshly grated ginger

2 tablespoons rice wine (mirin) or dry sherry

¼ firmly packed light brown sugar

4 turkey thighs, skin removed

blend the soy sauce, hoisin, garlic, ginger, rice wine, and brown sugar in a mixing bowl and stir to combine.

pour the marinade in a zipper-top plastic bag. Add the turkey thighs to the bag. Seal the bag and refrigerate for at least 8 hours or overnight. Pour the contents of the bag in the insert of a 5- to 7-quart slow cooker.

cover and cook on high for 3 to 4 hours, until the turkey is cooked through and registers 175°F on an instant-read thermometer.

remove the turkey from the slow cooker, cover with aluminum foil, and allow to rest for 20 minutes before serving.

serves **6**

Tea "Smoked" Turkey Legs

Tea-smoked duck or chicken dishes are common in Asian restaurants. The flavor of the tea infuses the poultry, giving it a smoky, exotic taste. Your slow-cooker rack helps you re-create the same flavor using turkey legs coated in soy and brown sugar and flavored with tea. Serve with flour tortillas, hoisin sauce, and sliced green onions and cucumber sticks.

2 cups chicken broth

8 bags Lapsang Souchong or black tea (see savvy)

4 slices fresh ginger

1 cinnamon stick

½ cup soy sauce

¼ cup hoisin sauce

6 turkey legs, skin removed

bring the broth to a boil in a saucepan and add the tea bags, ginger, and cinnamon. Allow the broth to cool, about 45 minutes. Strain the broth through a fine-mesh sieve into a bowl and whisk in the soy sauce and hoisin.

brush some of the sauce on the turkey legs with a silicone pastry brush. Pour the remaining sauce in the insert of a 5- to 7-quart slow cooker. Fit the rack in the slow cooker and place the turkey legs on the rack.

cover and cook on high for 5 hours, basting the turkey a few times during cooking.

slice the turkey legs into serving-size pieces and serve.

serves **6**

tea savvy
Most supermarket teas are combinations of various black teas. I recommend the Lapsang Souchong tea in this recipe because of its smoky character; ordinary Lipton or Tetley just didn't have the same flavor.

Artichoke-Stuffed Turkey Breast Cutlets

Artichoke hearts, pine nuts, cheese, and bread crumbs are spread on turkey breast cutlets, which then are braised in a sage and white wine sauce. This is a terrific do-ahead meal—the turkey cutlets can be rolled a day ahead of time and then put in the slow cooker the next day.

4 tablespoons (½ stick) unsalted butter

2 cloves garlic, minced

One 16-ounce package frozen artichoke hearts, defrosted and coarsely chopped

½ cup pine nuts (see savvy)

1 cup fresh bread crumbs

⅔ cup freshly grated Parmigiano-Reggiano cheese

4 leaves fresh basil, finely chopped

8 turkey breast cutlets, ¾ to 1 pound

1½ teaspoons salt

½ teaspoon freshly ground black pepper

½ cup finely chopped onion

1 teaspoon dried sage

2 tablespoons all-purpose flour

1 cup dry white wine or vermouth

1 cup chicken broth

melt 2 tablespoons of the butter in a large skillet over medium-high heat. Add the garlic and artichoke hearts and sauté until the liquid in the pan evaporates, 5 to 7 minutes.

transfer to a mixing bowl. Add the pine nuts, bread crumbs, cheese, and basil to the bowl and stir to combine. Place the cutlets on a cutting board, sprinkle evenly with the salt and pepper, and spread 2 tablespoons of the filling on each turkey breast.

roll the cutlets lengthwise and place seam-side down in the insert of a 5- to 7-quart slow cooker. Melt the remaining 2 tablespoons butter in the same skillet. Add the onion and sage and sauté until the onion is softened, about 3 minutes.

add the flour and cook for 3 minutes, stirring constantly. Deglaze the pan with the wine and chicken broth, scraping up any browned bits, and bring to a boil, whisking constantly. Pour the sauce over the turkey rolls.

cover and cook on high for 2 to 3 hours, until the turkey is tender.

serve from the cooker set on warm.

serves **6**

pine-nut savvy
There is no need to toast the pine nuts for this preparation; the stuffing is wet, and the toasted flavor will be lost in the moist ingredients.

Salsa Turkey Loaf

A south-of-the-border twist on traditional meat loaf, this spicy bite is terrific to serve with refried beans and rice to soak up the delicious sauce.

SAUCE

2 tablespoons olive oil

2 medium onions, coarsely chopped

2 medium red bell peppers, seeded and coarsely chopped

1 Anaheim chile, seeded and coarsely chopped

1 teaspoon ground cumin

½ teaspoon dried oregano

¼ teaspoon ancho chile powder

One 28- to 32-ounce can tomato purée

1½ teaspoons salt

MEAT LOAF

Four 6-inch flour tortillas, coarsely chopped

¼ cup milk

2 pounds ground turkey

½ cup finely chopped onion

1 clove garlic, minced

¼ cup finely chopped fresh cilantro

¼ cup prepared mild salsa

1 large egg, beaten

1 teaspoon salt

heat the oil in a sauté pan over medium-high heat. Add the onions, bell peppers, chile, cumin, oregano, and chile powder and sauté until the vegetables are softened, 5 to 7 minutes. Add the tomato purée and salt to the pan and stir to combine.

transfer the contents of the skillet to the insert of a 5- to 7-quart slow cooker. Cover and cook on low while making the meat loaf.

soak the tortillas in the milk in a large mixing bowl for 5 minutes, breaking them up with a fork.

add the remaining ingredients and stir to combine. Form the mixture into a 3-inch-wide by 8-inch-long loaf. Place the loaf on top of the sauce in the slow-cooker insert and spoon some of the sauce over it.

cover and cook on high for 3 hours, until the meat loaf is cooked through and registers 175°F on an instant-read thermometer. Skim off any fat from the surface of the sauce. Carefully remove the meat loaf from the sauce, cover with aluminum foil, and allow it to rest for 15 minutes.

slice the meat loaf and serve with the sauce on the side.

serves **6**

Asian Meatballs

Steeped in a soy and rice wine sauce, these delicious treats burst with the flavors of ginger, garlic, and green onions. Serve them as an entrée with stir-fried vegetables and steamed rice, or as a bite–size appetizer for entertaining, keeping them warm in the slow cooker.

SAUCE

1 cup soy sauce

⅔ cup rice wine (mirin) or dry sherry

2 cups chicken broth

½ cup white miso

1 clove garlic, sliced

2 dime-size slices fresh ginger

MEATBALLS

1 pound ground turkey

1 pound lean ground pork

2 teaspoons freshly grated ginger

1 clove garlic, minced

4 green onions, finely chopped, plus additional for garnish

1 large egg white, beaten

½ teaspoon hot sauce

2 tablespoons cornstarch mixed with ¼ cup water or chicken broth

Sesame seeds for garnish

put all the sauce ingredients in the insert of a 5- to 7-quart slow cooker and stir to combine.

cover and cook on high while preparing the meatballs.

combine all the meatball ingredients in a large bowl and stir. Roll the mixture into 2-inch balls and place in the slow-cooker insert.

cover and cook on high for 3 hours, until the meatballs are cooked through and register 175°F on an instant-read thermometer.

remove the meatballs from the sauce and transfer the sauce to a saucepan. Bring the sauce to a boil, add the cornstarch mixture, and bring back to a boil.

serve the sauce with the meatballs, and garnish with the additional green onions and sesame seeds

makes about **24** two-inch meatballs

Chicken Wings

Wings in the slow cooker make a terrific snack. During testing we found that they really need to be browned before going into the cooker though, or the skin, one of my favorite parts, becomes gummy. Once that step is done, it's just a matter of making a sauce, pouring it in the slow cooker, and cooking the wings in the sauce. Long, slow cooking gives the wings a deeper flavor than roasting or grilling. I prefer chicken wing drumettes because they are easier to handle at parties. If you aren't able to get drumettes, cut off the tips of whole chicken wings and separate the wing at the joint into two pieces with a sharp knife or cleaver.

Rosemary Lemon Wings

Lemon juice, zest, garlic, red pepper flakes, and pungent rosemary flavor these wings. They can be addictive, so don't plan on having any leftovers!

3 pounds chicken wing drumettes

¼ cup olive oil

1½ teaspoons salt

1 teaspoon sweet paprika

Freshly ground black pepper

SAUCE

½ cup lemon juice

Grated zest of 3 lemons

2 teaspoons salt

Pinch of red pepper flakes

½ cup extra-virgin olive oil

2 tablespoons red wine vinegar

6 cloves garlic, minced

1 tablespoon finely minced fresh rosemary

½ cup chicken broth

coat the insert of a 5- to 7-quart slow cooker with nonstick cooking spray. Preheat the broiler for 10 minutes.

combine the wings, olive oil, salt, paprika, and a generous grinding of pepper in a large mixing bowl and toss until the wings are evenly coated. Arrange the wings on a wire rack in a baking sheet and broil until the wings are crispy on one side, about 5 minutes.

turn the wings and broil until crispy and browned an additional 5 minutes.

remove the wings from the oven. If you would like to do this step ahead of time, cool the wings and refrigerate for up to 2 days. Otherwise, put the wings in the prepared cooker insert.

combine all the sauce ingredients in a mixing bowl and stir. Pour the sauce over the wings and turn to coat.

cover and cook on high for 3 hours, turning the wings several times to coat with the sauce.

serve the wings from the cooker set on warm.

serves **8**

Frank's Hot-Sauce Buffalo Wings

The Anchor Bar in Buffalo, New York, is renowned for cooking up the first wings bathed in hot sauce and butter. Frank's hot sauce is the sauce they still use to this day. You can use your favorite hot sauce for these buttery and deliciously spicy wings.

3 pounds chicken wing drumettes

¼ cup olive oil

1½ teaspoons salt

1 teaspoon sweet paprika

Freshly ground black pepper

SAUCE

1 cup (2 sticks) unsalted butter, melted

½ cup Frank's Red Hot Hot Cayenne Pepper Sauce

coat the insert of a 5- to 7-quart slow cooker with nonstick cooking spray. Turn the broiler on and preheat for 10 minutes.

put the wings, olive oil, salt, paprika, and a generous grinding of pepper in a large mixing bowl and toss until the wings are evenly coated. Arrange the wings on a wire rack in a baking sheet and broil until the wings are crispy on one side, about 5 minutes.

turn the wings, and broil until crispy and browned, an additional 5 minutes.

remove from the wings from the oven. If you would like to do this step ahead of time, cool the wings and refrigerate for up to 2 days. Otherwise, put the wings in the prepared cooker insert.

combine the butter and hot sauce in a mixing bowl and stir. Pour the sauce over the wings and turn to coat.

cover and cook on high for 3 hours, turning the wings several times to coat in the sauce.

serve from the cooker set on warm.

serves **8**

Thai Peanut Wings

Salty, smoky, and spicy, these wings bathe in a coconut-flavored peanut sauce.

3 pounds chicken wing drumettes

¼ cup olive oil

1½ teaspoons salt

1 teaspoon sweet paprika

Freshly ground black pepper

SAUCE

One 14-ounce can coconut milk

½ cup chicken broth

1 cup smooth peanut butter

¼ cup firmly packed brown sugar

2 tablespoons soy sauce

2 teaspoons freshly grated ginger

¼ teaspoon hot sauce

½ cup finely chopped fresh cilantro for garnishing

½ cup finely chopped roasted peanuts for garnishing

coat the insert of a 5- to 7-quart slow cooker with nonstick cooking spray. Preheat the broiler for 10 minutes.

put the wings, olive oil, salt, paprika, and a generous grinding of pepper in a large mixing bowl and toss until the wings are evenly coated. Arrange the wings on a wire rack in a baking sheet and broil until the wings are crispy on one side, about 5 minutes.

turn the wings and broil until crispy and browned, an additional 5 minutes.

remove the wings from the oven. If you would like to do this step ahead of time, cool the wings and refrigerate for up to 2 days. Otherwise, put the wings in the prepared cooker insert.

combine all the sauce ingredients in a small saucepan over medium heat and stir.

heat the sauce until it begins to boil. Pour the sauce over the wings and turn to coat.

cover and cook on high for 3 hours, turning the wings several times to coat in the sauce.

garnish the wings with the cilantro and peanuts and serve from the cooker set on warm.

serves **8**

Asian Honey Wings

Wings are one of those foods that most people can eat their own weight in; there is no such thing as too many wings! A slow cooker will keep the wings warm and bathed in sauce, but the meat needs to be browned ahead of time. Although this is a two-step process, the end result is easy for entertaining or for a weeknight meal.

3 pounds chicken wing drumettes

¼ cup olive oil

1½ teaspoons salt

1 teaspoon sweet paprika

½ teaspoon freshly ground black pepper

SAUCE

1 cup honey

½ cup soy sauce

½ cup hoisin sauce

¼ cup rice wine (mirin) or dry sherry

2 cloves garlic, minced

1 teaspoon freshly grated ginger

coat the insert of a 5- to 7-quart slow cooker with nonstick cooking spray. Turn the broiler on and preheat for 10 minutes.

put the wings, olive oil, salt, paprika, and pepper in a large mixing bowl and toss to coat the wings evenly. Arrange the wings on a rack in a baking sheet and broil until the wings are crispy on one side, about 5 minutes.

turn the wings and broil until crispy and browned, another 5 minutes

remove the wings from the oven. If you would like to do this step ahead of time, cool the wings and refrigerate for up to 2 days; otherwise, place the wings in the prepared cooker insert.

combine all the sauce ingredients in a mixing bowl and stir. Pour over the wings and turn to coat.

cover and cook on high for 3 hours, stirring twice during the cooking time to make sure the wings are cooking evenly.

serve from the cooker set on warm.

serves **6–8**

Le Bambou Vietnamese Wings

For this recipe, I went back to my favorite Vietnamese restaurant in Del Mar, California, for a bit of what I call reconnaissance, trying to figure out what is in the addictive barbecue sauce they serve on chicken and pork. I think I'm close to the original with this recipe. These wings will have you licking your fingers, they are so good. Flavored with soy, brown sugar, ketchup, coriander, ginger, and Asian fish sauce (which you can find in the Asian section of the supermarket), I also use this sauce on pork and chicken for outdoor grilling.

3 pounds chicken wing drumettes

¼ cup olive oil

1½ teaspoons salt

1 teaspoon sweet paprika

Freshly ground black pepper

SAUCE

2 tablespoons vegetable oil

1 medium onion, cut into half rounds

½ cup ketchup

¼ cup soy sauce

½ cup firmly packed light brown sugar

2 cloves garlic, minced

1 teaspoon freshly grated ginger

1 teaspoon ground coriander

2 tablespoons Asian fish sauce (Nuoc Nam)

½ cup chicken broth

½ cup finely chopped fresh cilantro for garnishing

coat the insert of of a 5- to 7-quart slow cooker with nonstick cooking spray. Preheat the broiler for 10 minutes.

put the wings, olive oil, salt, paprika, and a generous grinding of pepper in a large mixing bowl and toss until the wings are evenly coated. Arrange the wings on a wire rack in a baking sheet and broil until the wings are crispy on one side, about 5 minutes.

turn the wings and broil until crispy and browned, an additional 5 minutes.

remove the wings from the oven. If you would like to do this step ahead of time, cool the wings and refrigerate for up to 2 days. Otherwise, put the wings in the prepared cooker insert.

combine all the sauce ingredients in a mixing bowl and stir. Pour the sauce over the wings and turn to coat.

cover and cook for on high for 3 hours, turning the wings several times to coat in the sauce.

garnish the wings with the cilantro and serve from the cooker set on warm.

serves **8**

Chapter 4
Something Fishy Going On

When I first got my slow cooker I didn't cook seafood in it. Then I decided that there had to be a way to cook seafood in the pot without disintegrating. Soon, I realized that I could poach salmon perfectly, make a delicious Moroccan tagine, and prepare Mediterranean seafood stews without fear. The slow cooker takes great care of seafood and the result is a tender, moist, and flavor-filled dinner.

Acadiana Shrimp Barbecue

Shrimp cook quickly in a slow cooker, but the sauce for these succulent butter-soaked crustaceans can loll around in the pot all day, coaxing every bit of flavor out of the garlic, herbs, and spices. This dish is similar to many that are served in the French Quarter in New Orleans. Serve over rice or tossed with pasta, and with plenty of crusty bread to soak up the sauce.

1 cup (2 sticks) unsalted butter

¼ cup olive oil

8 cloves garlic, sliced

2 teaspoons dried oregano

1 teaspoon dried thyme

½ teaspoon freshly ground black pepper

Pinch of cayenne pepper

2 teaspoons sweet paprika

¼ cup Worcestershire sauce

¼ cup lemon juice

3 pounds large shrimp, peeled and deveined (see savvy)

½ cup finely chopped fresh Italian parsley

put the butter, oil, garlic, oregano, thyme, pepper, cayenne, paprika, Worcestershire, and lemon juice in the insert of a 5- to 7-quart slow cooker. Cover and cook on low for 4 hours.

turn the cooker up to high and add the shrimp, tossing them in the butter sauce. Cover and cook for an additional 10 to 15 minutes, until the shrimp are pink.

transfer the shrimp from the slow cooker to a large serving bowl and pour the sauce over the shrimp. Sprinkle with the parsley and serve.

serves **6–8**

seafood savvy
This dish is also delicious made with fish fillets; 2 pounds halibut, salmon, or sea bass fillets can be cooked for 1 to 1½ hours on high.

Beantown Scallops

Scallops have a clean, sweet taste, and although they have a tendency to get tough when overcooked, a sherry-butter sauce bath keeps them at a low and slow temperature, ensuring you will have scallop perfection.

1 cup (2 sticks) unsalted butter

2 tablespoons olive oil

2 cloves garlic, minced

2 teaspoons sweet paprika

¼ cup dry sherry

2 pounds dry-pack sea scallops (see savvy)

½ cup finely chopped fresh Italian parsley

put the butter, oil, garlic, paprika, and sherry in the insert of a 5- to 7-quart slower cooker.

cover and cook on low for 4 hours. Turn the cooker to high and add the scallops, tossing them in the butter sauce. Cover and cook on high for 30 to 40 minutes, until the scallops are opaque.

transfer the scallops and sauce from the slow cooker to a serving platter. Sprinkle with the parsley and serve.

serves **6**

scallop savvy
Look for "dry-pack" scallops—other scallops are injected with a preservative and are not as fresh, turning rubbery in the slow cooker. Dry-pack diver scallops will have been harvested recently and are far superior—you will pay a price, but it's well worth it.

Garlic Crab Claws

This is messy, but oh so good to eat! Spicy garlic wine butter coats these crab claws, and the pot can be put on the center of your dining table for everyone to serve themselves. Make sure to provide crackers, picks, and bibs for your family to be able to pick apart the crab. I crack the crab shells or cut them with kitchen shears. That way, more garlic butter will seep into the crab, giving it a more spicy, sweet flavor. Make this for a casual dinner on the porch or deck, and serve the claws in shallow bowls to catch the juices, accompanied

1 cup (2 sticks) unsalted butter

½ cup olive oil

10 cloves garlic, sliced (see savvy)

2 tablespoons Old Bay seasoning

2 cups dry white wine or vermouth

1 lemon, thinly sliced

3 to 4 pounds cooked crab legs and claws, cracked (see savvy)

put the butter, oil, garlic, seasoning, wine, and lemon in the insert of a 5- to 7-quart slow cooker.

cover and cook on low for 4 hours. Add the crab, spoon the sauce over the crab, and cook for an additional 1½ hours, turning the crab in the sauce during cooking.

serve the crab from the cooker set on warm.

serves **6–8**

garlic savvy
Why slice the garlic? The garlic in this dish will be cooking for a long time and will eventually become mellow like roasted garlic, the flavor I want, rather than the sharper flavor of minced garlic. Remember, the smaller the piece of garlic, the more intense the flavor.

crab savvy
I love to make this dish with frozen king crab legs, but it is also delicious with stone crab claws, snow crab claws, or Dungeness crab claws. Crab is usually processed on boats, meaning that it is already cooked, but the slow cooker steams it so that it doesn't dry out or get tough.

Bouillabaisse

Bouillabaisse comes from the Mediterranean region of France. Although there are many variations on the typical bouillabaisse, according to the late Julia Child, it has two components: a fish soup base made with the region's aromatic vegetables and herbs, and the fish. Since this is a typical fisherman's stew, made with what's left from the catch of the day, the fishy ingredients are left up to the cook. I've suggested a few that work best in the slow cooker.

¼ cup extra-virgin olive oil

3 leeks, cleaned and coarsely chopped, using the white and tender green parts

4 cloves garlic, sliced

1 bulb fennel, ends trimmed, coarsely chopped

Grated zest of 1 orange

1 teaspoon dried thyme

1 teaspoon saffron threads, crushed

Pinch of cayenne pepper

One 28- to 32-ounce can crushed tomatoes, with their juice

½ cup white wine or dry vermouth

3 cups clam juice

1 cup chicken broth

½ pound littleneck clams

½ pound mussels

3 pounds thick-fleshed fish, cut into 1-inch chunks

½ cup finely chopped fresh Italian parsley

heat the oil in a large skillet over medium-high heat. Add the leeks, garlic, fennel, zest, thyme, saffron, and cayenne and sauté until the vegetables are softened, about 2 minutes. Add the tomatoes and wine and cook down for 10 minutes, to concentrate the flavors. Transfer the mixture to the insert of a 5- to 7-quart slow cooker.

add the clam juice and broth to the slow-cooker insert and stir to combine. Cover and cook on low for 6 to 8 hours. Remove the cover and place the clams and mussels in the sauce.

place the fish on top of the shellfish and spoon the sauce over the top of the fish. Cover and cook on high for 45 minutes, until the fish is cooked through and opaque and the clams and mussels have opened.

discard any clams and mussels that haven't opened. Sprinkle with the parsley and serve immediately.

serves **6—8**

Catalan-Style Seafood Stew

Catalonia is a region of Spain that includes the beautiful city of Barcelona. *Zarzuela de marisco*, a Catalonian seafood stew, is decidedly spicier than its French cousin, bouillabaisse. A red pepper–based garlic, onion, and tomato mixture called *sofrito* starts the stew, with the addition of spicy sausage to add a smoky note. Recipes vary, but most include clams, fish, and prawns. For the slow cooker I've chosen clams and fish, which enhance the rich sauce nicely. Make sure to serve lots of crusty bread to soak up the sauce, and hand out bibs to catch any drips!

½ cup extra-virgin olive oil

2 medium onions, finely chopped

2 medium red bell peppers, seeded and finely chopped

6 cloves garlic, minced

1 teaspoon saffron threads, crushed

1 teaspoon hot paprika

1 cup finely chopped Spanish chorizo or sopressata salami

One 28- to 32-ounce can crushed tomatoes

2 cups clam juice

1 cup chicken broth

2 pounds firm-fleshed fish, such as halibut, monkfish, cod, or sea bass fillets, cut into 1-inch chunks

1½ pounds littleneck clams

½ cup finely chopped fresh Italian parsley

heat the oil in a large skillet over medium-high heat. Add the onions, bell peppers, garlic, saffron, paprika, and chorizo and sauté until the vegetables are softened, 5 to 7 minutes. Add the tomatoes and transfer the contents of the skillet to the insert of a 5- to 7-quart slow cooker. Add the clam juice and broth and stir to combine.

cover and cook on low for 6 hours. Add the fish and clams to the slow-cooker insert, spooning some of the sauce over the fish and pushing the clams under the sauce.

cover and cook for an additional 45 to 50 minutes, until the clams have opened and the fish is cooked through and opaque. Discard any clams that haven't opened.

sprinkle the parsley over the stew and serve immediately.

serves **6–8**

Poached Miso Salmon

Gorgeous pink salmon glazed with miso and flavored with ginger and a bit of honey is a simple dish to serve for dinner on a bed of stir-fried Napa cabbage or vegetables. Halibut or sea bass make equally delicious substitutions if salmon is not available.

3 pounds salmon fillets

3 tablespoons white Miso

3 tablespoons honey

¼ cup rice wine (mirin) or dry sherry

2 teaspoons freshly grated ginger

place the salmon in the insert of a 5- to 7-quart slow cooker.

combine the miso, honey, rice wine, and ginger in a mixing bowl and stir.

pour the sauce over the salmon in the slow cooker. Cover and cook on high for 1½ hours, until the salmon is cooked through and registers 165°F on an instant-read thermometer inserted in the center of a thick fillet.

carefully remove the salmon from the slow-cooker insert with a large spatula. Remove the skin from the underside of the salmon (if necessary) and arrange the salmon on a serving platter.

strain the sauce through a fine-mesh sieve into a saucepan. Boil the sauce, reduce it to a syrupy consistency, and serve with the salmon.

serves **8**

Poached Salmon Provençal

The herby aroma of the poaching liquid in this dish is intoxicating, and the gorgeously pink salmon covered with tomatoes is a sight to behold when you remove the cover of your slow cooker. The salmon is perfectly cooked, moist, flavorful, and tender, and the pan sauce makes a delicious accompaniment.

3 pounds salmon fillets

½ cup dry white wine or vermouth

4 cloves garlic, peeled

1½ teaspoons finely chopped fresh rosemary

2 teaspoons finely chopped fresh thyme leaves

2 teaspoons finely chopped fresh tarragon

½ cup olive oil

One 28- to 32-ounce can plum tomatoes, drained

½ cup heavy cream

Salt and freshly ground black pepper

place the salmon in the insert of a 5- to 7-quart slow cooker and pour in the white wine.

put the garlic, rosemary, thyme, tarragon, oil, and tomatoes in a food processor and process until smooth. Spoon the mixture over the salmon in the slow-cooker insert.

cover and cook on high for 1½ to 2 hours, until the fish is cooked through.

transfer the salmon from the slow-cooker insert to a serving platter and remove the skin.

transfer the sauce to a saucepan and bring to a boil, reducing the sauce by about ¼ cup. Add the heavy cream and stir to combine. Season with the salt and pepper.

serve the salmon and top with some of the sauce.

serves **6**

Olive Oil–Poached Tuna

Once you taste this tuna, you will never go back to the grocery store's tuna shelf again. Slow-poaching in olive oil makes the tuna succulent, like a duck confit. After making this once, you may want to experiment by adding red pepper flakes, lemon zest, or garlic to add flavor to the oil. The tuna will keep in the refrigerator for about one week, and it's delicious in Niçoise salad, pasta sauces, and tuna noodle casserole.

3 pounds tuna fillets

Olive oil to cover (about 3 cups)

1 teaspoon coarse sea salt

place the tuna in the insert of a 5- to 7-quart slow cooker and pour the oil over the tuna. The oil should cover the tuna, and depending on the shape of your slow cooker, you may need to add a bit more oil. Add the salt to the slow-cooker insert.

cover and cook on low for 3 to 4 hours, until the tuna is cooked through and is white. Remove the tuna from the oil and cool completely before using.

serves **6**

Sea Bass Tagine

Nothing could be easier than this simple, flavorful dish. I call sea bass the no-brainer of fish, because it's almost impossible to overcook. The sea bass' protein structure is quite different from that of other fish and has to be cooked longer and slower than its thick-fleshed counterparts like salmon and halibut. In this dish, the sea bass marinates in a cilantro and lemon mixture, and is then added to a tomato and cumin sauce. The fish has a buttery texture and is richly flavored from both the marinade and the sauce. Although couscous is the traditional accompaniment, I've added potatoes to the tagine as they absorb a lot of flavor from the sauce, making this a terrific one-pot meal.

2 pounds sea bass fillets

½ cup olive oil

Grated zest of 1 lemon

¼ cup lemon juice

1 teaspoon sweet paprika

½ cup finely chopped fresh cilantro

2 cloves garlic, chopped

1 medium onion, finely chopped

1 teaspoon ground cumin

½ teaspoon saffron threads, crushed

One 28- to 32-ounce can crushed tomatoes, with their juice

6 medium Yukon gold potatoes, quartered

1 teaspoon salt

½ teaspoon freshly ground black pepper

½ cup finely chopped fresh Italian parsley

place the fish in a zipper-top plastic bag.

whisk ¼ cup of the oil, the zest, lemon juice, paprika, and cilantro together in a small bowl. Pour the marinade over the fish in the bag. Seal the bag and refrigerate for at least 1 hour or up to 4 hours.

heat the remaining ¼ cup oil in a large skillet over medium-high heat. Add the garlic, onion, cumin, and saffron and sauté until the onion is softened, 5 to 7 minutes.

add the tomatoes and stir to combine. Place the potatoes in the bottom of the insert of a 5- to 7-quart slow cooker and sprinkle them evenly with the salt and pepper, tossing to coat. Add the tomato mixture to the insert. Cover and cook on low for 5 to 6 hours, until the potatoes are almost tender.

pour the marinade into the insert and stir the potatoes and sauce to combine. Put the fish on top of the potatoes and spoon some of the sauce over the top. Cook for an additional 1 to 1½ hours, until the sea bass is cooked through and is opaque in the center.

sprinkle the parsley evenly over the top of the sea bass and serve immediately, scooping up some potatoes and sauce with the fish.

serves **6**

Lemon, Garlic, and Butter Halibut

Halibut loves the slow cooker—it cooks evenly and remains moist and tender. Along with the lemon, garlic, and butter sauce flavored with chives, this makes a delightful dinner served over cheesy mashed potatoes or ratatouille.

1 cup (2 sticks) unsalted butter

½ cup olive oil

6 cloves garlic, sliced

1 teaspoon sweet paprika

½ cup lemon juice

Grated zest of 1 lemon

¼ cup finely chopped fresh chives

2 to 3 pounds halibut fillets

½ cup finely chopped fresh Italian parsley

combine the butter, oil, garlic, paprika, lemon juice, zest, and chives in the insert of a 5- to 7-quart slow cooker and stir to combine. Cover and cook on low for 4 hours.

add the halibut to the pot, spooning the sauce over the halibut. Cover and cook for an additional 40 minutes, until the halibut is cooked through and opaque.

sprinkle the parsley evenly over the fish, and serve immediately.

serves **6**

South-of-the-Border Halibut

This delicious recipe only needs five ingredients, and they all get tossed into the cooker—dinner is ready when you are! What's not to like about salsa-covered halibut with a garnish of melted Monterey Jack cheese? Serve this delicious fish in warm corn tortillas for a fish taco dinner, or serve it over steamed rice with a side of black beans.

3 cups prepared medium-hot salsa

2 tablespoons fresh lime juice

1 teaspoon ground cumin

2 to 3 pounds halibut fillets

1½ cup finely shredded Monterey Jack cheese (or pepper Jack for a spicy topping)

combine the salsa, lime juice, and cumin in the insert of a 5- to 7-quart slow cooker and stir. Cover the slow cooker and cook on low for 2 hours.

put the halibut in the cooker and spoon some of the sauce over the top of the fish. Sprinkle the cheese evenly over the fish. Cover and cook for an additional 30 to 45 minutes.

remove the halibut from the slow cooker and serve on a bed of the sauce.

serves **6**

Sole Pizzaiola

Simple, spicy, and delicate are all words that describe this dish. Ordinarily I wouldn't cook sole in the slow cooker because it's too thin and might disintegrate, but if it is rolled up, it cooks evenly and absorbs the garlic and oregano–flavored tomato sauce. Serve this over orzo to soak up the sauce.

PIZZAIOLA SAUCE

2 tablespoons extra-virgin olive oil

1 medium onion, finely chopped

2 teaspoons dried oregano

2 teaspoons dried basil

Pinch red pepper flakes

3 cloves garlic, minced

One 28- to 32-ounce cans crushed plum tomatoes, with their juice

1½ teaspoons salt

½ teaspoon freshly ground black pepper

½ cup olive oil

1 tablespoon Old Bay seasoning

2 pounds sole fillets

½ cup finely shredded mozzarella

½ cup freshly grated Parmigiano-Reggiano cheese

½ cup finely chopped fresh Italian parsley

heat the oil in a small saucepan over medium-high heat. Add the onion, oregano, basil, red pepper flakes, and garlic and sauté until the onion is softened, about 3 minutes.

add the tomatoes, salt, and pepper and stir to combine. Transfer to the insert of a 5- to 7-quart slow cooker.

cover and cook on low for 4 hours.

mix together the oil and seasoning in a shallow dish. Dip each fillet in the oil mixture and roll up from the narrow end.

place the rolled fillets in the slow cooker, wedging the pieces to fit. Spoon the sauce over each roll and sprinkle evenly with the cheese. Cover and cook on low for 35 to 45 minutes, until the fish is cooked through and flakes easily with a fork.

sprinkle the parsley over the fish and serve immediately.

serves 6–8

Miso-Glazed Cod

When Nobu Matsuhisa introduced this simple dish to New York City, everyone was raving about the delicious sweet, salty, and rich fish. Although the cod at Nobu is a bit different, the slow cooker poaches the cod in miso-flavored broth. You can then reduce the poaching liquid to a caramelized glaze and pour it over the top of the fish. Five-star restaurant food is only a few hours away!

½ cup white miso paste

¼ cup rice wine (mirin)

¼ firmly packed light brown sugar

1 teaspoon rice vinegar

1½ cups water

2 pounds black cod (if unavailable, use fresh cod, halibut, sea bass, or salmon)

6 green onions, finely chopped, using the white and tender green parts

¼ cup toasted sesame seeds for garnish

combine the miso, rice wine, sugar, rice vinegar, and water in the insert of a 5- to 7-quart slow cooker.

cover and cook on low for 4 hours. Add the cod, spooning the sauce over the top. Cover and cook for an additional 30 to 45 minutes.

remove the cod from the slow-cooker insert and cover with aluminum foil to keep warm. Pour the sauce in a saucepan. Bring to a boil and reduce by half until it begins to look syrupy, about 15 to 20 minutes. Add the green onions to the sauce.

serve each piece of cod in a pool of the sauce, and sprinkle each serving with sesame seeds. Serve any additional sauce on the side.

serves **6**

Poached Salmon Cakes in White Wine Butter Sauce

If you have leftover salmon or other fish, this is a terrific recycled dinner. Salmon, mixed with marinated artichokes, bread crumbs, and cheese, is formed into cakes and poached in a white wine and garlic-butter sauce that can be spooned over the cakes when serving.

WHITE WINE BUTTER SAUCE

½ cup (1 stick) unsalted butter

1 teaspoon Old Bay seasoning

2 cloves garlic, sliced

2 ½ cups white wine or vermouth

SALMON CAKES

4 cups cooked salmon, flaked

One 6-ounce jar marinated artichoke hearts, drained and coarsely chopped

1 cup fresh bread crumbs

½ cup freshly grated Parmigiano-Reggiano cheese

1 large egg, beaten

½ teaspoon freshly ground black pepper

put all the sauce ingredients in the insert of a 5- to 7-quart slow cooker and stir to combine. Cover and cook on low for 4 hours.

put all the salmon cake ingredients in a large mixing bowl and stir to combine. Form the mixture into 2-inch cakes. Place the cakes in the simmering sauce and spoon the sauce over the cakes.

cover and cook for an additional 1 hour, until the cakes are tender. Carefully remove the cakes to a serving platter.

strain the sauce through a fine-mesh sieve into a saucepan. Bring the sauce to a boil and reduce by half.

serve the sauce over the cakes, or serve on the side.

serves **6**

Pacifica Sweet-Hot Salmon

This sweet and spicy salmon is a terrific dish to serve for dinner any night of the week. Serve it hot or cold—the flavor is a real wake-up call, with hot English mustard pairing with honey and dill. Serve on a bed of rice pilaf or with a fennel gratin.

3 pounds salmon fillets

½ cup Colman's English mustard

¼ cup honey

2 tablespoons finely chopped fresh dill

place the salmon in the insert of a 5- to 7-quart slow cooker. Put the mustard, honey, and dill in a small bowl and stir to combine.

pour the mixture over the salmon, spreading evenly.

cover and cook on high for 1½ hours, until the salmon is cooked through.

serve the salmon from the slow cooker topped with some of the sauce.

serves **6**

Potato-Crusted Sea Bass

Thin slices of Creole-spiced Yukon gold potatoes surround sea bass in the slow cooker to create a terrific dinner to serve with your favorite green vegetable. The lemon-butter sauce is a nice contrast with the somewhat spicy potatoes.

1 cup (2 sticks) unsalted butter, melted and cooled

½ cup fresh lemon juice

Grated zest of 1 lemon

2 cloves garlic, minced

8 tablespoons olive oil

2 tablespoons Old Bay seasoning

2 to 3 pounds sea bass fillets, cut to fit the slow-cooker insert (see savvy)

6 medium Yukon gold potatoes, cut into ¼-inch-thick slices

stir the butter, lemon juice, zest, garlic, and 2 tablespoons of the olive oil together in a small bowl. Combine the remaining 6 tablespoons oil and the seasoning in a large mixing bowl.

paint the sea bass with some of the butter sauce and set aside. Toss the potatoes in the seasoned oil. Pour half the butter sauce in the insert of a 5- to 7-quart slow cooker.

place half the potatoes in the bottom of the slow cooker. Place the sea bass on top of the potatoes and pour half the remaining butter sauce over the sea bass. Place the remaining potatoes on top of the sea bass and drizzle with the remaining butter sauce.

cover and cook on high for 1½ hours, until the potatoes begin to turn golden and the sea bass is cooked through and opaque in the middle. Remove the cover and cook for an additional 15 to 20 minutes.

serve immediately.

serves **6**

 slow-cooker savvy
This recipe only worked with sea bass, which has a different protein structure than other fish. If you would like to use a different fish, I recommend you use two 16-ounce packages frozen and defrosted shredded hash browns instead of fresh potatoes, and proceed as directed.

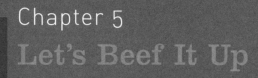

Chapter 5
Let's Beef It Up

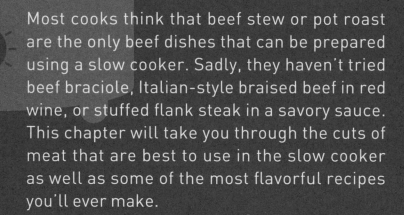

Most cooks think that beef stew or pot roast are the only beef dishes that can be prepared using a slow cooker. Sadly, they haven't tried beef braciole, Italian-style braised beef in red wine, or stuffed flank steak in a savory sauce. This chapter will take you through the cuts of meat that are best to use in the slow cooker as well as some of the most flavorful recipes you'll ever make.

Slow-cooked beef is a miracle in many ways. A slow cooker can take a tough, sinewy piece of meat, melt away all the fat and connective tissue, and give you a melt-in-your-mouth entrée. The sauce that comes from the slow cooker is concentrated not only with the beefy flavor, but also with the flavors that have been added to the pan before the lid is put on. Tough cuts, such as chuck, short ribs, bottom and top round, and rump all become fork-tender when they are braised in the slow cooker. Using these cuts, beef for dinner is a bargain, with short ribs, chuck, and rump all in the $4.00 per pound and under range. If you are able to get them on sale, your dinners can be even cheaper. Round and flank cuts make delicious meals in the slow cooker and, although they can be more expensive, they are virtually fat-free meats and can be stuffed and used for entertaining. Just set your slow cooker in the morning and a delicious meal awaits you and your company later that day.

In most of these recipes I recommend that you brown the meat before adding it to the slow-cooker insert. The reason for browning is because a layer of flavor is created that carries through the entire dish as it simmers. The caramelization that takes place on the outside of the meat helps to give a depth of flavor that you won't have if you just plop the meat and vegetables into the slow cooker and turn it on. Browning ahead of time to release the flavors of the meat produces a balanced and flavorful dish.

In recipes using chuck, brisket, or other fatty meats, use the minimum amount of liquid. These cuts actually contain a lot of water and fat, and, when braised, give off a lot of liquid. In order to concentrate flavors, use a little liquid to start with. By the end of cooking , however, there will be a good quantity of liquid to sauce the meat.

Straining sauces and thickening them are personal choices. If your family wants a smooth sauce without bits of onion or other aromatics, then strain the sauce before serving. But if you like the rustic feel of the bits in the sauce, leave them in. If you want a gravy or thickened sauce, there are several options. One is to transfer the sauce to a saucepan and add a "beurre manié" (see page 188) or add instant-blending flour such as Wondra brand. Either way, these two methods will thicken the sauce. Cornstarch mixed with water or stock will thicken sauces, as well. Sauces can also be puréed—the bits of onion and other vegetables will help to thicken the sauce without the addition of a thickener.

Labeling in the beef department is not as standardized as it is with poultry or pork. When I recommend a certain cut, I try to specify those that are readily available in most parts of the country. Most of the beef sold in supermarkets comes in three grades: Prime, which is the top of the line, heavily marbled with fat, and usually aged; Choice, the grade that I recommend for the slow cooker because it's not as pricey and still has good flavor; and Select, which will not have much marbling and, although it will be cheaper, I don't recommend that you buy it because the cuts aren't as flavorful.

GROUND BEEF

Meat Loaf
Meat Loaf Italiano with Chunky Tomato Sauce, 206
Diner-Style Meatloaf with Gravy, 208
Old-Fashioned Meat Loaf, 210

Meatballs and Variations
Meatballs Italiano, 212
Curried Meatballs, 213
Mom's Stuffed Cabbage Rolls, 214
Lazy-Day Cabbage Rolls, 215

FLANK STEAK
Flank Steak with Spinach, Bacon, and Mushroom Stuffing, 217
Artichoke-Stuffed Flank Steak with Red Wine Sauce, 218
Salsa Beef Fajitas, 219
Chicago-Style Italian Beef, 220

SHORT RIBS
Pacific Rim Braised Short Ribs, 222
Pub-Crawl Short Ribs, 223
Barbecue-Style Short Ribs, 224
Lemon Garlic Short Ribs, 225
Zinfandel-Braised Short Ribs, 226
Hot Italian Short Ribs, 227

VEAL
Veal Shanks Osso Bucco-Style, 229
Veal Chops Braised in White Wine and Sage, 230
Veal Chops Braised with Confetti Peppers, 231

VEAL STEWS
Veal Stew with Forty Cloves of Garlic, 233
Sage-Scented Veal and Sausage Stew, 234
Veal Paprikash, 235

Round

Round comes from the hind leg of the cow. It is leaner than most cuts and can tend to be dry, but when braised in the slow cooker it becomes tender. The best part about round is that it can usually be cut in neat slices so you can serve it arranged on a platter. When braising, I like to use rump roast or eye of the round, which have a layer of fat that helps to flavor the braise. Thinly sliced round steaks can be used in braciole or beef rolls, or braised until they are fall-apart tender.

Pot Roast Italiano

The aroma of beef, wine, and tomatoes will entice your family into your kitchen, waiting for the slow cooker to finish so they can eat this hearty, comforting pot roast. The addition of dried porcini mushrooms enhances and deepens the flavor of this savory stew, which is delicious served with garlic mashed potatoes, polenta, or pasta. Any leftovers can be frozen for up to 2 months.

1 tablespoon extra-virgin olive oil

1 bottom round roast (about 3 to 3½ pounds), tied with butcher's twine

3 cloves garlic, minced

Salt and freshly ground black pepper

2 large sweet onions, such as Vidalia, coarsely chopped

1 tablespoon dried rosemary, crumbled

1 cup Zinfandel wine

4 dried porcini mushrooms, crumbled

One 15-ounce can chopped tomatoes, with their juice

2 tablespoons all-purpose flour

2 tablespoons unsalted butter

¼ cup finely chopped fresh Italian parsley for garnish

heat the oil in a large skillet over high heat. Rub the meat with the garlic, 1½ teaspoons salt, and 1 teaspoon pepper. Add the meat to the skillet and brown on all sides.

transfer the browned meat to the insert of a 5- to 7-quart slow cooker. Add the onions and rosemary to the same skillet and sauté until they become fragrant and the onions begin to soften, about 3 minutes. Transfer the contents of the skillet to the slow-cooker insert.

add the wine, dried mushrooms, and tomatoes and stir to combine. Cover the slow cooker and cook on high for 4 to 5 hours or low for 10 hours, until the meat is tender.

remove the meat from the slow-cooker insert, cover with aluminum foil, and allow to rest for 15 minutes.

transfer the sauce to a saucepan and bring to a boil. Boil the sauce for about 10 minutes, to concentrate the flavor. Blend the flour and butter in a small bowl and stir to form a paste. Add the flour mixture to the saucepan a bit at a time, whisking until the sauce is thickened.

remove from the heat and stir in the parsley. Season with salt and pepper. Slice the meat, cover it with some of the sauce, and serve. Serve any additional sauce on the side.

serves 6—8

Not-So-Swiss Steak

Swiss steak is a blast from the past. A staple from the 1950s, when Campbell's Cream of Mushroom Soup was considered exotic, recipes called for round steak that was pounded until tender, coated with flour, and seared, then smothered with onions, tomatoes, and other flavors. For this version, you won't need to pound the meat because the slow cooker tenderizes it. The addition of meaty cremini mushrooms and a savory mix of Worcestershire sauce, ketchup, and smoked paprika makes this dish a delicious weeknight meal to serve with buttered noodles, mashed potatoes, or rice.

One 1-inch-thick beef round steak (3½ to 4 pounds), cut into 6 pieces

Salt and freshly ground black pepper

2 tablespoons olive oil

2 large sweet onions, such as Vidalia, coarsely chopped

1 pound cremini mushrooms, quartered

¼ cup Worcestershire sauce

1 cup ketchup

1 cup beef broth

1 teaspoon smoked paprika (see savvy)

sprinkle the meat evenly with 1½ teaspoons salt and 1 teaspoon pepper. Heat the oil in a large skillet over medium-high heat. Add the meat and brown on all sides.

transfer the meat to the insert of a 5- to 7-quart slow cooker. Add the onions to the same skillet and sauté until they are softened and are beginning to turn translucent, 5 to 7 minutes. Add the mushrooms and sauté until the mushrooms begin to color, 7 to 10 minutes.

add the Worcestershire, ketchup, broth, and paprika and stir to combine. Bring the sauce to a boil. Transfer the contents of the skillet to the slow-cooker insert, covering the beef with the sauce. Cover the slow cooker and cook on high for 4 to 5 hours or on low for 8 to 10 hours.

remove the meat and vegetables from the slow cooker, cover with aluminum foil, and allow to rest for 20 minutes.

thicken the sauce if desired using any of the methods discussed in the introduction. Season with salt and pepper.

cover the meat and vegetables with some of the sauce and serve. Serve any additional sauce on the side.

serves **6**

spice savvy
Paprika and other red spices (cayenne pepper, chili powder) can lose their potency quickly. Make sure that your red spices are bright red in color, not brown or dark rust. Paprika has a flavor—whether it is sweet, smoked, or hot—so make sure to smell it to see if it still has an aroma. If it doesn't, it's best to discard it and buy new. If you haven't cooked with smoked paprika, you are in for a delicious surprise; it adds a lot of personality to dishes.

Asian Braised Beef in Sake

When I lived in Japan, I was served hot sake at most restaurants, which was delicious after a day in the cold and damp Japanese winter, where the wind would chill you to the bone. Sake is used in many dishes in Japan, but the most famous is sukiyaki. This is a slow-cooked variation on that dish, and it always brings me back to a simpler place and that beautiful country. There is no browning in this recipe, but you will need to marinate the meat overnight. Serve this with sticky rice to soak up the delicious sauce.

⅔ cup soy sauce

½ cup sake

1 clove garlic, minced

½ teaspoon freshly ground black pepper

2 tablespoons sugar

2 to 3 pounds beef chuck, cut into 1-inch pieces

2 large onions, coarsely chopped

1 cup chicken broth

½ pound shiitake mushrooms, stems removed and caps sliced

Two 10-ounce bags baby spinach

2 tablespoons cornstarch mixed with ¼ cup water or chicken broth

combine the soy sauce, sake, garlic, pepper, and sugar in a large bowl and whisk.

add the meat and stir to coat. Cover and refrigerate for at least 4 hours or up to 36 hours.

put the beef and marinade in the insert of a 5- to 7-quart slow cooker. Add the onions and chicken broth and stir to combine.

cover and cook on high for 3 hours. Skim off any fat from the top of the stew. add the mushrooms, spinach, and cornstarch mixture and stir to combine. Cover and cook on low for an additional 1 hour, until the meat is tender and the sauce is thickened.

serve the beef from the cooker set on warm.

serves **8**

Southwestern Beef Rolls

A riff on braciole, these beef rolls are stuffed with roasted green chiles and chorizo sausage and braised in a hearty, tequila-spiked ranchero sauce, filled with colorful bell peppers and onions. This is comfort food with a kick. Serve with rice and beans for a fiesta with some frosty margaritas and south-of-the-border beer. You can make the beef rolls ahead of time, refrigerating for up to 24 hours before making the rest of the dish.

Eight 6-inch-square slices round steak (2 ½ to 3 pounds)

Salt and freshly ground black pepper

8 canned roasted green chiles, drained and rinsed

½ pound chorizo sausage, cooked and crumbled

5 tablespoons plus 1 teaspoon olive oil

2 large sweet onions, coarsely chopped

2 medium yellow bell peppers, seeded and coarsely chopped

2 medium red bell peppers, seeded and coarsely chopped

2 medium green bell peppers, seeded and coarsely chopped

1 teaspoon ground cumin

¼ teaspoon ancho chile powder

½ cup gold tequila (optional)

Two 28- to 32-ounce cans tomato purée

place the beef on a cutting board and sprinkle it with 2 teaspoons salt and 1 teaspoon pepper. Cut a slit in the side of each chile. Stuff the chiles with the cooked chorizo. Place a chile in the center of each beef slice.

roll the beef and secure the seams with a toothpick or skewer. Place the rolls seam-side down on a plate and set aside.

heat 2 tablespoons of the oil in a large skillet over medium-high heat. Add the rolls and brown on all sides. Transfer the beef to the insert of a 5- to 7-quart slow cooker. Heat the remaining 3 tablespoons plus 1 teaspoon oil in the skillet over medium-heat heat. Add the onions, bell peppers, cumin, and chile powder and sauté until the vegetables begin to soften, 5 to 7 minutes. Deglaze the pan with the tequila (if using; if not using, deglaze the pan with the tomato puree), scraping up any browned bits, add the tomato purée, and stir to combine.

transfer the contents of the skillet to the slow-cooker insert, covering the beef rolls. Cover and cook on high for 4 to 5 hours or low for 8 to 10 hours. Remove the meat from the sauce, cover with aluminum foil, and allow to rest for 10 to 15 minutes.

purée the sauce with an immersion blender. Season with salt and pepper.

remove the toothpicks from the rolls. Cut each roll in half and place on top of some sauce on a serving plate. Serve any additional sauce on the side.

serves **8**

Mediterranean Beef Rolls

Stuffed with salty feta cheese, spinach, and dill, these beef rolls are braised in a red wine sauce and are perfect for entertaining. A side of orzo and a crisp salad with red onions, Kalamata olives, and a red wine vinaigrette will round out your dinner.

Salt and freshly ground black pepper

½ cup all-purpose flour

4 tablespoons olive oil

2 cloves garlic, minced

2½ cups finely chopped sweet onion, such as Vidalia

2 tablespoons chopped fresh dill

Two 10-ounce packages baby spinach or one 16-ounce package frozen chopped spinach, defrosted

6 ounces feta cheese, crumbled

2 cups fresh bread crumbs

Eight 6-inch-square slices round steak (2½ to 3 pounds)

1 cup red wine, such as Barolo or Chianti

1½ cups beef broth

put 2 teaspoons salt, 1 teaspoon pepper, and the flour in a shallow dish and stir to combine. Set aside.

heat 2 tablespoons of the oil in a large skillet over medium-high heat. Add the garlic, ½ cup of the onion, and the dill and sauté until the onion is softened, 2 to 3 minutes. Add the spinach and sauté until the spinach is wilted and the moisture in the pan has evaporated, 3 to 5 minutes. Transfer the mixture to a bowl and allow to cool. Add the feta, bread crumbs, and ½ teaspoon pepper to the bowl and stir to combine.

place the meat slices on a cutting board and place 2 to 3 tablespoons of the filling on the meat. Roll the meat and secure the seams with a toothpick. Place the rolls in the shallow dish with the flour, coat the rolls with the flour, and shake off any excess. Heat the remaining 2 tablespoons oil in the same skillet over high heat. Add the rolls seam-side down and brown on all sides.

transfer to the insert of a 5- to 7-quart slow cooker. Add the remaining 2 cups onion to the skillet and sauté until the onion is translucent, about 7 minutes. Deglaze the pan with the wine and reduce the sauce slightly.

transfer the mixture to the slow-cooker insert and add the beef broth, scraping up any browned bits. Cover the slow cooker and cook on on high for 4 hours or low for 8 hours, until the beef is tender. Remove the beef from the cooker, cover with aluminum foil, and allow to rest for 15 minutes. Transfer the sauce to a saucepan and bring to a boil.

boil the sauce for 10 minutes, until it is reduced and begins to thicken. Skim off any fat and season with salt and pepper.

remove the toothpicks from the beef rolls. Slice each roll into 3 pieces and serve the rolls in a pool of sauce.

serves 8

Beef in Barolo

Slowly simmered and served over garlic mashed potatoes, pasta, polenta, or rice, this Italian beef stew will make everyone in your house cheer for snow days! Chuck roast becomes meltingly tender when it is braised in red wine, tomatoes, and aromatic herbs. Short ribs would also be a good choice for this recipe.

4 tablespoons olive oil

Salt and freshly ground black pepper

3 cloves garlic, minced

4 pounds beef chuck , cut into 1-inch pieces

2 large sweet onions, cut into half rounds

2 teaspoons sugar

1 tablespoon dried rosemary, crushed

½ cup red wine, such as Chianti or Barolo

One 32-ounce can crushed tomatoes, with their juice

put 2 tablespoons of the oil, 1½ teaspoons salt, ½ teaspoon pepper, and the garlic in a small bowl and stir to combine. Add the meat to the bowl and toss to coat in the mixture.

heat the remaining 2 tablespoons oil in a large skillet over high heat.

add the beef and brown on all sides. Transfer to a 5- to 7-quart slow cooker insert. Add the onions, sugar, and rosemary to the same skillet over medium-high heat and sauté until the onions begin to soften, 3 to 4 minutes.

transfer the contents of the skillet to the slow-cooker insert. Add the wine and tomatoes and stir to combine. Cover and cook on high for 4 hours, or low for 8 hours, until the beef is tender. Remove the beef from the slow cooker with a slotted spoon and cover with aluminum foil.

skim off the fat from the top of the sauce and season with salt and pepper.

serve the beef with the sauce on a platter.

serves 6–8

North African Beef Stew

The fragrance of Marrakech markets will perfume your home when cooking this succulent meat dish with spices from the Kasbah. Filled with hearty chunks of beef cooked until fork-tender, exotic spices, dried fruit, and garbanzo beans, it's a wonderful weeknight dinner served with rice or couscous.

3 tablespoons olive oil

3 pounds beef chuck roast, cut into 1-inch pieces

1½ teaspoons salt

1 teaspoon freshly ground black pepper

1 large onion, coarsely chopped

2 cloves garlic, sliced

4 medium carrots, coarsely chopped

2 teaspoons sweet paprika

1 teaspoon ground cumin

½ teaspoon ground cinnamon

3 cups beef broth

One 15-ounce can garbanzo beans, drained and rinsed

1 cup dried apricots, cut into ½-inch pieces

½ cup golden raisins

2 tablespoons cornstarch mixed with ¼ cup water

heat the oil in a large skillet over high heat. Sprinkle the meat evenly with the salt and pepper. Add the meat to the skillet a few pieces at a time and brown on all sides. Transfer the browned meat to the insert of a 5- to 7-quart slow cooker.

add the onion and garlic to the same skillet and sauté until the onion begins to soften, about 3 minutes. Add the carrots, paprika, cumin, and cinnamon and sauté until the spices are fragrant, about 2 minutes.

deglaze the skillet with 1 cup of the broth and scrape up any browned bits from the bottom of the pan. Transfer the contents of the skillet to the slow-cooker insert. Add the remaining 2 cups broth, the beans, apricots, and raisins.

cover the slow cooker and cook on low for 8 to 10 hours, until the meat is tender.

skim off any fat from the top of the stew. Add the cornstarch mixture and stir to combine. Cover the slow cooker and cook for an additional 20 to 30 minutes, until the sauce is thickened.

serve the stew warm from the cooker.

serves 8

Old-Fashioned Beef Stew with Vegetables

If you have a family that turns up their nose at a "new" beef stew, this one will look just like your usual one, but without the time-intensive cooking. Just load it in the cooker in the morning, and by dinnertime you've got a terrific one-pot meal. Chuck works well here. Your market may sell stew meat, but check the price—it may be cheaper to buy the chuck and cut it yourself. Stew meat is usually the leftovers from many different cuts of meat, so some pieces may become tender faster than others.

6 medium Yukon gold or red potatoes, quartered

4 medium carrots, cut into 1-inch lengths

3 medium onions, quartered

Salt and freshly ground black pepper

1 cup all-purpose flour

2 to 3 pounds beef chuck, fat trimmed and cut into 1-inch pieces

2 tablespoons olive oil

1½ cups beef broth

2 teaspoon dried thyme leaves

2 cups frozen petite peas, defrosted

2 cups frozen corn, defrosted

combine the potatoes, carrots, onions, 1 teaspoon salt, and ½ teaspoon pepper in the insert of a 5- to 7-quart slow cooker, and toss the vegetables to distribute the seasonings.

add 2 teaspoons salt, 1 teaspoon pepper, and the flour to a large plastic bag and stir to combine. Add the meat to the flour, toss to coat, and shake off any excess flour.

heat the oil in a large skillet over high heat. Add the meat and brown on all sides transfer the browned meat to the slow cooker insert.

deglaze the skillet with the broth and scrape up any browned bits from the bottom of the pan. Transfer the contents of the skillet to the slow-cooker insert and add the thyme. Cover and cook on low for 8 hours, until the meat is tender.

add the peas and corn and cook for an additional 1 hour. Season with salt and pepper before serving.

serves 8

OLD-FASHIONED BEEF STEW WITH VEGETABLES

CRANBERRY ORANGE PORK LOIN

OLD FASHIONED MAC AND CHEESE

HOT LEMON BLUEBERRY PUDDING CAKE

BRAISED LAMB WITH EGGPLANT, TOMATOES, AND FETA

CIOPPINO

RED WINE POACHED PEARS WITH STILTON

BEEF BRACIOLE

Beef Braciole

In this southern Italian dish, thinly sliced round steak is transformed into melt-in-your-mouth-tender rolls filled with savory goodness. Cooked in a tomato sauce flavored with golden raisins, the braciole is what the Italians describe as *agra dolce*, or "sweet and sour." This preparation provides an interesting balance of flavor and is just waiting to be served with soft polenta, pasta, or garlic mashed potatoes. You can make the beef rolls ahead of time, refrigerating for up to 24 hours before making the rest of the dish.

Eight 6-inch-square thin slices round steak, (2½ to 3 pounds)

Salt and freshly ground black pepper

8 thin slices prosciutto

8 tablespoons olive oil

2 cloves garlic, minced

Two 10-ounce packages baby spinach or one 16-ounce package frozen chopped spinach, defrosted and thoroughly drained

¼ teaspoon freshly grated nutmeg

2 cups fresh bread crumbs

⅓ cup freshly grated Pecorino-Romano cheese

2 large eggs, beaten

1 large sweet onion, such as Vidalia, coarsely chopped

2 teaspoons dried basil

Two 28- to 32-ounce cans crushed tomatoes, with their juice

1½ cups golden raisins

place the beef on a cutting board and sprinkle it with 2 teaspoons salt and 1 teaspoon pepper. Place a slice of prosciutto over each piece of beef and set aside.

heat 2 tablespoons of the oil in a medium skillet over medium-high heat. Add the garlic and sauté until it is fragrant, about 30 seconds. Add the spinach and sauté until it is wilted and the liquid in the pan has evaporated, 3 to 4 minutes. Add the nutmeg and season with salt and pepper. Allow to cool before proceeding.

put the bread crumbs and cheese in a large bowl and stir to combine. Add the spinach and eggs, and stir until the mixture comes together. Place 3 tablespoons of filling in the center of each piece of beef. Roll the beef and secure the seams with a toothpick or skewer. Place the rolls seam-side down on a platter.

heat the remaining 6 tablespoons oil in a large skillet over medium-high heat. Add the rolls seam-side down and brown on all sides. Transfer the rolls to the insert of a 5- to 7-quart slow cooker. Add the onion and basil to the same skillet over medium-high heat and sauté until the onion is fragrant and is softened, about 3 minutes. Add the tomatoes and raisins and stir to combine.

transfer the sauce to the slow-cooker insert, covering the beef rolls. Cover the slow cooker and cook on high for 4 to 5 hours or on low for 8 to 9 hours. remove the beef rolls from the cooker and cover with aluminum foil. Skim off any fat from the top of the sauce and season with salt and pepper.

remove the toothpicks from the rolls. Cut each roll in half and place on top of some sauce on a serving plate. Serve any additional sauce on the side.

serves **8**

Shirley's Sunday Pot Roast

My mother-in-law was the queen of chuck roasts—it was her go-to dish when company came or for Sunday dinner after church—and she loved its beefy flavor. She would cover a roast with sliced onions, salt, and pepper and then bake it for hours. The result was a beefy pot roast, but didn't have a great sauce. This pot roast uses chuck roast and is cooked with beef broth, sage, and root vegetables to add flavor and interest to the finished dish. Make sure to brown the meat evenly on all sides before loading in the slow cooker to ensure the maximum flavor.

3 tablespoons olive oil

4 cloves garlic, minced

2 teaspoons dried sage leaves, crushed

Salt and freshly ground black pepper

One 4-pound boneless chuck roast
(see savvy)

2 large sweet onions, such as Vidalia,
coarsely chopped

4 medium carrots, cut into 1-inch lengths,
or two cups baby carrots

2 medium parsnips, cut into 1-inch lengths

8 medium red potatoes, quartered

1½ cups beef broth

¼ cup soy sauce

2 tablespoons cornstarch mixed with
4 tablespoons water

add the oil, garlic, sage, 2 teaspoons salt, and 1 teaspoon pepper to a small bowl and stir to combine. Rub the meat with the oil mixture to coat. Put the onions, carrots, parsnips, and potatoes in the insert of a 5- to 7-quart slow cooker.

heat a large skillet over high heat. Add the meat and brown evenly on all sides. Transfer the browned meat to the slow-cooker insert. Add the broth and soy sauce to the cooker.

cover and cook on high for 4 to 5 hours or on low for 8 to 10 hours. Carefully remove the meat and vegetables from the insert and cover with aluminum foil. Skim off the fat from the surface of the sauce or pour the sauce into a fat separator. Season with salt and pepper.

transfer the sauce to a saucepan and bring to a boil. Add the cornstarch mixture and whisk until the sauce comes back to a boil. Remove from the heat.

cut the meat in serving-size portions and serve with some of the sauce spooned over. Serve any additional sauce on the side.

serves **6–8**

pot roast savvy
If the meat is too large for your insert, don't be afraid to cut it and wedge it in or stack it. Halfway through the cooking time, most of the collagen and fat will have melted away, and the pieces can then be set side by side in the slow cooker.

Beef Fajitas-Style

This simple recipe adds a punch of flavor to the beef, which is perfect served as fajitas, tacos, or in its sauce over rice with a side of refried beans. Braised in salsa, lime juice, and beer, the beef becomes so tender that you can pull the meat into shreds, like pulled pork, and serve it on warm flour tortillas. Any leftover beef and sauce can made into a beefy version of tortilla soup.

2 tablespoons olive oil

1 teaspoon ground cumin

½ teaspoon dried oregano

1 teaspoon ancho chile powder

One 4-pound boneless chuck roast

2 large white onions, coarsely chopped

Two 16-ounce jars medium-hot salsa (see savvy)

½ cup lime juice

One 12-ounce bottle beer

add the oil, cumin, oregano, and chile powder to a small bowl and stir to combine. Rub the mixture over the meat, coating evenly. Heat a large skillet over high heat.

add the meat and brown on all sides. Transfer to the insert of a 5- to 7-quart slow cooker. Add the onions to the skillet over medium-high heat and sauté until softened, 3 to 5 minutes. Transfer to the slow-cooker insert. Add the salsa, lime juice, and beer to the slow cooker and stir to combine.

cover and cook on high for 5 to 6 hours or on low for 10 to 12 hours. Remove the meat from the slow cooker, cover with aluminum foil, and allow to rest for 20 to 30 minutes.

transfer the sauce to a saucepan and bring to a boil. Boil the sauce to reduce to concentrate the flavor, about 10 minutes. Strain the sauce through a fine-mesh sieve, if desired.

shred the beef or return the sauce and beef to the slow cooker and serve from the cooker set on the warm setting.

serves **8**

salsa savvy
Although I love fresh salsa for dipping with chips, for this dish it is too watery to add to the cooker. Prepared salsa is perfect for this dish, and you can choose your favorite brand.

Hungarian Smoked Beef Braise

Spanish smoked paprika, bacon, Guinness, and a bit of chipotle turns chuck roast a glorious shade of red in the braising liquid and flavors it with a smoky and slightly sweet sauce. Adding root vegetables to the pot turns this into a one-pot meal, but if you decide to omit them (see savvy), the stew is delicious served over buttered noodles. Make sure to use smoked paprika in this dish—you can find it in many markets and gourmet retailers or online at www.penzeys.com.

6 medium Yukon gold or red potatoes, quartered

4 medium carrots, cut into 1-inch lengths

2 teaspoons salt

½ teaspoon freshly ground black pepper

4 strips thick-cut bacon, cut into ½-inch pieces

3 medium onions, cut into half rounds

2 teaspoons smoked paprika

2 chipotle chiles in adobo, minced

2 cloves garlic, minced

1 cup all-purpose flour

3½ to 4 pounds beef chuck, cut into 1-inch pieces

2 tablespoons canola or vegetable oil

One 14- to 15-ounce can chopped tomatoes, with their juice

One 12-ounce bottle Guinness or dark ale

arrange the potatoes, carrots, 1 teaspoon of the salt, and the pepper in the insert of a 5- to 7-quart slow cooker and stir to combine. Cook the bacon in a large skillet over medium heat until crisp.

transfer the bacon to the slow-cooker insert and remove all but 3 tablespoons of fat from the pan. Heat the remaining fat in the pan over medium-high heat. Add the onions, paprika, chiles, and garlic and sauté until the onions begin to soften 4 to 5 minutes.

transfer the mixture to the slow-cooker insert. Put the flour and the remaining 1 teaspoon salt in a large plastic bag. Put the meat in the flour, toss to coat, and shake off any excess flour.

heat the canola oil in the same skillet over high heat. Add the meat a few pieces at a time and brown on all sides. Transfer the browned meat to the slow-cooker insert. Deglaze the pan with the tomatoes, scraping up any browned bits from the bottom of the pan.

transfer the tomatoes to the slow-cooker insert. Add the Guinness and stir to combine. Cover the slow cooker and cook on high for 4 to 5 hours, until the meat and vegetables are tender.

skim off any fat from the top of the stew and serve the meat and vegetables from the slow cooker.

serves **8**

 slow-cooker savvy
If you decide to omit the vegetables, cook the stew for 4 hours on high.

Sirloin   Located near the hip area, sirloin is a popular choice for slow cooking. Not as tough as chuck, it has some marbling of fat to give it flavor. Sirloin has a great flavor and when slow cooked, it retains its shape, and slices into nice thin slices when allowed to rest after cooking.

Porcini Pot Roast

This melt-in-your mouth pot roast gets its punch from the addition of dried thyme and porcini mushrooms. The resulting braise, flavored with red wine and cremini mushrooms, is a great entrée for company, as well as a weeknight dinner.

One 4-pound sirloin roast

3 cloves garlic, minced

2 teaspoons salt

1 teaspoon freshly ground black pepper

2 tablespoons olive oil

2 large sweet onions, such as Vidalia, quartered

2 teaspoons dried thyme

1 pound cremini mushrooms, quartered

4 ounces dried porcini mushrooms

1 cup red wine

2 cups beef broth

2 teaspoons cornstarch dissolved in 2 tablespoons water or broth (see savvy)

rub the roast with the garlic, salt, and pepper, coating evenly. Heat the oil in a 5- to 6-quart dutch oven over medium-high heat. Add the roast and brown on all sides. Transfer the roast to a 5- to 7-quart slow-cooker insert.

add the onions and thyme to the pan over medium-high heat and sauté until the onions begin to soften, about 3 minutes. Add the cremini mushrooms and sauté about 5 minutes, until the mushroom liquid evaporates.

transfer the mixture to the slow-cooker insert. Put the porcini mushrooms and wine in a small bowl and soak the mushrooms for 10 minutes. Add the wine mixture and broth to the slow-cooker insert. Cover the slow cooker and cook on high for 3 to 4 hours or low for 8 hours, until the meat is fork tender.

remove the roast from the slow cooker, cover loosely with aluminum foil, and allow it to rest for 10 to 15 minutes. Skim off any fat from the top of the sauce. Strain the sauce through a fine-mesh sieve into a saucepan and bring it to a boil. Add the cornstarch mixture, stir to combine, and bring back to a boil.

slice the roast and serve the sauce on the side.

serves **8**

thickener savvy
An old chef's trick for thickening sauces is *beurre manié,* or kneaded butter. Take equal parts all-purpose flour and softened unsalted butter and knead them together to make a paste. Bring the sauce to a boil and whisk in a few bits of the beurre manié, bringing the sauce back to a boil after each addition. This is an easy way to fix a sauce that may not be as thick as you would like.

Sirloin Teriyaki

Sirloin marinated in Asian flavors and accompanied by sticky rice and an Asian slaw is the perfect dinner for friends and family. Marinate the meat the day before, put it all in the slow cooker, and inhale the delicious aromas of garlic, ginger, soy, and beef all day long.

⅔ cup soy sauce

¼ cup vegetable oil

½ cup rice wine (mirin)

¼ cup firmly packed light brown sugar

1 teaspoon freshly grated ginger

2 cloves garlic, minced

One 2½- to 3-pound sirloin roast (tri-tip or triangle sirloin works well here)

2 cups beef broth

2 large sweet onions, such as Vidalia, coarsely chopped

2 teaspoons cornstarch mixed with 2 teaspoons of water

Chopped green onions for garnishing

Sesame seeds for garnishing

combine the soy sauce, oil, rice wine, brown sugar, ginger, and garlic in a large zipper-top plastic bag. Add the sirloin to the bag, seal, and turn to coat the meat with the marinade. Refrigerate for at least 8 hours and up to 24 hours.

pour the marinade and the meat into the insert of a 5- to 7-quart slow cooker. Add the broth and onions. Cover and cook on high for 4 to 5 hours.

remove the meat from the insert, cover with aluminum foil, and allow to rest for 15 minutes. Strain the sauce through a fine-mesh sieve into a saucepan and bring to a boil. Taste the sauce and dilute it with water or broth if it is too strong.

add the cornstarch mixture and bring the sauce back to a boil, whisking constantly, until it is thickened. Keep the sauce warm on the stovetop, or transfer it to the slow cooker set on warm.

slice the meat and serve with the sauce, and garnish with the green onions and sesame seeds.

serves **6–8**

All-I-Want-Is-Meat-and-Potatoes Sirloin

When tasting recipes for this book, my husband longed for a simple meat-and-potatoes dinner. I was so focused on flavor combinations and international flavors that I left traditional ones behind. So, Dr. Chuck, this one's for you. We loved this served with crisp green beans dressed with extra-virgin olive oil.

One 2 ½- to 3-pound sirloin roast

Salt and freshly ground black pepper

3 tablespoons olive oil

2 large sweet onions, such as Vidalia, coarsely chopped

2 teaspoons dried thyme

3 cups beef broth

2 tablespoons Worcestershire sauce

24 golf ball–sized Yukon gold or red potatoes

2 tablespoons unsalted butter

2 tablespoons all-purpose flour

sprinkle the roast evenly with 1½ teaspoons salt and 1 teaspoon pepper. Heat the oil in a large skillet over high heat. Add the meat and brown on all sides.

transfer the meat to the insert of a 5- to 7-quart slow cooker. Add the onions and thyme to the same skillet and sauté until the onions begin to soften, 3 to 4 minutes. Transfer the onion mixture to the slow cooker. Add the broth, Worcestershire, and potatoes to the cooker, surrounding the meat.

cover the slow cooker and cook on high for 4 to 5 hours or on low for 8 to 9 hours. Remove the meat and potatoes from the slow cooker, cover with aluminum foil, and allow to rest for about 15 minutes.

skim off any fat from the surface of the sauce. Transfer the sauce to a saucepan and strain through a fine-mesh sieve, if desired. Put the butter and the flour in a small bowl and stir to form a paste.

bring the sauce to a boil and add the butter mixture in pieces to the sauce, bringing the sauce back to a boil after each addition. Season with salt and pepper.

slice the meat and serve napped with some of the sauce. Serve any additional sauce warmed on the side.

serves **6–8**

Red Wine–Marinated Sirloin

Julia Child once remarked that Boeuf Bourguignon was the best beef stew known to man. By marinating the meat in the wine and spices ahead of time, your stew will have a deep flavor and the slow cooker will melt the meat into a tender and delicious dinner, giving you the whole day to relax. A classic French beef stew flavored with bacon or salt pork and garnished with mushrooms and small pearl onions, when done right, this is heaven on a plate. The slow cooker takes over with its low and slow braising and gives you a melt-in-your-mouth dinner. Make sure to serve with a crusty loaf of French bread to dip in the sauce.

4 cups Burgundy wine

3 cloves garlic, minced

1 teaspoon dried thyme

1 bay leaf

2 tablespoons honey

1 teaspoon salt

½ teaspoon freshly ground black pepper

3 to 4 pounds beef sirloin, fat trimmed, cut into 1-inch pieces

6 strips thick-cut bacon, cut into ½-inch pieces

One 15-ounce can double-strength beef broth

4 tablespoons (½ stick) unsalted butter, at room temperature

1 pound small white button mushrooms

½ pound pearl onions, blanched and peeled

3 tablespoons all-purpose flour

combine the wine, garlic, thyme, bay leaf, honey, salt, and pepper in a large zipper-top plastic bag. Add the beef to the bag, seal, and turn to coat the meat with the marinade. Refrigerate for at least 8 hours and up to 24 hours, turning the bag a few times during refrigeration.

remove the meat from the marinade and set the marinade aside, removing the bay leaf. Cook the bacon in a large skillet until crisp and remove it to drain on paper towels. Add the meat to the bacon drippings and brown on all sides. Transfer the browned meat to the insert of a 5- to 7-quart slow cooker. Add the marinade to the skillet and bring to a boil, scraping up any browned bits from the bottom of the pan.

transfer the contents of the skillet to the slow-cooker insert and add the broth. Cover and cook on high for 3 hours, until the meat is tender. Melt 2 tablespoons of the butter in a large skillet over medium-high heat. Add the mushrooms and onions and sauté until they begin to turn golden and the liquid in the pan is evaporated. Set aside until ready to serve. (The mushrooms and onions may be refrigerated for up to 2 days.) Stir the flour into the remaining 2 tablespoons butter to form a paste.

when the stew is finished cooking, skim off any fat from the top of the sauce and stir in the butter and flour mixture. Add the mushroom mixture, reserved bacon, and stir to combine. Cover and cook for an additional 15 to 20 minutes, until the sauce is thickened, before serving.

serves 8

Santa Maria Tri-Tip for Fajitas

The area around Santa Barbara on the central coast of California is famous for its tri-tip sirloin-roast barbecues, which date back to the days of the Spanish ranchers. Generally this cut is barbecued and thinly sliced to serve with warm flour tortillas and condiments. The slow cooker mimics a covered grill and braises this delicious cut of meat to perfection. This preparation requires a cut of meat that can be hard to find in some areas, but ask your butcher for the "triangle sirloin" or "bottom sirloin triangle cut." If you have trouble finding it, 3-inch-thick top sirloin will work here. Just remember to slice the top sirloin thinly across the grain.

2 large onions, cut into half rounds

¼ cup firmly packed light brown sugar

2 tablespoons sweet paprika

2 teaspoons ancho chile powder

2 teaspoons garlic salt

1 teaspoon celery seeds

Two 1½- to 2-pound tri-tip roasts, fat trimmed, tied together with kitchen string or silicone loops

2 tablespoons olive oil

½ cup beef broth

spread the onions on the bottom of the insert of a 5- to 7-quart slow cooker. Combine the sugar, paprika, chile powder, garlic salt, and celery seeds in a small bowl. Rub the mixture evenly over the roasts.

heat the oil in a large skillet over high heat. Add the meat and brown on all sides.

transfer the meat to the slow-cooker insert. Deglaze the skillet with the broth and scrape up any browned bits from the bottom of the pan.

pour the broth over the meat in the slow-cooker insert. Cover and cook on high for 3 hours or on low for 6 to 7 hours, until the meat is tender.

remove the meat from the slow cooker, cover with aluminum foil, and allow to rest. Remove the strings from the meat. Slice the meat thinly against the grain and serve.

serves **8**

Barbecued Beef Sandwiches

My son Ryan was a fussy eater growing up, but he and his friends never could get enough of these sandwiches. They loved the slowly cooked, melt-in-your-mouth beef surrounded by the sweet and spicy barbecue sauce, especially when they could serve themselves from the slow cooker. I prefer tri-tip for this recipe because it's so lean and flavorful, but you can use other sirloin cuts as well.

2 tablespoons sweet paprika

1½ teaspoons salt

Pinch of cayenne pepper

Two 1½- to 2-pound tri tip roasts or one 3½- to 4-pound bottom sirloin roast, rolled and tied

2 tablespoons canola or vegetable oil

1 medium onion, finely chopped

2 cloves garlic, minced

2 cups tomato sauce

1 cup ketchup

2 tablespoons Worcestershire sauce

¼ cup molasses

2 tablespoons sugar

2 tablespoons Dijon mustard

8 Kaiser rolls or soft onion rolls

combine the paprika, salt, and cayenne in a small bowl, and rub the mixture evenly onto the roast. Heat the oil in a large skillet over high heat. Add the meat and brown on all sides.

transfer to the insert of a 5- to 7-quart slow cooker. Add the onion and garlic to the same skillet over medium-high heat and sauté until the onion is softened and the garlic is fragrant, 2 to 3 minutes. Pour in the tomato sauce and stir up any browned bits from the bottom of the pan.

transfer the contents of the pan to the slow cooker and stir in the remaining ingredients. Cover the slow cooker and cook on high for 3 to 4 hours or on low for 8 to 9 hours, until the meat is tender. Remove the meat from the cooker, cover with aluminum foil, and allow to rest for 10 minutes.

remove the strings from the meat and slice the meat across the grain. Skim off any fat from the top of the sauce. Return the meat to the slow cooker set on warm, and serve on the rolls.

serves 8

Shepherd's Pie

Cafeteria versions of shepherd's pie, with mystery meat shrouded in instant mashed potatoes, gave this delicious dish a bad rap. The best shepherd's pie has tender chunks of beef or lamb and vegetables simmered in hearty gravy, and is covered with rich whipped potatoes. No powdered things, please! Cook the stew in the slow cooker, and then cover the top of the finished stew with the potatoes, which can be kept warm for 2 to 3 hours before serving without a problem.

1½ teaspoons salt

½ teaspoon freshly ground black pepper

1 cup all-purpose flour

2½ to 3 pounds beef sirloin, cut into ½-inch pieces

2 tablespoons olive oil

1 medium onion, finely chopped

1½ teaspoons dried thyme

2 cups beef broth

3 medium carrots, cut into ½-inch rounds

8 ounces green beans, cut into 1-inch lengths

1½ cups frozen white corn, defrosted

Mashed Potatoes for Stews or Pot Pies (recipe follows; see savvy)

2 tablespoons unsalted butter, at room temperature

combine the salt, pepper, and flour in a large zipper-top plastic bag. Toss the beef to coat in the flour and shake off any excess.

heat the oil in a large skillet over high heat. Add the beef a few pieces at a time and brown on all sides. Transfer the meat to the insert of a 5- to 7-quart slow cooker.

add the onion and thyme to the same skillet over medium-high heat and sauté until the onion is softened, 2 to 3 minutes. Pour in the broth and scrape up any browned bits from the bottom of the pan.

pour the mixture over the beef in the cooker. Cover and cook on high for 3 hours, until the meat is tender. Add the vegetables to the stew and stir to combine. Cover the stew with the mashed potatoes, being careful not to push the potatoes into the stew.

dot the top of the potatoes with the butter. Cover and cook for an additional 1 hour, until the butter is melted.

serve the stew by scooping out a portion covered with mashed potatoes for each diner.

serves **8**

not-so-shepherd's-pie savvy
If you would prefer not to top the stew with potatoes, bake biscuits and split them, serving the stew over the biscuits.

mashed-potato savvy
Chef Laurent Tourondel, of BLT restaurant fame, suggests that the butter and cream be heated before adding to the potatoes, and I agree. The potatoes take on an ethereal quality that doesn't happen when you add cold cream and butter.

Mashed Potatoes for Stews or Pot Pies

Mashed potatoes that cover stews or pot pies have to be stiff, but that doesn't mean they have to be flavorless! These potatoes are filled with butter and sour cream, which give them terrific flavor, and they won't sink to the bottom of your stew. Make sure you add the liquid to the potatoes a bit at a time and keep the consistency stiff, not runny. Feel free to leave the peels on the potatoes if you like more texture. Lumpy mashed potatoes are fine, too! Great additions include your favorite cheeses, cooked crumbled bacon, and caramelized onions.

8 medium russet (baking) potatoes, peeled and cut into 1-inch chunks

2 medium shallots, finely chopped (see savvy)

4 tablespoons (½ stick) unsalted butter

¼ cup heavy cream

¼ cup sour cream

Salt and freshly ground pepper (see savvy)

¼ cup finely chopped chives for garnishing (optional)

combine the potatoes and shallots in a large pot and add water to cover. Bring to a boil and boil uncovered for 20 minutes, until a knife goes into the potatoes easily. Drain the potatoes thoroughly in a colander and return to the pot over low heat.

warm the butter and cream in a small pan until the butter is melted. Pour half the butter mixture in the pot and mash the potatoes until they are smooth. Add the sour cream, 1 teaspoon salt, ½ teaspoon pepper, and some additional butter mixture and mash to achieve a nice stiff texture.

transfer the potatoes to the top of the stew by lifting some of the potatoes onto a spatula and flattening to ½- to ¾-inch thick. Slide the potatoes onto the stew without pushing down on them. Continue until you have covered the stew. The potatoes can be made ahead of time and kept warm over boiling water. (Any leftover potatoes may be frozen for up to 3 months.)

season with salt and pepper and sprinkle the chives (if using) over the potatoes.

serves **8**

garlic-mashed savvy
If you would prefer garlic mashed potatoes, omit the shallots and add 3 garlic cloves, peeled and cut half to the potatoes.

pepper savvy
Many of my students will buy white pepper and use it once, then get it out several years later to use again only to find it's lost its taste and potency. If you use white pepper just once in a blue moon, don't waste your money on it and just add freshly ground black pepper instead.

Bistro Dijon Sirloin

French bistros serve an assortment of comfort foods, and many days there will be some type of stew on the menu. This stew is flavored with Dijon mustard, wine, tarragon, and shallots, and transports you to a sidewalk bistro in Paris. Serve this stew over noodles, or, my favorite, garlic mashed potatoes.

Salt and freshly ground black pepper,

3 pounds beef sirloin, cut into 1-inch pieces

2 tablespoons olive oil

6 medium shallots, cut into half rounds

1 cup dry white wine or vermouth

½ cup Dijon mustard

1 teaspoon dried tarragon

1 cup beef broth

2 tablespoons finely chopped fresh tarragon

2 tablespoons unsalted butter

2 tablespoons all-purpose flour

sprinkle 1½ teaspoons salt and ½ teaspoon pepper evenly over the meat. Heat the oil in a large skillet over high heat. Add the meat a few pieces at a time and brown.

transfer the meat to the insert of a 5- to 7-quart slow cooker. Add the shallots to the same skillet over medium-high heat and sauté for 1 minute, until they begin to soften. Deglaze the pan with the wine, scraping up any browned bits from the bottom of the pan, and add the mustard and dried tarragon.

transfer the mixture to the slow cooker and stir in the broth. Cover and cook on high for 3 hours, until the meat is tender. Skim off any fat from the top of the sauce and stir in the fresh tarragon.

mix the butter and the flour together to form a paste. Add the butter mixture in pieces to the cooker. Cover and cook for an additional 30 minutes, until the sauce is thickened.

season with salt and pepper before serving.

serves **6**

Brisket

Brisket is a cut that comes from the foreleg and just behind in the breast section of the cow, and tends to be very tough but has great flavor. When slowly cooked, brisket becomes tender and is the centerpiece of many great meals, such as pot roast and barbecued beef sandwiches. Corned beef can also be a brisket cut, and the flat, first cut is the piece to buy. Some wholesale clubs sell whole brisket for the barbecue, but for the slow cooker, you will need only one side of the brisket.

Corned Beef and Cabbage Braised in Riesling

Sweet, crisp Riesling adds a delicious counterpoint to the spicy and salty corned beef in this simple slow-cooker classic.

12 small Yukon gold potatoes, scrubbed

2 cups baby carrots

3 medium sweet onions, such as Vidalia, coarsely chopped

2 cups Riesling wine

½ cup whole-grain mustard

¼ cup Dijon mustard

¼ cup firmly packed light brown sugar

4 whole black peppercorns

2 bay leaves

One 3½- to 4-pound corned beef, rinsed and fat trimmed

1 large head green cabbage, cut in half, cored and thickly sliced (see savvy)

layer the potatoes, carrots, and onions in the insert of a 5- to 7-quart slow cooker. Whisk together the riesling, mustards, and sugar in a large bowl. Stir in the peppercorns and bay leaves.

place the brisket on top of the vegetables in the slow-cooker insert. (If you are using a 5-quart cooker, you may need to cut the brisket in half and stack the pieces to fit.) Pour the riesling mixture over the brisket and strew the cabbage over the top of the brisket.

cover the slow cooker and cook on low for 8 to 10 hours. Remove the brisket from the cooker, cover with aluminum foil, and allow to rest for about 20 minutes.

using a slotted spoon, remove the vegetables and arrange them on a platter. Slice the brisket across the grain and arrange over the vegetables. Strain the liquid from the cooker through a fine-mesh sieve and ladle a bit over the meat and vegetables before serving.

serves 6

cabbage savvy
Sliced cabbage blankets the brisket and adds some of the cabbage flavor when laid on the platter with the other vegetables. If you would like to serve quartered cooked cabbage with your corned beef, add it during the last 2 hours of cooking time. It will still retain its crispness.

Corned Beef with Guinness

Braised in ale with mustard seeds and brown sugar, this corned beef is terrific thinly sliced and served with whole-grain mustard on dark bread. This is great food for tailgating or watching sports on TV; the sliced beef can be returned to the cooker to stay warm for guests to serve themselves.

Two 12-ounce cans Guinness or other stout or dark ale

¼ cup firmly packed light brown sugar

2 teaspoons mustard seeds

6 whole black peppercorns

1 bay leaf

2 allspice berries

3 large sweet onions, such as Vidalia, sliced into ½-inch-thick half rounds

One 3½- to 4-pound corned beef, rinsed

stir the Guinness, sugar, mustard seeds, peppercorns, bay leaf, and allspice berries together in the insert of a 5- to 7-quart slow cooker. Add the onions and top with the corned beef. (Cut it in half to fit, if necessary.)

cover and cook on low for 8 to 10 hours, until the meat is fork tender. Remove the meat from the cooker, cover with aluminum foil, and allow to rest for 20 minutes.

remove the bay leaf, peppercorns, and allspice berries from the cooking liquid. Thinly slice the brisket across the grain to serve.

serves 6–8

Brisket with Dried Fruits

Intensely flavored brisket gets a sweet and savory touch in this dish. Dried fruits contribute to a delectable sauce that is terrific served over buttered noodles.

Salt and freshly ground black pepper

¼ cup Dijon mustard

¼ cup firmly packed light brown sugar

One 3- to 4-pound first-cut or flat-cut brisket, fat trimmed

3 tablespoons olive oil

3 large sweet onions, thinly sliced.

2 teaspoons dried thyme

½ cup red wine

½ cup beef broth

1 cup dried figs, halved

½ cup dried plums, halved

½ cup dried apricots, halved

2 tablespoons cornstarch dissolved in ¼ cup water or beef broth

combine 2 teaspoons salt, 1 teaspoon pepper, the mustard, and brown sugar in a small bowl. Rub the mixture over the brisket. Heat the oil in a large skillet over medium-high heat.

add the brisket and brown on all sides. Remove the brisket and transfer to the insert of a 5- to 7-quart slow cooker. Add the onions and thyme to the same skillet over medium-high heat and sauté until the onions are softened, 2 to 3 minutes. Deglaze the pan with the wine and broth, scraping up any browned bits, and bring the liquid to a boil.

pour the mixture into the slow-cooker insert and add the dried fruits around the brisket. Cover and cook on high for 4 to 5 hours or low for 8 to 10 hours, until the meat is fork tender. Remove the brisket and fruits from the insert and cover with aluminum foil.

transfer the liquid to a saucepan or saucier. Skim off any fat from the top of the sauce.

bring the sauce to a boil, add the cornstarch and stir, bringing the sauce back to a boil. Season with salt and pepper.

trim any fat from the brisket and thinly slice it across the grain. Serve the brisket surrounded with the fruit and napped with some of the sauce. Serve the remaining sauce on the side.

serves **8**

Old-Fashioned Beef Brisket with Root Vegetables

This savory braise of beef and vegetables in a rich, beefy gravy is one your family will love. The beef is melt-in-your-mouth tender after ten hours in the slow cooker and the vegetables are infused with the flavor of the meat. Brisket gives off at least three cups of liquid during the braise, making a delicious gravy with the flavors of the rub.

4 medium sweet onions, such as Vidalia, quartered

4 medium carrots, cut into 1-inch lengths

4 large red potatoes, quartered

3 medium parsnips, cut into 1-inch lengths

2 tablespoons sweet paprika

1 tablespoon garlic salt

1 teaspoon onion powder

2 teaspoons dried thyme

½ teaspoon freshly ground black pepper

1 teaspoon celery seeds

4 beef bouillon cubes, crumbled, or 4 teaspoons Better than Bouillon beef soup base

¼ cup firmly packed light brown sugar

2 tablespoons all-purpose flour

One 4-pound brisket, fat trimmed

combine the onions, carrots, potatoes, and parsnips in the insert of a 5- to 7-quart slow cooker. Mix the paprika, garlic salt, onion powder, thyme, pepper, celery seeds, bouillon, brown sugar, and flour together in a small bowl

rub the mixture over the brisket and transfer the brisket to the cooker. (If the brisket is too large, cut it in half and stack to fit.) Cover the cooker and cook on low for 10 hours, until the brisket is tender.

remove the brisket from the cooker and cover with aluminum foil. Carefully lift the vegetables from the sauce, arrange on a platter, and cover with aluminum foil.

skim off any fat from the sauce and leave in the cooker set on warm. Thinly slice the brisket across the grain and arrange it on a serving platter with the vegetables. Spoon some of the sauce over the top of the brisket, and serve any remaining sauce in a gravy boat.

serves 6–8

Barbecued Brisket

This recipe is an adaptation of one that was popular in the 1970s that used a can of beer, chili sauce, and Lipton's onion soup mix. It was a no-brainer to make, but the flavor just wasn't quite there. This version has onions and a simple sauce, with beef that is falling-apart tender and tastes like it belongs at the backyard barbecue. Serve the brisket on soft rolls with coleslaw or potato salad on the side.

4 tablespoons olive oil

3 cloves garlic, minced

1½ teaspoons salt

1 teaspoon freshly ground black pepper

One 4- to 5-pound flat cut brisket, fat trimmed

4 large onions, thinly sliced

1½ cups ketchup

2 cups tomato purée

1 teaspoon Tabasco sauce

½ cup firmly packed light brown sugar

¼ cup molasses

¼ cup Dijon mustard

combine 2 tablespoons of the oil, the garlic, salt, and pepper together in a small bowl. Rub the mixture all over the brisket.

heat the remaining 2 tablespoons oil in a large skillet over high heat. Add the meat and brown on all sides. Transfer the brisket to the insert of a 5- to 7-quart slow cooker. Add the onions to the same skillet over medium-high heat and sauté until the onions begin to soften, 5 to 7 minutes.

add the remaining ingredients to the skillet and stir to combine. Transfer the contents of the skillet to the cooker, lifting the meat, and evenly distribute it in the cooker. Cover and cook on high for 4 to 5 hours or on low for 8 to 10 hours.

remove the meat from the slow cooker, cover with aluminum foil, and allow to rest for 15 minutes. Skim off any fat from the sauce, pour the sauce into a saucepan, and boil to reduce and concentrate the flavor, about 10 minutes.

taste the sauce and adjust the seasonings. Slice the meat at an angle across the grain and transfer back to the slow cooker.

pour the sauce over the meat and leave in the cooker set on low until ready to serve, for up to 4 hours.

serves 6–8

Texas Smoked Brisket

Lighting the barbecue or the smoker in the dead of winter in Minnesota isn't my idea of a great time, but with a slow cooker, you can "smoke" a brisket and enjoy the flavor of barbecue all year-round! Spicy and smoky, this brisket is perfect to serve on rolls with pinto beans and slaw on the side. Yee haw!

4 medium onions, cut into half rounds

2 tablespoons sweet paprika

2 chipotle chiles in adobo, minced

1 teaspoon freshly ground black pepper

1 teaspoon ground cumin

¼ cup firmly packed light brown sugar

2 tablespoons Worcestershire sauce

2 tablespoons apple cider vinegar

One 4-pound brisket, fat trimmed

1 cup ketchup

spread the onions on the bottom of the insert of a 5- to 7-quart slow cooker and turn the machine on low. Stir the paprika, chiles, pepper, cumin, sugar, Worcestershire, and vinegar together in a small bowl.

rub the mixture over the brisket and place the brisket on top of the onions in the slow cooker. Cover and cook for 10 hours on low, until the brisket is tender. Remove the brisket from the cooker and cover with aluminum foil.

skim off any fat from the cooking liquid and strain through a fine-mesh sieve into a saucepan. Stir in the ketchup and simmer for 20 minutes, until thickened.

slice the brisket across the grain to serve, accompanied by some of the sauce.

serves **8**

Ground Beef

There are many varieties of ground beef. The leanest ground beef has only 5 percent fat but is usually not very tasty. I recommend using ground beef with 15 percent fat. Ground chuck generally has the most flavor, and you can ask the butcher to grind it fresh for you. Some fat is necessary to keep the beef moist and tasty.

Meat Loaf

Meat loaf, once relegated to the category of "mystery meat" in cafeterias around the country, has now gained recognition as a culinary comfort food. It's not just diner fare anymore! Meat loaf is a formula in some respects, with different seasonings and sauces changing the flavor. It's simple to prepare a meat loaf; the loaf can be shaped the day before and refrigerated until you are ready to place it in the slow cooker with the sauce. Meat loaf sandwiches are a great reward the day after! Make sure to cook the meat loaf on high for the first hour to guard against any bacteria growth in the raw meat.

Meat Loaf Italiano with Chunky Tomato Sauce

This meat loaf is one from my childhood. Redolent with garlic, herbs, and pungent Pecorino-Romano, it's delicious with pasta, polenta, or garlic mashed potatoes.

MEAT LOAF

3 slices soft-crusted Italian bread, torn into pieces (about ⅔ cup)

½ cup milk

1 pound 85% lean ground beef

8 ounces lean ground pork

8 ounces ground veal

8 ounces bulk Italian sweet sausage

2 tablespoons olive oil

1 cup finely chopped onion

3 cloves garlic, minced

1 teaspoon dried oregano

½ teaspoon dried basil

½ teaspoon dried marjoram

2 large eggs, beaten

½ cup freshly grated Pecorino-Romano cheese

put the bread and milk in a large mixing bowl and allow the bread to absorb the milk. Combine the meats in the bowl. Heat the oil in a small skillet over medium-high heat. Add the onion, garlic, oregano, basil, and marjoram and sauté until the onion and garlic are fragrant, about 3 minutes.

cool the mixture and transfer to the mixing bowl. Add the eggs and cheese. Using clean hands or a large wooden spoon, mix the ingredients until they are well combined, being careful not to compact the mixture.

pat the meat into a loaf 6 to 8 inches long, 3 inches wide, and 2 to 3 inches tall. Cover and refrigerate, up to 24 hours, while you make the sauce.

CHUNKY TOMATO SAUCE

2 tablespoons extra-virgin olive oil

4 cloves garlic, minced

1 medium red bell pepper, seeded and coarsely chopped

1 medium yellow bell pepper, seeded and coarsely chopped

2 teaspoons dried oregano

1 teaspoon dried basil

½ cup balsamic vinegar

Three 32-ounce cans peeled plum tomatoes, with their juice

3 tablespoons brown sugar

Salt and freshly ground black pepper

heat the oil in a large skillet over medium-high heat. Add the garlic, bell peppers, oregano, and basil and sauté until the bell peppers soften, about 3 minutes.

add the balsamic vinegar, reduce the heat, and cook, swirling the pan, until the vinegar is reduced by half and looks syrupy. Transfer the contents of the skillet to the insert of a 5- to 7-quart slow cooker. Stir in the tomatoes and brown sugar.

transfer the meat loaf to the cooker and spoon some of the sauce over the top. Cook the meat loaf on high for 1 hour, then reduce the heat to low and cook for 4 hours, until the meat loaf registers 165°F on an instant-read thermometer.

remove the meat loaf from the cooker, using two long and wide spatulas. Cover with aluminum foil and allow to rest for 15 minutes. Cut into ½-inch slices with a serrated knife and season with salt and pepper.

skim off any fat from the top of the sauce, and season with the salt and pepper.

serve the meat loaf napped with a bit of the sauce, and serve any remaining sauce on the side.

serves **8**

Diner-Style Meat Loaf with Gravy

Truck stops and diners serve what I call "the all-American meat loaf," with onions, green bell peppers, and whatever else the cook decides to add in. In some areas of the country, the traditional milk-soaked bread is replaced with rolled oats, while other areas use saltine or other cracker crumbs. Our nation has dined on this dish for years, usually served with a glue-like brown gravy; it was what my husband would tactfully call "warm and filling." This meat loaf, however, is moist and tender and crowned with a beautifully rich and scrumptious onion and mushroom gravy. You will be proud to serve it to anyone, even your mother-in-law! Mashed potatoes and two vegetables on the side will give you that famous combination found in the South called "meat and three." Leftovers make terrific sandwiches on grilled sourdough bread with a bit of your favorite cheese on top.

SAUCE

2 tablespoons unsalted butter

1 tablespoon olive oil

2 large onions, thinly sliced into half rounds

2 teaspoons dried thyme

1 pound cremini mushrooms, sliced

2 tablespoons all-purpose flour

3 cups beef broth

¼ cup soy sauce

Salt and freshly ground black pepper

heat the butter and oil in a large skillet over medium-high heat. Add the onions and thyme and sauté until the onions begin to soften, about 3 minutes.

add the mushrooms and sauté until they begin to color and the liquid in the pan evaporates. Transfer the contents of the skillet to the insert of a 5- to 7-quart slow cooker.

whisk the flour and ¼ cup of the broth together in a large bowl. Add the remaining broth and the soy sauce to the slurry and whisk until smooth.

pour the mixture into the cooker. Cover and cook on high while you prepare the meat loaf.

MEAT LOAF

2 tablespoons olive oil

1 medium onion, finely chopped

1 medium green bell pepper, seeded and finely chopped

1 teaspoon dried sage leaves, crumbled in the palm of your hand

1½ pounds 85% lean ground beef

2 tablespoons ketchup

2 tablespoons Worcestershire sauce

1 cup cracker crumbs (saltines or Ritz both work well here) or 1 cup dry unflavored bread crumbs

2 large eggs, beaten

1 teaspoon salt

½ teaspoon freshly ground black pepper

¼ cup beef broth

heat the oil in a small skillet over medium-high heat. Add the onion, bell pepper, and sage and sauté until the vegetables are softened, about 3 minutes. Cool the mixture and transfer to a large mixing bowl.

add the remaining ingredients. With clean hands or a large wooden spoon, mix together until well combined, being careful not to compact the mixture. Pat the meat into a loaf shape 6 inches long, 3 inches wide, and 2 to 3 inches tall.

set the loaf on top of the sauce in the slow cooker and cook on high for 1 hour. Reduce the heat to low and cook for 4 to 6 hours, until an instant-read thermometer inserted in the center reads 165°F.

remove the loaf from the cooker using two long, wide spatulas. Cover with aluminum foil and allow to rest for 15 minutes. Season the sauce with salt and pepper.

cut the loaf into ½-inch slices with a serrated knife and serve napped with some of the sauce. Serve any remaining sauce on the side.

serves **6**

Old-Fashioned Meat Loaf

As a child, the only meat loaf my mom made was a large Italian-style meatball in loaf form. I preferred the meat loaf my aunt made, which was seasoned with onion, thyme, and ketchup and then covered with bacon and baked in a barbecue sauce. I loved to eat it with lumpy mashed potatoes and green beans. I still love to eat meat loaf with mashed potatoes, but a green salad on the side is now my favorite!

MEAT LOAF

2 slices white sandwich bread, torn into pieces (use a sandwich bread with some structure like Pepperidge Farm)

¼ cup milk

1½ pounds ground 85% lean ground beef

½ cup ketchup

1 tablespoon Dijon mustard

2 tablespoons Worcestershire sauce

½ cup finely chopped onion

2 teaspoons dried thyme

1 large egg, beaten

1 teaspoon salt

½ teaspoon freshly ground black pepper

BARBECUE SAUCE

½ cup onion, finely chopped

2 cloves garlic, minced

1½ cups ketchup

1 cup tomato sauce

2 tablespoons soy sauce

½ cup firmly packed brown sugar

6 dashes Tabasco sauce

Salt and freshly ground black pepper

place the bread in a small bowl, pour the milk over the bread, and let soak for 5 minutes. Put the meat in a large mixing bowl and add the remaining ingredients, including the milk-soaked bread. Do not squeeze the moisture out of the bread because the milk actually helps tenderize the meat loaf.

using clean hands or a large spoon, stir the mixture together until the ingredients are thoroughly blended.

form the mixture into a loaf about 6 inches long and 3 inches wide and tall. Set aside while you mix the sauce ingredients, or cover and refrigerate for up to 24 hours.

stir together all the sauce ingredients in the insert of a 5- to 7-quart slow cooker and set the meat loaf in the sauce. Spoon some of the sauce over the top of the meat loaf to coat it.

cook the meat loaf on high for 1 hour. Reduce the heat to low and cook until an instant-read thermometer inserted in the center of the meat loaf registers 165°F, 5 to 6 hours. Using two long, wide spatulas, remove the meat loaf from the slow cooker, cover with aluminum foil, and allow to rest for 15 minutes.

season the sauce with salt and pepper. Cut the meat loaf into ½-inch-thick slices with a serrated knife. Serve with some of the sauce.

serves **6**

Meatballs and Variations

Although we all associate meatballs with Italian cuisine, you hardly ever see them on a menu in Italy. They are more home cooking than *ristorante* fare. That being said, meatballs make a terrific slow-cooker meal and they can be made into smaller sizes for appetizers to serve a crowd. Either way, there are quite a few recipes for meatballs in this book that use various meats and flavors. The following meatball recipes are two that I'm quite fond of and use ground beef as the main ingredient. The meat loaf recipes also make terrific meatballs—just use a scoop to shape them and then put them into the sauce. You can either sauté meatballs to get a nice, crispy crust on the outside or you can just plop them in the sauce. Plopping the meatballs into the sauce without browning actually makes them even more tender and delicious when they are slow cooked. In order for the meatballs to cook evenly, use a small scoop to form them so that each ball has the same density. I have a variety of scoops just for this purpose.

Meatballs Italiano

Actually called *polpette* in Italian, these little gems are terrific to serve in your favorite tomato sauce with pasta. The fact that this makes a lot of sauce and meatballs gives you the option of serving this to a crowd (see savvy), or being able to freeze the leftovers for another meal. *Mangia bene*, as Grandma used to say!

SAUCE

2 tablespoons extra-virgin olive oil

2 medium onions, coarsely chopped

3 cloves garlic, minced

2 teaspoons dried oregano

3 tablespoons sugar

1 ½ teaspoons salt

½ teaspoon freshly ground black pepper

Four 28- to 32-ounce cans whole plum tomatoes, with their juice

MEATBALLS

4 slices soft-crusted Italian bread, torn into pieces (about 1 cup)

⅔ cup milk

1 pound 85% lean ground beef

1 pound bulk Italian sweet pork sausage

1 pound lean ground pork

1 medium onion, finely chopped

¼ cup finely chopped fresh Italian parsley

1 cup freshly grated Parmesan cheese

3 eggs, beaten

1½ teaspoon salt

1 teaspoon freshly ground black pepper

¼ teaspoon freshly ground nutmeg

Vegetable oil for frying (optional)

heat the oil in a large sauté pan over medium-high heat. Add the onions, garlic, and oregano and sauté until the onions begin to soften.

transfer the mixture to the insert of a 5- to 7-quart slow cooker and stir in the sugar, salt, pepper, and tomatoes. cover and cook on high while making the meatballs.

put the bread and milk in a large mixing bowl and allow the bread to absorb the milk. When the bread has absorbed the milk, add the remaining ingredients. With clean hands or a large wooden spoon, stir the mixture to combine, being careful not to compact it. Using a scoop, form the meatballs, and place in the cooker.

cook on high for 1 hour, then reduce the temperature to low and cook for 3 hours, until the meatballs register 165°F on an instant-read thermometer.

(For crispier meatballs, heat ½ inch of oil in a large skillet over medium-high heat. Add the meatballs and brown, turning them when they begin to form a crust on each side. Transfer them to the slow cooker and cook as directed.)

serve the meatballs directly from the cooker set on warm, speared with 6-inch skewers.

makes about **24** two-inch meatballs

meatball savvy
If you would like to serve the meatballs for an appetizer, form them into ¾- to 1-inch balls (they will shrink during the cooking process), and cook as directed.

Curried Meatballs

These spicy meatballs are flavored with Indian spices and yogurt, and bubble away in a cinnamon-infused tomato sauce. They make a perfect nibble for a cocktail party (see savvy, page 212) or you could serve them over rice as a main course. Make sure to serve traditional *raita*, a cooling yogurt sauce, on the side to tame some of the spiciness.

SAUCE

2 tablespoons vegetable oil

4 cloves garlic, minced

2 large onions, coarsely chopped

2 teaspoon freshly grated ginger

½ teaspoon ground cumin

1 teaspoon sweet paprika

Pinch of cayenne pepper

¼ teaspoon ground cinnamon

Two 32-ounce cans tomato purée

MEATBALLS

1 pound 85% lean ground beef

1 teaspoon salt

¼ teaspoon ground cumin

¼ teaspoon garam masala

¼ cup finely minced fresh cilantro

½ cup nonfat yogurt

Vegetable oil for frying (optional)

heat the oil in a sauté pan over medium-high heat. Add the garlic, onions, ginger, cumin, paprika, cayenne, and cinnamon and sauté until the onions begin to soften, 4 to 5 minutes.

transfer the mixture to the insert of a 5- to 7-quart slow cooker and stir in the tomato purée. Cover and cook on high while making the meatballs.

combine the meatball ingredients in a large bowl. With clean hands or a large wooden spoon, stir the mixture to combine, being careful not to compact it. Using a scoop, shape the mixture into 2-inch balls.

place the meatballs in the sauce and cook for 1 hour on high, then reduce the temperature to low and cook for 3 hours, until the meatballs register 165°F on an instant-read thermometer. When the meatballs are done, they can be kept warm in the slow cooker or served immediately.

(For crispier meatballs, heat ½ inch of oil in a large skillet over medium-high heat. Add the meatballs and brown on all sides, turning them when they begin for form a crust. Transfer them to the slow cooker and cook as directed.)

serve the meatballs directly from the cooker set on warm, speared with 6-inch skewers.

serves **8**

Mom's Stuffed Cabbage Rolls

As a child, when I smelled this dish in my mom's kitchen I knew I was in for a treat. Beef rolled in cabbage leaves was simmered in a tangy tomato sauce for hours on the stovetop, resulting in a lovely package of tender beef and rice infused with the flavor of the sauce, sweet and a bit sour. Mom always served this with mashed potatoes, and it's terrific with some chunky applesauce on the side.

1 large head green cabbage

One 32-ounce can tomato purée

¼ cup firmly packed light brown sugar

2 tablespoons apple cider vinegar

One 6-ounce sauerkraut, drained and rinsed

1 large onion, sliced into half rounds

1 pound 85% lean ground beef

½ cup finely chopped onion

½ cup cooked white rice

½ cup ketchup

Salt and freshly ground black pepper

heat 6 quarts of salted water in a large pot and bring to a boil. Core the cabbage and separate the leaves carefully so they don't tear. Blanch the cabbage a few leaves at a time in the boiling water and remove after about 30 seconds.

drain the cabbage leaves in a large colander and repeat until all the leaves are blanched. Set aside 8 large leaves and coarsely chop any remaining cabbage. Put the chopped cabbage, tomato purée, sugar, vinegar, sauerkraut, and onion in the insert of a 5- to 7-quart slow cooker.

stir the mixture to combine. Cover and cook on high while making the rolls.

blend the beef, onion, rice, ketchup, 1 teaspoon salt, and ½ teaspoon pepper in a large mixing bowl. Divide the mixture into 8 portions. Place one portion in the center of each cabbage leaf and roll the leaf around the filling, tucking in the sides. Place the rolls seam-side down in the sauce in the slow cooker.

cook on high for 1 hour then cook on low for 4 to 5 hours, until the meat reaches 165°F on an instant-read thermometer. Season the sauce with salt and pepper. Skim off any fat from the sauce.

serve the rolls from the cooker set on warm.

serves 6–8

Lazy-Day Cabbage Rolls

My friend Andy Gnoza gave me this idea. *Golabki*, as stuffed cabbage rolls are called in Polish, were a staple in the bachelor pad he shared with my soon-to-be husband, Chuck. He came up with this idea when he was too tired to blanch the cabbage but still wanted the delicious stick-to-your-ribs fare that he remembered from his mom's house. This is a simple supper that is perfect to serve right from the slow cooker.

One 32-ounce can tomato purée

¼ cup granulated sugar

¼ cup white vinegar

½ cup golden raisins

8 ounces lean ground pork

8 ounces 85% lean ground beef

½ cup cooked rice

½ cup finely chopped shallot

½ cup ketchup

1 teaspoon salt

½ teaspoon freshly ground black pepper

1 large head green cabbage, cut into ½-inch-thick slices

1 large onion, sliced into half rounds

One 15-ounce can sauerkraut, drained and rinsed

stir the tomato purée, sugar, vinegar, and raisins together in the insert of a 5- to 7-quart slow cooker. Stir the pork, beef, rice, shallot, ketchup, salt, and pepper together in a large mixing bowl. Form the mixture into 3-inch oval patties and set aside.

lay half the cabbage, onion, and sauerkraut in the bottom of the cooker with the sauce. Top with all the meat patties and spread the remaining cabbage, onion, and sauerkraut on top of the meat.

cover the cooker and cook on high for 1 hour. Spoon some of the sauce over the top of the cabbage and cook on low for 4 to 5 hours, until the meat registers 165°F on an instant-read thermometer.

serve from the cooker set on warm.

serves **8**

Flank Steak

My local supermarket has what they call the "gourmet meal" section, where you can buy stuffed flank steaks, stuffed chicken breasts, and other seemingly complicated dishes to take home and bake. I always wonder how long they have been sitting there, and then whether anyone would buy another one after finding them to be tough and lacking flavor. Stuffed flank steak needs to be braised and cooked low and slow for the lean meat to become tender. The basic recipe for stuffing and cooking is the same, but the flavorings may be mixed and matched to suit your preference.

Flank Steak with Spinach, Bacon, and Mushroom Stuffing

2 tablespoons olive oil

1 large onion, coarsely chopped

2 cloves garlic, minced

4 strips bacon, cut into ½-inch pieces

2 medium shallots, finely chopped

½ pound white button mushrooms, coarsely chopped

Two 10-ounce packages baby spinach

1 teaspoon salt

½ teaspoon freshly ground black pepper

1 cup fresh bread crumbs

½ cup finely shredded white Cheddar cheese

One 1 ½- to 2-pound flank steak

One 28- to 32-ounce can crushed tomatoes with their juice

toss the oil, onion, and garlic together in the insert of a 5- to 7-quart slow cooker. Cover and cook on high while making the filling.

cook the bacon in a medium skillet until crisp and remove it to paper towels to drain. Add the shallots and mushrooms to the same skillet and sauté until the liquid in the pan evaporates and the mushrooms begin to color.

transfer the contents of the skillet to a mixing bowl and add the bacon. Add the spinach to the same skillet and sauté until it wilts, about 3 minutes. Stir in the salt and pepper.

transfer the spinach to the mixing bowl and allow the vegetables to cool. Add the bread crumbs and cheese and mix to blend.

place the flank steak on a cutting board and starting on one long side of the steak, cut the steak horizontally in half almost but not quite through the other side. Open the steak like a book. Spread the filling over the steak. Roll the steak up from one long side and tie with kitchen string or silicone loops. Add the tomatoes to the slow cooker and arrange the steak in the braising liquid.

cover and cook on high for 3 to 4 hours, until the meat is tender. Carefully lift the meat out of the pan, cover with aluminum foil, and allow to rest for at least 15 minutes. Cut the strings from the meat and cut into ½-inch-thick slices.

serve the meat napped with some of the sauce.

serves 6–8

Artichoke-Stuffed Flank Steak with Red Wine Sauce

Stuffed with piquant marinated artichokes, sharp Asiago cheese, and prosciutto, this flank steak is braised in a red wine sauce that makes it tender and delicious.

4 tablespoons (½ stick) unsalted butter

2 medium onions, finely chopped

3 cloves garlic, minced

1 teaspoon dried basil

½ teaspoon dried oregano

3 tablespoons all-purpose flour

2 cups full-bodied red wine

1 cup beef broth

Two 6-ounce jars marinated artichoke hearts, drained and coarsely chopped

6 thin slices prosciutto, cut into julienne strips

½ cup finely shredded Asiago cheese

1 cup fresh bread crumbs

One 1 ½- to 2-pound flank steak

melt the butter in a medium saucepan over medium-high heat. Add the onions, garlic, basil, and oregano and sauté until the onions are softened, about 3 minutes. Whisk in the flour and cook for 3 minutes.

add the wine and bring to a boil, whisking constantly, until the sauce is thickened. Transfer the sauce to the insert of a 5- to 7-quart slow cooker and stir in the beef broth. Combine the artichokes, prosciutto, cheese, and bread crumbs together in a small bowl.

place the flank steak on a cutting board and starting on one long side of the steak, cut the steak horizontally in half almost but not quite through the other side. Open the steak like a book. Spread the mixture over the flank steak. Roll the steak up from one long side and tie with kitchen string or silicone bands.

arrange the steak in the slow-cooker insert, cover, and cook on high for 3 hours. Remove the steak from the slow cooker, cover with aluminum foil, and allow to rest for 15 minutes. Skim off any fat from the sauce.

slice the meat. Serve it with some of the sauce.

serves 6—8

Salsa Beef Fajitas

This slow-cooker recipe couldn't be easier, and it's delicious! Load the flank steak, salsa, and seasonings into the cooker, and then read romance novels all day long, until it's time for dinner. Make sure to use a prepared salsa rather than fresh salsa, which will lose its flavor in the low slow cooking process. Serve the fajitas with warm tortillas, pinto beans, or Refried Bean Casserole (page 334) along with an assortment of condiments.

4 cups prepared salsa

1½ teaspoons ground cumin

¼ cup freshly squeezed lime juice

Two 1½-pound flank steaks

combine the salsa, cumin, and lime juice in the insert of a 5- to 7-quart slow cooker. Roll the flank steaks from the short side and place in the slow cooker.

cover and cook on low for 8 to 10 hours, until the meat is tender. Remove the meat from the sauce, allow it to rest for 15 minutes, and shred, using two forks.

skim off any fat from the top of the sauce and return the meat to the slow cooker. Stir to blend with the sauce.

serve the meat directly from the cooker.

serves **8**

Chicago-Style Italian Beef

Walk along any street in Chicago, and you will find little diners serving Italian beef sand-wiches. Many hot dog street vendors sell them as well. The meat is cooked in a highly spiced broth, thinly sliced, and topped with a mélange of sautéed and pickled peppers. For this recipe, the peppers and beef are cooked together so you can serve dinner right out of the slow cooker. You won't have leave town to try this Windy City sandwich!

Three 1½- to 2-pound flanks steaks

4 cloves garlic

1 teaspoon dried oregano

1 teaspoon dried basil

1 bay leaf

2 shallots, coarsely chopped

½ cup soy sauce

½ cup red wine vinegar

½ teaspoon freshly ground black pepper

¼ cup extra-virgin olive oil

4 large onions, cut into half rounds

2 medium green bell peppers, seeded and thinly sliced

2 medium red bell peppers, seeded and thinly sliced

Two 15-ounce cans double-strength beef broth

8 crusty rolls (see savvy)

put the flank steaks into a 2-gallon zipper-top plastic bag. Mix the garlic, oregano, basil, bay leaf, shallots, soy sauce, vinegar, pepper, and 2 tablespoons of the oil together in a bowl. Pour the marinade into the bag and toss with the meat to coat. Seal the bag and refrigerate for at least 6 hours or overnight.

remove the meat from the marinade and discard the mari-nade. Roll the steaks from the short side and place them in the bottom of the insert of a 5- to 7-quart slow cooker. Heat the remaining oil in a large skillet over medium-high heat. Add the onions and sauté until they are softened and begin to turn translucent, 5 to 7 minutes. Add the bell peppers and sauté until they are softened, about 5 minutes.

transfer the onions and bell peppers to the cooker and stir in the broth. Cover and cook on low for 8 hours, until the meat is tender.

remove the meat from the cooker, cover with aluminum foil, and allow to rest for at least 15 minutes. Skim off any fat from the top of the sauce. Unroll the meat on a cutting board and cut across the grain into thin slices. Return the meat to the slow cooker.

serve the meat, onions, and peppers from the cooker along with the crusty rolls.

serves **8**

 italian beef savvy
Use firm-crusted rolls for this sandwich so you can dip them into the beef juice, as it is done in Chicago. A crusty roll can withstand the extra moisture, whereas soft-crusted rolls will shrink and become gummy.

Short Ribs

Short ribs come from the end of the rib section and can be sold with or without pieces of bone. I recommend that you buy boneless short ribs because they cook faster than those with bones, and you won't have to take the meat off the bone to serve it.

Pacific Rim Braised Short Ribs

This succulent dish is a great way to jump-start a weeknight dinner. The Asian flavors highlight the beefy short ribs, and when served with soba noodles or sticky rice and an Asian cabbage salad, your family will be asking for seconds!

1½ tablespoons vegetable oil

½ cup firmly packed light brown sugar

4½ pounds boneless short ribs, fat trimmed (see savvy)

½ teaspoon freshly ground black pepper

4 cups sliced sweet onions, such as Vidalia or red onions (about 4 medium to large)

6 cloves garlic, minced

1 teaspoon freshly grated ginger

2 tablespoons hoisin sauce

½ cup soy sauce

1½ cups chicken broth

Chopped green onions for garnishing

Toasted sesame seeds for garnishing

heat the oil in a large skillet over medium-high heat. Pat half the brown sugar onto the ribs. Add the ribs a few at a time to the skillet and brown on all sides, being careful not to burn the sugar.

transfer the ribs to the insert of a 5- to 7-quart slow cooker. Add the onions, garlic, and ginger to the skillet over medium-high heat and sauté until the onions and garlic are fragrant, about 4 minutes.

transfer the contents of the skillet to the slow-cooker insert and stir in the remaining sugar, the hoisin, soy sauce, and broth. Sprinkle with the pepper. Cover the slow cooker and cook on high for 8 hours or on low for 3½ to 4 hours, until the meat is tender.

remove the meat from the slow-cooker insert. Skim off any fat from the sauce and pour some of the sauce over the meat. Serve any remaining sauce on the side. Garnish the ribs with the green onions and sesame seeds.

serves 4–6

short ribs savvy
You may not be able to get exactly 4½ pounds of short ribs—it may be 5 pounds or it may be 4 pounds. I recommend purchasing 7 boneless ribs no matter what the weight comes to, that way you have about 1½ ribs per person, once all the fat and collagen has melted away.

Pub-Crawl Short Ribs

My daughter lived in London for a while, and I was delighted to spend a week with her exploring the new "gastro pubs" that emphasize interesting food. These short ribs remind me of that delicious week of sampling new British cuisine. Because pub mustard and Guinness are strong flavors, I've added sweet carrots and parsnips to the braise to balance the flavors.

Salt and freshly ground black pepper

¼ cup Colman's English mustard or Stonewall Kitchen Pub Style mustard (see savvy)

4½ pounds boneless short ribs, fat trimmed

1½ tablespoons canola oil

4 cups coarsely chopped sweet onions, such as Vidalia

2 teaspoons dried thyme

2 cups baby carrots

2 cups peeled parsnips, cut into chunks

1 tablespoon prepared horseradish

1 cup Guinness stout

1 cup double-strength beef broth

2 tablespoons unsalted butter, at room temperature (optional)

2 tablespoons all-purpose flour (optional)

mix 1½ teaspoons salt, ½ teaspoon pepper, and the mustard together in a small bowl. Rub the mixture over the short ribs and allow the ribs to sit at room temperature for about 15 minutes.

heat the oil in a large skillet over high heat. Add the ribs a few at a time and brown on all sides. Transfer to the insert of a 5- to 7-quart slow cooker.

add the onions and thyme to the same skillet over medium-high heat and sauté until the onions are softened and fragrant. Transfer the onions to the slow cooker and stir in the carrots, parsnips, horseradish, stout, and broth.

cover the slow cooker and cook on low for 8 hours or on high for 3½ to 4 hours. Remove the meat and vegetables from the pan, cover with aluminum foil, and allow to rest for 15 minutes. If you would like a smooth sauce, strain it through a fine-mesh sieve. Skim off any fat from the sauce and season with salt and pepper.

serve the ribs and vegetables with the sauce. If you would like to thicken the sauce, transfer it to a saucepan and bring it to a boil. Stir the butter and flour together and add it in pieces to the boiling sauce, whisking constantly. Bring the sauce back to a boil after each addition. Serve immediately.

serves 4–6

mustard savvy
Colman's and the other pub-style mustards are not powdered —they have a saucy consistency and can be found in the mustard section of your grocery store or gourmet retailer.

Barbecue-Style Short Ribs

Simple, homey, and reminiscent of summer barbecues, this dinner cries out for slaw or potato salad on the side! You can use a bottled barbecue sauce, instead of the homemade version here, but try this one first. It's sweet, with a touch of heat.

2 cups ketchup

1 tablespoon Dijon mustard

½ cup firmly packed light brown sugar

2 tablespoons Worcestershire sauce

½ teaspoon cayenne pepper

1½ tablespoons vegetable oil

4½ pounds boneless short ribs, fat trimmed

1 cup coarsely chopped red onion

combine the ketchup, mustard, brown sugar, Worcestershire, and cayenne in the insert of a 5- to 7-quart slow cooker, cover, and set on low while you brown the meat.

heat the oil in a large skillet over high heat.

add the short ribs a few at a time and brown on all sides. Transfer them to the slow-cooker insert when they are browned. Add the onion to the same skillet and sauté until it begins to soften.

transfer the onion to the insert, stir the sauce to combine, cover, and cook on high for 3½ to 4 hours or on low for 8 hours. Remove the meat from the slow-cooker insert and cover with aluminum foil. Let the meat rest for 10 to 15 minutes. Skim off any fat from the sauce.

serve the beef with the sauce.

serves 4–6

Lemon Garlic Short Ribs

A taste of the Mediterranean flavors these short ribs. The bright scent of lemon zest makes them sparkle with a pleasing aroma. The rub can be done the night before, then just layer your ingredients in the slow cooker in the morning. Great sides with this dish are orzo or couscous, and sautéed spinach.

Grated zest of 2 lemons

2 tablespoons olive oil

2 teaspoons dried oregano

1 teaspoon dried rosemary, crushed in the palm of your hand

6 cloves garlic, minced

Pinch of red pepper flakes

1 teaspoon salt

4 ½ pounds beef short ribs, fat trimmed

½ cup dry red wine

1 cup beef broth

mix the lemon zest, oil, oregano, rosemary, garlic, red pepper flakes, and salt together in a small bowl. Rub the mixture over the meat until it is well coated. Cover and refrigerate for at least 4 hours but preferably overnight.

remove the meat from the refrigerator at least 30 minutes before sautéing. Heat a large skillet over medium-high heat. Add the beef a few pieces at a time and sauté until browned on all sides. Remove the meat to the insert of a 5- to 7-quart slow cooker.

add the wine and beef broth to the skillet and scrape up the browned bits on the bottom of the pan. Transfer the liquid to the slow cooker. Cover and cook on high for 3½ to 4 hours or on low for 8 hours. Remove the beef from the slow cooker and cover with aluminum foil. Let meat rest for 10 to 15 minutes. Skim off any fat from the sauce, then taste and adjust the seasoning.

serve the beef with the sauce spooned over the top.

serves 4-6

Zinfandel-Braised Short Ribs

Zinfandel is a great wine for braising beef, with its bold flavor and hint of sweet berries. Since it is a reasonably priced wine, you can use it in the braise and also serve it with dinner or sip it while the slow cooker is doing its thing. Serve this dinner with pasta or steamed new potatoes and braised escarole or spinach on the side. A crisp green salad dressed with red wine vinaigrette would also make a great accompaniment.

4½ pounds boneless short ribs, fat trimmed

2 teaspoons salt

1 teaspoon freshly ground black pepper

2 tablespoons extra-virgin olive oil

2 cups red onions, cut into half rounds

6 cloves garlic, minced

1 tablespoon dried thyme

2 cups Zinfandel wine

4 dried porcini mushrooms, crumbled

sprinkle the beef ribs evenly with the salt and pepper. Heat the oil in a large skillet over medium-high heat. Add the beef a few pieces at a time and brown on all sides. Remove the meat to the insert of a 5- to 7-quart slow cooker.

add the onions, garlic, and thyme to the skillet and sauté until the onions are softened and fragrant, about 3 minutes. Stir in the wine and mushrooms, stirring up any browned bits from the bottom of the skillet, and then transfer to the slow-cooker insert.

cover and cook on high for 3½ to 4 hours or on low for 8 hours.

remove the beef from the slow cooker and cover with aluminum foil. Let the meat rest for 10 to 15 minutes. Skim off any fat from the sauce.

serve the meat with the sauce.

serves 4

Hot Italian Short Ribs

This recipe will give new meaning to the words "playing with fire." The ribs are braised with hot pickled Italian peppers, and the result is addictive! My grandmother used to make a dish similar to this, which she served at room temperature with crusty bread. Although it was hot, it was the type of dish where you'd take one bite, think to yourself that's a little hot, and immediately want to eat some more. This is not for the faint of heart, so make sure you know who's coming to dinner. It's about a seven on a ten-point heat meter.

4½ pounds boneless short ribs, fat trimmed

2 teaspoons salt

1 teaspoon freshly ground black pepper

2 tablespoons extra-virgin olive oil

2 cups coarsely chopped sweet onion, such as Vidalia

6 cloves garlic, minced

2 medium red bell peppers, seeded and thinly sliced

4 hot pickled Italian peppers, drained, stems removed, and excess seeds removed

1 cup red wine

1 cup beef broth

sprinkle the short ribs evenly with the salt and pepper. Heat the oil in a large skillet over high heat. Add the beef a few pieces at a time and brown on all sides.

transfer the browned meat to the insert of a 5- to 7-quart slow cooker. Add the onion, garlic, and bell peppers to the skillet and sauté until the onion and bell peppers become soft, about 4 minutes.

add the pickled peppers, wine, and broth to the skillet and scrape up any browned bits from the bottom of the pan. Transfer the contents of the skillet to the slow-cooker insert.

cover and cook on high for 3½ to 4 hours or on low for 8 hours. Remove the meat from the insert and cover with aluminum foil. Let the meat rest for 10 to 15 minutes. Skim off any fat from the sauce.

serve the meat with some of the vegetables and sauce poured over top and the remaining sauce on the side.

serves 4–6

Veal

Veal is the meat from a four-month-old calf and is not as popular in the United States as it is in Europe. I grew up on veal that my Italian grandmother prepared in so many delicious ways. I love its flavor and tenderness. The slow cooker does a great job with veal chops, braising them to melt-in-your-mouth goodness.

Veal Shanks Osso Bucco–Style

Osso bucco is a well-known dish from Lombardy and is traditionally served with risotto. Gremolata, a spicy mixture of garlic, lemon and orange zests, and Italian parsley, is typically sprinkled over the top of the finished dish, but adding it to the pot in the last hour of cooking brings a sparkle and intensity of flavor to the veal shanks. This stew is the perfect dish to serve to your family and friends when it's cold and gray outside. Don't forget the risotto!

½ cup all-purpose flour

1 teaspoon salt

½ teaspoon freshly ground black pepper

6 meaty slices veal shank, cut 1½ to 2 inches thick

2 tablespoons olive oil

2 tablespoons unsalted butter

1 medium onion, finely chopped

3 medium carrots, finely chopped

¼ cup tomato paste

⅔ cup dry white wine or vermouth

1 cup chicken broth

½ cup beef broth

2 cloves garlic, minced

Grated zest of 2 lemons

Grated zest of 1 orange

½ cup finely chopped Italian parsley

mix the flour, salt, and pepper in a large zipper-top plastic bag. Coat the veal shanks in the flour mixture and shake off the excess. Heat the oil and butter in a large skillet over high heat. Add the shanks a few at a time and brown on all sides.

transfer the shanks to the insert of a 5- to 7-quart slow cooker. Add the onion and carrots to the same skillet and sauté until the onion is softened, about 3 minutes. Add the tomato paste and stir to combine. Add the wine and bring to a boil.

transfer the contents of the skillet to the slow-cooker insert Add the broths and stir. Cover and cook on low for 4 hours. Combine the garlic, citrus zests, and parsley in a small bowl. Add the garlic mixture to the stew and stir to combine. Cook the stew for another hour, until the veal is tender.

taste and adjust the seasoning and serve.

serves 6

osso bucco savvy
Osso bucco literally means "bone with a hole." Traditionally the shank is served with a tiny spoon to scoop out the marrow from the bone, which is considered a delicacy. I generally will scoop out the marrow and add it to the sauce for additional flavor.

Veal Chops Braised in White Wine and Sage

Veal chops are a luxury, and while expensive, they can be some of the best eating, especially when they are braised and served falling off the bone. Tomato, garlic, wine, balsamic vinegar, and sage make these veal chops a delicious meal. Serve on a bed of polenta or with a side of asparagus or butternut squash risotto. Pork chops, which are less expensive, may be substituted for the veal. Use the same preparation and cooking times.

1½ teaspoons salt

½ teaspoon freshly ground black pepper

3 cloves garlic, minced

1 tablespoon finely chopped dried sage leaves (see savvy)

3 tablespoons extra-virgin olive oil

6 veal chops, 1 to 1½ inches thick

1 cup dry white wine or vermouth

One 15-ounce can crushed plum tomatoes, with their juice

¼ cup balsamic vinegar

½ cup golden raisins

make a paste with the salt, pepper, garlic, sage, and 1 table-spoon of the oil in a small bowl. Rub the chops evenly with the mixture. Heat the remaining 2 tablespoons oil in a large skillet over high heat. Add the chops a few at a time and brown on both sides.

transfer the chops to the insert of a 5- to 7-quart slow cooker. You may have to stack the chops in two layers, depending on the size of your pot.

add the wine to the same skillet and allow some of it to evaporate. Add the tomatoes and scrape up any browned bits from the bottom of the pan. Transfer the contents of the skillet to the slow-cooker insert.

add the vinegar and raisins and stir to combine.

cover and cook on low for 5 to 6 hours, until the chops are tender. Carefully remove the chops from the sauce to a platter and cover with aluminum foil. Pour the sauce into a small saucepan, bring it to a boil, and continue to boil until the sauce is reduced and concentrated.

taste and adjust the seasoning. Serve the chops napped with some of the sauce and serve additional sauce on the side.

serves **6**

sage savvy
Sage is a pungent herb and is available both fresh and dried. For this dish, whole fresh leaves are best.

Veal Chops Braised with Confetti Peppers

This delightfully rustic dish makes the most of tastes of the Mediterranean. Colorful peppers and red onion highlight a braising liquid flavored with red wine, orange zest, oregano, and tomatoes. This dish makes a terrific weeknight dinner. Serve it with pasta or crusty bread to soak up the sauce.

1½ teaspoons salt

½ teaspoon freshly ground black pepper

3 cloves garlic, minced

1½ teaspoons dried oregano

3 tablespoons extra-virgin olive oil

6 veal chops, 1 to 1½ inches thick

2 medium onions, coarsely chopped

2 medium red bell peppers, seeded and cut into ½-inch slices

2 medium yellow bell peppers, seeded and cut into ½-inch slices

1 cup full-bodied red wine, such as Chianti or Barolo

One 15-ounce can crushed tomatoes, with their juice

Grated zest of 2 oranges

½ cup beef broth

1 cup chicken broth

make a paste with the salt, pepper, garlic, oregano, and 1 tablespoon of the olive oil in a small bowl. Rub the veal chops evenly with the paste. Heat the remaining 2 tablespoons oil in a large skillet over high heat. Add the chops a few at a time and brown on both sides.

transfer the veal to the insert of a 5- to 7-quart slow cooker. Add the onions and bell peppers to the same skillet and sauté until the vegetables begin to soften. Add the wine to the skillet and scrape up any browned bits from the bottom of the pan. Transfer the contents of the skillet to the slow-cooker insert. Add the tomatoes, orange zest, and both broths and stir to combine.

cover and cook on low for 4½ to 5½ hours, until the chops are tender. Taste and adjust the seasoning before serving.

serves **6**

Veal Stews

Each of the three stews here has a different flavor, but they are all prepared using essentially the same technique, just with a few different herbs, spices, and vegetables. Since most of us don't have veal stock in the freezer, a good approximation is a mixture of one part beef broth and two parts chicken broth. If you absolutely want to use veal stock, there are many mail-order companies that will ship it, and many gourmet retailers carry it as well.

Veal Stew with Forty Cloves of Garlic

A chicken dish called *poulet sauté dauphinois*, made famous by American chef, writer, and icon James Beard, has been prepared in the French region of Provence for years. Beard shocked his devotees by adding forty whole cloves of garlic to the stew, which became mellow, smoky, and sweet when simmered for a long period of time. In this slow-cooker meal, we'll use veal stew meat, rather than chicken, which gives the dish a richer flavor and pairs well with cheesy mashed potatoes.

½ cup all-purpose flour

1½ teaspoons salt

½ teaspoon freshly ground black pepper

2½ pounds boneless veal shoulder or shank, cut into 1-inch pieces

3 tablespoons extra-virgin olive oil

¼ cup tomato paste

1 teaspoon dried thyme

½ cup dry white wine or vermouth

1 cup chicken broth

½ cup beef broth

1 bay leaf

40 cloves garlic, peeled

mix the flour, salt, and pepper in a large zipper-top plastic bag. Add the veal, toss to coat, and shake off any excess. Heat the oil in a large skillet over high heat. Add the veal a few pieces at a time and sauté until browned on all sides.

transfer the browned meat to the insert of a 5- to 7-quart slow cooker. When all the veal is browned, add the tomato paste, thyme, and white wine to the skillet and scrape up any browned bits from the bottom of the pan. Add both broths and stir to combine.

pour the contents of the skillet over the veal in the slow cooker, add the bay leaf and garlic, and stir to distribute the ingredients. Cover and cook the veal on low for 6 to 7 hours, until it is tender. Remove the veal from the cooker with a slotted spoon.

mash the garlic cloves and stir them into the sauce. Taste and adjust the seasoning. Return the veal to the cooker and serve the stew.

serves **6**

Sage-Scented Veal and Sausage Stew

Flavors of the Umbrian region of Italy define this braised stew, fragrant with sage, white wine, sweet Italian sausages, and artichoke. Serve this over pasta, polenta, or mashed potatoes for a hearty dish to soothe the soul.

12 baby artichokes, stems trimmed, cut in half and any tough leaves removed

1½ teaspoons salt

⅛ teaspoon red pepper flakes

3 tablespoons extra-virgin olive oil

2½ pounds boneless veal shoulder or shank, cut into 1-inch pieces

6 cloves garlic, sliced

8 Italian sweet sausages

6 fresh sage leaves, plus finely chopped leaves for garnishing

1 cup dry white Italian wine, such as Pinot Grigio

1 cup chicken broth

½ cup beef broth

place the cleaned and trimmed artichokes in the insert of a 5- to 7-quart slow cooker. Sprinkle the salt and red pepper flakes evenly over the veal.

heat the oil in a large skillet over high heat. Add the veal a few pieces at a time and brown on all sides. Transfer the browned veal to the cooker. Add the garlic and sausages to the pan and brown the sausages on all sides.

add the 6 sage leaves and the wine and cook, stirring, until the wine is evaporated by about one-fourth. Transfer the contents of the skillet to the slow cooker. Add both broths and stir to combine.

cover and cook on low for 4½ to 5½ hours, until the veal and artichokes are tender and the sausage is cooked through.

remove the solids from the cooker with a slotted spoon. Strain the liquid through a fine-mesh sieve into a small saucepan. Bring to a boil and reduce the liquid to about 1½ cups. Cut the sausage into ½-inch rounds.

arrange the artichokes, sausages, and veal on a serving platter and spoon the sauce over the top. Or, return the meat, vegetables, and sauce to the slow cooker set on warm, and serve directly from there. Garnish with the finely chopped sage leaves before serving.

serves **6**

Veal Paprikash

There is nervous laughter in my cooking classes when I show students bright red paprika and tell them that if theirs is brown or if it's the same jar they bought when they moved into their first apartment, it's time to get rid of it. Paprika isn't just for sprinkling on potato salads and deviled eggs. It's a flavoring, and nowhere is this more apparent than in this traditional Hungarian dish fragrant with paprika, tomato, and bell peppers. The flavors in this dish are rounded out with the addition of sour cream at the end. Paprikash is traditionally served with either dumplings or spaetzel-style noodles.

5 strips thick-cut bacon, cut into ½-inch pieces

½ cup all-purpose flour

1 teaspoon salt

¼ teaspoon hot paprika

2½ pounds boneless veal shoulder or shank, cut into 1-inch pieces

3 tablespoons olive oil

¼ cup sweet paprika

1 teaspoon dried marjoram

1 teaspoon dried thyme

1 large green bell pepper, seeded and coarsely chopped

1 large red bell pepper, seeded and coarsely chopped

1 large yellow bell pepper, seeded and coarsely chopped

One 15-ounce can crushed plum tomatoes, with their juice

1 cup chicken broth

½ cup beef broth

1 bay leaf

1 cup sour cream at room temperature

cook the bacon in a large skillet until crisp and transfer it to the insert of a 5- to 7-quart slow cooker. Remove all but 3 tablespoons of the drippings in the pan.

mix the flour, salt, and hot paprika in a large zipper-top plastic bag. Add the veal to the flour mixture, toss to coat, and shake off the excess. Heat the bacon drippings over medium-high heat.

add the veal a few pieces at a time and brown on all sides.

transfer the browned veal to the slow-cooker insert. Add the oil to the skillet over medium-high heat. Stir in the sweet paprika, marjoram, thyme, and bell peppers and sauté until the bell peppers begin to soften, 4 to 5 minutes.

add the tomatoes and both broths to the skillet and scrape up any browned bits from the bottom of the pan. Transfer the contents of the skillet to the slow-cooker insert. Add the bay leaf and stir to combine the ingredients.

cover the slow cooker and cook on low for 4½ to 5½ hours. Remove the bay leaf. Taste the stew and adjust the seasonings. Stir in the sour cream and serve the stew immediately.

serves **6**

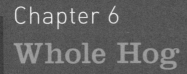

Chapter 6

Whole Hog

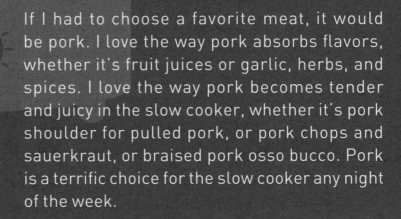

If I had to choose a favorite meat, it would be pork. I love the way pork absorbs flavors, whether it's fruit juices or garlic, herbs, and spices. I love the way pork becomes tender and juicy in the slow cooker, whether it's pork shoulder for pulled pork, or pork chops and sauerkraut, or braised pork osso bucco. Pork is a terrific choice for the slow cooker any night of the week.

Shoulder

There are two different cuts of pork shoulder available in the market; one is the Boston shoulder, which weighs about six to nine pounds with the bone in, and the other is the boneless picnic shoulder, weighing in at between three and five pounds. Whatever it's called, it's a succulent piece of meat that has a lot of fat (great for keeping the meat moist), and it needs to be braised or slow roasted. According to the pork producers' Web site, the names and weights can vary, and we found that to be true of the pork we tested (testers in Pennsylvania, Indiana, Ohio, and Florida)—some regions call these cuts different things because different names appeal in different areas. Furthermore, pork raised in California weighs in differently than that raised in the Midwest, where the feed mixture is different. There is no real standard weight here, but the averages given are just as close as we can get.

Pulled Pork

The quintessential barbecue flavors of pork and barbecue sauce combine in this dish for some lip-smacking good eats. Pile the meat onto soft rolls and serve with a side of slaw and some baked beans. Any leftovers will freeze well for up to 2 months.

½ cup vegetable oil

¼ cup red wine vinegar

½ cup firmly packed dark brown sugar

½ cup soy sauce

2 cups ketchup

1 teaspoon garlic powder or garlic salt

1 large onion, coarsely chopped

2 tablespoons Worcestershire sauce

One 5-pound boneless pork shoulder roast, fat trimmed

Barbecue sauce for serving

whisk the oil, vinegar, brown sugar, soy sauce, ketchup, garlic powder, onion, and Worcestershire together in a mixing bowl. Pour into a large zipper-top plastic bag. Place the pork in the bag with the marinade, seal the bag, and turn the pork in the bag to coat. Refrigerate overnight, turning the bag once or twice. Pour the entire contents of the bag into the insert of a 5- to 7-quart slow cooker.

cover and cook on low for 10 hours, until the pork is fork tender. Remove the pork from the insert, cover with aluminum foil, and allow to rest for 15 minutes. Skim off any fat from the top of the sauce with a spoon and discard.

shred the meat with two forks and return it to the sauce. (At this point, the pork may be refrigerated for up to 5 days or frozen for up to 2 months). Warm the pork in the slow cooker on low if desired. Serve with additional barbecue sauce.

serves 10–12

Cinco de Mayo Pork

Pork shoulder is a favorite for the slow cooker, and this south-of-the-border entrée will have your family celebrating Cinco de Mayo even in December! Serve with warm flour or corn tortillas, or ladle it over steamed rice. The pork is meltingly tender and accented with salsa and sweet corn.

2 tablespoons vegetable oil

1 teaspoon ground cumin

½ teaspoon chili powder (I prefer ancho chile powder, but an all-purpose blend is fine as well)

2 cloves garlic, minced

3 pounds boneless pork shoulder meat, excess fat removed, cut into 2-inch pieces

2 teaspoons salt

1 cup prepared salsa (medium, or hot if you like a bit more heat)

½ cup beef broth

One 16-ounce package frozen corn, defrosted

Flour or corn tortillas for serving

heat the oil in a large skillet over medium heat. Add the cumin, chili powder, and garlic and sauté until the garlic and spices are fragrant, about 1 minute.

sprinkle the meat with the salt and brown the pork on all sides in the seasonings. Transfer the pork to the insert of a 5- to 7-quart slow cooker. Add the salsa and broth to the skillet, scraping up any browned bits from the bottom.

transfer the contents of the skillet to the insert and add the corn. Stir to combine. Cook on on high for 4 hours or low for 8 hours, until the meat is tender. Serve the pork with warmed tortillas.

serves 6–8

slow-cooker savvy
Some treatments for pork shoulder are no-brainers, so try these when you need some magic from your pantry to flavor a 4- to 5-pound pork shoulder:
- 3 cups prepared barbecue sauce; cook on high for 6 hours (reduce the sauce on the stovetop after cooking)
- 3 cups prepared teriyaki sauce; cook on high for 6 hours and serve in flour tortillas with hoisin sauce and green onions
- 3 cups prepared salsa; cook on high for 6 hours and serve for fajitas
- 3 cups prepared Caesar dressing; cook on high for 6 hours

Pork Shoulder Shanghai-Style

I love to serve this red-cooked pork in flour tortillas with hoisin sauce, green onions, and cucumber slices. The pork is infused with a delicious marinade of soy, rice wine, brown sugar, and ketchup, then slowly cooked until it is fall-apart tender. If you prefer, you can serve this with sticky rice and an Asian slaw.

1 cup soy sauce

1 cup rice wine (mirin) or dry sherry

½ cup firmly packed light brown sugar

½ cup ketchup

½ teaspoon five-spice powder

2 cloves garlic, minced

1 teaspoon freshly grated ginger

One 3- to 4-pound boneless pork shoulder, tied with kitchen string

2 tablespoons cornstarch mixed with ¼ cup water

combine the soy sauce, rice wine, sugar, ketchup, five-spice powder, garlic, and ginger in a large zipper-top plastic bag. Add the pork to the bag, seal, and turn to coat the meat with the marinade. Refrigerate for at least 8 hours or up to 24 hours.

pour the meat and marinade into the insert of a 5- to 7-quart slow cooker. Cover and cook on high for 5 to 6 hours, until the meat is tender. Remove the meat from the slow cooker and allow to rest for 15 minutes.

shred the meat using two forks. Skim off the fat from the sauce and stir in the cornstarch mixture. Return the meat to the sauce, cover, and cook for an additional 30 minutes, until the sauce is thickened.

serve the pork from the slow cooker set on warm.

serves **6–8**

Pork Chalupa-Style

Chalupa in Spanish means "small boat," and the chalupas that are sold on the street in Mexico are shells of corn flour that are deep fried and then filled with shredded pork and pinto beans, along with cilantro, onion, and maybe a bit of chipotle chile. This slow-cooker dish combines pork, beans, and chipotle for a great stick-to-your-ribs dinner. Serve it on tostada shells or alongside Spanish rice and a pico de gallo salad.

3 tablespoons vegetable oil

3 cloves garlic, minced

2 chipotle chiles in adobo, minced, with about ½ teaspoon adobo

Salt

1 teaspoon ground cumin

½ teaspoon ground cinnamon

One 3-pound pork shoulder roast, excess fat removed, cut into 2-inch chunks (see savvy)

1½ cups coarsely chopped white onion

½ cup gold tequila (optional)

Four 15-ounce cans refried beans (nonfat are okay here)

1 cup beef broth

Freshly ground black pepper

16 tostada shells

½ cup finely chopped fresh cilantro for garnishing

1½ cups sour cream for garnishing

1½ cups shredded mild Cheddar cheese or crumbled queso fresco for garnishing

in a small bowl, combine 1 tablespoon of the oil with the garlic, chipotles, 2 teaspoons salt, the cumin, and cinnamon to make a paste. Using rubber gloves to protect your hands from the chiles, slather the paste onto the pork and massage it into the meat. Heat the remaining 2 tablespoons oil in a large skillet over high heat.

add the meat and brown on all sides a few pieces at a time, being careful not to crowd the pan. Transfer it to the insert of a 5- to 7-quart slow cooker. Add the onion to the same skillet, adding oil if the pan is dry, and sauté until the onion begins to soften, about 3 minutes. Add the tequila (if using) and allow the liquid to evaporate by half.

transfer the mixture to the slow-cooker insert. Stir the beans and beef broth together in a bowl. Add to the slow cooker and stir to combine.

cook the stew on high for 4 to 5 hours or on low for 8 to 10 hours, until the meat is tender and the beans are thick. Skim off any fat from the surface of the sauce. Season with salt and pepper.

ladle some of the meat and beans onto a tostada shell and top with cilantro, sour cream, and cheese. Serve two per person if the tostada shells are smaller than 6 inches across.

serves **8**

pork savvy
Pork shoulder is usually cheaper with the bone in, even though you are paying for the weight of the bone. With a dish like this, you can buy it on the bone and cut away the bone before cutting it into cubes. Some markets offer already-cut-up shoulder meat.

Umbrian Porchetta

Several years ago, my husband and I set off on what I called the "Roots Tour" of Italy. My grandmother was born in a small hill town in Umbria, and I set out to find the family. Umbria is home to many wonderful culinary pleasures, chief among them a roasted pork called *porchetta*, which is not only served in restaurants, but also at roadside stands dotting the countryside. The pork is butterflied and stuffed with aromatic herbs, onion, garlic, and, sometimes, fennel, then slow roasted for hours. The result is meltingly tender pork perfumed with the flavors of the stuffing. This is my take on this traditional Umbrian dish.

One 4-pound boneless pork shoulder, butterflied

2 teaspoons salt

1 teaspoon freshly ground black pepper

½ cup extra-virgin olive oil

4 cloves garlic, minced

1 tablespoon finely chopped fresh rosemary

1 teaspoon fennel seeds

2 medium onions, finely chopped

1 bulb fennel, ends trimmed, finely chopped

1 cup dry white wine or vermouth

place the pork fat-side down on a cutting board and sprinkle with some of the salt and pepper. Stir together the remaining salt and pepper, the oil, garlic, rosemary, and fennel seeds. rub this mixture all over the pork.

roll up the pork from the short side and tie with kitchen string or silicone loops. Spread the onions and fennel over the bottom of the insert of a 5- to 7-quart slow cooker. Pour in the wine and place the pork on top of the vegetables.

cover and cook on high for 4 to 5 hours or on low for 8 to 10 hours. Remove the meat from the slow cooker, cover with aluminum foil, and allow to rest for 20 minutes. Strain the contents of the slow cooker through a fine-mesh sieve into a saucepan and skim off any fat from the surface.

bring the sauce to a boil and reduce by half. Cut the strings from the roast. Cut the meat into ½-inch-thick slices or shred the meat with two forks.

serve piled on a platter and accompany with the sauce.

serves **8**

Pork Chops with Sauerkraut and Apples

Pork chops can sometimes be dry and tough, but in the slow cooker they turn into a meltingly tender and succulent entrée. These chops rest on thinly sliced sweet apples, flavored with Dijon mustard and brown sugar, and are covered with onions and sauerkraut. This one-pot meal is terrific to serve with mashed potatoes and applesauce.

½ cup (1 stick) unsalted butter, melted

4 Braeburn apples, peeled, cored, cut into ½-inch-thick slices

½ cup Dijon mustard

½ cup firmly packed light brown sugar

Six 1-inch-thick pork loin chops

2 medium sweet onions, cut into half moons

One 1-pound bag sauerkraut, rinsed and drained

½ cup apple juice

pour half the butter into the insert of a 5- to 7-quart slow cooker. Add the apples and toss to coat. Stir the mustard and sugar together in a small bowl and dot the apples with ¼ cup of the mustard mixture.

paint the pork chops with the remaining mustard mixture and put the pork chops on the apples. Heat the remaining butter in a large skillet over medium-high heat. Add the onions and sauté until they begin to turn golden, about 15 minutes.

add the sauerkraut to the onions and stir to combine. Spread the sauerkraut mixture over the pork and pour in the apple juice. Cover and cook on high for 3½ to 4 hours or on low for 6 to 8 hours, until the pork is tender and cooked through.

serve the pork chops with the apples and sauerkraut.

serves **6**

pork chop savvy
Chops are cut from the loin. Thick center-cut pork chops are the best choice for a slow cooker.

South-of-the-Border Pork Chops

A terrific weekend dinner, these chili-rubbed pork chops simmer in a sweet pepper and onion sauce. Serve this with steamed rice and refried beans for a weekend fiesta.

4 tablespoons olive oil

2 medium onions, cut into half rounds

2 medium red bell peppers, seeded and cut into ½-inch slices

2 medium yellow bell peppers, seeded and cut into ½-inch slices

1 teaspoon ground cumin

1 teaspoon sugar

1 teaspoon salt

½ teaspoon freshly ground black pepper

One 28- to 32-ounce can crushed tomatoes, with their juice

1 teaspoon ancho chile powder

Six 1-inch-thick pork loin chops

heat 2 tablespoons of the oil in a large skillet over medium-high heat. Add the onions, bell peppers, cumin, sugar, salt, and pepper and sauté until the onions begin to turn translucent, about 10 minutes. Add the tomatoes and stir to combine. Transfer the mixture to the insert of a 5- to 7-quart slow cooker. Cover the cooker and set on low.

heat the remaining 2 tablespoons oil in the skillet over medium-high heat. Sprinkle the chile powder evenly over the chops and add to the skillet. Brown the chops on all sides. Transfer the chops to the slow- cooker insert and spoon some of the sauce over the chops.

cover the slow cooker and cook on high for 3½ to 4 hours or on low for 6 to 8 hours, until the pork is tender.

serve the pork chops with the sauce.

serves 6

Pork Chops with Sage and Balsamic Vinegar

Sweet balsamic vinegar, dried figs, aromatic sage, and pork chops are braised together to succulent perfection in the slow cooker. The sauce is delicious served with polenta or roasted potatoes.

¼ cup olive oil

1 teaspoon salt

½ teaspoon freshly ground black pepper

Six 1-inch-thick pork loin chops

12 dried figs, cut in half

2 medium onions, cut into half rounds

2 teaspoons finely chopped fresh sage leaves

½ cup balsamic vinegar

¼ cup chicken broth

2 tablespoons unsalted butter

heat the oil in a large skillet over high heat. Sprinkle the salt and pepper evenly over the pork chops and add the pork to the skillet.

brown the pork on all sides. Transfer to the insert of a 5- to 7-quart slow cooker. Add the figs to the slow-cooker insert. Add the onions and sage to the same skillet and sauté until the onions are softened, about 5 minutes. Deglaze the skillet with the vinegar and scrape up any browned bits from the bottom of the pan. Transfer the contents of the skillet to the slow-cooker insert and pour in the broth.

cover and cook on high for 3½ to 4 hours or on low for 6 to 8 hours. Carefully remove the pork from the pot and cover with aluminum foil. Using an immersion blender, purée the sauce and whisk in the butter.

return the pork to the slow cooker and set on warm to serve.

serves **6**

Smothered Pork Chops

This recipe is an improvement on the one from the Campbell's soup company that cooked pork chops in cream of mushroom soup on the stovetop. Don't be worried about the amount of onions, for they add sweetness to the sauce. If you have family members who aren't onion fans, purée the sauce before serving, and it will be our little secret!

6 strips bacon, cut into ½-inch pieces

¼ cup all-purpose flour

1 teaspoon salt

½ teaspoon freshly ground black pepper

8 center-cut ¾-inch-thick pork chops

4 tablespoons (½ stick) unsalted butter

4 large onions, cut into ¼-inch-thick slices

1 teaspoon dried sage leaves, crushed in the palm of your hand

½ teaspoon dried thyme

2 tablespoons sugar

1 cup beef broth

2 cups chicken broth

cook the bacon in a large skillet until crisp and remove it to paper towels to drain. Combine the flour, salt, and pepper in a zipper-top plastic bag, add the chops, and shake to coat.

add the chops to the bacon drippings and brown on both sides. Transfer the chops to the insert of a 5- to 7-quart slow cooker. If the chops don't fit snugly in one layer, put some on top of each other.

melt the butter in the same skillet over medium-high heat. Add the onions, sage, thyme, and sugar and sauté until the onions begin to turn golden but not brown. Pour the beef broth into the skillet and scrape up any browned bits from the bottom of the pan. Transfer the contents of the skillet to the slow-cooker insert and add the chicken broth.

cover the slow cooker and cook on low for 7 to 8 hours, until the pork is tender. Stir in the bacon.

serve the pork chops covered with some of the sauce.

serves **6–8**

Sweet Potato Pork Chop Supper

Most of us think of serving sweet potatoes during the Thanksgiving and Christmas holidays, when in fact they are delicious year-round and don't just complement turkey or chicken. This hearty one-dish meal of pork chops slowly cooked with orange-and-thyme-flavored sweet potatoes is sure to become a family favorite. The best news is that once it goes into the slow cooker, you've got it made!

2 teaspoons dried thyme

2 teaspoons salt

1 teaspoon freshly ground black pepper

8 center-cut 1-inch-thick boneless pork loin chops

2 tablespoons vegetable oil

½ cup (1 stick) unsalted butter

1 large sweet onion, such as Vidalia, thinly sliced into half rounds

4 medium sweet potatoes, peeled and cut into ½-inch slices

1 cup orange juice

combine the thyme, salt, and pepper in a small bowl. Sprinkle half the mixture over both sides of the pork chops. Heat the oil in a large skillet over medium-high heat.

add the pork chops and brown on both sides. Transfer the pork to the insert of a 5- to 7-quart slow cooker. Melt the butter in the same skillet over medium-high heat. Add the remaining thyme mixture and sauté for 1 minute.

add the onion and sauté until the onion is beginning to soften, about 3 minutes. Transfer the onion to the slow-cooker insert, leaving some of the butter in the skillet. Cover the onion with the sweet potato slices and pour the orange juice over all.

drizzle the potatoes with the butter remaining in the skillet. Cover the slow cooker and cook on high for 3 hours or on low for 6 hours, until the sweet potatoes and pork chops are tender.

serve the pork chops with the sweet potatoes and some of the sauce.

serves 6–8

Just-Peachy Pork Chops

These pork chops are a terrific weeknight meal and give a sweet and savory spin to the traditional pork chop. Peaches, cippolini onions, and balsamic vinegar combine to make a delicious sauce perfectly balanced for serving with scalloped potatoes or rice.

¼ cup all-purpose flour

Salt and freshly ground black pepper

4 tablespoons (½ stick) unsalted butter

6 center-cut, bone-in, 1-inch-thick pork chops

2 cups cippolini or small pearl onions, peeled and left whole

2 teaspoons dried sage leaves, crumbled in the palm of your hand

2 tablespoons light brown sugar

1 cup peach preserves (see savvy)

¼ cup balsamic vinegar

¼ cup beef broth, plus ¼ cup (optional)

2 tablespoons cornstarch (optional)

combine the flour, 2 teaspoons salt, and 1 teaspoon pepper in a shallow dish. Dip each chop in the flour, coating both sides lightly and shaking off any excess flour. Melt 2 tablespoons of the butter in a large skillet over medium heat. Add half the chops and brown on both sides. Repeat with the remaining chops.

transfer the chops to the insert of a 5- to 7-quart slow cooker. Melt the remaining 2 tablespoons butter in the same skillet. Add the onions, sage, and sugar and sauté until the onions begin to turn golden, about 10 minutes. Add the preserves, vinegar, and ¼ cup broth and stir to blend.

cover the chops with the onion mixture. Cover the slow cooker and cook on high for 3 hours or on low for 6 hours. Remove the cover from the slow cooker. Season with salt and pepper.

(If you would like to thicken the sauce, mix 2 tablespoons cornstarch with ¼ cup beef broth. Thirty minutes before the chops are done. remove the cover and stir in the cornstarch mixture. Cover the cooker and cook on high for an additional 30 minutes, until the sauce is thickened.)

serve the chops napped with some of the sauce and onions.

serves **6**

preserves savvy
Try to find preserves marked "simply fruit," with less sugar, otherwise this dish will be way too sweet. If you can't find preserves without sugar added, then omit the brown sugar in the recipe.

Maple Bourbon Pork Chops

Sweet and smoky, with a touch of heat, these pork chops will become a new favorite at your house. Serve them with rice or polenta to soak up the delicious sauce.

2 tablespoons olive oil

1½ teaspoons salt

½ teaspoon freshly ground black pepper

Six 1-inch-thick pork loin chops

2 tablespoons unsalted butter

2 medium onions, finely chopped

½ cup ketchup

½ cup bourbon

¼ cup pure maple syrup

1 teaspoon Tabasco sauce

1 teaspoon dry mustard

½ cup beef broth

heat the oil in a large skillet over high heat. Sprinkle the salt and pepper evenly over the pork chops and add to the skillet.

brown the chops on both sides, adding a few at a time, being careful not to crowd the pan, and transfer to the insert of a 5- to 7-quart slow cooker.

melt the butter in the skillet over medium-high heat. Add the onions and sauté until they begin to soften, about 5 minutes. Add the remaining ingredients and scrape up any browned bits from the bottom of the pan. Transfer the contents of the skillet to the slow-cooker insert.

cover and cook on high for 3 to 4 hours or on low for 6 to 8 hours. Skim off any fat from the top of the sauce.

serve from the cooker set on warm.

serves **6**

Plum Sauce Pork Chops

Plum preserves, Dijon mustard, and lemon juice are braised with pork chops for a delicious dinner entrée. Serve with rice pilaf or wild rice. Cherry preserves may also be used in place of the plum preserves.

¼ cup olive oil

1 teaspoon salt

½ teaspoon freshly ground black pepper

Six 1-inch-thick pork loin chops

2 medium onions, finely chopped

1 cup plum preserves

2 tablespoons Dijon mustard

2 tablespoons fresh lemon juice

Grated zest of 1 lemon

½ cup ketchup

heat the oil in a large skillet over high heat. Sprinkle the salt and pepper evenly over the pork chops and add to the skillet. Brown the pork on all sides.

transfer to the insert of a 5- to 7-quart slow cooker. Lower heat to medium-high. Add the onions to the skillet and sauté until the onions are softened, about 3 to 5 minutes. Add the preserves to the skillet and scrape up any browned bits from the bottom of the pan. Transfer the contents of the skillet to the slow-cooker insert.

add the mustard, lemon juice and zest, and ketchup and stir to combine. Cover and cook on high for 3½ to 4 hours or on low for 6 to 8 hours. Skim off any fat from the surface of the sauce.

serve the pork chops from the slow cooker set on warm.

serves **6**

Loin   Think of a bone-in pork chop. The smaller side of the chop is the tenderloin, and the other side is the loin. When the bone is removed, the meat—both tenderloin and loin—is rolled and tied into one compact piece called a "whole" pork loin. Sometimes the tenderloin is removed, leaving only the loin, a solid piece of delicious eating. Pork loin can be roasted and served in any number of ways. I like to braise it, or brine it and then roast it with garlic and herbs. I trim the fat from the roast after it has finished cooking, not before, because the fat helps keep the meat moist while cooking.

Cranberry Orange Pork Loin

This gorgeous red pork roast is the perfect entrée to serve during fall and winter, especially at the holidays. The pork is infused with the flavors of orange and cranberry, and the resulting sauce is delicious spooned over the roast or served on the side. A wild rice pilaf with dried cranberries and bits of orange zest would be an ideal side dish.

2 tablespoons olive oil

One 3- to 4-pound pork loin roast, tied

Salt and freshly ground black pepper

1 large sweet onion, such as Vidalia, coarsely chopped

Two 16-ounce cans whole-berry cranberry sauce

Grated zest of 2 oranges

Juice of 2 oranges (about 1 cup)

2 teaspoons dried thyme leaves

½ cup beef broth

spray the insert of a 5- to 7-quart slow cooker with nonstick cooking spray or line it with a slow-cooker liner according to the manufacturer's directions.

heat the oil in a large sauté pan over high heat. Sprinkle the roast with 1½ teaspoons salt and 1 teaspoon pepper and add to the pan.

sauté the pork on all sides until browned. Transfer the roast to the slow-cooker insert. Add the remaining ingredients and stir to combine. Cover the slow cooker and cook the roast on high for 4 hours or on low for 8 hours.

remove the cover, transfer the roast to a cutting board, and cover loosely with aluminum foil. Let the meat rest for 15 minutes. Skim off any fat from the top of the sauce. Stir the sauce and season with salt and pepper.

slice the roast and nap with some of the sauce. Serve the remaining sauce in a gravy boat on the side.

serves 6–8

Pork Loin Braised in Cider with Apples and Cream

This flavorful dish is reminiscent of those served in bistros on the Normandy coast of France. The succulent pork, infused with the sweetness of cider, is perfect over buttered noodles. Leftover pork and sauce may be refrigerated for up to three days or frozen for up to six weeks.

2 tablespoons olive oil

½ cup Dijon mustard

½ cup firmly packed light brown sugar

One 2½- to 3-pound pork loin roast, rolled and tied

1 large onion, finely sliced

2 teaspoons dried thyme

½ cup apple cider

1 cup beef stock

4 large Gala or Braeburn apples, peeled, cored, and cut into 8 wedges each

¾ cup heavy cream (see savvy)

Salt and freshly ground black pepper

1 pound buttered cooked wide egg noodles

heat the oil in a large sauté pan over medium-high heat. Make a paste of the mustard and sugar and spread over the roast on all sides. Add the roast to the pan and brown on all sides. Add the onion and thyme to the sauté pan and cook until the onion is softened, 3 to 5 minutes.

transfer the roast, onion, and any bits from the bottom of the pan to the insert of a 5- to 7-quart slow cooker. Add the cider and beef stock. Cover the slow cooker and cook on high for 3 hours. Remove the cover and add the apples and cream. Cover and cook on high for an additional 1 hour.

remove the pork from the slow-cooker insert, cover with aluminum foil, and allow to rest for 15 minutes. Season the sauce with salt and pepper. Remove the strings from the roast, cut into thin slices, and serve the pork on the buttered noodles, napping both with some of the sauce.

serves 6—8

low-fat savvy
For a sauce with less fat, omit the cream. The cream rounds out the sauce and gives it a luxurious flavor, but it's good without the cream as well.

Pork Loin in Plum Bourbon Sauce

Pork loin is made sweeter with the addition of dried plums, and a smoky quality comes from the addition of bourbon to flavor the braise. The flavors are a terrific combination and pair well with scalloped potatoes or a vegetable gratin.

24 dried plums

1½ cups beef broth

One 4-pound pork loin roast, rolled and tied

½ cup Dijon mustard

⅔ cup firmly packed dark brown sugar

1 tablespoon vegetable oil

⅓ cup bourbon

1 teaspoon dried sage

1½ teaspoons dried thyme

1 tablespoon cornstarch mixed with 2 tablespoons water

¼ cup chopped fresh Italian parsley

combine the plums and beef broth in the insert of a 5- to 7-quart slow cooker. Dry the outside of the roast with paper towels. Rub the meat all over with the mustard, then roll it in the brown sugar, coating it evenly.

heat the oil in a large skillet over medium-high heat. Add the roast and brown on all sides, making sure the sugar doesn't burn. Transfer the pork to the slow-cooker insert. Add the bourbon, sage, and thyme to the skillet and scrape up any browned bits from the bottom of the pan. Transfer to the slow-cooker insert. Cover and cook on high for 4 to 5 hours or on low for 8 to 10 hours. Transfer the pork and plums to a serving platter. Cover with aluminum foil, and allow the roast to rest for 20 minutes.

strain the cooking liquid through a fine-mesh sieve into a saucepan and skim off as much fat as possible from the top of the sauce. Bring to a boil and taste and adjust the seasonings. Stir in the cornstarch mixture and bring to a boil, stirring constantly. Reduce the heat to medium and stir in the parsley.

cut the strings on the meat and cut into ½-inch-thick slices. Serve the pork and plums with the sauce on the side.

serves **8**

Orange Chipotle Pork Loin

Smoky chipotle chiles and sunny oranges are a stellar combination when slow cooking pork loin. The same sauce can be used also for slow cooking pork shoulder for carnitas. Serve the pork loin with rice and refried beans for a casual dinner.

2 tablespoons olive oil

One 4-pound pork loin roast, rolled and tied

1½ teaspoons salt

½ teaspoon freshly ground black pepper

1½ cups coarsely chopped onion

2 cloves garlic, minced

2 canned chipotle chiles in adobo (or to taste), finely chopped, with 1 teaspoon adobo

1 teaspoon ground cumin

1 cup orange marmalade

¼ cup fresh orange juice

2 teaspoons fresh lime juice

4 navel oranges, thinly sliced for garnishing

heat the oil in a large skillet over medium-high heat. Sprinkle the roast evenly with the salt and pepper and add to the skillet. Brown on all sides and transfer to the insert of a 5- to 7-quart slow cooker.

add the onion, garlic, chiles, and cumin to the same skillet and sauté until the onion is softened, about 3 minutes. Add the marmalade, orange juice, and lime juice and stir to combine, scraping up any browned bits from the bottom of the pan.

transfer the contents of the skillet to the slow-cooker insert. Cover and cook on high for 4 to 5 hours or on low for 8 to 10 hours, until the roast is tender.

remove the roast from the slow-cooker insert, cover with aluminum foil, and allow the meat to rest for 15 to 20 minutes. Taste the sauce for seasoning and adjust if needed.

slice the meat and strain the sauce. Serve the roast napped with some of the sauce, garnished with orange slices and additional sauce on the side.

serves 10

Sugar and Spice Pork Loin

Spice rubs work wonders for slow-cooked meats, because they not only flavor the meat but also add seasoning to the pan sauce. This rub, with a shot of brown sugar and strong flavors like cumin, fennel, and cinnamon, is perfect for pork. Its flavors blend nicely with the root vegetables surrounding the meat.

2 medium sweet potatoes, peeled and cut into 1-inch chunks or wedges

2 medium Yukon gold potatoes, peeled and cut into 1-inch chunks or wedges

2 medium red onions, cut into quarters

½ cup olive oil

1 teaspoon ground cumin

1½ teaspoons fennel seeds

½ teaspoon ground cinnamon

½ teaspoon ground ginger

¼ cup firmly packed light brown sugar

2 teaspoons salt

1 teaspoon freshly ground black pepper

One 4-pound pork loin roast, rolled and tied

½ cup chicken broth

arrange the vegetables in the insert of a 5- to 7-quart slow cooker. Drizzle ¼ cup of the oil over the vegetables and toss to coat. Combine the cumin, fennel seeds, cinnamon, ginger, sugar, salt, and pepper in a small bowl. Sprinkle 1 tablespoon of the rub over the vegetables and toss again.

pat the rest of the rub over the meat, place the meat on the vegetables, and drizzle with the remaining ¼ cup olive oil. Pour in the chicken broth. Cover and cook on high for 4 to 5 hours or on low for 8 to 10 hours, until the pork and vegetables are tender. (The roast should register 175°F on an instant-read thermometer.)

transfer the pork to a cutting board, cover with aluminum foil, and let rest for 20 minutes. Cut the meat into ½-inch-thick slices and arrange on the center of a platter. Spoon the vegetables around the meat and serve.

serves **6–8**

Apricot-Mustard Glazed Pork Loin

Simple, homey, and, oh, so good, this pork loin is sweet and tangy, and the fruity mustard pan sauce is delicious over rice or noodles. Try to find apricot preserves that aren't sweetened—the jar should read "pure fruit." If the preserves have a lot of sugar in them, omit the brown sugar in the recipe.

2 cups apricot preserves

½ cup Dijon mustard

2 tablespoons fresh lemon juice

¼ cup fresh orange juice

¼ cup beef broth

1 teaspoon dried thyme

One 4-pound pork loin roast, rolled and tied

1 teaspoon salt

½ teaspoon freshly ground black pepper

½ teaspoon ground ginger

combine the preserves, mustard, lemon and orange juices, broth, and thyme in the insert of a 5- to 7-quart slow cooker. Sprinkle the roast evenly with the salt, pepper, and ginger.

place the roast in the slow-cooker insert and spoon some of the sauce over the roast. Cover and cook on high for 4 to 5 hours or on low for 8 to 10 hours, until the meat is tender. (The roast should register 175°F on an instant-read thermometer.)

transfer the roast to a cutting board, cover with aluminum foil, and allow to rest for 20 minutes before carving. Skim off any fat from the surface of the sauce and taste and adjust the seasoning.

cut the roast into ½-inch-thick slices and arrange on a platter. Serve the sauce on the side.

serves **6–8**

Braised Pork Loin with Riesling and Red Cabbage

The ruby red color of this dish makes it a stand out any night of the week. Sweet, crisp Riesling wine flavors red cabbage and sauerkraut and helps flavor the pork loin as it braises low and slow. The finished dish has a lovely sweet-and-sour quality that pairs well with root vegetable gratins, applesauce, or mashed potatoes on the side.

2 tablespoons olive oil

1½ teaspoons salt

½ teaspoon freshly ground black pepper

One 4-pound pork loin roast, rolled and tied

4 tablespoons (½ stick) unsalted butter

2 medium onions, cut into half rounds

1 small head red cabbage, cored and thinly sliced (3 to 4 cups)

2 cups Riesling wine

½ cup firmly packed light brown sugar

One 1-pound bag sauerkraut, rinsed and drained

heat the oil in a large skillet over medium-high heat. Sprinkle the salt and pepper evenly over the roast. Add the roast to the skillet and brown on all sides.

transfer to the insert of a 5- to 7-quart slow cooker. Melt the butter in the same skillet over medium-high heat. Add the onions and cabbage and sauté until the onions are softened and begins to turn translucent.

add the wine, brown sugar, and sauerkraut to the skillet, and stir to scrape up any browned bits from the bottom of the pan. Bring to a boil.

transfer the contents of the skillet to the slow-cooker insert. Lift the pork and spoon some of the vegetables under the pork. Cover and cook on high for 4 to 5 hours or low for 8 to 10 hours. Transfer the roast to a cutting board, cover with aluminum foil, and allow to rest for 20 minutes.

cut the roast into ½-inch-thick slices and serve with the sauerkraut.

serves 6–8

Tenderloin

The tenderloin is the filet mignon of pork. Because it has no fat, it needs a marinade or brine to keep it juicy and tender during cooking. Most pork tenderloins weigh about one pound. The tenderloin has what is called silver skin, which is a sheath that runs the length of the meat; you will need to trim and discard that. Simply run a thin, sharp knife underneath it, separating it from the meat. If you don't trim the silver skin, it will cause the meat to buckle when it cooks and it won't cook evenly.

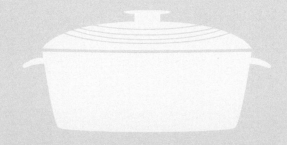

Pork Tenderloin Osso Bucco–Style

The traditional veal dish is made here with pork tenderloin instead, and the results are deeply flavored and delicious. Serve with risotto, polenta, or pasta.

2 tablespoons unsalted butter

1 tablespoon olive oil

4 pounds pork tenderloin, silver skin removed, cut into 1-inch cubes

1½ teaspoons salt

1 teaspoon freshly ground black pepper

1 cup finely chopped onion

1 cup finely chopped carrots

1 cup finely chopped celery

1 teaspoon dried sage

½ cup dry white wine or vermouth

½ cup chicken broth

½ cup beef broth

One 15-ounce can chopped plum tomatoes, with their juice

4 cloves garlic, minced

Grated zest of 1 lemon

Grated zest of 1 orange

½ cup finely chopped fresh parsley

heat the butter and oil in a large skillet over medium-high heat. Sprinkle the pork with the salt and pepper. Add to the skillet in several batches and brown until nicely crusted on all sides.

transfer the pork to the insert of a 5- to 7-quart slow cooker. Add the onion, carrots, celery, and sage to the same skillet and cook, stirring, until the onion begins to soften and turn translucent, about 5 minutes.

add the wine and scrape up any browned bits from the bottom of the pan. Transfer to the slow-cooker insert. Add both broths and the tomatoes and stir to combine. Cover and cook on low for 6 hours, until the meat is fork tender.

skim off any fat from the top of the sauce. Stir in the garlic, lemon and orange zests, and parsley.

serve from the cooker set on warm.

serves **10**

Pork Tenderloin Stuffed with Cranberry Wild Rice with Cranberry Sauce

A delicious stuffing made with wild rice and orange zest bursts from this butterflied pork tenderloin, which is braised in a cranberry and port sauce. Your family will wonder what you are up to when you serve this elegant dish on a weeknight.

2 tablespoons unsalted butter

1 cup finely chopped onion

1 cup finely chopped celery

1 teaspoon dried thyme

1 teaspoon grated orange zest

3 cups cooked wild rice

Two 1-pound pork tenderloins

2 teaspoons salt

1 teaspoon freshly ground black pepper

Two 14- to 15-ounce cans jellied cranberry sauce

¼ cup Ruby Port

¼ cup fresh orange juice

¼ cup beef broth

1 teaspoon finely chopped fresh rosemary

2 tablespoons olive oil

melt the butter in a large skillet over medium-high heat. Add the onion, celery, thyme, and orange zest and sauté until the vegetables are softened, about 5 minutes. Transfer to a mixing bowl and stir in the wild rice.

remove the silver skin from the outside of the pork with a boning knife and discard. Cut each tenderloin lengthwise in half to within ½ inch of the other side and open it like a book. Place the meat on a cutting board, cover with a piece of plastic wrap, and pound the pork evenly ½ inch thick.

sprinkle one tenderloin with half the salt and pepper. Spread half the wild rice mixture over the meat. Roll up the meat from one long side and tie at 1-inch intervals with kitchen string or silicone loops. Repeat with the second tenderloin.

combine the cranberry sauce, port, orange juice, broth, and rosemary in the insert of a 5- to 7-quart slow cooker.

heat the oil in a large skillet over high heat. Brown each pork tenderloin on all sides. Transfer them to the slow-cooker insert and spoon some of the sauce over the pork. Cover and cook on high for 3 hours or on low for 5 to 6 hours, until the pork is tender. (The pork should register 175°F on an instant-read thermometer.)

remove the pork from the slow-cooker insert, cover with aluminum foil, and allow to rest for 20 minutes. Skim off any fat from the top of the sauce. Remove the strings from the meat and cut into ½-inch-thick slices. Serve with the sauce.

serves 6–8

Pork Tenderloin Stuffed with Cornbread Dressing with Red Wine Sauce

Stuffed pork chops are on many dinner tables during the week, so I've dressed this one up at bit and given it a rich red-wine sauce to complement the sweet cornbread filling. The slow cooker takes care of all the simmering, and you can lift the lid and surprise your family with this delicious down-home-dish-with-a-twist.

2 tablespoons unsalted butter

1 cup finely chopped onion

1 cup finely chopped celery

1 teaspoon dried sage leaves

4 cups crumbled stale cornbread

1 large egg, beaten

Two 1-pound pork tenderloins

2 teaspoons salt

1 teaspoon freshly ground black pepper

2 tablespoons olive oil

1 tablespoon cornstarch

½ cup red wine such as Pinot Noir or Syrah

½ cup chicken broth

1 cup beef broth

1 teaspoon dried thyme

melt the butter in a large skillet over medium-high heat. Add the onion, celery, and sage and sauté until the vegetables are softened, about 5 minutes. Transfer to a mixing bowl and allow to cool. Stir in the cornbread and egg.

remove the silver skin from the outside of the pork with a boning knife and discard. Cut each roast lengthwise in half to within ½ inch of the other side and open it like a book. Place the meat on a cutting board, cover with a piece of plastic wrap, and pound the pork evenly ½ inch thick.

sprinkle one tenderloin with half the salt and pepper. Spread half the cornbread stuffing mixture over the meat. Roll up the meat from one long side and tie at 1-inch intervals with kitchen string or silicone loops. Repeat with the second tenderloin.

heat the oil in a large skillet over high heat. Brown each pork tenderloin on all sides. Transfer to the slow-cooker insert. Dissolve the cornstarch in the wine, then add the wine, both broths, and thyme to the skillet. Cook, scraping up any browned bits from the bottom of the pan, until the sauce thickens. Pour the sauce into the slow-cooker insert.

cover and cook on high for 3 hours or on low for 5 to 6 hours, until the pork is tender. (The pork should register 175°F on an instant-read thermometer.)

remove the pork from the slow-cooker insert, cover with aluminum foil, and allow to rest for 20 minutes. Skim off any fat from the top of the sauce. Remove the strings from the meat and cut into ½-inch-thick slices. Serve with the sauce.

serves 6–8

Jamaican Jerk Pork Tenderloin in Mango Sauce

Braised on a bed of tropical fruit, the spicy pork tenderloins in this dish become sweet and juicy. Serve the pork with steamed rice and black beans.

4 tablespoons (½ stick) unsalted butter, melted

2 large mangoes, peeled, pitted, and coarsely chopped

2 navel oranges, peeled and sectioned

2 tablespoons soy sauce

½ cup dark rum

½ cup beef broth

Two 1-pound pork tenderloins

2 tablespoons Jamaican jerk seasoning

6 green onions, finely chopped, using the white and tender green parts for garnishing

stir the butter, mangoes, oranges, soy sauce, rum, and broth together in the insert of a 5- to 7-quart slow cooker. Remove the silver skin from the outside of the pork with a boning knife and discard.

rub the jerk seasoning on the pork and arrange it in the slow cooker. Cover and cook on high for 3 hours, until the pork is tender and cooked through. (The pork should register 175°F on an instant-read thermometer.)

remove the pork from the sauce, cover with aluminum foil, and allow to rest for 20 minutes. Skim off any fat from the top of the sauce.

slice the meat and garnish with the green onions. Serve the sauce on the side.

serves 6

Chile Relleno Pork Tenderloin with Ranchero Sauce

This pork dish takes the idea of a chile relleno, a batter-fried cheese-stuffed pepper, to another level. When the pork is sliced, the chiles and melting cheese are revealed. The combination with the ranchero sauce is scrumptious. Serve this over rice or polenta, which will absorb the sauce.

SAUCE

2 tablespoons vegetable oil

2 large onions, thinly sliced

2 cloves garlic, minced

1 medium green bell pepper, seeded and cut into thin strips

1 medium red bell pepper, seeded and cut into thin strips

1 teaspoon ground cumin

1 teaspoon salt

⅛ teaspoon chili powder

2 tablespoons tequila

4 cups tomato purée

heat the oil in a large skillet over medium-high heat. Add the onions and sauté, stirring, until softened, about 3 minutes. Add the garlic, bell peppers, cumin, salt, and chili powder and cook, stirring, for 5 to 7 minutes. The vegetables should be soft and the garlic and onions almost translucent.

add the tequila and allow it to evaporate, about 1 minute. Stir in the tomato purée and bring to a boil.

transfer to the insert of a 5- to 7-quart slow cooker and prepare the pork.

PORK AND CHILES

Two 6-ounce cans roasted green chiles, rinsed and drained

8 ounces Monterey Jack cheese, cut into 3-by-1-inch strips

Two 1-pound pork tenderloins

2 teaspoons salt

1 teaspoon freshly ground black pepper

2 tablespoons olive oil

slit each chile down one side. Stuff each chile with a strip of cheese. Remove the silver skin from the outside of the pork with a boning knife and discard.

cut each tenderloin lengthwise in half to within ½ inch of the other side and open it like a book. Place the meat on a cutting board, cover with a piece of plastic wrap, and pound the pork evenly ½ inch thick. Sprinkle one tenderloin with half the salt and pepper. Arrange 4 or 5 stuffed chiles on the meat, lining the chiles up parallel with the ends of the meat.

roll up the meat from the short side and tie at 1-inch intervals with kitchen string or silicone loops. Repeat with the second pork tenderloin.

heat the oil in a large skillet over high heat. Add one tenderloin at a time and brown on all sides. Transfer to the slow-cooker insert and spoon the sauce over the pork.

cover and cook on high for 3 hours or on low for 5 to 6 hours, until the pork is tender. (The pork should register 175°F on an instant-read thermometer.)

remove the pork from the slow-cooker insert, cover with aluminum foil, and allow to rest for 20 minutes. Skim off any fat from the top of the sauce. Remove the strings from the meat and cut into ½-inch-thick slices. Serve with the sauce.

serves 6–8

Teriyaki Pork Tenderloin

Marinated in teriyaki sauce and then slow cooked, these tenderloins are delicious served on a bed of sesame noodles or an Asian slaw. You also can slice the pork, return it to the sauce, and serve it with skewers as an appetizer.

2 tablespoons vegetable oil

2 cloves garlic, minced

1 teaspoon grated fresh ginger

1 cup soy sauce

¼ cup rice vinegar

3 tablespoons light brown sugar

Two 1-pound pork tenderloins

whisk the oil, garlic, ginger, soy sauce, vinegar, and sugar together in a bowl until blended. Remove the silver skin from the outside of the pork with a boning knife and discard.

place the tenderloins in a 1-gallon zipper-top plastic bag or 13-by-9-inch baking dish. Pour the marinade over the tenderloins and seal the bag or cover the dish with plastic wrap.

marinate for at least 4 hours or overnight, turning the meat once or twice during that time. Place the marinade and pork in the insert of a 5- to 7-quart slow cooker. Cover and cook on high for 3 hours.

remove the meat from the sauce, cover loosely with aluminum foil, and allow the meat to rest for about 10 minutes. Skim off any fat from the top of the sauce.

cut the meat diagonally in ½-inch-thick slices. Nap each serving of pork with some of the sauce.

serves **6**

Ribs

Ribs are messy and finger-licking-good food to serve for a casual backyard picnic or cut down and served as finger food at indoor parties. Spareribs are meatier than baby back ribs, and you will need to cut them into manageable pieces when they are cooked. This is easily accomplished with a cleaver or other sharp knife. So-called country-style spareribs are really blade pork chops that have been split. They are delicious when braised, and the slow-cooker takes good care of them.

Baby Back Ribs

Baby back ribs become sticky and fall-apart tender in the slow cooker. You can serve them as appetizers, but I really prefer them for dinner. The basic preparation is the same. You could vary the sauce to highlight a different cuisine every week and not have a repeat.

Country-Style Ribs

Meaty ribs like these need to be braised in liquid for the meat to fall off the bone and the sauce to absorb the flavors. The basic preparation is the same: the ribs are submerged in the flavorful liquid and cook all day.

Asian Barbecued Baby Back Ribs

Soy and ginger flavor these sticky ribs. Serve them as an appetizer or with rice and Asian slaw for a simple supper with lots of flavor.

½ cup soy sauce

¼ cup hoisin sauce

2 teaspoons grated fresh ginger

2 cloves garlic, minced

¼ cup firmly packed light brown sugar

1 tablespoon toasted sesame oil

½ cup chicken broth

4 green onions, finely chopped, using the white and tender green parts

4 pounds baby back ribs (about 3 slabs), cut to fit the slow cooker

stir the soy sauce, hoisin, ginger, garlic, sugar, sesame oil, broth, and green onions together in the insert of a 5- to 7-quart slow cooker. Add the ribs and push them down into the sauce.

cover and cook on low for 7 to 8 hours, until the meat is tender. Remove cover and cook for an additional 30 to 35 minutes.

serve the ribs with the remaining sauce on the side.

serves **6**

Barbecued Baby Back Ribs

When my husband and I met, he did quite a bit of cooking at his bachelor pad. One of his favorites was barbecued chicken with apple jelly and bottled barbecue sauce. He's graduated since then, and now we like this sweet and spicy apple-flavored homemade sauce over ribs.

½ cup apple cider

½ teaspoon ground ginger

½ cup firmly packed light brown sugar

¼ cup Dijon mustard

1 tablespoon Worcestershire sauce

2 cups ketchup

2 tablespoons rice vinegar

1 teaspoon Tabasco sauce

4 pounds baby back ribs (about 3 slabs), cut to fit the slow-cooker

stir together all the ingredients except the ribs in the insert of a 5- to 7-quart slow cooker. Add the ribs to the pot and push them down into the sauce.

cover and cook on low 7 to 8 hours, until the meat is tender.

serve the ribs with the remaining sauce on the side.

serves **6**

Mediterranean-Style Spareribs

Red pepper flakes, garlic, oregano, red wine, and tomato flavor these ribs. They are superb over pasta or polenta.

3 pounds country-style spareribs

1½ teaspoons salt

2 tablespoons extra-virgin olive oil

3 medium onions, finely chopped

⅛ teaspoon red pepper flakes

3 cloves garlic, minced

1 teaspoon dried oregano

½ cup red wine, such as Chianti or Barolo

One 28- to 32-ounce can crushed tomatoes, with their juice

sprinkle the ribs with the salt and arrange in the insert of a 5- to 7-quart slow cooker. Heat the oil in a large skillet over medium-high heat. Add the onions, red pepper flakes, garlic, and oregano and sauté until the onions are softened, about 5 minutes.

add the wine to the skillet and stir up any browned bits from the bottom of the pan. Transfer the contents of the skillet to the slow-cooker insert and stir in the tomatoes. Cover and cook on low for 8 to 10 hours, until the meat is tender. Skim off any fat from the surface of the sauce.

serve the ribs from the cooker set on warm.

serves **6**

Country-Style Ribs with Sauerkraut

Caraway, beer, and sauerkraut flavor these meaty ribs, bringing Oktoberfest into your kitchen any time of the year. Serve the ribs with applesauce and mashed potatoes, and don't forget the cold beer!

3 pounds country-style spareribs

1 teaspoon salt

½ teaspoon freshly ground black pepper

2 tablespoons unsalted butter

2 medium onions, cut into half rounds

2 teaspoons caraway seeds

One 1-pound bag sauerkraut, rinsed and drained

¼ cup whole-grain mustard

One 12-ounce bottle dark beer

sprinkle the ribs with the salt and pepper and arrange in the insert of a 5- to 7-quart slow cooker. Melt the butter in a large skillet over medium-high heat.

add the onions and caraway seeds and sauté until the onions are softened, about 5 minutes. Transfer the contents of the skillet to the slow-cooker insert and stir in the sauerkraut, mustard, and beer. Cover and cook on low for 8 to 10 hours, until the meat is tender. Skim off any fat from the top of the liquid in the pot.

serve from the cooker set on warm.

serves **6**

Braised Asian Spareribs

These ribs turn a mahogany red when braised low and slow in aromatic liquid. Serve these ribs over soba noodles with stir-fried vegetables.

2 cups soy sauce

1 cup rice wine (mirin)

1 teaspoons freshly grated ginger

¼ cup hoisin sauce

¼ cup rice vinegar

2 tablespoons sugar

3 pounds country-style spareribs

stir the soy sauce, rice wine, ginger, hoisin, rice vinegar, and sugar together in the insert of a 5- to 7-quart slow cooker.

add the ribs to the pot and spoon the liquid over the ribs. Cover and cook on low for 8 to 10 hours, until the ribs are tender. Skim off any fat from the sauce.

serve the ribs from the cooker set on warm.

serves **6**

Sausage

There are myriad choices when it comes to sausages, and they all do well in the slow cooker. It's really your choice as to whether the sausage is sweet, spicy, or hot, and those I call for in the recipes are only suggestions. Have fun with this, because sausage is comfort food. It's all about what makes you happy at the table!

MEXICAN CHORIZO

This is a sausage made from pork and chiles. It must be removed from its casing and cooked like ground beef before using.

SPANISH CHORIZO

Made from pork, it is a dried sausage and can be used as is. It is great in paella.

ITALIAN SAUSAGE

Either sweet or hot, Italian sausages are pork based and can be flavored with fennel seeds or whatever is common in the region. Most sweet Italian sausage sold here has fennel seeds and black pepper added to it. Hot sausages are heated with red pepper flakes added to the mix.

SMOKED SAUSAGE

Kielbasa is made from ground beef and pork sausage and is then smoked. Since it's already cooked, you can eat it right out of the package, but it's terrific to cook with sauerkraut or potatoes.

ANDOUILLE

Smoked with garlic and black and red peppers, this sausage is Creole to the core. Use it in gumbo and jambalaya.

BOCKWURST

Made with pork, veal, and seasonings, this delicate sausage works well in the slow cooker.

BAVARIAN WURST

Already cooked, it's similar to its cousin bockwurst.

KNOCKWURST

This sausage made with beef, pork, and garlic is generally smoked. Heat and serve.

BRATWURST

Made from pork, sometimes with veal added, bratwurst can be smoked or fresh. Make sure to cook the fresh thoroughly. They do well in the slow cooker.

Choucroute Garni

Most versions of this dish, basically a peasant stew made with sauerkraut and pork, contain some type of sausage as the pork component. This simple supper will be a welcome dinner on a cold winter night. It is stick-to-your-ribs fare with a flair. Serve with stone-ground mustard and spicy applesauce.

4 medium Yukon gold potatoes, scrubbed and cut into ½-inch-thick slices

2 Granny Smith apples, peeled, cored, and cut into ½-inch-thick slices

2 large sweet onions, such as Vidalia, coarsely chopped

1½ teaspoons salt

½ teaspoon freshly ground black pepper

3 tablespoons olive oil

4 cloves garlic, sliced

2 pounds smoked sausages, cut into 1-inch rounds, or your favorite sausage (see savvy)

4 cups sauerkraut, rinsed and drained

2 tablespoons Dijon mustard

1 cup Riesling or other sweet white wine

arrange the potatoes, apples, onions, salt, pepper, oil, and garlic in the insert of a 5- to 7-quart slow cooker and toss to coat all the ingredients. Spread them in an even layer.

cover the potato mixture with the sausages and top with the sauerkraut. Mix the mustard and wine and pour over the top of the ingredients. Cover and cook on high for 4 hours or on low for 8 hours. At the end of the cooking time, make sure the potatoes are cooked through and tender.

serve each person a portion of the potato mixture, sausages, and sauerkraut, using a slotted spoon to drain off any additional liquid.

serves **8**

sausage savvy
If you would like to make this with uncooked sausages, such as bratwurst, or with pork chops, make sure to brown the meat first and then add them to the slow cooker.

Brats 'n' Beer

This is the way to get your friends' attention: throw an Oktoberfest party and serve them brats braised in your favorite local brew with onions and sauerkraut. The brats emerge from the slow cooker succulent and juicy. Serve them on rolls with the onions and sauerkraut from the cooker, along with an assortment of mustards, chunky applesauce, and more of your favorite brew.

2 tablespoons butter

2 large onions, cut into half rounds

2 teaspoons caraway seeds

¼ cup firmly packed light brown sugar

¼ cup Dijon or whole-grain mustard

32 ounces or (about 4 cups) sauerkraut, rinsed and drained

10 bratwurst

Two 12-ounce bottles dark lager or your favorite beer

melt the butter in a large skillet over medium-high heat. Add the onions and caraway seeds and sauté until the onions begin to turn golden.

add the sugar and mustard and stir to blend. Transfer the contents of the skillet to the insert of a 5- to 7-quart slow cooker. Add the remaining ingredients and stir to combine. Cover and cook on high for 4 hours or on low for 8 hours, until the brats are cooked through.

serve the brats and sauerkraut from the slow cooker.

serves **8**

Pushcart Sausage and Peppers

Walk along the streets of New York and you will smell grilled Italian sausages with onions and peppers being served at pushcarts on nearly every street corner. The cooked sausages are stuffed into rolls and covered with the onions and peppers, which have cooked down until they are almost melted. In the slow cooker, the sausage seasons the peppers and onions as they become sweet with the long, slow cooking.

2 tablespoons extra-virgin olive oil

1½ teaspoons salt

½ teaspoon freshly ground black pepper

1 tablespoon light brown sugar

2 tablespoons tomato paste

2 medium onions, cut into half rounds

3 medium red onions, cut into half rounds

2 medium red bell peppers, seeded and sliced

2 medium yellow bell peppers, seeded and sliced

2 medium orange bell peppers, seeded and sliced

3 pounds sweet Italian sausages

mix the oil, salt, pepper, sugar, and tomato paste in the insert of a 5- to 7-quart slow cooker. Add the onions and bell peppers and toss to coat.

add the sausages, cover, and cook on high for 5 hours, until the sausages are cooked through. Skim off any fat from the sauce.

serve from the slow cooker set on warm.

serves 6–8

Smoky Sausage in Barbecue Sauce

In the area around Charleston, South Carolina, barbecue shacks serve a mustard-based sauce that is delicious when paired with smoked sausages or pulled pork. Serve the sausages on rolls with plenty of cooling slaw.

2 cups yellow mustard

1 cup apple cider

¾ cup firmly packed light brown sugar

¼ cup molasses

1 tablespoon sweet paprika

1 teaspoon Worcestershire sauce

½ teaspoon cayenne pepper

½ teaspoon ground white pepper

3 pounds smoked sausages, such as kielbasa, cut into 3-inch lengths

6 to 8 hot dog rolls

mix the mustard, cider, sugar, molasses, paprika, Worcestershire, cayenne, and white pepper in the insert of a 5- to 7-quart slow cooker.

add the sausages, pushing them into the sauce, cover, and cook on high for 4 hours, until the sausages are heated through and the sauce is thickened.

serve the sausage in hot dog rolls with some of the sauce.

serves 6–8

Old-Fashioned Franks and Beans

Known as "beanie weenies" in New England, no household would go through a weekend without this dish! The franks float in the baked beans, flavoring the sauce, and the whole deal is served with plenty of steamed brown bread on the side. The cooker does a great job with baked beans. This is the recipe from my grandmother on my Irish side, hence, no basil or Parmigiano in the recipe!

2 cups small dried white beans, soaked overnight in water to cover and drained

6 strips thick-cut bacon, cut into 2-inch pieces

2 medium onions, finely chopped

1 clove garlic, minced

5 cups vegetable broth

¼ cup dark molasses

¼ cup yellow mustard

2 tablespoons light brown sugar

1 teaspoon dried thyme

¼ teaspoon ground ginger

2 teaspoons salt

1 bay leaf

12 premium all-beef hot dogs (see savvy)

add the soaked beans to the insert of a 5- to 7-quart slow cooker. Cook the bacon in a medium skillet over medium heat until it renders some fat. Add the onions and garlic and sauté until the onion is softened.

add 1 cup of the broth to the skillet and scrape up any browned bits from the bottom of the pan. Transfer the contents of the skillet to the slow-cooker insert. Add the remaining 4 cups broth and the remaining ingredients. Cover and cook on low for 10 hours, until the beans are tender.

serve the franks and beans from the cooker set on warm.

serves 6–8

slow-cooker savvy
For a variation, substitute two 1¼-pound ham steaks, cut into 6 serving pieces, for the hot dogs and proceed as directed.

Hawaiian Sausages

This is a simple dish to serve as part of a brunch, and goes together in a wink. Link sausages are cooked and glazed with pineapple, and make a nice pairing with a savory strata or frittata.

3 pounds link pork sausages

2 cups pineapple juice

3 tablespoons cornstarch

1 teaspoon curry powder

1 ripe large pineapple, peeled and cored, and cut into 1-inch chunks (about 4 cups)

sauté the sausages in a large skillet until browned on all sides. Transfer the sausages to the insert of a 5- to 7-quart slow cooker.

mix the pineapple juice, cornstarch, and curry powder in a mixing bowl, and pour into the slow-cooker insert. Add the pineapple, cover, and cook on low for 4 to 5 hours, until the sausages are cooked through and the sauce is thickened.

serve from the cooker set on warm.

serves 6–8

Ham   A fully cooked ham is a great way to serve a lot of people at once. Ham should be warmed before serving, and a glaze adds visual interest as well as a nice contrast to the smoky flavor. A large slow-cooker insert is required, and most will not hold a ham that is more than 6 inches tall.

See party in a pot (page 450) for slow cooking and glazing.

Crocked Ham and Scalloped Potatoes

One definition of "an eternity" is two people and a ham, and those words were never truer than when you are trying to find ways to recycle the leftovers. This is a very traditional recipe for scalloped ham and potatoes, but instead of cubing the ham, you cut it into matchsticks and layer it with potatoes and onions. Feel free to use your favorite cheeses in this dish. I love the nutty flavor of Gruyère, but other Swiss cheeses work well, as does Cheddar, Havarti, fontina, or provolone.

5 medium Yukon gold or red potatoes, scrubbed and cut into ¼-inch-thick slices

1 medium onion, cut into half rounds

4 tablespoons (½ stick) unsalted butter, melted

1½ teaspoons salt

1 teaspoon freshly ground black pepper

2 cups leftover ham, cut into matchsticks (about 8 slices)

2 cups heavy cream

1 cup whole milk

1 tablespoon Dijon mustard

2 cups finely shredded Gruyère cheese

½ cup grated Parmigiano-Reggiano cheese

coat the insert of a 5- to 7-quart slow cooker with nonstick cooking spray or line it with a slow-cooker liner according to the manufacturer's directions.

combine the potatoes, onion, butter, salt, and pepper in a mixing bowl. Arrange a layer of the potato mixture in the bottom of the slow cooker and top with a layer of ham. Repeat the layers, ending with potatoes. (You should have 3 layers of potatoes.) Whisk the cream, milk, and mustard together and pour over the potatoes. Sprinkle evenly with the cheeses.

cover and cook on low for 5 hours, until the potatoes are tender. Remove the cover and cook for an additional 30 to 45 minutes.

serve the potatoes from the cooker set on warm.

serves 6–8

Barbecue-Style Ham Loaf

Ham loaf, a staple of the 1950s, makes a comeback in the slow cooker, but this time with a South Carolina mustard-based barbecue sauce that gives it a lot of personality. The smoky thyme-flavored loaf is terrific sliced and served with slaw or fruit salad. Any leftovers make terrific sandwiches for lunches later. This is a great way to use up leftover ham, and you can freeze the loaf for up to 6 weeks after it is cooked.

SOUTH CAROLINA BARBECUE SAUCE

2 tablespoons vegetable oil

1 cup finely chopped onion

1 teaspoon dried thyme leaves

Pinch of red pepper flakes or cayenne pepper

1 cup ketchup

½ cup chicken broth

½ cup whole-grain mustard

½ cup firmly packed light brown sugar

HAM LOAF

2 slices sturdy white bread, such as Pepperidge Farm, torn into pieces

¼ cup milk

2 cups ground smoked ham (about 12 to 16 ounces)

12 ounces lean ground pork

¼ cup finely chopped shallots

1 teaspoon dried thyme leaves

2 large eggs, beaten

¼ cup ketchup

1 tablespoon whole-grain or Creole mustard

preheat a 5- to 7-quart slow cooker, with the insert uncovered, on high for 20 minutes. Add the oil, onion, thyme, and red pepper flakes and stir until the onion is coated with the oil.

stir in the ketchup, broth, mustard, and sugar. Cover and cook on high while assembling the ham loaf.

soak the bread in the milk in a large bowl until the milk is absorbed. Add the ham, pork, shallots, thyme, eggs, ketchup, and mustard and stir until blended.

wet your hands with warm water and shape the loaf into a rectangle that is about 2½ to 3 inches tall and wide, so that it will fit into the slow cooker with space around the sides.

place the loaf on top of the sauce in the slow cooker and spoon some of the sauce over the top. Cover and cook on high for 3 hours or on low for 6 hours, until the internal temperature registers 165°F on an instant-read thermometer.

transfer the loaf, using two wide spatulas, from the slow cooker to a cutting board. Cover loosely with aluminum foil and allow to rest for 10 minutes. Skim off any fat from the top of the sauce.

slice the loaf and serve with the sauce on the side.

serves **6**

Chapter 7
Ewe'll Love This!

Lamb sold in the United States is either imported from New Zealand or Australia or farm raised in the States. Both types are fine, but the most widely available is the farm raised. Most markets carry "choice" grade lamb, which is well marbled and tender and the best buy pound for pound.

Slow-cooked lamb is tender and falling-apart delicious. Whether it's a leg of lamb, lamb shanks, or lamb shoulder for stew, lamb makes a great dinner in the slow cooker. Less-expensive shoulder meat and blade chops are transformed into delicious dinners with herbs, spices, and wine added to help flavor the meat. Lamb meat loaf is also terrific slow cooked and served with a complimentary sauce. Lamb curries and tagines cook to perfection in the slow cooker; all you need to add is steamed rice or couscous.

···

LEG
Leg of Lamb Stuffed with Mint Pesto, 289

Zinfandel-Braised Leg of Lamb, 290

Lamb Tex-Mex–Style with Pinto Beans, 291

Lemon Dijon Leg of Lamb, 292

SHANKS
Lamb Shanks Braised Osso Bucco–Style, 294

Lamb Shanks Braised in Ale, 295

Lamb Cassoulet with White Beans and Rosemary, 296

SHOULDER
Lamb Curry, 298

Lamb Tagine, 299

Braised Lamb with Eggplant, Tomatoes, and Feta, 300

Mediterranean Lamb with Green Beans, Potatoes, and Mint, 301

North African Lamb with Lemon and Artichokes, 302

Lentils and Lamb, Mediterranean-Style, 303

Tandoori-Style Lamb, 304

Cottage Pie, 305

Dubliner Stew, 306

GROUND LAMB
Curried Lamb Meatballs, 308

Mediterranean Gyros-Style Meatballs, 309

···

Leg Boneless leg of lamb becomes moist and delicious after a long braise in the slow cooker. I like to stuff a leg of lamb with savory stuffing and braise it in an aromatic liquid so the meat is flavorful all the way through. Marinating the lamb first helps ramp up the flavor as well as tenderize the meat. For slow-cooker preparations, a boneless leg of lamb is a must, since a bone-in leg of lamb will not fit into even the largest slow cooker.

Leg of Lamb Stuffed with Mint Pesto

Remembering my father's fondness for leg of lamb and the goopy mint jelly he had to have with it, I thought I might honor the pairing but update the presentation. This leg of lamb is slathered inside with a garlicky mint pesto (see savvy) and then braised in a delicious wine sauce. The result is a tender roast with a surprising swirl of bright green pesto in the center.

MINT PESTO

1 cup packed fresh mint leaves

4 cloves garlic

1 tablespoon rice vinegar or white vinegar

¼ cup olive oil

6 or 7 leaves fresh oregano

1 teaspoon salt

⅛ teaspoon cayenne pepper

2 large onions, cut into half rounds

1 cup dry white wine

1 cup beef broth

One 3- to 4-pound leg of lamb, boned and butterflied

put all the pesto ingredients in a food processor or blender and process until the ingredients are a paste. Cover and refrigerate for up to 4 days.

spread the onions over the bottom of the insert of a 5- to 7-quart slow cooker. Pour in the wine and beef broth. Lay the lamb, fat-side down, boned-side up on a cutting board or flat surface and spread all the pesto over the surface of the lamb.

roll up the meat, starting from the short end, and tie with kitchen string or silicone loops. Arrange on top of the onions in the slow-cooker insert. Cover and cook on low for 8 to 10 hours, until the lamb is tender. Remove the lamb from the slow-cooker insert, cover with aluminum foil, and allow to rest for 20 minutes.

strain the sauce through a fine-mesh sieve into a saucepan and remove any fat from the surface. Boil the sauce until it is reduced by about one quarter, 10 to 15 minutes.

remove the strings from the lamb, cut into ½-inch-thick slices, and serve with the sauce on the side.

serves **8**

pesto savvy
Not the traditional pesto alla Genovese, with its garlic, pine nuts, and Parmesan, this pesto is made with fresh mint, oregano, and garlic. The herb paste not only flavors the meat but also seeps into the sauce.

Zinfandel-Braised Leg of Lamb

This leg of lamb is almost too simple to include, but sometimes the simplest preparations deliver the most extraordinary results. Marinate the lamb overnight in a Zinfandel marinade, then pour everything into the cooker and fire it up! The meat is infused with the flavor of the wine, garlic, and herbs, and the marinade cooks down into a delicious sauce (see savvy) to serve over the meat at the end.

One 3- to 4-pound boneless leg of lamb, butterflied

4 cups Zinfandel wine

¼ cup olive oil

6 cloves garlic, sliced

1 tablespoon finely chopped fresh rosemary

¼ cup honey

1 teaspoon salt

½ teaspoon freshly ground black pepper

2 bay leaves

put the lamb in a zipper-top plastic bag. Whisk the remaining ingredients together in a mixing bowl and pour over the lamb in the bag. Seal the bag and refrigerate for at least 8 hours or up to 24 hours.

put the marinade in the insert of a 5- to 7-quart slow cooker and tie the lamb at 1-inch intervals with kitchen string or silicone loops. Cover and cook on high for 3 to 4 hours, until the meat is tender.

carefully remove the meat from the slow cooker, cover with aluminum foil, and allow to rest for 20 minutes. Strain the sauce through a fine-mesh sieve into a saucepan and remove any fat from the surface. Boil the sauce until reduced by half.

slice the meat and serve with the sauce napped over the lamb.

serves **8**

saucing savvy
If you would like to thicken this sauce, it does well with buerre maine, 1 part unsalted butter and 1 part flour kneaded together and whisked into the boiling liquid.

Lamb Tex-Mex–Style with Pinto Beans

Straight from the Lone Star state, this dish is hearty stick-to-your-ribs fare. I prefer to cut up the leg of lamb, rather than cook it whole with the beans, because the lamb falls apart and mingles with the beans creating lamb-and-bean stew. This makes a terrific supper to serve at a make-your-own-burrito bar with tortillas, shredded cheeses, pico de gallo, and sour cream.

2 cups pinto beans, soaked overnight in water to cover and drained

¼ cup olive oil

3 pounds leg of lamb, cut into 1-inch chunks

½ teaspoon chili powder

2 medium onions, coarsely chopped

2 Anaheim chiles, seeded and coarsely chopped

1 teaspoon ground cumin

½ teaspoon dried oregano

One 14- to 15-ounce can chopped tomatoes, with their juice

1½ cups beef broth

put the beans in the bottom of the insert of a 5- to 7-quart slow cooker. Heat the oil in a large skillet over medium-high heat.

sprinkle the meat with the chili powder. Add the meat a few pieces at a time to the skillet and brown on all sides. Transfer the browned meat to the slow-cooker insert. Add the onions, chiles, cumin, and oregano to the same skillet and cook until the onions are softened, about 5 minutes.

add the tomatoes to the skillet and heat, stirring up any browned bits from the bottom of the pan.

transfer the contents of the skillet to the cooker and stir in the broth. Cover and cook on low for 8 to 10 hours, until the meat and beans are tender.

remove any fat from the top of the stew and serve from the cooker set on warm.

serves **8**

Lemon Dijon Leg of Lamb

Tangy Dijon mustard, lemon, oregano, and garlic all contribute to the flavor of this delicious leg of lamb. It is perfect paired with orzo and grilled vegetables.

½ cup Dijon mustard

¼ cup fresh lemon juice

Grated zest of 2 lemons

6 garlic cloves, minced

¼ cup extra-virgin olive oil

1 teaspoon dried oregano

1 teaspoon salt

½ teaspoon freshly ground black pepper

One 3- to 4-pound boneless leg of lamb, butterflied, fat trimmed

1 cup dry white wine

½ cup finely chopped fresh Italian parsley

combine the mustard, lemon juice, zest, garlic, oil, oregano, salt, and pepper in a mixing bowl. Pour the marinade into a zipper-top plastic bag, add the lamb to the bag, and turn it to coat. Seal the bag and refrigerate for at least 8 hours or up to 24 hours.

drain the marinade, and roll the meat into a compact cylinder, tying the meat at 1-inch intervals with kitchen string or silicone loops, and put the lamb in insert of a 5- to 7-quart slow cooker. Add the wine. Cover and cook on high for 3 to 4 hours, until the meat is tender. Remove the meat from the slow cooker, cover with aluminum foil, and allow to rest for 20 minutes.

strain the sauce through a fine-mesh sieve into a saucepan and remove any fat from the surface. Boil until the sauce is reduced by half. Taste and adjust the seasonings, adding the parsley to the sauce.

cut the meat into ½-inch-thick slices and serve with the sauce on the side.

serves **8**

Shanks

Perfect for long braises, lamb shanks make delicious stews because the bones contribute flavor and the meat falls into the rich sauce. Lamb shoulder can be substituted for the shanks in any of these recipes; you will need ten to twelve ounces boneless shoulder to replace each lamb shank.

Lamb Shanks Braised Osso Bucco–Style

Lamb shanks are some of the best eating in the world, but most people walk right by them at the butchers. The meat becomes fall-apart tender after a long braise in the slow cooker. The shank bones flavor the sauce when cooked in the same style as osso bucco, with tomato, vegetables, wine, garlic, and citrus zest to brighten the stew. Serve the lamb shanks with pappardelle or other wide flat noodles to soak up the sauce.

6 meaty lamb shanks (about 1 pound each), fat trimmed

2 teaspoons salt

1 teaspoon freshly ground black pepper

2 tablespoons olive oil

1 medium onion, finely chopped

3 medium carrots, finely chopped

3 cloves garlic, minced

Grated zest of 2 lemons

Grated zest of 1 orange

⅔ cup full-bodied red wine

One 18-ounce can tomato purée

1 cup beef broth

½ cup chicken broth

½ cup finely chopped fresh Italian parsley

2 tablespoons unsalted butter, at room temperature

2 tablespoons all-purpose flour

sprinkle the lamb shanks evenly with the salt and pepper. Heat the oil in a large skillet over high heat. Add as many lamb shanks as will fit in a single layer and brown on all sides. Transfer the browned shanks to the insert of a 5- to 7-quart slow cooker. Brown any remaining shanks and transfer them to slow-cooker insert.

add the onion, carrots, garlic, and citrus zests to the same skillet and sauté until the onion begins to soften. Add the wine and heat, scraping up any browned bits from the bottom of the pan.

transfer the contents of the skillet to the slow-cooker insert. Stir in the tomato purée and both broths. Cover and cook for 6 hours on low. Remove the shanks from the cooker and cover with aluminum foil to keep warm. Pour the sauce into a saucepan and boil for 10 to 15 minutes, until the sauce has reduced a bit. Add the parsley to the sauce.

mix the butter and flour until smooth in a small bowl and whisk, a bit at a time, into the sauce, bringing it back to a boil after each addition. Taste and adjust the seasoning.

return the sauce and the shanks to the slow cooker and keep warm until ready to serve.

serves **6**

Lamb Shanks Braised in Ale

Lamb shanks take on a sweet flavor when braised in Guinness with carrots, parsnips, and onions. The resulting stew is a terrific dish to serve on a cold winter's night with plenty of mashed potatoes to soak up the hearty sauce.

½ cup all-purpose flour

1½ teaspoons salt

½ teaspoon freshly ground black pepper

6 meaty lamb shanks, fat trimmed (lamb shanks range in size from 12 to 16 ounces, depending on the size of the bone)

¼ cup olive oil

3 large onions, cut into half rounds

One 12-ounce bottle Guinness or other dark ale

4 medium carrots, cut into 1-inch lengths

4 medium parsnips, cut into 1-inch lengths

2 tablespoons tomato paste

½ cup beef broth

mix the flour, salt, and pepper in a large zipper-top plastic bag. Add the meat, toss to coat, and shake off any excess flour. Heat the oil in a large skillet over high heat. Add the meat a few pieces at a time and brown on all sides. Transfer the browned meat to the insert of a 5- to 7-quart slow cooker.

add the onions to the same skillet and sauté until they begin to soften and turn translucent, 4 to 5 minutes. Pour in the Guinness and scrape up any browned bits from the bottom of the pan.

transfer the contents of the skillet to the slow-cooker insert, add the carrots and parsnips, and stir to distribute evenly. Stir the tomato paste into the broth and pour into the insert. Cover and cook on low for 10 to 12 hours, until the meat is tender. Skim off any fat from the top of the sauce.

serve the lamb directly from the cooker set on warm.

serves **6**

Lamb Cassoulet with White Beans and Rosemary

Lamb in rosemary-scented stew, thickened with white beans, makes a hearty dish to feed and soothe the hungry on a cold winters' night. Cassoulet, made with duck and sometimes pork, is found on bistro menus throughout France, but lamb and rosemary are a classic combination that also pair well with the creamy beans.

1 pound dried white beans (in France they use the larger white beans), soaked in water to cover overnight and drained

½ cup extra-virgin olive oil

6 meaty lamb shanks, fat trimmed

1½ teaspoons salt

½ teaspoon freshly ground black pepper

3 medium onions, coarsely chopped

4 cloves garlic, minced

4 medium carrots, coarsely chopped

4 stalks celery, coarsely chopped

1 tablespoon fresh rosemary leaves, finely chopped

One 28- to 32-ounce can crushed tomatoes, with their juice

5 cups chicken broth

3 cups beef broth

1 bay leaf

TOPPING

1½ cups fresh bread crumbs

½ cup freshly grated Parmigiano-Reggiano cheese

4 cloves garlic, minced

½ cup finely chopped fresh Italian parsley

place the beans in the insert of a 5- to 7-quart slow cooker. Heat the oil in a large skillet over medium-high heat. Sprinkle the meat evenly with the salt and pepper. Add as many lamb shanks as will fit in a single layer and brown on all sides. Transfer the browned shanks to the slow-cooker insert. Brown any remaining shanks and transfer them to the slow-cooker insert.

add the onions, garlic, carrots, celery, and rosemary to the same skillet and sauté until the vegetables are softened, 5 to 7 minutes. Add the tomatoes and 1 cup of the chicken broth to the skillet and heat, scraping up any browned bits from the bottom of the pan. Transfer the tomato mixture to the slow-cooker insert and stir in the remaining broths, and the bay leaf. Cover and cook on high for 6 to 8 hours or low for 10 to 12 hours, until the beans and lamb are tender.

combine all the ingredients for the topping in a small bowl while the lamb is cooking,. Cover and refrigerate.

uncover the cooker and spoon off any fat on the surface. Taste and adjust with the seasoning. Sprinkle the topping over the cassoulet, cover, and cook on high another 30 minutes.

serve the cassoulet from the cooker set on warm.

serves **6**

Shoulder

Lamb shoulder, cut from the foreleg, is generally tough and needs to braise in liquid to become rich and tender. Shoulder meat and blade-cut chops are great choices for the slow cooker. The lamb melts into the sauce as it cooks and becomes flavorful and tender. Lamb shoulder is generally inexpensive, and the rewards from the slow cooker are delicious curries, Mediterranean stews, Moroccan tagines, and, that old English favorite, cottage pie.

Lamb Curry

Fragrant lamb becomes succulent in this coconut milk–and-curry-flavored sauce. With potatoes and green beans cooking along with the lamb, this dish makes a terrific one-pot meal. Serve this slow-cooked meal with flatbread (see savvy) and condiments on the side. If you would prefer, beef may be used instead of lamb.

4 tablespoons olive oil

3 pounds lamb shoulder meat, fat trimmed, cut into 2-inch cubes

1½ teaspoons salt

½ teaspoon freshly ground black pepper

2 medium onions, coarsely chopped

4 garlic cloves, minced

2 tablespoons grated fresh ginger

2 tablespoons sweet curry powder

Pinch of red pepper flakes

One 14-ounce can coconut milk

One 15-ounce can diced tomatoes, drained

1 cup chicken broth

8 medium Yukon gold potatoes, quartered

8 ounces green beans, ends snipped and cut into 1-inch pieces

2 bay leaves

CONDIMENTS

Major Grey's chutney

Chopped green onions

Raisins (dark or golden)

Toasted unsweetened coconut

Chopped roasted peanuts or cashews

Dried banana chips

Lime pickle

heat 2 tablespoons of the oil in a large skillet over high heat. Sprinkle the meat evenly with the salt and pepper. Add the meat to the skillet and brown on all sides. Transfer the meat to the insert of a 5- to 7-quart slow cooker.

add the remaining 2 tablespoons oil to the same skillet and heat over medium-high heat. Add the onions, garlic, ginger, curry powder, and red pepper flakes and sauté to release the oils in the spices and to soften the onions, 2 to 3 minutes. Add the coconut milk to the skillet and heat, scraping up any browned bits from the bottom of the pan.

transfer the contents of the skillet to the slow-cooker insert and stir in the tomatoes, broth, potatoes, beans, and bay leaves. Cover and cook on low for 6 to 8 hours, until the lamb is tender. Remove any fat from the top of the sauce, discard the bay leaves.

serve the lamb with the condiments.

serves **8**

flatbread savvy
Traditional Naan flatbreads are sold in stores such as Whole Foods and Trader Joes, or in ethnic markets. Pita may be used as a substitute if Naan isn't available.

Lamb Tagine

A *tagine* is both a vessel and a method of preparation for Moroccan dishes. A tagine slow cooks meats and poultry until they are tender and fragrant with the flavors of the Kasbah. The slow cooker will give you the same delicious results without having to watch a pot on the stovetop.

½ cup all-purpose flour

1 teaspoon salt

½ teaspoon freshly ground black pepper

3 pounds lamb shoulder meat, fat trimmed, cut into 1-inch pieces

½ cup olive oil

3 large onions, coarsely chopped

2 cloves garlic, chopped

1 teaspoon ground cumin

½ teaspoon ground cinnamon

½ teaspoon ground ginger

Pinch of saffron threads

1 cup chicken broth

1 cup beef broth

1 cup pitted dates, quartered

¼ cup finely chopped fresh cilantro

mix the flour, salt, and pepper in a large zipper-top plastic bag. Add the meat, toss to coat, and shake off any excess flour. Heat ¼ cup of the oil in a large skillet over high heat.

add the meat a few pieces at a time and brown on all sides. Transfer the browned meat to the insert of a 5- to 7-quart slow cooker. Add the remaining oil to the same skillet and heat over medium-high heat. Add the onions, garlic, cumin, cinnamon, ginger, and saffron and sauté until the onions begin to soften, about 5 minutes.

pour the chicken broth into the skillet and heat, scraping up any browned bits from the bottom of the pan.

transfer the contents of the skillet to the slow cooker and stir in the beef broth and dates. Cover and cook on low for 6 to 7 hours, until the lamb is tender. Skim off any fat from the top of the sauce and stir in the cilantro.

serve from the cooker set on warm.

serves **8**

Braised Lamb with Eggplant, Tomatoes, and Feta

This boldly flavored lamb and eggplant stew, redolent with garlic, tomato, and oregano and finished with salty feta cheese, makes a terrific dish to serve to guests. You can serve it right from the slow cooker, and accompany it with orzo and a salad.

¼ cup extra-virgin olive oil

3 pounds lamb shoulder, fat trimmed, cut into 1-inch chunks

1½ teaspoons salt

½ teaspoon freshly ground black pepper

2 large onions, coarsely chopped

4 cloves garlic, sliced

4 Japanese eggplants (about 1 pound), cut into ½-inch cubes (see savvy)

1 teaspoon dried oregano

½ cup dry white wine or vermouth

One 28- to 32-ounce can chopped tomatoes, with their juice

½ cup finely chopped fresh Italian parsley

1 cup crumbled feta cheese for garnishing

heat the oil in a large skillet over medium-high heat. Sprinkle the lamb evenly with the salt and pepper, add a few pieces at a time to the skillet, and brown on all sides. Transfer the browned meat to the insert of a 5- to 7-quart slow cooker.

add the onions, garlic, eggplants, and oregano to the skillet and sauté until the onions begin to soften and turn translucent, 5 to 7 minutes. Add the wine to the skillet and heat, scraping the browned bits from the bottom of the pan. Transfer the contents of the skillet to the slow-cooker insert and stir in the tomatoes.

cover and cook on high 3 to 4 hours or low for 7 to 8 hours. Skim off any fat from the top of the stew and stir in the parsley. Keep the stew in the cooker set on warm until ready to serve.

garnish each serving with a sprinkling of feta.

serves **8**

eggplant savvy
Japanese eggplants are small and do not require salting, peeling, and draining before going into the pot. If you cannot find them, 1 medium purple eggplant may be substituted. Peel a large eggplant, cut it into cubes, toss with 2 teaspoons salt in a colander, and let drain for 20 minutes. Press the cubes between paper towels to remove excess water.

Mediterranean Lamb with Green Beans, Potatoes, and Mint

In this terrific one-pot meal, the lamb melts into fork-tender chunks seasoned with tomato and mint, along with green beans, and garlicky potatoes. Serve this with a green salad for a memorable weeknight meal or casual weekend dinner.

½ cup extra-virgin olive oil

2 to 2½ pounds small Yukon gold potatoes, cut in half

1 pound green beans, ends snipped, cut into 1-inch lengths

6 cloves garlic, sliced

2 teaspoons salt

1 teaspoon freshly ground black pepper

2½ pounds lamb shoulder, fat trimmed, cut into 1-inch chunks

1 medium onion, finely chopped

¼ cup dry white wine or vermouth

¼ cup tomato paste

½ cup chicken broth

3 tablespoons finely chopped fresh mint

toss together ¼ cup of the oil, the potatoes, green beans, garlic, 1 teaspoon of the salt, and ½ teaspoon of the pepper in the insert of a 5- to 7-quart slow cooker. Sprinkle the lamb with the remaining salt and pepper.

heat the remaining oil in a large skillet over high heat. Add the meat and brown on all sides. Transfer the browned meat to the slow-cooker insert. Add the onion to the same skillet and sauté until it is softened and beginning to turn translucent, about 4 minutes. Add the wine, tomato paste, and broth to the skillet and heat, scraping up any of the browned bits from the bottom of the pan.

transfer the contents of the skillet to the slow cooker. Don't stir up the vegetables on the bottom; just pour the liquids in and add the mint. Cover and cook on high for 4 to 5 hours or low for 8 to 10 hours, until the potatoes are tender and the meat is fork tender.

skim off any fat from the top of the stew. Using a slotted spoon, transfer the meat and vegetables to a serving bowl, then spoon the sauce over the top.

serves **8**

North African Lamb with Lemon and Artichokes

Braised with piquant lemon zest, spices from the Kasbah, and artichokes, this stew is nothing like your mama's. If you are looking for a new dish to serve your guests, this one is sure to please with its lovely wine-and-lemon sauce. Serve with couscous or steamed rice.

½ cup olive oil

1½ teaspoons salt

1 teaspoon ground cumin

Pinch of cayenne pepper

1 teaspoon sweet paprika

3 pounds lamb shoulder meat, fat trimmed, cut into 1-inch chunks

4 leeks, cut into ½-inch pieces, using the white and tender green parts

4 garlic cloves, minced

1 cup dry white wine

½ cup chicken broth

Grated zest of 2 lemons

One 16-ounce package frozen artichoke hearts, defrosted and drained

mix ¼ cup of the oil, the salt, cumin, cayenne, and paprika in a large bowl. Add the meat and toss to coat with the spice mixture. Heat the remaining oil in a large skillet over medium-high heat. Add the meat a few pieces at a time and brown on all sides. Transfer the browned meat to the insert of a 5- to 7-quart slow cooker.

add the leeks and garlic to the same skillet and sauté until the leeks are softened, 3 to 4 minutes. Add the wine, broth, and zest and heat, scraping up any browned bits from the bottom of the pan.

pour the contents of the skillet over the lamb and add the artichokes, stirring to distribute the ingredients in the pot. Cover and cook on low for 8 hours, until the lamb is tender.

using a slotted spoon, carefully transfer the lamb and artichokes to a serving bowl. Strain the sauce through a fine-mesh sieve into a saucepan. Skim off any fat from the top and bring to a boil. Boil until the sauce is reduced to about 1½ cups to concentrate the flavor. Taste and adjust the seasoning.

spoon the sauce over the lamb and artichokes and serve.

serves 6–8

Lentils and Lamb, Mediterranean-Style

Stretching the protein in your slow-cooker dishes not only saves you money but also introduces legumes into your family's diet. In this dish, which is served frequently in French bistros, lentils pair well with lamb and help thicken the thyme-flavored sauce.

¼ cup extra-virgin olive oil

2 pounds lamb shoulder meat, fat trimmed, cut into 1-inch chunks

1½ teaspoons salt

½ teaspoon freshly ground black pepper

2 medium onions, coarsely chopped

3 medium carrots, cut into 1-inch lengths

3 stalks celery, coarsely chopped

2 teaspoons dried thyme

One 14- to 15-ounce can crushed tomatoes, with their juice

1 cup green lentils (see savvy)

2 cups chicken broth

heat the oil in a large skillet over medium-high heat. Sprinkle the lamb evenly with the salt and pepper. Add the meat a few pieces at a time to the skillet and brown on all sides. Transfer the meat to the insert of a 5- to 7-quart slow cooker.

add the onions, carrots, celery, and thyme to the same skillet and sauté until the vegetables begin to soften and the onions begin to turn translucent. Add the tomatoes and heat, scraping up any browned bits from the bottom of the pan.

transfer the contents of the skillet to the slow-cooker insert and stir in the lentils and chicken broth. Cover and cook on low for 8 to 10 hours, until the meat and lentils are tender. Skim any fat from the top of the stew.

serve from the cooker set on warm.

serves **6–8**

lentil savvy
If you can only find brown lentils, increase the broth to 3 cups and add about 40 minutes to the cooking time.

Tandoori-Style Lamb

A *tandoor* is an oven used in India. Meat for the tandoor is usually marinated in spices and yogurt and then roasted with very high heat. Although the slow cooker doesn't roast at a high temperature, it can deliver the flavor and tenderness of tandoori with its long, slow, moist cooking. Tandoori seasonings, such as ginger, garlic, coriander, cumin, and garam masala, can all be found in your supermarket, and there are now tandoori spice blends that you can purchase. This same recipe will work as well for boneless skinless chicken thighs.

1½ cups plain yogurt (see savvy)

2 tablespoons fresh lemon juice

4 cloves garlic, minced

1½ teaspoons ground cumin

1½ teaspoons garam masala

1 teaspoon ground coriander

Pinch of cayenne pepper

1 teaspoon salt

3 pounds lamb shoulder, fat trimmed, cut into 1-inch chunks

4 medium Yukon gold potatoes, cut into quarters

3 medium carrots, cut into 1-inch lengths

½ cup chicken broth

whisk together the yogurt, lemon juice, garlic, and spices in a large bowl. Add the lamb and toss to coat well with the marinade. Cover and refrigerate for at least 2 hours or overnight.

drain the marinade and add the lamb to the insert of a 5- to 7-quart slow cooker. Add the vegetables and broth and stir to combine. Cover and cook on high for 3 hours, until the lamb is tender and the vegetables are cooked through. Skim off any fat from the top of the sauce.

serve from the cooker set on warm.

serves **8**

yogurt savvy
Full-fat yogurt is used in this dish because the nonfat variety will separate and leave you with too much liquid in the cooker. If you strain nonfat yogurt through cheesecloth or a coffee filter to eliminate the water, it's perfectly fine to use after discarding the liquid.

Cottage Pie

Lidgate, a butcher shop in London's Holland Park area, sells cottage pie to bake at home, and it is divine. My daughter lived around the corner from this wonderful store, and we frequently bought meats there for dinner when I visited. But on nights when we didn't feel like cooking, the cottage pie would soothe us after a long day on the go. Cottage pie should consist of lamb and vegetables in a rich sauce, covered by rich mashed potatoes. The whole shebang cooks in the slow cooker, which will keep it warm until you are ready to serve it.

1 cup all-purpose flour

1 ½ teaspoons salt

½ teaspoon freshly ground black pepper

2½ to 3 pounds lamb shoulder, fat trimmed, cut into ½-inch chunks

2 tablespoons olive oil

1 medium onion, finely chopped

1½ teaspoons dried thyme

1 cup chicken broth

½ cup beef broth

3 medium carrots, cut into ½-inch dice

1 cup frozen petite size peas, defrosted

1½ cups frozen white corn, defrosted

Mashed Potatoes for Stews or Pot Pies (page 195)

2 tablespoons unsalted butter, at room temperature

mix the flour, salt, and pepper in a large zipper-top plastic bag. Add the lamb, toss to coat, and shake off the excess flour. Heat the oil in a large skillet over high heat. Add the lamb a few pieces at a time and brown on all sides. Transfer the browned meat to the insert of a 5- to 7-quart slow cooker.

add the onion and thyme to the skillet and sauté until the onion is softened, 2 to 3 minutes. Pour in both broths and heat, scraping up any browned bits from the bottom of the pan. Pour the contents of the skillet over the lamb. Cover and cook for 3 hours on high, until the meat is tender. Add the vegetables to the stew and stir to combine.

cover the stew with the mashed potatoes, being careful not to push the potatoes into the stew. Dot the top of the potatoes with the butter. Cover and cook for another 1 hour, until the butter is melted.

scoop servings of the stew covered with mashed potatoes onto each plate.

serves 8

Dubliner Stew

Ireland is famous for their lamb stews, and this one is traditional home cooking—just meat, vegetables (potatoes, of course!), and a delicious slow-simmering sauce. Serve this with Irish soda bread to sop up the wonderful sauce, or hollow out small round loaves of bread and serve the stew in the bread bowls.

12 to 14 baby carrots

14 to 16 tiny new or white creamer potatoes

¼ cup olive oil

3 pounds lamb shoulder meat, fat trimmed, cut into 1-inch chunks

1½ teaspoons salt

½ teaspoon freshly ground black pepper

2 cups pearl onions, peeled

1½ cups chicken broth

1 cup beef broth

1 teaspoon dried thyme

2 cups petite frozen peas, defrosted

2 tablespoons unsalted butter, at room temperature

2 tablespoons all-purpose flour

arrange the carrots and potatoes in the insert of a 5- to 7-quart slow cooker. Heat the oil in a large skillet over medium-high heat. Sprinkle the meat evenly with the salt and pepper. Add the meat a few pieces at a time to the skillet and brown on all sides. Transfer the meat to the slow-cooker insert.

add the onions to the same skillet and cook until the onions begin to color a bit, about 4 minutes. Add the chicken broth to the skillet and heat, scraping up any browned bits from the bottom of the pan. Transfer the contents of the skillet to the slow-cooker insert and stir in the beef broth and thyme. Cover and cook on on high for 3½ to 4 hours or low for 7 to 8 hours.

skim off any fat from the top of the stew. Stir the peas into the stew. Mix the butter and flour until smooth and stir a bit at a time into the stew as well. Cover and cook for another 30 minutes on high until the sauce is thickened.

serve the stew from the cooker set on warm.

serves **6–8**

Ground Lamb

Ground lamb isn't found as often as ground beef or pork in the supermarket, but it makes some terrific meatballs or meat loaf for dinner in the slow cooker. Think about using lamb for meatballs at your next party because they are flavorful and tender when cooked in their sauce in the slow cooker. All the meatball mixtures in the recipes that follow can also be shaped into a meat loaf; cook on low for five hours until the internal temperature is 185°F.

Curried Lamb Meatballs

Called *koftas* in India, these delicious meatballs are full of flavor from the usual suspects: garlic, ginger, coriander, cumin, and garam masala. Cooked in a spicy tomato sauce, they are soft and flavored with the cooking liquid. I like to serve these as an appetizer for parties because they tend to wake up my guests. But they are also a delicious main dish served over steamed rice.

SAUCE

2 tablespoons vegetable oil

2 medium onions, finely chopped

2 cloves garlic, minced

1 teaspoon grated fresh ginger

1 teaspoon sweet curry powder

Pinch of cayenne pepper

One 28- to 32-ounce can tomato purée

½ cup chicken broth

MEATBALLS

2 pounds ground lamb

½ cup finely chopped onion

½ teaspoon grated fresh ginger

1 clove garlic, minced

½ teaspoon ground coriander

¼ teaspoon ground cumin

½ teaspoon garam masala

½ teaspoon salt

½ cup soft fresh bread crumbs

½ cup chopped fresh cilantro

heat the oil in a skillet over medium-high heat. Add the onions, garlic, ginger, curry powder, and cayenne and sauté for 2 minutes, until the mixture is fragrant.

add the tomatoes and broth and heat, scraping up any of the spices that have stuck to the bottom of the pan.

transfer the sauce to the insert of a 5- to 7-quart slow cooker and keep warm while making the meatballs.

combine all the meatball ingredients except the cilantro in a large mixing bowl and mix until well blended. Shape into 2-inch meatballs and drop into the sauce in the slow cooker.

cover and cook on high for 3 to 4 hours or on low for 6 to 8 hours, until the meatballs are cooked through. Skim off any fat from the sauce and stir in the cilantro.

serve the meatballs with skewers from the cooker set on warm.

serves **6–8**

Mediterranean Gyros-Style Meatballs

Gyros are made from highly seasoned lamb and beef, spit roasted so the outside is crispy and the inside is juicy. Thinly sliced and packed into pita bread with cucumber yogurt sauce, tomatoes, and lettuce, the meat makes a delicious sandwich. Instead of spit roasting lamb, however, we'll form the meat into balls and cook them in a red wine sauce. These meatballs are highly spiced with garlic, lemon zest, onion, and oregano and are terrific served over pasta or stuffed into pita with salad. Or, they can be served with skewers from the slow cooker for a party.

SAUCE

2 tablespoons extra-virgin olive oil

½ cup finely chopped onion

2 tablespoons all-purpose flour

2 cups red wine, such as Chianti, Barolo, or Zinfandel

1 cup beef broth

1 cup chicken broth

MEATBALLS

1 pound lean ground lamb

1 pound lean ground beef

3 cloves garlic, minced

1 cup finely chopped yellow onion

2 teaspoons dried oregano

1 teaspoon dried rosemary, crushed in the palm of your hand

2 slices bread, crusts removed, torn into pieces

¼ cup milk

2 teaspoons salt

1 teaspoon freshly ground black pepper

Grated zest of 1 lemon

½ cup finely chopped fresh parsley

heat the oil in a saucepan over medium-high heat. Add the onion and sauté for 3 minutes, until softened.

stir in the flour and cook, stirring, for 3 minutes. Add the wine and whisk until the mixture boils. Transfer to the insert of a 5- to 7-quart slow cooker and stir in the broths.

cover and keep warm while making the meatballs.

combine all the meatball ingredients except the parsley in a largemixing bowl and mix until well blended. Shape into 2-inch balls and carefully place in the sauce.

cover and cook on high for 3 to 4 hours or on low for 6 to 8 hours, until the meatballs are cooked through. Skim off any fat from the top of the sauce and stir in the parsley.

serve from the cooker set on warm.

serves **6–8**

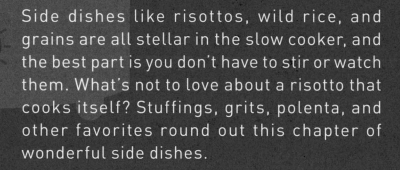

Chapter 8
On the Side

Side dishes like risottos, wild rice, and grains are all stellar in the slow cooker, and the best part is you don't have to stir or watch them. What's not to love about a risotto that cooks itself? Stuffings, grits, polenta, and other favorites round out this chapter of wonderful side dishes.

Saffron Rice

I've always been partial to the flavor of saffron, which is a spice from the stigma of the crocus plant. It takes a lot of these to make an ounce of saffron, but the flavor is sublime and it colors rice (and risotto) a bright yellow. Buy your saffron from Penzey's or a local gourmet retailer because what you get in your supermarket is typically an inferior product.

½ cup (1 stick) unsalted butter

½ cup finely chopped shallots

About 1 teaspoon saffron threads, crushed in the palm of your hand

3 cups converted white rice

4½ to 5½ cups chicken broth (see savvy)

2 cups frozen petite peas, defrosted

spray the insert of a 5- to 7-quart slow cooker with nonstick cooking spray or line it with a slow-cooker liner according to the manufacturer's directions.

melt the butter in a small sauté pan over medium-high heat. Add the shallots and saffron and sauté until the shallots are softened, about 3 minutes. Transfer to the slow-cooker insert.

add the rice and 4½ cups of the broth and stir to combine. cover and cook on high for 2 hours, until the rice is tender and the liquid is absorbed. Uncover the cooker and stir in the peas.

serve from the cooker set on warm.

serves 8–10

broth savvy

Depending on the brand of rice and size and shape of your slow cooker, you may find that you need to add more broth to the rice. I find it's a good idea to be prepared and have additional broth on hand. If you don't use it, label and freeze it in zipper-top plastic bags.

Bulgur with Basil, Mint, and Tomato

This simple dish is a terrific side for lamb, with its tomato and mint flavors mingling with the chewy bulgur. Serve this mounded on a platter, surrounded by lamb or gyros for a delicious meal. Once the bulgur has been cooked, you can store it in the refrigerator for up to 3 days and reheat in the slow cooker for another meal.

2 cups medium bulgur

2 tablespoons extra-virgin olive oil

1 medium onion, finely chopped

3 cloves garlic, minced

Pinch of red pepper flakes

One 14- to 15-ounce can chopped tomatoes, drained but juice reserved

3½ cups chicken or vegetable broth

1 teaspoon salt

¼ cup finely chopped fresh basil

¼ cup finely chopped fresh mint

coat the insert of a 5- to 7-quart slow cooker with nonstick-cooking spray and add the bulgur. Heat the oil in a large skillet over medium-high heat. Add the onion, garlic, and red pepper flakes and sauté until the onion is softened, about 3 minutes. Add the drained tomatoes and cook until there is no liquid left in the pan.

pour the broth in the skillet and scrape up any browned bits on the bottom of the pan. Transfer the contents of the skillet to the slow-cooker insert and stir in the reserved tomato juice and the salt. Cover and cook on low for 5 to 6 hours, until the bulgur is tender and the liquid is absorbed.

stir in the basil and mint and serve from the cooker set on warm.

serves **8**

Polenta

Polenta is a fine Italian dish that up until now required constant stirring to become creamy, but with your slow cooker, you can have delicious polenta any day of the week. The slow cooker does all the work.

6 cups chicken or vegetable broth

2 cups cornmeal for polenta

1 teaspoon salt

4 tablespoons (½ stick) unsalted butter, melted and slightly cooled

coat the insert of a 5- to 7-quart slow cooker with nonstick cooking spray or line it with a slow-cooker liner according to the manufacturer's directions.

pour the broth, cornmeal, salt, and butter into the slow-cooker insert and stir to blend. Cover and cook on high for 1½ to 2 hours, until the polenta is smooth and creamy.

serve from the cooker set on warm.

serves **6**

GORGONZOLA POLENTA

stir in 1½ cups crumbled Gorgonzola cheese just before serving.

SAGE AND PARMESAN POLENTA

stir in 1 tablespoon finely chopped fresh sage and 1 cup freshly grated Parmigiano-Reggiano cheese just before serving.

PORCINI POLENTA

add 4 ounces dried porcini mushrooms along with the broth and cornmeal and proceed as directed.

Risotto Risottos are made with a medium-grain rice usually labeled Arborio or Carnaroli (my favorite). Risottos can be finicky. If you have watched any Italian food preparation, you know that making risotto on the stovetop involves a lot of stirring and ladling hot broth into the pan. The slow cooker makes a delicious risotto, and you don't have to baby it at all. However, as with traditional risotto, you do have to cook the rice in butter or oil first, so don't skip any of the steps.

Risotto alla Milanese

Who said one can't improve on a classic? If I can set the risotto and forget it for 2½ hours, then I think that's a huge improvement! Cooked with saffron and white wine and finished with butter and Parmigiano-Reggiano, this risotto is delicious with any entrée!

½ cup (1 stick) unsalted butter

2 tablespoons olive oil

1 teaspoon saffron threads

½ cup finely chopped shallots (about 4 medium)

1½ cups Arborio or Carnaroli rice

¼ cup dry white wine or vermouth

4 cups chicken broth

½ cup freshly grated Parmigiano-Reggiano cheese

coat the insert of a 5- to 7-quart slow cooker with nonstick cooking spray or line it with a slow-cooker liner according to the manufacturer's directions.

melt ¼ cup of the butter with the oil in a large saucepan over medium-high heat. Add the saffron and shallots and cook, stirring, until the shallots are softened. Add the rice and cook, coating the rice with the butter, until the rice begins to look opaque. Add the wine and allow it to evaporate.

transfer the contents of the saucepan to the slow-cooker insert. Add the broth and stir to incorporate it. Cover and cook on high for 2½ hours; check the risotto at 2 hours to make sure that the broth hasn't evaporated. At the end of the cooking time, the risotto should be tender and creamy. Stir in the remaining ¼ cup butter and ¼ cup of the cheese.

serve the risotto with the remaining cheese on the side.

serves 4–6

risotto savvy
The risotto should be served immediately; it will thicken into an unappetizing lump if it's left in the slow cooker. Leftover risotto can be made into a layered rice dish and baked in oven.

Butternut Squash Risotto

My agent, Susan Ginsburg, and I had a butternut squash risotto at Gramercy Tavern in New York City that I am still dreaming about. This one is a close second, although the chef there would probably scream that it wasn't true risotto! The squash actually cooks with the risotto and becomes creamy along with the rice.

½ cup (1 stick) unsalted butter

2 tablespoons olive oil

½ cup finely chopped shallots (about 4 medium)

2 cups diced peeled and seeded butternut squash

1½ cups Arborio or Carnaroli rice

¼ cup dry white wine or vermouth

4¼ cups chicken broth

½ cup freshly grated Parmigiano-Reggiano cheese

coat the insert of a 5- to 7-quart slow cooker with nonstick cooking spray or line it with a slow-cooker liner according to the manufacturer's directions.

heat ¼ cup of the butter with the oil in a large saucepan over medium-high heat. Add the shallots and squash and sauté until the shallots are softened, about 3 minutes. Add the rice and cook, tossing to coat with the butter, until the rice is opaque. Add the wine and cook until the wine evaporates.

transfer the mixture to the slow-cooker insert and stir in the broth. Cover and cook on high for 2½ hours; check the risotto at 2 hours to make sure the broth hasn't evaporated. Stir in the remaining ¼ cup butter and ¼ cup of the cheese.

serve the risotto immediately with the remaining cheese on the side.

serves 4–6

Risotto with Gorgonzola

Sweet, salty, and creamy, Gorgonzola pairs well with the creamy rice in this dish. I love to serve this with grilled steak and an arugula salad.

½ cup (1 stick) unsalted butter

2 tablespoons olive oil

½ cup finely chopped shallots (about 4 medium)

1½ cups Arborio or Carnaroli rice

¼ cup dry white wine or vermouth

4 cups chicken broth

1 cup crumbled Gorgonzola cheese

coat the insert of a 5- to 7-quart slow cooker with nonstick cooking spray or line it with a slow-cooker liner according to the manufacturer's directions.

heat ¼ cup of the butter with the oil in a large saucepan over medium-high heat. Add the shallots and sauté until softened, about 4 minutes. Add the rice and cook, stirring to coat with the butter, until the rice begins to look opaque. Add the wine and cook until the wine evaporates.

transfer the mixture to the slow-cooker insert and stir in the broth. Cover and cook on high for 2½ hours; check the risotto at 2 hours to make sure that the broth hasn't evaporated.

stir in the remaining butter and Gorgonzola before serving immediately.

serves 4–6

Pilaf   Pilaf dates back to ancient times, and is common throughout the Middle East, Asia, and South America. Grain (usually rice) is sauteed in butter or oil, and then cooked in a seasoned broth. The slow cooker not only helps to make a fluffy pilaf but also will keep it warm until serving.

Bulgur and Shiitake Mushroom Pilaf

Bulgur, which is wheat that has been steamed, dried, and cracked, makes a nice change of pace for a side dish. The slightly crunchy texture, flavored here with soy and shiitake mushrooms, contrasts nicely with grilled meats, chicken, or seafood. Bulgur comes in several different sizes: very fine, coarse, and medium. I recommend the medium texture for these dishes.

2 cups medium bulgur

2 tablespoons extra-virgin olive oil

1 medium onion, finely chopped

2 cloves garlic, minced

8 ounces fresh shiitake mushrooms, stems removed, caps sliced

¼ cup soy sauce

4 cups beef broth (substitute vegetable or chicken broth if desired)

4 ounces dried shiitake mushrooms, crumbled.

coat the insert of a 5- to 7-quart slow cooker with nonstick cooking spray and add the bulgur. Heat the oil in a large skillet over medium-high heat. Add the onion, garlic, and fresh mushrooms and sauté until the onion is softened and translucent and the liquid in the pan has evaporated. Remove from the heat, pour in the soy sauce, and scrape up any remaining bits from the bottom of the pan.

transfer the contents of the skillet to the slow-cooker insert and stir in the broth and dried mushrooms. Cover and cook on low for 5 to 6 hours, until the bulgur is tender and the broth is absorbed.

serve from the cooker set on warm.

serves 8

White and Wild Rice Pilaf

Crunchy wild rice and white rice combine in this classic side dish. You might think this dish old-fashioned, but the classics often remind us that simple foods are the best, and this is no exception. The pilaf, rich with the flavor of chicken broth and filled with vegetables, not only looks beautiful but also tastes great! Try serving it mounded in the center of a serving platter surrounded by roasted meat, poultry, or seafood.

2 cup converted white rice

2 cups wild rice, rinsed with cold water and drained twice

½ cup (1 stick) unsalted butter

2 medium onions, finely chopped

4 medium carrots, cut into ½-inch dice

4 stalks celery, cut into ½-inch dice

1 teaspoon dried thyme

½ teaspoon dried sage leaves, crushed in the palm of your hand

6 to 7 cups chicken broth

coat the insert of a 5- to 7-quart slow cooker with nonstick cooking spray or line it with a slow-cooker liner according to the manufacturer's directions.

pour the white and wild rice into the slow-cooker insert. Melt the butter in a large skillet over medium-high heat. Add the onions, carrots, celery, thyme, and sage and sauté until the onions are translucent and softened, about 6 minutes. Add 1 cup of the broth to the skillet and heat, scraping up any browned bits from the bottom of the pan. Add the contents of the skillet and remaining chicken broth to the rice (see savvy).

cover and cook on low for 5 hours, until the rice is tender but not mushy and the liquid is absorbed. Remove the lid from the slow cooker and cook for an additional 30 minutes.

serve the rice from the cooker set on warm.

serves **8–10**

wild rice savvy
Each brand of wild rice is different, and you may need to add more broth during the last hour of cooking. If the wild rice is not yet tender and the liquid is absorbed, add more broth, then cover and continue to cook. If the rice is tender but there is still liquid in the cooker, uncover and cook on high for 30 to 45 minutes to evaporate the liquid.

Fruited Wild Rice Pilaf

Wild rice is an aquatic grain that is raised in the northern regions of North America. I like to serve wild rice with roasted meats and poultry, and it makes a delicious stuffing for poultry and butterflied pork tenderloin. This wild rice pilaf is cooked with plump dried apricots and cranberries, giving the rice a sweet and crunchy flavor.

2 cups wild rice, rinsed with cold water and drained twice

½ cup (1 stick) unsalted butter

1 medium onion, finely chopped

3 stalks celery, finely chopped

1 teaspoon dried marjoram

4 to 5 cups chicken broth

½ cup finely chopped dried apricots

½ cup dried cranberries

½ teaspoon freshly ground black pepper

½ cup sliced almonds, toasted

coat the insert of a 5- to 7-quart slow cooker with nonstick cooking spray or line it with a slow-cooker liner according to the manufacturer's directions.

pour the rice into the slow-cooker insert. Melt the butter in a large skillet over medium-high heat. Add the onion, celery, and marjoram and sauté until the vegetables are softened, about 4 minutes.

transfer the vegetables to the slow-cooker insert. Stir in the broth, apricots, cranberries, and pepper. Cover and cook on high for 2½ to 3 hours or on low for 7 hours, until the rice is tender. Check at intervals to make sure there is still liquid in the slow cooker, and add more broth if needed. Uncover the slow cooker and cook for another 30 to 45 minutes on low. Stir in the almonds.

serve from the cooker set on low.

serves **8–10**

Basil and Pine Nut Pilaf

Basil and crunchy toasted pine nuts give this pilaf terrific flavor and texture. I like to serve this with grilled seafood; it adds color, aroma, and flavor to the plate. Any leftovers make a terrific rice salad, tossed with vinaigrette and with strips of cooked chicken, fish, or beef added.

2 tablespoons unsalted butter

1 cup pine nuts

3 cups converted white rice

4½ to 5½ cups chicken or vegetable broth (see savvy page 320)

1 teaspoon freshly ground black pepper

½ cup finely chopped fresh basil, plus additional whole leaves for garnishing

coat the insert of a 5- to 7-quart slow cooker with nonstick cooking spray or line it with a slow-cooker liner according to the manufacturer's directions.

melt the butter in a small sauté pan over medium-high heat. Add the pine nuts and sauté until they begin to color, about 4 minutes. Set aside.

combine the rice, 4½ cups broth, and the pepper in the slow-cooker insert. Cover and cook on high for 1 hour.

stir in the pine nuts and chopped basil. Cover and cook for 1½ hours, until the rice is tender and liquid is absorbed.

serve from the cooker set on warm, garnished with the whole basil leaves.

serves 8-10

Bread Stuffings

Stuffings and dressings are part and parcel of what make holidays so special. Your slow cooker makes these stuffings, which are really savory bread puddings, moist and delicious, and delivers the added bonus of keeping them warm until you're ready to serve.

Classic Bread Stuffing

I've never met a starch I didn't like, and stuffing is a guilty pleasure for me. I eat it while I'm making it, I've been known to sneak tastes while it's being cooked, and I've been caught eating the leftovers cold! This is the stuffing my mom made when I was a child, and I still love its herby flavor, especially with gravy!

8 cups stale white bread cubes
(a sturdy bread, such as Pepperidge Farm)

½ cup (1 stick) unsalted butter

2 medium onions, finely chopped

4 stalks celery with leaves, finely chopped

2 teaspoons finely chopped fresh sage leaves

2 teaspoons finely chopped fresh thyme leaves

¼ cup finely chopped fresh Italian parsley

2 to 3 cups chicken broth

1½ teaspoons salt

1 teaspoon freshly ground black pepper

3 large eggs, beaten

coat the insert of a 5- to 7-quart slow cooker with nonstick cooking spray or line it with a slow-cooker liner according to the manufacturer's directions. Place the bread in a large mixing bowl and set aside.

melt the butter in a large skillet over medium-high heat. Add the onions, celery, sage, thyme, and parsley and sauté until the onions and celery begin to soften. Transfer the mixture to the bowl with the bread.

whisk together the broth, salt, pepper, and eggs in another mixing bowl. Pour over the bread mixture and stir until well combined. Add the stuffing mixture to the slow-cooker insert and cover. Cook on high for 1 hour, then reduce the heat to low. Cook for 4 to 5 hours, until cooked through, 170°F on an instant-read thermometer.

serve from the cooker set on warm.

serves 10–12

Cornbread Stuffing

This savory dressing is filled with nuggets of smoked ham, flavored with rosemary and sage, and scattered with bits of onion, celery, and dried apricots for a little sweetness. Many grocery stores sell cornbread in their bakeries around the holidays, but if you can't find cornbread, it's easy enough to make either from scratch or using a packaged mix.

8 cups crumbled stale cornbread

½ cup (1 stick) unsalted butter

2 medium onions, finely chopped

4 stalks celery, finely chopped

2 cups finely diced smoked ham

2 teaspoons finely chopped fresh rosemary

1 tablespoon finely chopped fresh sage

2 tablespoons finely chopped fresh Italian parsley

1 cup chopped dried apricots

1 teaspoon hot sauce

1 cup whole milk

2 to 3 cups chicken broth (see savvy)

3 large eggs, beaten

coat the insert of a 5- to 7-quart slow cooker with nonstick cooking spray or line it with a slow-cooker liner according to the manufacturer's directions. Put the cornbread in a large mixing bowl and set aside.

melt the butter in a large skillet over medium-high heat. Add the onions, celery, ham, rosemary, sage, and parsley and sauté until the onions and celery are softened. Transfer to the bowl with the cornbread and add the apricots. Put the hot sauce, milk, broth, and eggs in another bowl and whisk until blended. Pour over the cornbread mixture and stir until well combined. Transfer the stuffing to the slow-cooker insert.

cover and cook on high for 1 hour, then reduce the heat to low. Cook for 4 to 5 hours, until cooked through, 170°F on an instant-read thermometer.

serve the stuffing directly from the slow cooker.

serves **12**

stuffing savvy
You may need more broth depending upon how dry the bread is. Use the lesser amount called for, and if the stuffing appears dry, add more chicken broth.

French Onion Stuffing

This savory bread pudding is loaded with caramelized onions and Gruyère cheese chunks that melt into the stuffing. Serve this instead of mashed potatoes the next time you make a roast beef. It tastes something like the best bowl of French onion soup.

8 cups stale white bread cubes with crusts removed

2 cups Gruyère cheese, cut into ½-inch cubes (about 8 ounces)

3 tablespoons unsalted butter

1 tablespoon olive oil

3 large onions, thinly sliced

1 tablespoon sugar

2 teaspoons dried thyme

1½ teaspoons salt

½ teaspoon freshly ground black pepper

3 cloves garlic, mashed

5 large eggs

2 cups heavy cream

½ teaspoon Tabasco sauce

1 teaspoon Worcestershire sauce

¼ cup chopped fresh Italian parsley

coat the insert of a 5- to 7-quart slow cooker with nonstick cooking spray or line it with a slow-cooker liner according to the manufacturer's directions. Combine the bread and cheese in the slow cooker.

heat the butter with the oil in a large skillet over medium heat until the butter melts and the foam subsides. Add the onions, stir to coat with the butter, and cook until they begin to turn translucent. Sprinkle with the sugar, thyme, salt, pepper, and garlic and cook, stirring, until the onions become golden. Remove from the skillet and allow to cool.

whisk together the eggs, cream, Tabasco, Worcestershire, and parsley, in a large bowl, and stir in the cooled onions. Pour the egg mixture over the bread and cheese and press down on the bread to saturate it. Cover and cook on high for 2½ to 3 hours, until the stuffing is puffed and registers 185°F on an instant-read thermometer. Uncover and allow to rest for 15 to 30 minutes.

serve from the cooker set on warm.

serves **8**

Colonial Williamsburg Spoon Bread

Spoon bread is a creamy cornbread that was served in colonial days. You don't see this on many restaurant menus anymore, except at historic inns and taverns in the South, and that's a shame because it is a delicious accompaniment to roasted meats, pork, and poultry. At Christiana Campbell's tavern in Williamsburg, they actually spoon it out of a large cast-iron pot. I love to serve this with maple syrup or honey on the side.

3 cups cornmeal

3 cups water

3 cups milk

⅓ cup sugar

2 tablespoons baking powder

½ cup (1 stick) unsalted butter, melted and cooled slightly

8 large eggs

coat the insert of a 5- to 7-quart slow cooker with nonstick cooking spray.

put the cornmeal, water and milk in a large mixing bowl and stir for 3 to 5 minutes. (This will ensure a light spoon bread). Add the sugar, baking powder, butter, and eggs and beat with a wooden spoon until the mixture is smooth.

transfer the mixture to the slow-cooker insert.

cover and cook on high for 3 hours, until the top is set. Uncover and cook for an additional 30 minutes.

serve the spoon bread from the cooker set on warm.

serves **8**

Grits　Grits cook up creamy and smooth in a slow cooker. All that's left for you to do is to add flavor and pizzazz to this classic Southern dish. I'm not fond of plain grits, but you can definitely make them in your slow cooker, especially if you like them for breakfast. My favorites are dishes where the grits peek out from under a stellar entrée such as barbecued shrimp New Orleans–style, a lamb shank, or a pot roast. Any way you decide to make them, the slow cooker will treat them well.

Basic Grits

This recipe contains just a few ingredients and is for the purists in the crowd who love plain grits with eggs over-easy in the morning. If you want to dress this up, substitute chicken broth for the water, and add one to two cups shredded cheese at the end for a simple side dish. For grits casseroles, see the recipes on the facing page.

1¼ cups stone-ground grits

5½ cups water

1 teaspoon salt

2 tablespoons unsalted butter, melted, plus more for serving

coat the insert of a 4- to 5-quart slow cooker with nonstick cooking spray or line it with a slow-cooker liner according to the manufacturer's directions.

stir all the ingredients together in the insert. Cover and cook on low for 8 hours, until the grits are creamy.

serve from the cooker set on warm with additional butter on the side.

serves **8**

Cheesy Grits Casserole

This delicious casserole will be a star at your next dinner. The grits are cooked in broth, rather than water, for a richer flavor, and then further enriched with eggs, cream, and cheese halfway through the cooking. This dish is a standout with grilled meats, poultry, and seafood. I love to serve New Orleans-style barbecued shrimp over these grits.

1 cup stone-ground grits

4½ cups chicken broth

4 tablespoons (½ stick) unsalted butter, melted and slightly cooled

2 large eggs, beaten

½ cup heavy cream

2 cup finely shredded mild Cheddar cheese (see savvy)

coat the insert of a slow cooker with nonstick cooking spray or line it with a slow-cooker liner according to the manufacturer's directions.

stir the grits, broth, and butter together in the slow-cooker insert. Cover and cook on low for 4 hours. Stir in the eggs, cream, and cheese. Cover and cook for an additional 4 hours, until the grits are creamy and the cheese has melted.

serve from the cooker set on warm.

serves **8**

GARLIC CHEESE GRITS

mince 3 cloves garlic, sauté in the butter, and add along to the slow cooker with the grits and broth. Proceed as directed.

SMOKED BACON AND CHEDDAR CHEESE GRITS

cook 8 ounces thick-cut Applewood smoked bacon until crisp. Drain; then crumble and set aside while the grits cook. Substitute sharp white Cheddar cheese for the mild cheese and add ½ teaspoon Tabasco sauce along with the eggs, cream, and cheese. Stir the bacon into the grits just before serving.

cheese savvy
You can substitute your favorites here: Swiss, Havarti with dill, sharp Cheddar, Asiago, provolone, Monterey Jack, and pepper Jack are all great choices.

Chapter 9
Eat Your Veggies

Whether or not you have vegetarians in your life, the slow cooker can be used to make a wide variety of vegetable dishes, including potato casseroles, root vegetable braises, eggplant Parmesan—the list goes on! Vegetables in the slow cooker can be an accompaniment or main course any night of the week. Vegetables and side dishes seem to require a lot of forethought for some home cooks, but the slow cooker takes out a lot of the guesswork. The ingredients are layered, the machine turned on low, and hours later a delicious vegetable dish emerges from the slow cooker.

Refried Bean Casserole

An easy Southwestern side dish, these beans are spicy, creamy, smooth and cheesy. Serve them at a build-your-own-taco bar or with carne or pollo asada.

2 tablespoons canola or vegetable oil

1 medium onion, finely chopped

1 jalapeño pepper, seeded and finely chopped

1 teaspoon ground cumin

½ teaspoon dried oregano

Four 14- to 15-ounce cans refried beans

1½ cups sour cream

2 cups shredded mild Cheddar cheese

1 cup shredded pepper Jack cheese

coat the insert of a 5- to 7-quart slow cooker with nonstick cooking spray or line it with a slow-cooker liner according to the manufacturer's directions.

heat the oil in a small skillet over medium-high heat. Add the onion, jalapeño, cumin, and oregano and sauté until the onion is softened, about 3 minutes.

transfer to a mixing bowl and stir in the refried beans and sour cream. Spoon half the mixture into the slow-cooker insert and sprinkle with the Cheddar cheese. Top with the remaining beans and sprinkle with the pepper Jack cheese.

cover and cook on low for 4 to 5 hours, until the beans are heated through and the cheese is melted.

serve the beans from the cooker set on warm.

serves **8**

Caribbean Black Beans

Black beans, fragrant with island spices and cooked in the slow cooker, are a great side dish to serve at a barbecue or as part of a Southwestern dinner. Black beans need to be covered with liquid at all times, so this is one recipe where lifting the lid and stirring is encouraged!

1 pound black turtle beans, soaked overnight in water to cover and drained

2 tablespoons olive oil

2 medium red onions, finely chopped

2 cloves garlic, minced

1 Anaheim chile, seeded and finely chopped

1 medium red bell pepper, seeded and finely chopped

1 teaspoon jerk seasoning

1 bay leaf

One 14- to 15-ounce can crushed plum tomatoes, with their juice

2 tablespoons fresh lime juice

5 cups chicken broth

pour the beans in the insert of a 5- to 7-quart slow cooker. Heat the oil in a large skillet over medium-high heat. Add the onions, garlic, chile, bell pepper, jerk seasoning, and bay leaf and sauté until the vegetables are softened.

add the tomatoes and transfer the contents of the skillet to the slow-cooker insert. Stir in the lime juice and broth.

cover and cook on high for 5 hours. Check the level of the liquid after 3 and 4 hours of cooking; stir and add more chicken broth if needed. The beans should be tender and creamy.

serve the beans from the cooker set on warm.

serves **8**

Creamy White Beans

White beans are a staple in the Mediterranean, and this simple dish flavored with extra-virgin olive oil, garlic, and rosemary is a winner any night of the week. The beans become creamy as they cook and are terrific served as a bed for lamb or chicken. The leftovers can be puréed and served as a dip or spread, like hummus.

2 cups dried small white beans, soaked overnight in water to cover and drained

½ cup extra-virgin olive oil

6 cloves garlic, sliced

1 tablespoon finely chopped fresh rosemary

6 to 8 cups chicken broth

1½ teaspoons salt

½ teaspoon freshly ground black pepper

pour the beans in the insert of a 5- to 7-quart slow cooker. Heat the oil in a small skillet over very low heat. Add the garlic and rosemary and cook for about 10 minutes, taking care that the garlic doesn't brown.

add the contents of the skillet to the slow-cooker insert and stir in 6 cups chicken broth. Cover and cook on high for 3 hours. Check to make sure that the beans are not sticking to the pot and add more broth if needed. Cover and cook for an additional 1 hour. Season with the salt and pepper.

serve from the cooker set on warm.

serves **6**

Veggie Cassoulet

A terrific vegetarian entrée or side dish, cassoulet is usually made with lots of meats, including duck and sausages, but for this cassoulet, we'll forgo the meats and use legumes, chunky vegetables, and tangy orange zest to fortify the pot. I actually like this better the next day, after the flavors have gotten to know each other.

2 cups Great Northern beans, soaked overnight in water to cover and drained

½ cup brown lentils

½ cup yellow split peas

½ cup extra virgin olive oil

2 medium onions, coarsely chopped

5 cloves garlic, minced

1 teaspoon dried thyme

Pinch of red pepper flakes

4 medium carrots, cut into ½-inch rounds

4 stalks celery, cut into ½-inch pieces

2 parsnips, cut into ½-inch rounds

1 cup red wine, such as Burgundy

Grated zest of 1 orange

One 14- to 15-ounce can crushed tomatoes

8 cups chicken or vegetable broth

1 bay leaf

Salt and freshly ground black pepper

2 tablespoons butter, melted

1 cup fresh bread crumbs

⅓ cup grated Parmesan cheese

½ cup finely chopped Italian parsley

combine the beans, lentils, and split peas in the insert of a 5- to 7-quart slow cooker. Heat the oil in a large skillet over medium-high heat. Add the onions, garlic, thyme, and red pepper flakes and sauté until the onions are softened.

transfer the contents of the skillet to the slow-cooker insert. Stir in the carrots, celery, parsnips, wine, zest, tomatoes, broth, and bay leaf. Cover and cook on high for 5 to 6 hours, until the beans are tender. Check after several hours to see if the beans need additional broth.

remove the bay leaf and season with salt and pepper. Combine the butter, bread crumbs, cheese, and parsley in a mixing bowl and sprinkle over the top of the cassoulet. Cook uncovered for another 30 minutes.

serve from the cooker set on warm, as a side dish or vegetarian main dish.

serves **8**

Cowboy-Style Baked Beans

Robust and bursting with chunks of sausage in a savory sauce, these beans are terrific for a barbecue. Serve alongside burgers, hot dogs, grilled meats, or pulled pork. If you have an outdoor kitchen, plug in the cooker and keep the beans warm.

1½ pounds bulk pork sausage (Jimmy Dean is a good brand)

2 medium onions, chopped

2 chipotle chiles in adobo, minced

Four 16-ounce cans plain baked beans

½ cup ketchup

¼ cup maple syrup

2 tablespoons Worcestershire sauce

2 tablespoons Dijon mustard

brown the sausage in a large skillet over high heat, breaking up any large chunks with the back of a spoon. Add the onions and chiles and sauté until the onions are softened. Drain off any excess fat.

transfer the contents of the skillet to the insert of a 5- to 7-quart slow cooker. Add the remaining ingredients and stir to combine. Cover and cook on low for 5 to 7 hours, until the beans are tender.

serve the beans from the cooker set on warm.

serves **8**

Garbanzos Tuscan-Style

Garbanzo beans (or chickpeas) are a staple in Mediterranean cooking, and these beans become soft and creamy in your slow cooker. Fragrant with garlic, rosemary, tomatoes, and a bit of red wine, the beans make a terrific side dish to serve with grilled meats or seafood.

2 tablespoons extra-virgin olive oil

3 cloves garlic, minced

1 medium onion, finely chopped

2 teaspoons fresh rosemary leaves, finely chopped

Two 14- to 15-ounce cans crushed tomatoes

2 tablespoons dry red wine

Four 14- to 15-ounce cans garbanzo beans, rinsed and drained (see savvy)

1½ teaspoons salt

½ teaspoon freshly ground black pepper

½ cup finely chopped fresh Italian parsley

heat the oil in a medium skillet over medium-high heat. Add the garlic, onion, and rosemary and sauté until the onion is softened, about 3 minutes. Add the tomatoes and wine and swirl in the pan to combine.

transfer the contents of the skillet to the insert of a 5- to 7-quart slow cooker and stir in the beans along with the salt and pepper. Cover and cook on low for 6 to 7 hours, until the beans are soft and creamy.

stir in the parsley and serve.

serves 6–8

bean savvy
I am a spur-of-the-moment cook in many ways, and sometimes I won't have thought to soak dried beans the night before. If you plan ahead and want to use dried garbanzo beans in this recipe, instead of canned beans, soak them overnight in water to cover, drain, and cook as directed but increase the cooking time to 8 to 10 hours.

Southern-Style Green Beans

Southern cooks are proud of their green beans, which are typically slowly simmered with bacon, giving the beans their distinctive flavor. My version of this dish has whole garlic cloves and chicken broth added for more flavor. I love to serve these beans with fried chicken, mashed potatoes, and cream gravy.

6 strips bacon, cut into 1-inch pieces; reserve some for garnish

2 pounds green beans, ends snipped, cut into 1-inch pieces

1 medium onion, coarsely chopped

1½ cups chicken broth

4 cloves garlic, peeled

6 whole black peppercorns

combine all the ingredients in the insert of a 5- to 7-quart slow cooker. Cover and cook on low for 6 hours, until the beans are tender.

drain the beans and discard the peppercorns and garlic.

serve garnished with the reserved bacon.

serves 6–8

Roasted Beets with Goat Cheese and Pomegranate Dressing

This recipe is similar to one I have enjoyed at a local restaurant. The pomegranate dressing has a sweet-and-sour quality that gives the beets a nice flavor, and the goat cheese adds a tangy note. The dressing is equally good on field greens, or you can serve the beets on a bed of field greens, garnished with some Spicy Crocked Nuts (page 465). Roasting beets develops the sugars and makes them not only sweet but also full flavored. I recommend beets that are around two to two-and-a-half inches in diameter. Baby beets, generally about one inch in diameter, are expensive, and it would take a boatload to fill your cooker. Once the beets are cooked, they keep refrigerated for several days and stay nicely in the vinaigrette for three to four days.

6 to 8 medium beets, scrubbed, stem ends trimmed

1 cup canola or vegetable oil

½ cup pomegranate juice

¼ cup rice vinegar

2 shallots, finely chopped

2 teaspoons sugar

1 teaspoon salt

½ teaspoon freshly ground black pepper

¼ cup thinly sliced fresh basil for garnishing

8 ounces goat cheese, crumbled for garnishing

wrap each beet individually in aluminum foil and arrange in the insert of a 5- to 7-quart slow cooker. Cover and cook on high for 5 hours, until the tip of a knife inserted into the thickest part of the beet goes in without any resistance.

remove the beets from the slow-cooker insert and allow them to cool. Unwrap the beets and slip the skins off with a sharp paring knife.

cut the beets into wedges and transfer to a bowl. Whisk together the oil, pomegranate juice, vinegar, shallots, sugar, salt, and pepper in a mixing bowl. Pour the mixture over the beets and toss to coat.

marinate the beets for at least 2 hours or up to 3 days.

drain the beets and arrange on a serving platter and sprinkle with the basil and goat cheese.

serves 6–8

Eggplant Parmigiana

Eggplant is one of my favorite vegetables, and a slow cooker does a great job on this casserole of layered eggplant, garlicky tomato sauce, and cheese. Make sure to use a slow-cooker liner, or coat the insert of the slow cooker with nonstick cooking spray, for easy cleanup. I actually like this dish the day after, so you can definitely layer everything and refrigerate it, then bring it to room temperature and cook the next day.

1 large purple eggplant (about 1 ½ pounds), peeled and cut into ½-inch rounds

3 tablespoons salt

GARLIC MARINARA SAUCE

2 tablespoons extra-virgin olive oil

4 cloves garlic, minced

Pinch of red pepper flakes

2 teaspoons dried basil

One 28- to 32-ounce can crushed tomatoes

½ cup finely chopped fresh Italian parsley

1½ teaspoons salt

½ teaspoon freshly ground black pepper

1 teaspoon sugar

8 ounces fresh mozzarella, cut into ¼-inch-thick slices

1 cup freshly grated Asiago cheese

1 cup freshly grated Parmigiano-Reggiano cheese

arrange the eggplant slices on a baking sheet lined with paper towels. Salt the eggplant generously. (This step will remove the excess water from the eggplant, giving you a nice dish rather than a slow cooker full of water). After 10 minutes, turn the eggplant and salt the other side. Let stand for another 10 minutes. Blot the slices dry with paper towels and set aside while making the sauce.

heat the oil in a small saucepan over medium-high heat. Add the garlic, red pepper flakes, and basil and sauté until the garlic is fragrant but not browned, about 1 minute. Stir in the tomatoes, parsley, salt, pepper, and sugar; simmer uncovered for 30 minutes. Taste and adjust the seasoning.

coat the insert of a 5- to 7-quart slow cooker with nonstick cooking spray or line it with a slow-cooker liner according to the manufacturer's directions.

spread a layer of the sauce on the bottom of the slow-cooker insert, then top with a layer of the eggplant. Spread an even layer of the mozzarella over the eggplant and sprinkle with some of the Asiago and Parmigiano. Top with a bit of the sauce. Continue to layer the sauce, eggplant, and cheeses, ending with the last bit of Asiago and Parmigiano.

cover and cook on low for 4 hours, until the casserole is heated through and the cheese is melted in the center. Allow the casserole to rest for 10 minutes before serving.

serves 6–8

Ratatouille

A dish from Provence, ratatouille was made famous by a Pixar movie starring a gourmand named Remy, a rodent to rival Mickey. In order to appeal to a food critic, Remy went back to the man's roots and prepared a dish his mama used to make: ratatouille. Comfort foods soothe the soul, and in this instance, the Gallic soul. Ratatouille is a mélange of eggplant, zucchini, onions, and tomatoes, seasoned with the herbs of Provence, cooked low and slow. It can be served as a side dish or as main course with salad and a cheese course. Make sure to salt the vegetables before cooking to eliminate any excess liquid in the finished dish.

1 large eggplant (about 1½ pounds), peeled and cut into ½-inch cubes

3 medium zucchini or yellow summer squash, cut into ½-inch pieces

3 tablespoons salt

¼ cup extra-virgin olive oil

4 cloves garlic, sliced

2 medium onions, cut into half rounds

2 medium red bell peppers, seeded and sliced ½ inch thick

2 teaspoons herbes de Provence (see savvy)

1 bay leaf

¼ cup dry red wine

One 14- to 15-ounce can whole plum tomatoes, crushed in the palm of your hand, drained

½ teaspoon freshly ground black pepper

put the eggplant and zucchini in a large colander and sprinkle with the salt. Let the vegetables stand in the colander for 1 hour, tossing them every 10 minutes or so. Press any excess water out of the vegetables by pressing down on them in the colander and then blotting with paper towels. Set aside.

heat the oil in a large skillet over medium-high heat. Add the garlic, onions, bell peppers, herbs, and bay leaf and sauté until there is no liquid left in the skillet, about 7 minutes. Transfer the contents of the skillet to the insert of a 5- to 7-quart slow cooker.

stir in the eggplant and zucchini, the wine, tomatoes, and pepper. Cover and cook on high for 2 to 3 hours, until the vegetables are tender and the sauce is thickened. Remove the cover and discard the bay leaf. Cook on low for 30 minutes.

serve the ratatouille hot, warm, or at room temperature.

serves **8**

provence savvy
You can make your own combination of herbes de Provence by combining 1 teaspoon dried tarragon, ½ teaspoon dried rosemary, 1 teaspoon dried thyme, 1 teaspoon dried chervil, and ½ teaspoon dried basil.

Caponata

This delicious sweet and savory dish is terrific to serve as a topping for bruschetta and is a delicious complement for grilled meats, seafood, and poultry. The slow-cooked eggplant, onion, tomatoes, and aromatics combine with salty capers, olives, and golden raisins to melt into a sweet, salty, and flavor-packed condiment. The recipe for caponata depends on the region in Italy it is made, so you should feel free to add or subtract ingredients as you like. Just make sure that you keep the liquid measures the same. Caponata is best served at room temperature, actually gets better after a few days, and will keep for one week in the fridge.

2 tablespoons extra-virgin olive oil

1 medium red onion, finely chopped

3 cloves garlic, minced

3 stalks celery, finely chopped

2 medium purple eggplants, finely diced (see savvy)

2 medium red bell peppers, seeded and cut into ½-inch pieces

1 teaspoon dried oregano

1 teaspoon salt

Pinch of red pepper flakes

¼ cup balsamic vinegar

One 15-ounce can diced tomatoes, with their juice (see savvy)

1 cup golden raisins (see savvy)

¼ cup brined capers, drained

½ cup pitted Kalamata olives (or your favorite olive)

½ cup finely chopped fresh Italian parsley

heat the oil in a large skillet over medium-high heat. Add the onion, garlic, and celery and sauté until the onion is softened, about 3 minutes.

transfer the contents of the skillet to the insert of a 5- to 7-quart slow cooker. Add the eggplants, bell peppers, oregano, salt, and red pepper flakes to the skillet and sauté until the eggplant begins to soften, 4 to 5 minutes. Add the vinegar and allow it to evaporate a bit, then stir in the tomatoes and raisins.

transfer the contents of the skillet to the slow-cooker insert and stir to combine. Cover and cook on low for 5 hours. Stir in the capers, olives, and parsley and cook for an additional 1 hour, until the eggplant is tender.

remove the caponata from the slow cooker and serve it cold or at room temperature.

makes about **6** cups

eggplant savvy
I usually leave the skin on the eggplant because it adds color and texture to the dish. Make sure the eggplant you buy has a smooth unblemished skin and isn't wrinkly at all.

tomato savvy
If you prefer a less chunky version of this dish, use one 15-ounce can tomato purée instead of the diced tomatoes.

raisin savvy
In testing this recipe, I found the flavor of golden raisins much more to my liking than that of dark brown raisins.

Fennel Gratin

Fennel is a delicate anise-flavored vegetable that doesn't make it to many dinner tables, which is a shame because it is has an unusual and delicious flavor. This simple recipe pairs fennel with onions, potatoes, and Swiss cheese; the result is a spectacular side dish to serve with grilled or roasted meats or poultry.

3 bulbs fennel, stalks and root ends trimmed, cut into ½-inch slices

2 medium onions, cut into ½-inch half rounds

3 medium red or Yukon gold potatoes, scrubbed and cut into ¼-inch-thick slices

1½ cups heavy cream

1 cup chicken broth

2 teaspoons salt

1 teaspoon Tabasco sauce

1 cup finely shredded Gruyère cheese

coat the inside of the insert of a 5- to 7-quart slow cooker with nonstick cooking spray or line it with a slow-cooker liner according to the manufacturer's directions.

toss the vegetables together in a mixing bowl, put them in the slow-cooker insert, and press them down. Whisk together the cream, broth, salt, and Tabasco in a mixing bowl and pour over the vegetables.

cover and cook on high for 2 hours, until the potatoes are tender. Sprinkle with the cheese, cover, and cook for another 30 minutes.

serve the gratin from the slow cooker set on warm.

serves **6**

A Word about Potatoes

There are lots of potatoes to choose from in your supermarket, and each variety has its own special quality. Frankly I've never met a potato I didn't like, but some potatoes are better than others for particular preparations. I've made suggestions for each recipe, but these are some of their characteristics.

RUSSET OR IDAHO BAKING POTATOES

These potatoes are high in starch. They're great mashed, baked, stuffed, or fried.

RED, YUKON GOLD, OR WHITE CREAMERS

These are lower in starch, and are sometimes labeled as "new" even though they haven't been new for months. Use these potatoes in dishes, where they will absorb liquids, like gratins; in salads, where they will absorb dressing; or roasted whole or in wedges. You can mash them, but they are waxier than russets and will need more liquid to make them smooth and creamy.

FINGERLINGS

These tiny potatoes look like stubby fingers, hence the name. They can be expensive, but they are perfect to substitute for red and yukon gold varieties.

SWEET POTATOES

You may see these labeled as "yams" in the supermarket, when in fact yams are native to Africa and Asia and have a yellow color. Sweet potatoes have orange flesh and a high sugar content. They are terrific roasted, baked, or mashed. Roasting causes the sugars to caramelize, which makes the potatoes delicious with or without that ubiquitous marshmallow topping. If you buy a "yam" that has red-colored flesh, it is probably a Louisiana "yam," but is still a sweet potato. This is probably more than you wanted to know, but you may need dinner conversation at the next Thanksgiving meal!

Potatoes Baked in the Crock

Baking potatoes in a slow cooker may not seem like a brilliant idea, but in the heat of the summer, if you don't have to turn on your oven, you'll be very happy to have this recipe! A recent magazine article stated that baking potatoes low and slow in the oven yielded a much more delicious potato as compared to conventional high-heat baking. Once the potatoes are baked, they can be kept warm in the slow cooker until you are ready to serve them. These potatoes can be a jumping-off point for twice-baked potatoes, which can be reheated in the slow cooker on high for 1 hour.

8 russet baking potatoes, scrubbed

½ cup extra-virgin olive oil

3 tablespoons salt

1 teaspoon coarsely ground black pepper

prick each potato several times with the tip of a sharp knife. Combine the oil, salt, and pepper in a bowl and rub the potatoes all over the oil mixture.

arrange the potatoes in the insert of a 5- to 7-quart slow cooker. Cover and cook on high for 3 to 4 hours or on low for 7 to 8 hours.

remove the potatoes from the slow cooker and serve, or serve from the cooker set on warm.

serves 8–10

Rosemary and Garlic Potatoes

Coated with olive oil infused with garlic and rosemary, red potatoes become sweet when roasting low and slow for hours. The aromas from the slow cooker will have your family waiting by the cooker for the timer to go off.

½ cup extra-virgin olive oil

6 cloves garlic, sliced

2 teaspoons fresh rosemary leaves, finely chopped

2 teaspoons coarse salt

1 teaspoon coarsely ground black pepper

16 to 20 small (2-inch) red potatoes, scrubbed

combine all the ingredients in the insert of a 5- to 7-quart slow cooker cover and cook on high for 4 hours, stirring after 2 hours to bring the potatoes from the bottom to the top.

serve immediately, or keep warm for up to 2 hours in the cooker set on warm.

serves **8**

German Potato Salad with Sausage

German potato salad is one of the first recipes that was included with slow-cooker instruction books; unfortunately that salad was bland and didn't have the pizzazz that you would expect from a dish with sausage, onion, vinegar, and mustard. This recipe will give you the zesty flavor, and the tender potatoes will be a crowd pleaser at your next barbecue. I love Yukon gold potatoes for their flavor and color in this dish, but red potatoes or white creamers will work as well.

6 to 8 medium (3-inch) Yukon Gold potatoes, scrubbed and cut into ¼-inch-thick slices

1 medium red onion, coarsely chopped

2 stalks celery, coarsely chopped

½ pound kielbasa or other smoked sausage, cut into ½-inch dice

⅓ cup rice vinegar

¼ cup Dijon mustard

2 tablespoons olive oil

3 tablespoons light brown sugar

½ teaspoon mustard seeds

½ teaspoon celery seeds

½ cup finely chopped fresh Italian parsley

combine the potatoes, onion, celery, and sausage in the insert of a 5- to 7-quart slow cooker. Whisk together the vinegar, mustard, oil, sugar, and mustard seeds and celery seeds in a mixing bowl.

pour over the potatoes and toss to combine. Cover and cook on low for 4 to 5 hours, until the potatoes are tender.

remove the cover and sprinkle with the parsley. Reduce the temperature to warm and serve directly from the cooker.

serves **8**

Ultimate Mashed Potatoes

I teach this dish to students across the country in my Do-Ahead Thanksgiving classes. Although the entire casserole is prepared outside the slow cooker, you can place it in a slow-cooker liner and refrigerate or freeze it before Thanksgiving Day, then simply pull it out of the fridge or defrost it and add it to the slow cooker when you are ready. The potatoes are whipped into an ethereal mound and garnished with grated Parmesan cheese and butter—heaven on a plate! You'll be so smug at holiday time when you are able to keep the mashed potatoes warm and delicious for your family and friends.

8 large russet baking potatoes, peeled and cut into 1-inch chunks

4 tablespoons (½ stick) unsalted butter

½ cup freshly grated Parmesan cheese

One 8-ounce package cream cheese, softened

1 cup sour cream

¼ cup finely chopped fresh chives (optional)

Salt and freshly ground black pepper

coat the insert of a 5 to 7-quart slow cooker with nonstick cooking spray or line it with a slow-cooker liner according to the manufacturer's directions.

cook the potatoes in salted water to cover until they are tender when pierced with the tip of a sharp knife.

drain the potatoes thoroughly and put them in the bowl of an electric mixer. Add 2 tablespoons of the butter, ¼ cup of the Parmesan, the cream cheese, and sour cream and beat until fluffy and light. Stir in the chives (if using). Season with salt and pepper.

transfer the potato mixture to the slow-cooker insert and top with the remaining 2 tablespoons butter and ¼ cup Parmesan. Cook on low for 3 to 4 hours, until the butter is melted and the potatoes are heated through.

serve the potatoes from the cooker set on warm.

serves **8**

VARIATIONS

omit the Parmesan and add 1½ cups crumbled blue cheese to the potatoes when beating the potatoes with cream cheese.

cook 6 to 8 strips bacon until crisp, then drain and crumble. Add the bacon when beating the potatoes.

substitute finely shredded white Cheddar cheese for the Parmesan (also great with bacon).

add ½ to ¾ cup caramelized sliced onions while beating the potatoes.

substitute 8 ounces herbed goat cheese for the cream cheese.

substitute one 2-ounce package Boursin cheese for the cream cheese.

Mom's Buttered and Parsleyed Potatoes

Multicolor fingerling potatoes take a bath in butter and seasonings, then receive a dusting of fresh parsley and grated Parmesan. Serve this side dish with roasted meats or poultry. If fingerlings aren't available, small (about 1 inch in diameter) red potatoes, Yukon golds, or white creamers work well here.

2½ pounds fingerling potatoes (about twenty-four 2½-inch potatoes), scrubbed and cut in half

½ cup (1 stick) unsalted butter, melted

¼ cup olive oil

6 fresh sage leaves, finely chopped

1½ teaspoons salt

½ teaspoon freshly ground black pepper

¼ cup finely chopped fresh Italian parsley for garnishing

¼ cup freshly grated Parmesan cheese for garnishing

put the potatoes in the insert of a 5- to 7-quart slow cooker. Add the butter, oil, sage, salt, and pepper and stir to distribute the ingredients. Cover and cook on low for 4 to 5 hours, until the potatoes are tender.

combine the parsley and cheese in a small bowl and sprinkle over the top of the potatoes.

serve the potatoes immediately.

serves **6**

Potatoes Boulangerie

The story is told that in France, at the end of the day, after the boulangerie had baked its bread, it would make its ovens available to its customers for them to roast their meats. The meat would roast on a top rack, and a gratin of potatoes would bake below, collecting the drippings from the roasts. This dish is similar, with its flavor derived from bacon, leeks, and double-strength chicken broth, and finished with a bit of cream. The low and slow heat cooks the potatoes evenly, and this dish is perfect to serve with roasted meats or poultry. A mandoline or food processor makes short work of the potatoes.

6 medium russet potatoes, peeled and cut into ¼-inch-thick slices

6 strips bacon, cut into ½-inch pieces

3 leeks, thinly sliced, using the white and some of the tender green parts

2 teaspoons dried thyme

1 cup double-strength chicken broth

1½ teaspoons salt

1 teaspoon Tabasco sauce

1 cup heavy cream

coat the insert of a 5- to 7-quart slow cooker with nonstick cooking spray or line it with a slow-cooker liner according to the manufacturer's directions. Arrange the potatoes in the cooker and set aside.

cook the bacon in a large skillet until crisp, then transfer to paper towels to drain. Cook the leeks and thyme in the bacon drippings until the leeks are soft, 2 to 3 minutes.

add the chicken broth, salt, and Tabasco to the skillet and heat, scraping up any browned bits from the bottom of the pan. Pour the contents of the skillet over the potatoes and pour the heavy cream evenly over the potatoes. Cover and cook on high for 2½ to 3 hours, until the potatoes are tender.

serve from the slow cooker set on warm.

serves 6–8

Potatoes Pizzaiola

The aroma of tomatoes and oregano coming from your slow cooker will have your family clamoring to know what's for dinner! These potatoes are layered with onion, oregano, tomato sauce, and cheeses for a delicious side dish to pair with roasted or grilled meats and chicken.

4 tablespoons extra-virgin olive oil

2 cloves garlic, minced

2 teaspoons dried oregano

One 28- to 32-ounce can crushed tomatoes

2½ teaspoons salt

1 teaspoon freshly ground black pepper

8 medium red potatoes, scrubbed and cut into ¼-inch-thick slices

½ medium red onion, cut into thin half rounds (about ¼ cup)

2 cups shredded mozzarella

1 cup freshly grated Parmigiano-Reggiano cheese

coat the insert of a 5- to 7-quart slow cooker with nonstick cooking spray or line it with a slow-cooker liner according to the manufacturer's directions.

heat 2 tablespoons of the oil in a large saucepan over medium-high heat. Add the garlic and oregano and sauté for 30 seconds, until fragrant.

add the tomatoes, 1 teaspoon of the salt, and ½ teaspoon of the pepper and stir to combine. Simmer uncovered for 30 to 45 minutes. Taste and adjust the seasoning. Put the potatoes, onion, remaining 1½ teaspoons salt, ½ teaspoon pepper, and 2 tablespoons oil in a large mixing bowl and toss until the potatoes and onion are coated. In another bowl, mix together the cheeses.

pour ½ to ¾ cup of the sauce to cover the bottom of the slow-cooker insert. Top with half the potatoes and sprinkle with half the cheese. Spoon an even layer of sauce over the top. Repeat the layers with the remaining potatoes, cheese, and sauce (see savvy). Cover and cook on high for 5 hours or on low for 8 hours.

serve from the cooker set on warm.

serves 6–8

slow-cooker savvy
It's important to remember that the cookers are different sizes and shapes, so the amount of the sauce and number of layers will differ with each, but there should be an even number of layers.

Five-Spice-Glazed Sweet Potatoes

Asian five-spice powder has a smoky, complex flavor and pairs well with sweet potatoes. The addition of a bit of soy sauce and rice wine to the pot gives you a delicious side dish to serve with pork or poultry.

4 large sweet potatoes, peeled, cut into ½-inch-thick slices

4 tablespoons (½ stick) unsalted butter, melted and cooled slightly

2 tablespoons vegetable oil

2 tablespoons soy sauce

2 tablespoons rice wine (mirin) or dry sherry

2 tablespoons light brown sugar

1 teaspoon five-spice powder

coat the insert of a 5- to 7-quart slow cooker with nonstick cooking spray or line it with a slow-cooker liner according to the manufacturer's directions.

arrange the sweet potatoes in the slow-cooker insert. Combine the remaining ingredients in a mixing bowl and pour over the potatoes in the slow-cooker insert.

cover and cook on low for 5½ to 6 hours, until the sweet potatoes are tender when pierced with the tip of a paring knife.

serve the sweet potatoes from the cooker set on warm.

serves 6—8

Maple Chipotle–Glazed Sweets

Wedges of sweet potatoes glazed with smoky chipotle chile and sweet maple syrup are a wake-up call for your appetite! Serve these at your next potluck, and wait for the compliments!

8 medium sweet potatoes, peeled, halved lengthwise, and cut into wedges

2 tablespoons unsalted butter, melted

2 tablespoons canola oil

4 chipotle chiles in adobo, minced

¼ cup maple syrup

coat the insert of a 5- to 7-quart slow cooker with nonstick cooking spray or line it with a slow-cooker liner according to the manufacturer's directions.

arrange the sweet potatoes in the slow cooker. Combine the remaining ingredients in a small bowl, pour over the potatoes, and stir to coat the wedges. Cover and cook on high for 4 hours, until the wedges are tender when pierced with the tip of a paring knife.

serve the potatoes from the cooker set on warm.

serves **6–8**

Crock-Baked Sweets

Baking sweet potatoes in the slow cooker will save you the hassle of turning on the oven. You can arrange the potatoes in the slow cooker and then go off and enjoy the next six hours without worrying. The potatoes are delicious split open and slathered with butter, especially maple or honey-flavored, or you can mash them with your favorite seasonings.

6 to 8 medium sweet potatoes, scrubbed

prick each potato a few times with the tip of a sharp paring knife. Arrange the potatoes in the insert of a 5- to 7-quart slow cooker. Cover and cook on low for 6 hours, until the potatoes are tender when pierced with the tip of a knife.

serve the potatoes split open.

serves 6–8

Apple Praline Sweet Potato Gratin

This simple gratin-with-a-twist combines sweet potatoes, tart apples, and pecans in an apple cider and brown sugar glaze. It's more of a pie than a side dish. Equally at home on the weeknight table as it is on a holiday buffet, it's delicious paired with ham, roasted pork, chicken, or turkey.

4 large sweet potatoes, peeled and cut into ½-inch-thick slices

2 large Granny Smith apples, peeled, cored, and cut into ½-inch-thick slices

½ cup (1 stick) unsalted butter, melted

½ cup firmly packed light brown sugar

¼ cup dark corn syrup

½ cup apple cider or apple juice

1 teaspoon ground cinnamon

1 cup pecans, toasted, for garnish

coat the insert of a 5- to 7-quart slow cooker with nonstick cooking spray or line it with a slow-cooker liner according to the manufacturer's directions.

layer the sweet potatoes and apples in the slow cooker. Combine all the remaining ingredients except the pecans in a small mixing bowl and pour over the potatoes and apples in the cooker. Cover and cook on low for 7 hours, until the potatoes are tender when pierced with the tip of a paring knife.

sprinkle the top of the casserole with the pecans. Serve from the cooker set on warm.

serves 6–8

Orange-Thyme Glazed Carrots

Carrots are a kid-friendly option for side dishes, and this dish uses so-called baby carrots, with orange, honey, and thyme to glaze them. These are a winner at holiday meals.

½ cup (1 stick) unsalted butter, melted

¼ cup honey

1 cup orange juice

Grated zest of 1 orange

1 teaspoon dried thyme

½ cup chicken broth

Two 16-ounce bags baby carrots (see savvy)

coat the insert of a 5- to 7-quart slow cooker with nonslick cooking spray or line it with a slow-cooker liner according to the manufacturer's directions.

combine all the ingredients in the slow cooker and stir to coat the carrots. Cover and cook on low for 4 to 6 hours, until the carrots are tender.

serve the carrots from the cooker set on warm.

serves 6–8

carrot savvy
If you would prefer to use large whole carrots, you will need 2 pounds, and I recommend that you peel and cut them into 1-inch lengths.

Caramelized Onions

Sweet, golden brown, and melting into their own sauce, these onions are a terrific addition to soups or stews and make a terrific topping for burgers, grilled meats, or sandwiches. Make sure to use sweet onions, like Vidalia, Walla Walla, Texas 1015's, or Maui onions; these onions have 6 percent sugar and are the only ones that can carry the label "sweet." Ordinary brown onions will give you a harsh-flavored dish. Store in an airtight container in the refrigerator for up to 3 days or in the freezer for up to 2 months.

½ cup (1 stick) unsalted butter, melted

2 tablespoons canola or vegetable oil

2 tablespoons sugar

1½ teaspoons salt

1 teaspoon Tabasco sauce

1 teaspoon dried thyme

¼ cup chicken broth

6 large sweet onions, cut into half rounds (see savvy)

combine all the ingredients except the onions in the insert of a 5- to 7-quart slow cooker. Add the onions and toss to coat. Cover and cook on low for 10 to 12 hours, until the onions are golden brown.

stir several times during the cooking process, and check them at 10 hours, to make sure they don't burn. Remove the onions from the cooker and cool before serving.

makes about **5** cups

onion savvy
Brown onions are stored for months, and do not add a sweet flavor to dishes. Yellow onions are sometimes labeled "sweet (and are *not* okay to use)," and red onions are a fair substitute for the sweet onions called for. Once cooked, the onions may be refrigerated for up to three days or frozen for up to two months.

Creamed Pearl Onions with Sherry and Mushrooms

A tradition for my family at Thanksgiving dinner is to have creamed onions in a sherry and mushroom sauce. This dish doesn't contain any cream; instead the onions become tender and creamy in the low and slow braise and are mixed with with cremini mushrooms and sherry.

½ cup (1 stick) unsalted butter, melted

½ cup double-strength chicken broth

1½ teaspoons salt

1 teaspoon freshly ground black pepper

⅛ teaspoon freshly grated nutmeg

1 pound pearl onions, peeled (see savvy)

1 pound cremini mushrooms, sliced

combine all the ingredients in the insert of a 5- to 7-quart slow cooker. Cover and cook on low for 4 to 5 hours, until the onions are tender and ready to serve.

serves **8**

onion savvy
To peel pearl onions, bring a large pot of salted water to a boil, drop the onions in the water, and bring back to a boil. Drain the onions and let stand until cool enough to handle. Cut the root end from each onion and slip off the peels.

Stuffed Onions

Stuffed onions were a staple of the 1950s and 1960s when onions were inexpensive and could be stuffed with everyday ingredients. I love what the slow cooker does to make them tender, caramelized, and scrumptious, and they can be stuffed with a variety of fillings. Follow the basic instructions for preparation, and make a filling that will suit your main course. I like to serve these on a platter surrounding grilled or roasted meats.

8 medium sweet onions, such as Vidalia

Fillings (facing page)

½ cup (1 stick) unsalted butter, melted

2 tablespoons olive oil

2 tablespoons sugar

½ cup double-strength chicken broth

cut the top off each onion and peel back the skins to the root end. Cut off the skins, leaving the root end intact. Place the onions in a large skillet and add enough water to come halfway up the onions. Bring the water to a boil and continue to boil for 10 to 15 minutes, until the onions are tender but not cooked through. You just want the onions to be pliable so that you can scoop out the center. Remove the onions from the pan and cool.

using a sharp paring knife, cut around the center of the onion on the stem end, leaving at least two layers of the onion on the outside. Reserve the centers to use for the filling. Stuff the onions with one of the fillings.

combine the butter, oil, sugar, and broth in the insert of a 5- to 7-quart slow cooker and arrange the stuffed onions in the cooker. Spoon some of the liquid over the onions. Cover and cook on low for 6 hours or on high for 3 hours, until the onions are tender.

serve the onions ladeling any juice from the cooker over them.

serves 6–8

stuffed onion savvy
Since all onions are not alike, you may have a bit of stuffing left over; I usually surround the stuffed onions with the leftover stuffing in the bottom of the cooker, and serve those bits as well.

CHEESY CHIPOTLE SWEET ONION FILLING

¼ cup (½ stick) unsalted butter

1½ cups finely chopped reserved onions

2 chipotle chiles in adobo, minced

3 cups fresh bread crumbs

2 cups finely shredded white Cheddar cheese

melt the butter in a medium skillet over medium-high heat. Add the chopped onions and chiles and sauté until the onions begins to turn golden, 5 to 6 minutes.

transfer the contents of the skillet to a mixing bowl and allow to cool a bit. Add the bread and cheese and mix together.

SAUSAGE FILLING

8 ounces bulk pork sausage

1½ cups finely chopped reserved onions

3 cups fresh bread crumbs

2 cups finely shredded Swiss cheese

brown the sausage in a large skillet, breaking up any large pieces. Add the chopped onions to the skillet and cook until softened, about 3 minutes.

transfer the contents of the skillet to a mixing bowl and allow to cool a bit. add the bread and cheese and mix together. Stuff the cooked onions with the mixture.

BLUE PORT FILLING

½ cup (1 stick) unsalted butter

1½ cups finely chopped reserved onions

3 cups fresh bread crumbs

2 cups crumbled blue cheese

2 tablespoons Ruby Port

melt the butter in a small skillet over medium-high heat. Add the chopped onions and sauté until the onions begin to soften and turn translucent, about 5 minutes.

transfer the mixture to a bowl and allow to cool a bit. Add the bread, blue cheese, and port and mix together.

Cippolini Onions with Balsamic Glaze

Cippolini are tiny sweet onions that are great accompaniments for grilled meats, poultry, or seafood. I love these glazed onions stuffed into sandwiches, served atop a juicy burger, or as part of an antipasto platter.

½ cup (1 stick) unsalted butter

¼ cup firmly packed light brown sugar

½ cup balsamic vinegar

⅓ cup double-strength chicken broth

1½ pounds cippolini onions, peeled (see savvy)

put all the ingredients in the insert of a 5- to 7-quart slow cooker and stir to coat the onions.

cover and cook on low for 3 to 4 hours, until the onions are tender and glazed with the sauce.

cool and serve at room temperature or store in the refrigerator for up to 4 days.

serves **8**

onion savvy
Since cippolini many not be available in all areas of the country, you may want to use pearl onions for this dish. Follow the instructions for peeling on page 362.

Braised Root Vegetables

Root vegetables become sweet, creamy, and full of flavor when braised in the slow cooker. Try your favorite combinations. Make sure to cut each vegetable to the same size so they all cook in the same amount of time.

2 medium sweet potatoes, peeled and cut into ½-inch pieces

3 medium carrots, peeled and cut into ½-inch pieces

2 medium parsnips, peeled and cut into ½-inch pieces

2 medium red or Yukon gold potatoes, scrubbed and cut into ½-inch pieces

2 cups ½-inch pieces peeled and seeded butternut squash

2 medium red onions, quartered and separated

½ cup (1 stick) unsalted butter, melted

½ cup chicken or vegetable broth

1 teaspoon dried thyme

2 teaspoons salt

1 teaspoon freshly ground black pepper

stir together all the ingredients in the insert of a 5- to 7-quart slow cooker. Cover and cook on high 2½ to 3 hours or on low for 4 to 5 hours.

remove the vegetables from the slow cooker with a slotted spoon and arrange on a serving platter. Spoon some of the sauce over the vegetables and serve.

serves 6–8

Cabbage Braised with Riesling and Caraway

Braised cabbage becomes sweet in the slow cooker with the addition of Riesling and the piquant flavor of caraway. Serve this as a side dish with pork or chicken.

2 tablespoons olive oil

2 medium sweet onions, finely chopped

2 teaspoons caraway seeds

10 cups thinly sliced green cabbage (about 2 medium heads)

2 cups Riesling wine

1 teaspoon freshly ground black pepper

heat the oil in a large skillet over medium-high heat. Add the onions and caraway seeds and sauté until the onions are softened, about 3 minutes. Transfer the contents of the skillet to the insert of a 5- to 7-quart slow cooker.

add the cabbage, Riesling, and pepper and stir to coat the cabbage and distribute the ingredients. Cover and cook on low for 4 to 5 hours, until the cabbage is tender.

serve from the cooker set on warm.

serves 6–8

Cider-Braised Red Cabbage

This dish of brilliant red cabbage and red onions braised in apple cider with tart Granny Smith apples is a great choice to serve with pork or poultry. Leftover cabbage may be stored in the refrigerator for up to three days; reheat gently to serve.

2 medium red onions, cut into half rounds

10 cups thinly sliced red cabbage
(about 2 large heads)

2 medium Granny Smith apples, peeled, cored, and cut into ½-inch-thick slices

1 cup apple cider or apple juice

2 whole cloves

2 tablespoons light brown sugar

2 tablespoons balsamic vinegar

combine all the ingredients in the insert of a 5- to 7-quart slow cooker and toss to coat and combine. Cover and cook on low for 4 to 5 hours, until the cabbage is tender.

remove the cloves. Serve the cabbage from the cooker set on warm.

serves 6—8

Spinach Parmesan Strata

A mixture of creamy spinach and Parmesan puffs up in the slow cooker, making a delicious side dish to serve with prime rib or roasted chicken. A *strata* is a casserole made with bread, eggs, milk, and cheese. It is usually served for brunch or a light dinner, but this one is great as a side dish or vegetarian entrée.

2 tablespoons unsalted butter

2 medium shallots, finely chopped

Two 16-ounce packages frozen chopped spinach, defrosted and drained

¼ teaspoon freshly grated nutmeg

6 large eggs

2 cups milk

1½ teaspoons salt

1 teaspoon Tabasco sauce

6 cups bread cubes, crusts removed (a sturdy bread like Pepperidge Farm)

1 cup freshly grated Parmesan cheese

coat the inside of the insert of a 5- to 7-quart slow cooker with nonstick cooking spray or line it with a slow-cooker liner according to the manufacturer's directions.

melt the butter in a medium skillet over medium-high heat. Add the shallots and sauté for 2 minutes, until softened. Add the spinach and nutmeg and sauté until the liquid in the pan is evaporated. Set aside to cool.

whisk together the eggs, milk, salt and Tabasco in a large bowl. Arrange half the bread in the slow-cooker insert. Top with half of the spinach mixture and half the cheese. Layer the remaining bread, spinach, and cheese. Pour the egg mixture over the casserole and press down to make sure the bread has absorbed the egg mixture. Cover and cook on low for 3 to 3½ hours, until the strata is cooked through.

serve from the cooker set on warm.

serves **6–8**

SPINACH PARMESAN STRATA

FRUITED CHICKEN TAGINE

CHICKEN TORTILLA SOUP

PIZZA DIP

CREAMY LOADED BAKED-POTATO SOUP

ALPHABET BEEF VEGETABLE SOUP

ULTIMATE MASHED POTATOES

BUTTERNUT SQUASH BRAISED WITH THYME AND CIDER

Butternut Squash Braised with Thyme and Cider

Sweet butternut squash is a perfect vegetable to braise in the slow cooker because it becomes caramelized and tender when cooked low and slow. The addition of thyme and apple cider gives this squash lots of personality. Serve the squash with pork or poultry as a colorful and interesting side dish (see savvy).

½ cup (1 stick) unsalted butter, melted

¼ cup firmly packed light brown sugar

1 cup apple cider

2 teaspoons dried thyme

4 cups 1-inch chunks peeled and seeded butternut squash

combine all the ingredients in the insert of a 5- to 7-quart slow cooker. Cover and cook on high for 3½ to 4 hours, until the squash is tender.

serve the squash from the cooker set on warm.

serves **6–8**

slow-cooker savvy
This squash is also delicious puréed. When the squash is tender, use an immersion blender to purée it. Serve the squash in the cooker set on warm.

Apples and Sauerkraut

My friend Martha Mand made an Estonian dish called *Hapukapsa*, a caramelized apple and sauerkraut dish that she serves stuffed in a crown roast of pork at holidays. Martha's recipe translates well to the slow cooker, which allows the apples and sauerkraut to caramelize with a long slow braise. Serve this dish with pork or alongside corned beef.

½ cup (1 stick) unsalted butter

2 large onions, coarsely chopped

¼ cup sugar

6 cups finely shredded green cabbage (about 1 ½ medium heads)

Three 15-ounce cans sauerkraut, rinsed, drained, and squeezed dry

2 medium Granny Smith apples, peeled, cored, and thinly sliced

melt the butter in a large skillet over medium-high heat. Add the onions and sugar and sauté until the onions begin to soften, 3 to 4 minutes.

transfer the mixture to the insert of a 5- to 7-quart slow cooker. Add the remaining ingredients and stir to combine. Cover and cook on low for 4 to 5 hours, until the cabbage is tender.

serve the sauerkraut from the cooker set on warm.

serves 6–8

Peperonata

Confetti-colored bell peppers and onions combine to make a delicious side dish or topping for grilled meats, sausages, chicken, or seafood. This also makes a terrific topping for crostini or bruschetta, served at room temperature. Peperonata may be kept in the refrigerator for up to one week.

2 tablespoons extra-virgin olive oil

¼ cup tomato paste

2 teaspoons dried oregano

1 teaspoon dried basil

1 teaspoon sugar

½ teaspoon freshly ground black pepper

½ teaspoon finely chopped fresh rosemary

2 tablespoons balsamic vinegar

3 medium red onions, cut into half rounds

2 medium red bell peppers, seeded and sliced

2 medium yellow bell peppers, seeded and sliced

2 medium orange bell peppers, seeded and sliced

1 teaspoon salt

combine the oil, tomato paste, oregano, basil, sugar, pepper, rosemary, and vinegar in the insert of a 5- to 7-quart slow cooker and stir to blend.

add the vegetables and stir to coat. Cover and cook on low for 4 to 5 hours, until the peppers are tender. Season the peperonata with the salt.

serve from the cooker set on warm.

serves 6–8

Stuffed Peppers

Stuffed peppers, like many other foods, got a bad rap from cafeteria service, where the tired peppers looked like little green sagging buckets filled with crusty ground beef and rice. No one wants to eat that! These peppers are stuffed with a creamy chicken filling and are cooked in a marinara sauce. They turn out creamy, and, most of all, delicious.

4 cups marinara sauce, either fresh (page 398) or prepared

¼ cup dry red wine

2 tablespoons unsalted butter

2 tablespoons olive oil

2 medium shallots, finely chopped

4 ounces smoked ham, finely chopped

4 ounces white button mushrooms, finely chopped

8 ounces ground chicken or turkey

3 tablespoons all-purpose flour

½ cup chicken broth

1 tablespoon cream sherry

1½ cups heavy cream

⅛ teaspoon freshly grated nutmeg

½ cup freshly grated Parmigiano-Reggiano cheese

¼ cup finely chopped fresh Italian parsley

6 medium red bell peppers, tops removed, and reserved, seeds and membrane removed

pour the marinara into the insert of a 5- to 7-quart slow cooker and stir in the wine. Melt the butter with the oil in a large skillet over medium-high heat. Add the shallots, ham, and mushrooms and sauté until the mushroom liquid is evaporated. Add the chicken to the skillet and sauté, breaking up any large pieces, until it is no longer pink.

sprinkle the flour over the mixture and cook for 3 minutes, stirring to scrape up any browned bits from the bottom of the pan. Gradually stir in the broth and add the sherry. Bring the mixture to a boil. Stir in the cream, nutmeg, cheese, and parsley.

spoon the mixture into the bell peppers, set the peppers in the slow-cooker insert, and cover with the reserved tops. Cover and cook on high for 2½ hours or on low for 5 hours, until the peppers are tender and the filling is heated through. Carefully remove the bell peppers from the cooker.

serve each pepper in a pool of the marinara sauce on a dinner plate.

serves **6**

Stuffed Tomatoes

Stuffed tomatoes were a staple at my mother's house in the summer when the tomatoes were picked ripe from the vines. Mom would split them and top them with a delicious mixture of fresh bread crumbs, Romano and Parmesan cheeses, garlic, and fresh parsley and basil. She would cook them on the stovetop, but the slow cooker does a great job with these tomatoes. They are a stars during the summer months, served with grilled meats, fish, or chicken. The tomatoes are best warm or at room temperature.

½ cup olive oil

3 large meaty tomatoes, cut horizontally in half

Salt and freshly ground black pepper

4 cups fresh bread crumbs

½ cup freshly grated Romano cheese

½ cup freshly grated Parmesan cheese

4 cloves garlic, minced

¼ cup finely chopped fresh Italian parsley

¼ cup finely chopped fresh basil

pour ¼ cup of the oil into the insert of a 5- to 7-quart slow cooker. Arrange the tomato halves in the slow-cooker insert and sprinkle with salt and pepper. Combine the bread crumbs, both cheeses, the garlic, parsley, basil, and ¼ teaspoon pepper in a bowl.

mound the mixture on the tomato halves and drizzle with the remaining ¼ cup oil. Cover and cook on low for 3½ to 4 hours, until the tomatoes are cooked through.

spoon some of the pan juices over the tomatoes, turn off the cooker, and serve the tomatoes warm.

serves 6

All-American Stewed Tomatoes

When the tomatoes in your garden are threatening to overrun everything else, put your slow cooker to work and make this flavorful stewed tomato dish. Keep them on hand to use as you would canned tomatoes, or serve them covered with buttered bread crumbs as a side dish. The tomatoes will keep in in the refrigerator for up to one week or in the freezer for up to six months; store them in zipper-top plastic bags.

2 tablespoons olive oil

1 medium onion, coarsely chopped

1 medium green bell pepper, seeded and coarsely chopped

10 large tomatoes, peeled, cored, and cut into wedges

3 tablespoons brown sugar

1½ teaspoons salt

½ teaspoon freshly ground black pepper

combine all the ingredients in the insert of a 5- to 7-quart slow cooker. Cover and cook on low for 8 hours, until the tomatoes are tender.

allow the tomatoes to cool before serving.

serves 6—8

South-of-the-Border Stewed Tomatoes

A variation on All-American Stewed Tomatoes, this south-of-the-border version can be used to make all manner of Southwestern dishes, or it can be served as a sauce over grilled meats, chicken, or fish. Store in airtight containers in the refrigerator for up to five days or in the freezer for up to six months.

2 tablespoons olive oil

1 medium onion, coarsely chopped

2 Anaheim chiles, seeded and coarsely chopped

1 teaspoon ground cumin

1 teaspoon dried oregano

2 tablespoons sugar

1½ teaspoons salt

10 large tomatoes, peeled, cored, and cut into wedges

heat the oil in a large skillet over medium-high heat. Add the onion, chiles, cumin, and oregano and sauté until the onion begins to soften, 4 to 5 minutes.

transfer the mixture to the insert of a 5- to 7-quart slow cooker and stir in the sugar, salt, and tomatoes. Cover and cook on low for 8 hours.

allow the tomatoes to cool before serving.

serves 6

Herbed Cherry Tomatoes

Multicolored cherry or grape tomatoes, roasted slowly with olive oil, garlic, and herbs, create a lovely side dish for any main course. The tomatoes can also be served as a relish or condiment.

½ cup extra-virgin olive oil

6 cloves garlic, sliced

2 teaspoons dried tarragon

1 teaspoon dried chervil

½ teaspoon dried dill

6 cups varicolored cherry or pear tomatoes

combine all the ingredients in the insert of a 5- to 7-quart slow cooker. Cover and cook on high for 1½ hours or on low for 3 hours.

serve the tomatoes at room temperature.

serves **6**

Zucchini, Tomato, and Leek Gratin

Zucchini the size of baseball bats can appear in your garden without notice; that's when you start shredding the zucchini and freezing it in four-cup packages for this terrific gratin, layered with leeks, tomato, and tarragon. Salt the zucchini and tomatoes before layering in the casserole to eliminate any excess moisture.

4 cup shredded zucchini

3 tablespoons salt

3 medium tomatoes, cut into ½-inch-thick slices

2 leeks, coarsely chopped, using the white and tender green parts

4 tablespoons extra-virgin olive oil

2 teaspoons dried tarragon

½ teaspoon freshly ground black pepper

2 tablespoons tomato paste

½ cup chicken broth

Freshly grated Parmigiano-Reggiano cheese for garnishing

place the zucchini in a colander, sprinkle with 1 teaspoon of the salt, and press any moisture out of the zucchini. Sprinkle the tomatoes with 1 teaspoon salt and let drain on paper towels.

toss the leeks with 2 tablespoons of the oil and pour the remaining 2 tablespoons oil in the insert of a 5- to 7-quart slow cooker. Combine the tarragon, pepper, tomato paste, remaining salt and the broth in a small bowl. Arrange a layer of tomatoes in the slow-cooker insert and sprinkle with 2 tablespoons of the tomato paste mixture. Top with a layer of zucchini, sprinkle with 2 tablespoons of the tomato paste mixture, and top with some of the leeks. Continue to layer the ingredients, and pour the remainder of tomato paste mixture over the vegetables.

cover and cook on high for 1½ to 2 hours, until the vegetables are tender. Remove the cover and cook on low another hour.

serve the gratin warm or at room temperature with a sprinkling of grated Parmigiano-Reggiano.

serves 6–8

Yellow Squash Crock Casserole

Yellow squash casseroles are legendary in the South; you can count on a squash casserole to be on the table at most potlucks, with the guests evaluating whether it's worthy of the rest of the spread! This casserole, with its creamy, cheesy sauce, filled with nuggets of squash and ham and then covered with buttered cracker crumbs, is the perfect dish to serve with meats, chicken, or seafood.

6 medium yellow squash, cut into ½-inch pieces

1 teaspoon salt

4 tablespoons unsalted butter, plus 2 tablespoons, melted

1 medium onion, finely chopped

1 teaspoon dried thyme

¼ cup all-purpose flour

½ cup chicken broth

2 cups heavy cream

1 teaspoon Tabasco sauce

2½ cups finely shredded sharp white or mild Cheddar cheese

1 cup finely chopped ham

10 buttery crackers, crushed (about ½ cup)

¼ cup finely chopped fresh Italian parsley

¼ cup freshly grated Parmesan cheese (see savvy)

coat the insert of a 5- to 7-quart slow cooker with nonstick cooking spray or line it with a slow-cooker liner according to the manufacturer's directions.

place the squash in a colander and sprinkle with the salt. Set the squash aside for 30 minutes to drain excess moisture.

melt the 4 tablespoons butter in a medium saucepan over medium-high heat. Add the onion and thyme and sauté until the onion is softened, about 4 minutes. Sprinkle the flour into the saucepan and cook, stirring, for 3 minutes. Stir in the chicken broth, cream, and Tabasco and bring the sauce to a boil, stirring constantly. The sauce should be quite thick. Pour the sauce into the slow-cooker insert and fold in the Cheddar cheese and ham. Press out any excess moisture from the squash with paper towels and add the squash to the slow-cooker insert. Stir to distribute the ingredients.

cover and cook on high for 1½ to 2 hours, until the casserole is heated through and the squash is tender. While the casserole is cooking, stir together the melted butter, crushed crackers, parsley, and Parmesan.

sprinkle the top of the casserole with the buttered cracker crumbs and serve from the cooker set on warm.

serves 6–8

parmigiano savvy
Parmigiano-Reggianno is made only in the Parma region of Italy; it is stamped, so you know what you are buying, and it can be expensive. With that in mind, I recommend Parmigiano when I think the taste of the dish depends on its use, but in other instances, when strong flavors are used in a dish, as they are here, it is perfectly fine to use a domestic Parmesan to sprinkle over the top of the casserole.

Tomato, Corn, and Yellow Squash with Dill Butter

A no-brainer never tasted so delicious. This combination of cherry tomatoes, fresh corn cut off the cob, yellow squash, and dill butter is a terrific side dish for almost any entrée, and the creamy corn gives a sweet and crunchy texture to the dish. If you can't find decent fresh corn (in the dead of winter in Minnesota), you can use frozen corn that has been defrosted, but add it during the last hour of cooking time.

½ cup (1 stick) unsalted butter, melted

1 teaspoon salt

½ teaspoon freshly ground black pepper

2 tablespoons finely chopped fresh dill

6 cups fresh corn kernels (6 to 8 medium ears)

2 cups cherry tomatoes

4 yellow squash, cut into ½-inch pieces

combine all the ingredients in the insert of a 5- to 7-quart slow cooker. Cover and cook on high for 1½ to 2 hours, until the corn and tomatoes are tender.

serve from the slow cooker set on warm.

serves 6–8

Ultimate Creamed Corn

A favorite recipe from my Thanksgiving Dinner classes, this corn is simple but incredibly delicious. The corn may be made the day before and refrigerated before cooking.

½ cup (1 stick) unsalted butter, melted

¼ cup all-purpose flour

1 teaspoon salt

1 teaspoon sugar

1 cup milk

1½ cups heavy cream

Three 16-ounce packages frozen corn, defrosted

½ cup grated Parmesan cheese

coat the insert of a 5- to 7-quart slow cooker with nonstick cooking spray or line it with a slow-cooker liner according to the manufacturer's directions.

whisk the butter, flour, salt, sugar, and milk in a mixing bowl until smooth. Add to the slow-cooker insert and stir in the cream and corn. Sprinkle the cheese over the top. Cover and cook on high for 2½ to 3 hours, until the corn is thick and bubbling.

serve the corn from the cooker set on warm.

serves **8**

Corn on the Cob, Slow Cooked

A big problem at any barbecue is having enough corn on the cob for everyone, and keeping it warm. This recipe is the solution. Foil-wrapped corn bathes in flavored butter and keeps warm in the slow cooker until you are ready to serve it.

½ cup (1 stick) unsalted butter, at room temperature

2 teaspoons salt

½ teaspoon freshly ground black pepper

½ teaspoon sweet paprika

6 to 8 large ears fresh corn, shucked and silks removed

mix the butter, salt, pepper, and paprika in a small bowl. Break each ear of corn in half and place each half on a square of aluminum foil that is 1-inch larger than the ears. Spread 2 teaspoons of the butter on each ear of corn and wrap the corn in the foil.

place the ears in the slow cooker. Cover and cook on high for 1 to 2 hours, until the corn feels tender when the ear is squeezed.

serve the corn from the cooker set on warm.

serves 6—8

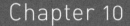

Chapter 10

Something Saucy and Spicy Going On

Sauces cooked in the slow cooker take on a smooth, rounded flavor, due to their long, slow simmering. Not only savory sauces but also sweet sauces, such as pumpkin butter, applesauce, chutney, and berry jam, are great choices for slow cooking. The cooker is also ideal for keeping sauces warm at a constant temperature for serving, especially gravies and sauces for those holiday meals that can seem so hectic for many hosts.

Sausage Gravy

When my daughter attended college in the South, I became a connoisseur of sausage gravy and would try it at most of the breakfast places while visiting. I decided that the quality of the gravy definitely depended on the quality of the sausage, so make sure to use a good-quality sausage when you make this. Keep it warm in the slow cooker when serving biscuits and eggs for breakfast. It's a real crowd pleaser!

3 pounds bulk pork sausage (Jimmy Dean is a good brand)

½ cup all-purpose flour

1 teaspoon dried sage

1 teaspoon dried thyme

2 cups chicken broth

4 cups milk

Salt and freshly ground black pepper

cook the sausage in a large skillet over high heat until it is no longer pink. Transfer it to the insert of a 5- to 7-quart slow cooker. Add the flour, sage, and thyme to the same skillet and cook for 3 minutes, whisking constantly.

whisk in the chicken broth and bring to a boil. Transfer the mixture to the slow cooker and stir in the milk. Cover and cook on low for 2 hours. Season with salt and pepper.

serve from the cooker set on warm.

makes about **7** cups

Chicken Gravy

Creamy chicken gravy is the only sauce to serve with fried chicken and mashed potatoes, but it also comes in handy for serving with plain grilled chicken or over plain steamed rice. The gravy will stay warm in the slow cooker for hours, so you can set it and forget it while you go about your day. Any leftover gravy can be frozen for up to three months.

6 cups chicken broth

3 cups milk

½ cup (1 stick) unsalted butter, melted

½ cup all-purpose flour

¼ cup reconstituted demi-glace or pan drippings from a chicken, fat skimmed

Salt and freshly ground black pepper

pour the broth and milk into the insert of a 5- to 7-quart slow cooker. Stir together the butter, flour, and any drippings in a small bowl.

whisk the mixture into the chicken broth in the slow cooker. Cover and cook on high for 4 hours or on low for 7 to 8 hours, until the gravy is thickened. Season with salt and pepper.

serve from the cooker set on warm.

makes about **10** cups

Turkey Gravy

If you are roasting a turkey, the drippings from the turkey will give your gravy a beautifully rich golden color. If you are making gravy for a slow-cooked turkey breast, you won't have drippings, because the turkey is steamed rather than roasted; in that case, I recommend that you use a demi-glace to further enhance the flavor and color of your gravy.

½ cup (1 stick) unsalted butter

½ cup all-purpose flour

⅓ cup reconstituted demi-glace or pan drippings from a turkey

8 cups chicken or turkey broth

Salt and freshly ground pepper

melt the butter in a medium saucepan over medium-high heat. Add the flour and cook, whisking constantly, for 3 minutes. Whisk in the drippings and broth and bring to boil.

transfer to the insert of a 5- to 7-quart slow cooker. Cover and cook on high for 4 hours or on low for 7 to 8 hours. Season with salt and pepper.

serve from the cooker set on warm.

makes about **10** cups

Beef Gravy

Rich beef gravy is a delicious addition to dinner, especially accompanying a standing rib roast and ladled over mashed potatoes. I highly recommend using reconstituted demi-glace for this gravy, because the flavor is outstanding. Any leftover gravy can be used for hot roast beef sandwiches or frozen for up to three months.

½ cup (1 stick) unsalted butter

½ cup all-purpose flour

1½ teaspoons dried thyme

1 cup reconstituted demi-glace or pan drippings from a roast

8 cups beef broth

melt the butter in a large saucepan over medium-high heat. Add the flour and cook for 3 minutes, whisking constantly.

whisk in the thyme, demi-glace, and broth and bring to a boil. Transfer to the insert of a 5- to 7-quart slow cooker. Cover and cook on high for 4 hours or on low for 7 to 8 hours.

serve from the cooker set on warm.

makes about 10 cups

Red Wine and Beef Sauce

Red wine reduction sauces are delicious, and this sauce cooks with the lid off and perfumes your home with the flavors of bold red wine, shallots, thyme, and beef stock. When the sauce is reduced, a simple beurre manié is whisked in just before serving. This reduction is great to have on hand in the freezer. I generally make a batch and use some of it, then freeze the rest for up to three months.

½ cup (¼ stick) unsalted butter, melted

½ cup finely chopped shallots

2 teaspoons dried thyme

2 cups full-bodied red wine

8 cups beef broth or reconstituted demi-glace

½ teaspoon freshly ground black pepper

¼ cup all-purpose flour

combine ¼ cup of the butter, the shallots, thyme, red wine, broth, and pepper in the insert of a 5- to 7-quart slow cooker. Cook uncovered on high for 4 hours, until the mixture is reduced by one-third.

stir the remaining melted butter and the flour together, then whisk into the sauce. Cover and cook for an additional 45 minutes, until the sauce is thickened.

serve from the cooker set on warm.

makes about **10** cups

Tomato Sauces

Pasta sauces and sauces for grilled or roasted entrées are great to have in your freezer ready and waiting. On a day when your slow cooker isn't otherwise employed, put it to use making a sauce that can be used at another time. Most of the sauces require a bit of sautéing, but then it's time to let the machine work its magic.

Marinara Sauce

Marinara is a plain tomato sauce that you can flavor however you choose. The initial sauté and subsequent slow cooking result in a delicious sauce to use on pasta, pizza, meats, and vegetables. Marinara will keep in the freezer for up to six months and is terrific to have on hand when you want to make a favorite Italian dish.

¼ cup extra-virgin olive oil

1 medium onion, finely chopped

2 cloves garlic, minced

Pinch of red pepper flakes (optional)

1 teaspoon dried herbs (basil, oregano, and/or rosemary)

Three 28- to 32-ounce cans crushed tomatoes and their juices

2 teaspoons salt

1 teaspoon freshly ground black pepper

½ cup finely chopped fresh Italian parsley (optional)

heat the oil in a small sauté pan over medium-high heat. Add the onion, garlic, red pepper flakes (if using), and dried herbs and sauté until the onion is softened and begins to turn translucent, about 5 minutes.

transfer the contents of the skillet to the insert of a 5- to 7-quart slow cooker and stir in the tomatoes, salt, and pepper. Cover and cook on high for 4 hours or on low for 8 to 9 hours.

taste and adjust the seasoning. Stir in the parsley (if using).

serve from the cooker set on warm.

makes about **12** cups

Bolognese Sauce

Bologna, Italy, is renowned for its culinary riches: mortadella, tortellini, balsamic vinegar, Parmigiano-Reggiano, rich dishes fortified with butter and cream, and, my favorite, pasta with Bolognese sauce. True Bolognese is simmered low and slow on the stovetop, with milk, which enriches the sauce, giving it a luxurious flavor. My favorite pasta to serve with this is wide pappardelle, but choose any noodle you like.

1 tablespoon unsalted butter

2 tablespoons olive oil

1 large sweet onion, such as Vidalia, finely chopped

1 cup finely diced carrot

1 cup finely diced celery

1 clove garlic, minced

1 pound lean ground pork

8 ounces ground veal

8 ounces lean ground beef

⅛ teaspoon ground nutmeg

⅛ teaspoon ground cinnamon

1 cup whole milk

1 cup dry white wine or vermouth

Three 32-ounce cans crushed plum tomatoes (San Marzano tomatoes are best)

Salt and freshly ground black pepper

melt the butter in the oil in a large skillet over medium heat. Add the onion, carrot, celery, and garlic and sauté until the vegetables are softened. Add the meats and sauté until no longer pink, breaking up any large chunks with a wooden spoon.

spoon off any fat or water from the pan until the pan is dry (see savvy). Add the nutmeg and cinnamon and sauté for another 2 minutes to allow the flavors to blend. Stir in the milk and boil until the milk has just about evaporated.

transfer the contents of the skillet to the insert of a 5- to 7-quart slow cooker. Add the wine and tomatoes and stir to blend. Cover and cook the sauce on high for 6 to 7 hours. Season with salt and pepper.

serve from the cooker set on warm.

makes **10** cups sauce

fat savvy
A great way to remove fat and water from the skillet is to use a bulb baster (it's not just for turkey!). Don't pour the fat down your drain because it could clog it. Instead, cool the fat, pour it into a zipper-top plastic bag, and dispose of it in the garbage.

Vegan Pasta Sauce

When a friend's daughter and son-in-law were coming to visit, she was panicking about what to cook for them because they were vegan, meaning they ate no animal products, thus eliminating any dishes with butter, cheese, or eggs. Since pasta is a great entrée, I developed this sauce recipe for them, and it's terrific to simmer in the slow cooker. Whether you are a vegan or not, the chunky vegetables and aromatic herbs make this a delicious sauce for pasta, but it can also be used for pizza. For meat eaters, it is also terrific over grilled chicken, fish, or beef.

2 tablespoon extra-virgin olive oil

2 cloves garlic, minced

½ teaspoon red pepper flakes

1 large onion, coarsely chopped

2 portobello mushrooms, coarsely chopped

1 medium red bell pepper, seeded and coarsely chopped

1 medium yellow bell pepper, seeded and coarsely chopped

1 tablespoon dried oregano

2 teaspoons dried basil

Salt

2 tablespoons balsamic vinegar

Two 32-ounce cans crushed plum tomatoes (see savvy)

Freshly ground black pepper

heat the oil in a large sauté pan over medium-high heat. Add the garlic and red pepper flakes, and sauté until the garlic is fragrant, about 1 minute. Add the onion and sauté until the onion begins to soften, another 2 minutes. Add the remaining vegetables, the oregano, basil, and 2 teaspoons salt and sauté until the vegetables give off some liquid, about 5 minutes.

using a slotted spoon, transfer the vegetables to the insert of a 5- to 7-quart slow cooker. Stir in the vinegar and tomatoes. Cover and cook on high for 4 hours or on low for 8 hours. Season with salt and pepper.

serve from the cooker set on warm.

makes **8** cups

tomato savvy
If you have cans of whole plum tomatoes, crush the tomatoes in your hand and add to the sauce along with their juices.

sauce savvy
Because this recipe makes 8 cups, there will be extra to freeze for another meal. Generally 2 cups of sauce is enough for 1 pound pasta, but many people like a lot of sauce. The sauce may be frozen for up to 4 months, without any problem, and will keep refrigerated for up to 1 week.

Mom's Sunday Sauce

Every Sunday morning in many parts of Italy, Mama will begin her "Sunday sauce," a deeply flavored tomato sauce bubbling with assorted meats and flavored with basil, parsley, and, sometimes, fennel, depending upon which region she's in. When the sauce has simmered all day, she serves it with pasta for Sunday dinner, and there is usually enough left over for meals during the week. Sunday sauce is a slow-simmering delight, and the slow cooker was made for it. The meats braise gently in the sauce, and the flavors come together without your ever having to stir during the day.

1½ pounds boneless beef short ribs, cut into 1-inch chunks

2 teaspoons salt

1 teaspoon freshly ground black pepper

2 tablespoons olive oil

1½ pounds sweet Italian sausages

2 pounds ground pork

2 cups chopped sweet onion, such as Vidalia

1 tablespoon dried basil

1 tablespoon dried parsley

Three 32-ounce cans crushed tomatoes in thick purée (you can also use tomato purée, or canned plum tomatoes in their juice; just make sure to crush them before adding)

3 tablespoons sugar

pat the short ribs dry with paper towels and sprinkle evenly with some of the salt and pepper. Heat the oil in a large skillet over high heat. Add the ribs and brown on all sides. Transfer to the insert of a 5- to 7-quart slow cooker. Add the sausages to the skillet and sauté over medium-high heat until browned on all sides. Transfer to the slow-cooker insert. Add the pork to the skillet and sauté until the meat loses its pink color.

drain off any excess water or fat that may have accumulated in the pan and add the onion, basil, parsley, and remaining salt and pepper. Sauté until the onion is translucent, 5 to 7 minutes. Transfer the contents of the skillet to the slow-cooker insert. Gently pour in the tomatoes and add the sugar. Stir the sauce until the mixture is well combined.

cover and cook on high for 4 to 5 hours or low for 8 to 10 hours. At the end of the cooking time, taste the sauce for salt, pepper, and sugar and add if necessary.

serve the meat separately from the sauce.

makes **8–12** cups

VARIATIONS

substitute a 3-pound chuck roast for the short ribs and sausage. Brown both as directed before adding to the slow cooker. When the sauce is finished cooking, remove the roast from the sauce, scrape off any fat from the meat, and cut into serving pieces.

substitute 2 pounds pork shoulder, trimmed of fat and cut into 1-inch pieces, for the ground pork.

substitute hot Italian sausage for the sweet sausage.

Sweet and Saucy

The slow cooker takes the guesswork out of sweet sauces, jams, marmalades, and chutneys. When fruits are in season, I'm at the farm stands stocking up for slow-cooked sauces that will keep in the freezer. Serve these sauces alongside entrées, or for dessert over ice cream, cake, or cream pie. With these sauces, the slow cooker relieves you of having to watch the sauce or jam constantly. The slow cooker takes good care of your fruits and turns them into splendid sauces.

Berry Good Sauce

I love blackberries, but then again I love all berries. When they are in season, you will see me loading up the back of the car with berries to make into this sauce. Not only do I make this sauce for myself, but I also make it for my friends so that they can share in my obsession. This deep purple sauce is a mixture of berries in lemon-flavored syrup thickened with cornstarch. You can choose your favorite berries, mixing and matching, or use only one type. Serve this sauce over ice cream. It's delicious hot or cold over cake, waffles, pancakes, or as a sauce to serve over cream pie or cheesecake. It's also delicious layered with cake and whipped cream in parfait glasses.

2 pints fresh blackberries

2 pints fresh strawberries, hulled, cut into quarters if large

2 pints fresh blueberries, picked over for stems

1 to 1½ cups sugar (depending on the sweetness of the berries)

2 tablespoons fresh lemon juice

Grated zest of 1 lemon

2 tablespoons cornstarch

mix all the ingredients together in the insert of a 5- to 7-quart slow cooker. Cover and cook on low for 4 hours, stirring twice during the cooking time.

allow the sauce to cool before removing from the cooker. Store in airtight containers in the refrigerator for up to 1 week or in the freezer for up to 3 months.

makes about **10** cups

slow-cooker savvy
Frozen fruit doesn't really work well in this sauce. It tends to fall apart, and the resulting sauce is mushy and the fruit unrecognizable.

Strawberry Rhubarb Sauce

This ruby-red sauce flavored with orange and a hint of nutmeg is terrific over ice cream, served with French toast for breakfast, or alongside scones or biscuits. Rhubarb is sold in stalks, and the redder the stalk, the more flavorful the rhubarb. When cooked, the rhubarb melts into the sauce and is almost indiscernible, except for its tart flavor. The sauce is delicious warm, cold, or at room temperature.

2 pints strawberries, hulled

2½ cups granulated sugar, plus more as needed

4 to 6 stalks rhubarb (about 12 ounces), tough ends trimmed, cut into 1-inch pieces

¼ cup orange juice

⅛ teaspoon freshly grated nutmeg

place the strawberries, 2½ cups sugar, rhubarb, and orange juice in the insert of a 5- to 7-quart slow cooker and stir to combine. Cover and cook on high for 2½ to 3 hours or low for 6 hours. At the end of the cooking time, stir in the nutmeg and taste for sugar. If the sauce is too tart, add up to ½ cup additional sugar and cook for another 1 hour on low.

remove the sauce from the insert and allow the sauce to cool. Store in airtight containers in the refrigerator for up to 1 week or the freezer for up to 6 months.

makes about **4** cups

Applesauce

Highly spiced with cinnamon, this applesauce will wake folks up when they taste it. The apple flavor is very intense and delicious. If you like Granny Smith apples, I recommend you use half Granny Smith and another cooking apple (see savvy), because the tart Granny Smiths will need more sugar.

10 cups peeled, cored, and quartered cooking apples (about 12 large)

1⅔ cups sugar

2 teaspoons ground cinnamon

½ teaspoon salt

½ cup apple juice

⅛ teaspoon freshly grated nutmeg

combine the apples, sugar, cinnamon, salt, and apple juice in the insert of a 5- to 7-quart slow cooker. Cover and cook on high for 4 hours or on low for 8 to 10 hours. Using an immersion blender or potato masher, purée the applesauce.

stir in the nutmeg and let the applesauce cool to room temperature. Store in airtight containers in the refrigerator for up to 1 week or the freezer for up to 3 months.

makes about 10 cups

apple savvy
Preferences for cooking apples will vary by region; these are some that work well in this recipe: Braeburn, Fuji, Rome, and Granny Smith.

Pumpkin Butter

Pumpkin butter is a smooth, intensely flavored pumpkin spread that can be used on toast, scones, or biscuits. A delicious addition to your holiday table, its maple-and-spice flavor will complement any type of roll or bread that is served.

Three 28- to 32-ounce cans pumpkin purée

¼ cup maple syrup

1⅔ cup firmly packed light brown sugar

2 teaspoons pumpkin pie spice

2 teaspoons vanilla extract or vanilla bean paste

4 tablespoons (½ stick) unsalted butter

combine all the ingredients in the insert of a 5- to 7-quart slow cooker. Cover and cook on low for 5 to 6 hours, until thickened and fragrant.

cool to room temperature and store in airtight containers in the refrigerator for up to 2 weeks or in the freezer for up to 3 months.

makes about **6** cups

Pear Butter

Similar to apple butter, and intensely flavored with cinnamon, cloves, and ginger, pear butter can be served like pumpkin or apple butter with breads, biscuits, and cornbread. Pear butter makes a nice gift for a hostess or special friend.

12 medium Bosc or Anjou pears, peeled, cored, and cut into chunks

½ cup pear nectar or apple juice

1 cup firmly packed light brown sugar

¾ cup sugar

1 teaspoon ground cinnamon

½ teaspoon ground cloves

½ teaspoon ground ginger

combine all the ingredients in the insert of a 5- to 7-quart slow cooker. Cover and cook on low for 5 hours, until the pears are soft. Using a potato masher or immersion blender, purée the butter.

cool to room temperature and store in airtight containers in the refrigerator for up to 2 weeks or in the freezer for up to 3 months.

makes about 10 cups

Five-Spice Pear Sauce

Smoky Chinese five-spice powder, juicy red pears, and orange-flavored syrup combine to make a sauce that is delectable to serve anytime in place of applesauce. You will love the interesting flavors in this sauce, especially with roasted pork or poultry.

12 ripe red pears, peeled, halved, and cored

1 cup orange juice

½ cup rice wine (mirin)

1½ cups firmly packed light brown sugar

1 teaspoon five-spice powder

Grated zest of 1 orange

combine all the ingredients in the insert of a 5- to 7-quart slow cooker. Cover and cook on high for 3½ to 4 hours or on low for 7 to 8 hours, until the pears are soft.

uncover the slow cooker, and, using an immersion blender or potato masher, purée the pear sauce.

cool to room temperature and store in airtight containers in the refrigerator for 1 week or the freezer for up to 3 months.

makes about **10** cups

Just-Peachy Sauce

This luxurious sauce made with fresh or frozen peaches is delicious as a topping for ice cream, pound cake, French toast, bread pudding, or ice cream pies, or as a layer between ladyfingers or cake for a trifle. Easily put together in the slow cooker, the sauce will perfume your home with the aromas of peaches and cinnamon.

½ cup peach nectar or apple juice

3 tablespoons cornstarch

10 cups large ripe peaches (10 to 12 large), peeled, pitted and cut into thick wedges, or three 16-ounce bags frozen sliced peaches, defrosted

3 cups sugar

2 tablespoons fresh lemon juice

1 tablespoon ground cinnamon

¼ teaspoon ground nutmeg

put the peach nectar and cornstarch in the insert of a 5- to 7-quart slow cooker and stir to dissolve the cornstarch. Add the remaining ingredients and stir well.

cover the slow cooker and cook on high for 3½ to 4 hours or on low for 8 hours, until the sauce is thick and glossy.

remove from the slow cooker and allow to cool before storing in airtight containers. Refrigerate the sauce for up to 1 week or freeze for up to 2 months.

makes 4–5 cups

Peach Melba Sauce

Peche Melba is a classic French dessert consisting of poached peaches covered with raspberry sauce. This combination of flavors also makes a great sauce. Try using it on ice cream, plain cheesecake, or layered with crème fraîche in parfait glasses.

Three 16-ounce bags frozen sliced peaches, defrosted and coarsely chopped, or 9 cups peeled, pitted, and coarsely chopped fresh peaches

Two 16-ounce bags unsweetened raspberries, defrosted, or 6 cups fresh raspberries, rinsed and picked over

2½ cups sugar

Grated zest of 1 orange

2 tablespoons cornstarch

combine all the ingredients in the insert of a 5- to 7-quart slow cooker. Cover and cook on high for 3 to 4 hours, until the fruit is softened and the sauce is thickened. Cool to room temperature. Using an immersion blender, purée the sauce, then push the purée through a fine-mesh sieve.

store the sauce in airtight containers in the refrigerator for up to 1 week or the freezer for up to 1 month.

makes about **10** cups

Mango Chutney

Chutney is a sweet and savory condiment that is served with Indian foods. When mangoes are on sale at my local grocer or farmers' market, I'm there grabbing the plumpest ones for this terrific chutney. I will give this away as gifts in pretty jars to my friends at Christmastime; I'll include the recipe to go with it, too. The chutney is traditionally served with curry, but it also can be spooned over a block of softened cream cheese and served with crackers. It's delicious as well stirred into mayonnaise and used to dress chicken salad.

10 large ripe mangoes, peeled, pitted, and cut into ½-inch dice

½ cup cider vinegar

1 cup firmly packed dark brown sugar

1 cup golden raisins

1 teaspoon freshly grated ginger

1 jalapeño pepper, seeded and finely chopped

3 cloves garlic, minced

1 teaspoon ground cumin

½ teaspoon ground coriander

½ teaspoon turmeric

Two 4-inch cinnamon sticks

combine all the ingredients in the insert of a 5- to 7-quart slow cooker. Cover and cook on high for 4 hours, until the mixture is thickened and the mangoes are soft.

cool to room temperature, remove the cinnamon sticks, and store in airtight containers in the refrigerator for up to 4 weeks or in the freezer for up to 1 month.

makes about **10** cups

Apple Pear Chutney

Autumn fruits pair in this sweet and savory condiment that is terrific served with pork or poultry. Try using this chutney to glaze a ham or pork roast; the sauce from the roasting pan will be a delicious combination of the drippings and the chutney.

1½ cups cider vinegar

1½ cups firmly packed dark brown sugar

2 teaspoons crystallized ginger, finely chopped

Two 4-inch cinnamon sticks

1 cup golden raisins

1 cup dark raisins

1 medium onion, finely chopped

Grated zest of 1 lemon

Pinch of cayenne pepper

6 under ripe pears, peeled, cored, and coarsely chopped

6 crisp cooking apples, peeled, cored, and coarsely chopped

combine all the ingredients in the insert of a 5- to 7-quart slow cooker. Cover and cook on high for 4 to 5 hours, until the chutney is thick and the apples and pears are softened.

cool to room temperature, remove the cinnamon sticks, and store in airtight containers in the refrigerator for up to 4 weeks or in the freezer for up to 1 month.

makes about **10** cups

Cranberry Chutney

This sweet and savory sauce is scrumptious served alongside poultry and pork. I serve this at Thanksgiving classes to rave reviews, but it's so good that many students make this all year-round to glaze ham or pork loins.

Two 12-ounce packages fresh or frozen cranberries, defrosted, washed and picked over (discard any white cranberries)

Two 16-ounce bags frozen sliced peaches, defrosted and coarsely chopped

3½ cups sugar

2 medium onions, chopped

1 teaspoon ground cinnamon

½ teaspoon ground ginger

2 cups pecan halves

combine all the ingredients in the insert of a 5- to 7-quart slow cooker. Cover and cook on high for 3 to 4 hours, until the cranberries have popped and the chutney is thickened.

cool to room temperature and store in airtight containers in the refrigerator for up to 4 weeks or in the freezer for up to 3 months.

makes about 8 cups

Apple Cranberry Compote

Dried fruits make terrific compotes to serve on the side with roasted or grilled entrées, particularly pork or chicken. Fragrant with sweet Riesling, cinnamon, and dried fruits, this compote is also delicious spooned over vanilla ice cream.

4 cups Riesling wine

3 cups dried apples, coarsely chopped

1 cup dried cranberries (craisins work, too)

Two 4-inch long cinnamon sticks

1 cup firmly packed dark brown sugar

combine all the ingredients in the insert of a 5- to 7-quart slow cooker. Cover and cook on low for 5 hours, until the liquid has been absorbed and the fruit is plump.

cool to room temperature, remove the cinnamon sticks and store in airtight containers in the refrigerator for up to 4 weeks or in the freezer for up to 3 months.

makes about **4** cups

Cranberry Port Sauce

Scents of the holidays will waft from your slow cooker when this sauce is bubbling away. Fragrant with ginger, cinnamon, and cloves, the sauce is terrific for Thanksgiving dinner but also complements chicken and pork. It can be used to glaze ham or pork roasts and is terrific on a turkey sandwich the day after Thanksgiving!

Two 12-ounce packages cranberries, washed and picked over (discard any white cranberries)

1 cup granulated sugar

¾ cup firmly packed light brown sugar

½ teaspoon ground ginger

1 teaspoon ground cinnamon

⅛ teaspoon ground cloves

2 cups golden raisins

1 cup ruby port

2 tablespoons balsamic vinegar

combine all the ingredients in the insert of a 5- to 7-quart slow cooker. Cover and cook on high for 2½ to 3 hours, until the cranberries have popped and the sauce is thickened.

cool to room temperature and store in airtight containers in the refrigerator for up to 2 weeks or the freezer for up to 3 months. If the sauce is frozen, defrost it in the refrigerator for 36 hours before planning to serve.

makes about **6** cups

Margarita Cranberry Sauce

A friend's dad makes a jalapeño turkey every Thanksgiving, and I thought, "What better condiment for it than a margarita-flavored cranberry sauce?" Lime is one of my favorite flavors, and the contrast with the cranberries is scrumptious. Serve with pork or poultry.

3 cups sugar

1 cup water

⅓ cup fresh lime juice

½ cup tequila

Two 12-ounce bags fresh cranberries washed and picked over (discard any white cranberries)

½ teaspoon ground ginger

½ teaspoon ground allspice

combine all the ingredients in the insert of a 5- to 7-quart slow cooker. Cover and cook on high for 2 to 3 hours, until the sauce is thickened and the cranberries have popped.

cool the sauce and refrigerate for up to 2 weeks.

makes about **4** cups

Not-Your-Mom's Cranberry Orange Sauce

I remember during my childhood a relative once made cranberry orange relish, which I didn't like much. I think the bitterness from the orange pith put me off. Since that time, I've learned to make an orange cranberry sauce, without bitterness, in the slow cooker. The orange and cranberry flavors melt together with cinnamon, clove, and ginger to give you a sauce you'd be proud to have grace your celebration table.

2 cups sugar

1½ cups orange juice

Grated zest of 2 oranges

Two 12-ounce packages fresh cranberries washed and picked over (discard any white cranberries)

1 teaspoon ground cinnamon

½ teaspoon ground ginger

¼ teaspoon ground cloves

combine all the ingredients in the insert of a 5- to 7-quart slow cooker. Cover and cook on high for 2 to 3 hours, until thickened and the cranberries have split.

allow the sauce to cool to room temperature and store in airtight containers in the refrigerator for up to 2 weeks.

makes about **4** cups

Jammin' Jams are foolproof when made in the slow cooker, but you do need to stir them a few times during the cooking process to make sure they aren't sticking. Once the jam is made, it can be refrigerated for two weeks or frozen for up to two months.

Strawberry Jam

Follow this basic recipe for any type of berry you would like to make into jam; the proportions should be the same. This recipe will give you six one-pint jars that can be refrigerated or frozen.

12 cups (3 quarts) strawberries, hulled and cut into quarters

10 cups sugar

⅔ cup fresh lemon juice

combine all the ingredients in the insert of a 5- to 7-quart slow cooker. Cover and cook on high for 2½ hours. Uncover the cooker, stir the jam, and cook covered for another 2 hours.

cool to room temperature and store in airtight containers for 2 weeks in the refrigerator or 2 months in the freezer.

makes about 12 cups

Bellini Peach Jam

Prosecco syrup combines with peaches to create a jam with the taste of the delicious effervescent cocktail that originated at Harry's Bar in Venice, the Bellini. In Venice, white peaches are juiced, and the pits are left in the peach juice to give it a pink tone. The juice is poured into champagne flutes and topped with Prosecco, an Italian sparkling wine.

2 cups Prosecco

10 cups sugar

16 cups peeled, pitted, and coarsely chopped firm but not overly ripe fresh peaches

One 7.5-ounce box powdered pectin

bring the Prosecco to a boil in a saucepan. Add the sugar and boil, stirring, until the mixture is thickened. (It should coat a spoon.) Transfer to the insert of a 5- to 7-quart slow cooker. Add the peaches and pectin and stir to blend. Cover and cook on high for 2 1/2 hours. Uncover the slow cooker, stir the jam, and cook covered for an additional 2 hours.

cool to room temperature and store in airtight containers in the refrigerator for up to 2 weeks or in the freezer for up to 2 months.

makes about 12 cups

Orange Margarita Marmalade

Brilliantly colored and intensely flavored, this marmalade makes it worth getting up in the morning. I have made this with pink oranges and blood oranges, and they are spectacular, but even regular navel oranges will turn out a fine marmalade. The addition of lime that has been cooked in tequila sugar syrup gives this marmalade a delicious new twist. It's important to wash the fruit thoroughly, because the peel will be a major player in the finished marmalade; if it has any wax on it, it will affect the taste of your marmalade.

2 cups tequila (white tequila is fine for this)

8 cups sugar

1 medium lime, washed thoroughly, cut in half, and thinly sliced

1 cup orange juice

16 large navel oranges, washed thoroughly, cut in half, and thinly sliced

stir the tequila, sugar, lime, and orange juice together in a large saucepan. Bring to a boil and continue to boil, stirring, until the mixture becomes thick, about 5 minutes. Transfer to the insert of a 5- to 7-quart slow cooker. Add the oranges and stir to combine. Cover and cook on high for 3 hours. Uncover the cooker, stir the marmalade, and cook coverwed for an additional 3 hours.

cool to room temperature. Transfer the marmalade to airtight containers and store in the refrigerator for up to 4 weeks. The marmalade doesn't freeze very well, so I don't recommend it.

makes about 12 cups

Chapter 11
What's for Dessert?

Desserts in the slow cooker can be anything from a fruit cobbler, rice pudding, bread pudding, hot fudge cake to brandied peaches. All require only a few minutes of prep work and then a long, slow cooking time to bring out the best in the ingredients. You may wonder why you would want to make a dessert in the slow cooker, but if oven space is a concern or if you want to make something and not have to tend it during a busy day, the slow cooker is your ticket. Also, in the heat of summer, a slow cooker can take the place of your oven, so that your hot fudge cake does not heat up the kitchen as well.

PUDDING

Brandied Peaches

Peaches poached in brandy with cloves and cinnamon are delicious served with a dollop of crème fraîche in the center, or warm over ice cream, or garnishing a platter of roasted meats. The peaches keep in the refrigerator for up to two weeks.

½ cup brandy

½ cup (1 stick) unsalted butter, melted

1½ cups firmly packed light brown sugar

Two 4-inch cinnamon sticks

4 whole cloves

½ cup peach nectar

8 large large peaches, peeled, halved, and pitted

combine the brandy, butter, sugar, cinnamon sticks, cloves, and nectar in the insert of a 5- to 7-quart slow cooker and stir to dissolve the sugar. Add the peaches to the slow-cooker insert and turn to coat them with the syrup.

cover and cook on high for 2 hours. Allow the peaches to cool slightly. Using a slotted spoon, remove the spices from the sauce.

serve the peaches with the sauce poured over

serves **8**

Crock-Baked Apples

Soft, tender baked apples are nostalgia food from the nursery, but there is no need any longer to crank up the oven to make these. They are simple to load into the slow cooker, and then simmered low and slow until they are tender and delicious. This version stuffs the apples with a mixture of walnuts and golden raisins flavored with cinnamon and rum.

8 medium apples (see savvy)

½ cup golden raisins

½ cup finely chopped walnuts

1 cup firmly packed light brown sugar

1 teaspoon ground cinnamon

2 tablespoons dark rum

4 tablespoons (½ stick) unsalted butter, melted and slightly cooled

1½ cups apple juice or apple cider

Unsweetened whipped cream for garnishing

Cinnamon sugar for garnishing

core the apples. Place them in the insert of a 5- to 7-quart slow cooker. Stir together the raisins, walnuts, sugar, cinnamon, rum, and butter in a mixing bowl and fill the apples with the mixture. Pour the apple juice into the bottom of the slow-cooker insert. Cover and cook on low for 2½ to 3 hours on high, until the apples are tender.

remove the apples using a spatula to catch any filling that may fall out of the bottom of the apple.

serve the apples with some of the sauce from the bottom of the slow cooker and a dollop of whipped cream, sprinkled with cinnamon sugar.

serves **8**

apple savvy
This preparation works with any apple; my favorites are Granny Smith, Gala, Fuji, Braeburn, and Rome.

Amaretto Poached Pears

When amaretto, brown sugar, and pears are cooked together, the pears are infused with a caramelized almond flavor. A sprinkling of crushed amaretti cookies and chopped toasted almonds completes this delicious dessert. Serve warm or at room temperature. Refrigerate any leftover pears and syrup for up to three days.

½ cup amaretto liqueur

1 cup pear nectar

1½ cups firmly packed light brown sugar

½ cup (1 stick) unsalted butter, melted

6 firm red pears, peeled and cored (see savvy)

½ cup crushed amaretti cookies (about 6)

½ cup chopped almonds, toasted

combine the amaretto, nectar, sugar, and butter in the insert of a 5- to 7-quart slow cooker and stir until the sugar is dissolved. Stand the pears in the liquid, stem-ends up. Cover and cook on low for 4 hours until the pears are tender.

combine the cookie crumbs and almonds in a small bowl and set aside. Uncover the pears and allow to cool.

serve each pear in a pool of the sauce and sprinkled with some of the almond mixture.

serves **6–8**

pear savvy
The easiest way to core the pears is to use a melon baller and go up through the bottom of the pear.

Red Wine Poached Pears with Stilton

The slow cooker takes very good care of pears in this dessert, poaching them in red wine and spices, to pair with tangy Stilton, an English blue cheese. Make sure the pears are not soft but rather under-ripe, otherwise they will fall apart in the slow cooker.

1 cup full-bodied red wine

1 cup Ruby Port

1½ cups firmly packed light brown sugar

One 4-inch cinnamon stick

6 large firm red pears, halved and cored

6 ounces Stilton cheese, at room temperature

combine the wine, port, brown sugar, and cinnamon stick in the insert of a 5- to 7-quart slow cooker. Add the pears to the slow-cooker insert, arranging them in layers, and spoon some of the sauce over the pears.

cover and cook on high for 2 to 2½ hours, until the pears are softened. Uncover the slow cooker and allow the pears to cool to room temperature. Carefully remove them from the cooker and arrange them on a platter. Strain the sauce through a fine-mesh sieve and boil for 5 to 10 minutes until the sauce becomes syrupy.

spoon the syrup over the pears on the platter and scoop a bit of Stilton into the center of each pear. Serve at room temperature.

serves 6–8

Five-Spice Asian Pears

Poached pears infused with five-spice powder make a delicious dessert to serve with green tea ice cream or crème fraîche. They are also terrific as a garnish for a large platter of roasted pork or chicken. Or chop the pears and spoon them over hot cereal for a breakfast treat.

½ cup (1 stick) unsalted butter, melted

1½ cups firmly packed light brown sugar

½ cup dry sherry

1 teaspoon five-spice powder

1 cup pear nectar

8 firm pears, peeled, halved, and cored

mix together the butter, sugar, sherry, five-spice powder, and pear nectar in the insert of a 5- to 7-quart slow cooker. Add the pears to the slow-cooker insert and turn to coat them with the liquid. Cover and cook on high for 2½ hours until tender.

remove the pears with a slotted spoon to a serving bowl and spoon the liquid from the slow cooker over the pears. Serve warm or chilled.

serves **8**

Strawberry Rhubarb Crumble

Sweet red strawberries and tart rhubarb cook together beneath a layer of oatmeal and white chocolate crumble, creating a delectable dessert to serve with vanilla ice cream.

4 cups strawberries, hulled and cut into quarters

4 stalks bright red rhubarb, cut into ½-inch slices

1½ cups granulated sugar

1 teaspoon ground cinnamon

Grated zest of 1 orange

1 tablespoon cornstarch

⅔ cup old-fashioned rolled oats

¾ cup firmly packed light brown sugar

½ cup finely chopped white chocolate

1 cup all-purpose flour

½ cup (1 stick) unsalted butter, chilled and cut into ½-inch pieces

Vanilla ice cream for serving

coat the insert of a 5- to 7-quart slow cooker with nonstick cooking spray. Stir the berries, rhubarb, granulated sugar, cinnamon, zest, and cornstarch together in the insert. Set aside while making the crumble.

stir together the oats, brown sugar, chocolate, and flour in a mixing bowl. Add the butter and cut the butter into the dry ingredients, using a blending fork or pastry blender, until the mixture forms coarse crumbs about the size of peas.

sprinkle the crumble over the fruit. Cover and cook on low for 2½ hours, until the crumble is set and the fruit is bubbling. Uncover the slow cooker and allow to cool for 30 minutes.

serve warm with vanilla ice cream.

serves **8**

Almond Pear Crumble

Amaretto, pears, cinnamon, and nutmeg bake under an almond crumble topping. Choose pears that are firm so they don't disintegrate when cooked. Serve the crumble with a large dollop of whipped cream.

1 cup firmly packed light brown sugar

¼ cup amaretto liqueur

¾ cup (1½ sticks) unsalted butter, melted

8 large firm pears, peeled, cored and coarsely chopped

½ cup granulated sugar

½ cup all-purpose flour

¾ teaspoon ground cinnamon

¼ teaspoon freshly grated nutmeg

⅔ cup sliced almonds

Whipped cream for serving

coat the insert of a 5- to 7-quart slow cooker with nonstick cooking spray. Add the brown sugar, amaretto, and ½ cup of the butter to the slow-cooker insert and stir until blended. Add the pears and turn the pears to coat with the syrup.

stir together the granulated sugar, flour, cinnamon, nutmeg, and almonds in a small bowl. Drizzle the remaining ¼ cup butter into the flour mixture and stir with a fork until the mixture begins to form crumbs. Sprinkle over the top of the pears. Cover and cook on high for 2½ hours, until a skewer inserted into the crumble comes out clean. Uncover and allow to cool for 30 minutes.

serve the crumble warm with a dollop of whipped cream.

serves **8**

Caramel Peaches with Praline Crumble

Juicy peaches bake in a caramel sauce under a brown sugar–pecan crumble. Make this when peaches are in season for the most delicious crumble you will ever eat! Of course, ice cream is the perfect accompaniment, but you can also serve this with unsweetened whipped cream.

2½ cups firmly packed dark brown sugar

¼ teaspoon ground ginger

½ teaspoon ground cinnamon

2 tablespoons cornstarch

2 tablespoons bourbon

8 large ripe peaches, peeled, pitted, and cut into wedges

¾ cup (1½ sticks) unsalted butter

1 cup all-purpose flour

¼ teaspoon freshly grated nutmeg

1 cup chopped pecans

Vanilla ice cream for serving

coat the insert of a 5- to 7-quart slow cooker with nonstick cooking spray. Add 1½ cups of the sugar, the ginger, cinnamon, cornstarch, and bourbon to the slow-cooker insert and stir until blended. Add the peaches and stir to coat them with the sugar. Melt ¼ cup of the butter, add it to the slow-cooker insert, and stir to blend. Stir together the flour, remaining 1 cup sugar, and the nutmeg in a mixing bowl.

add the remaining ½ cup butter to the mixing bowl and cut it in, using a blending fork or pastry blender, until the mixture resembles coarse crumbs.

sprinkle over the top of the peaches and spread the pecans evenly over the crumble. Cover and cook on high for 2 to 2½ hours, until a skewer inserted into the crumble comes out clean. Uncover the cooker and allow to cool for 30 minutes.

serve with vanilla ice cream.

serves **8**

Apple Cranberry Cobbler

Sweet Golden Delicious apples are paired with tart cranberries and bubble under a buttery cobbler topping flavored with maple syrup. With its tantalizing aromas of cinnamon, apples, and cloves, this cobbler will remind you of fall.

6 large Golden Delicious apples, peeled, cored, and coarsely chopped

One 12-ounce package fresh cranberries washed and picked over (discard any white cranberries)

2½ cups sugar

1 tablespoons cornstarch

1 teaspoon ground cinnamon

1 teaspoon cloves

⅛ teaspoon ground ginger

1½ cups (3 sticks) unsalted butter, melted

2 cups unbleached all-purpose flour

¼ cup maple syrup

2 large eggs, beaten

Vanilla ice cream for serving

coat the insert of a 5- to 7-quart slow cooker with nonstick cooking spray. Add the apples, cranberries, 1 cup of the sugar, the cornstarch, cinnamon, cloves, and ginger to the slow-cooker insert and stir to combine.

stir together the butter, flour, remaining 1½ cups sugar, the maple syrup, and eggs in a mixing bowl and spread the batter over the apple mixture. Cover and cook on high for 2½ hours, until a skewer inserted into the center of the batter comes out clean. Uncover and cool for 30 minutes.

serve the cobbler warm with vanilla ice cream.

serves **8**

Hot Lemon Blueberry Pudding Cake

Traditional soufflé pudding cakes puff up and separate into a pudding-like layer on the bottom covered by a sponge cake on the top. This pudding cake takes that one step further and incorporates blueberries into the pudding layer for a delicious surprise. Serve the cake warm.

1 cup fresh blueberries

4 large eggs, separated

Grated zest of 1 lemon

⅓ cup fresh lemon juice

4 tablespoons (½ stick) butter, at room temperature

1⅔ cups milk

1 cup sugar

⅓ cup all-purpose flour

⅛ teaspoon salt

coat the insert of a 5- to 7-quart slow cooker with nonstick cooking spray. Spread the blueberries over the bottom of the slow-cooker insert. Beat the egg whites in a large mixing bowl until soft peaks form, and set aside.

whisk the egg yolks in another mixing bowl. Add the zest and juice, butter, and milk and whisk until blended. Stir together the sugar, flour, and salt in another bowl and add to the egg yolk mixture. Beat until smooth, then fold into the reserved egg whites.

transfer the batter to the slow cooker. Cover and cook on high for 2½ hours.

allow the cake to cool slightly before serving.

serves **6**

Hot Fudge Upside-Down Cake

I will readily admit that I am not a baker, because baking involves science and following directions to the letter. I look for dessert recipes that are simple to make yet produce amazing results. This cake is just one of those recipes that I go back to time and time again. The top layer is an intensely flavored, tender chocolate cake, while the bottom layer is a cross between hot fudge sauce and chocolate pudding. I've adapted this recipe for the slow cooker, which keeps the cake moist on the top and saucy on the bottom.

½ cup milk

3 tablespoons unsalted butter, melted

1 teaspoon vanilla bean paste

1 cup granulated sugar

1 cup all-purpose flour

½ cup cocoa powder (make sure to use natural cocoa powder and not Dutch process)

2 teaspoons baking powder

¾ cup firmly packed light brown sugar

1¾ cups boiling water

Vanilla ice cream or unsweetened whipped cream for serving

coat the insert of a 5- to 7-quart slow cooker with nonstick cooking spray. Stir together the milk, butter, and vanilla bean paste in a mixing bowl. Gradually stir in the granulated sugar, flour, ¼ cup of the cocoa powder, and the baking powder. Spread the batter in the prepared slow-cooker insert.

mix together the brown sugar and remaining ¼ cup cocoa powder in a small bowl and sprinkle evenly over the batter. Pour in the boiling water (do not stir). Cover and cook on high for 2 hours, until a skewer inserted into the center comes out clean. Uncover and allow to cool for about 20 minutes.

serve in bowls with vanilla ice cream.

serves **4-6**

Mexican Hot Chocolate Lava Cake

A guilty pleasure when the weather gets cool here in San Diego is a steaming mug of Mexican hot chocolate, fragrant with cinnamon and a touch of coffee. This cake has all those flavors and separates like Hot Fudge Upside-Down Cake (facing page). It is perfect served with cinnamon gelato or coffee ice cream.

½ cup milk

3 tablespoons unsalted butter, melted

1 teaspoon instant espresso powder

½ teaspoon ground cinnamon

1 cup granulated sugar

1 cup all-purpose flour

½ cup cocoa powder (make sure to use natural cocoa powder and not Dutch process)

2 teaspoons baking powder

¾ cups firmly packed light brown sugar

1¾ cups boiling water

Cinnamon gelato or coffee ice cream for serving

coat the insert of a 5- to 7-quart slow cooker with nonstick cooking spray. Stir together the milk, butter, espresso powder, and cinnamon in a mixing bowl. Gradually stir in the granulated sugar, flour, ¼ cup of the cocoa powder, and the baking powder.

spread the batter in the prepared slow-cooker insert. Mix together the brown sugar and remaining ¼ cup cocoa powder in a small bowl and sprinkle evenly over the batter. Pour in the boiling water (do not stir).

cover and cook on high for 2 hours, until a skewer inserted into the center comes out clean. Uncover and allow to cool for about 20 minutes.

serve in bowls with cinnamon gelato.

serves 4–6

Perfect Crème Brûlée

Crème brûlée is said to have been first served at Trinity College in Cambridge, England, where my daughter studied during college. She lived in a turret (literally) while there, and I have a feeling that pub grub was on the menu for her more times than crème brûlée! Originally called "burnt cream," crème brûlée will sometimes get grainy in the oven if your oven doesn't heat evenly. In the slow cooker with its constant temperature, custard comes out silky and delicious.

8 to 10 cups boiling water

3½ cups heavy cream

⅔ cup superfine sugar

10 large egg yolks

1 tablespoon vanilla bean paste

¼ cup raw sugar

place a rack on the bottom of a 5- to 7-quart slow-cooker insert and set out eight 4-ounce ramekins.

pour in enough of the boiling water to come halfway up the sides of the ramekins when they are eventually added to the cooker. Cover the cooker and set on high to keep the water hot.

whisk together the cream, superfine sugar, and egg yolks in a large mixing bowl until blended. Add the vanilla bean paste and whisk until the vanilla is incorporated. Pour the custard into the ramekins, cover each one with aluminum foil, and set on the rack in the slow-cooker insert.

cover and cook on high for 1½ to 2 hours, until the custards are set. They may be a bit jiggly in the middle but will firm as they cool. Take the cover off the cooker and allow the custards to cool. Remove the foil, replace with plastic wrap, and refrigerate until chilled.

just before serving, sprinkle the raw sugar over each custard. Using a torch or under a preheated broiler, heat the sugar until it begins to bubble and caramelize. If you are broiling, caramelize just a few custards at a time.

allow to cool slightly and serve.

serves **6–8**

Pots de Crème

Chocolate custard cooked to silky perfection in the slow cooker is one of life's guilty pleasures. No need to worry about the eggs curdling because the cooker will keep the custard at a constant temperature, making this chocolate dessert perfect. The custards will keep in the refrigerator for up to two days.

8 to 10 cups boiling water

¾ cup whole milk

¾ cup heavy cream

1 cup chopped semisweet chocolate

4 large egg yolks

⅓ cup sugar

Unsweetened whipped cream for serving

place a slow-cooker insert rack on the bottom of a 5- to 7-quart slow cooker and set out six 4-ounce ramekins.

pour in enough of the boiling water to come halfway up the sides of the ramekins when they are eventually added to the cooker. Cover the cooker and set on high to keep the water hot.

heat the milk and cream in a medium saucepan until small bubbles begin to form around the edges of the pan. Remove from the heat, add the chocolate, and stir until the chocolate is melted and the mixture is slightly cooled.

whisk together the egg yolks and sugar in a mixing bowl, then whisk in the chocolate mixture. Strain the custard through a fine-mesh sieve into a large measuring cup. Pour the custard into the ramekins, cover each one with aluminum foil, and set on the rack in the slow cooker insert.

cover and cook on high for 1½ to 2 hours, until set. They may be a bit jiggly in the middle but they will firm as they cool. Remove the foil, allow the custards to cool to room temperature, and refrigerate until chilled.

serve the pots de crème with a dollop of whipped cream on top.

serves **6**

Pudding

One look into cookbooks from the 1800s, and you will find recipes for rice pudding. They are simple, silken, and delicious when cooked low and slow in the cooker. The basic formula and timing are the same, but the ingredients and flavorings can be quite different. Use a medium-grain rice here; Arborio produces the best results.

Mom's Old-Fashioned Rice Pudding

Generally made with a milk or cream base and flavored with nutmeg, rice pudding has been comfort food for generations. Raisins and other flavors can be added if you are in the mood, but this is your basic recipe. The pudding will keep in the refrigerator for up to three days.

5 cups whole milk

2 cups heavy cream

1¼ cups sugar

1 teaspoon vanilla bean paste

½ teaspoon freshly grated nutmeg

1 cup Arborio or other medium-grain rice, rinsed several times with cold water and drained

coat the insert of a 5- to 7-quart slow cooker with nonstick cooking spray. Whisk together the milk, cream, sugar, vanilla bean paste, and nutmeg in a large bowl and pour into the slow-cooker insert. Add the rice and stir to combine.

cover and cook on low for 2½ to 3 hours, until the pudding is soft and creamy and the rice is tender. Remove the cover, turn off the cooker, and allow to cool for 30 minutes.

serve warm, at room temperature, or chilled.

serves 6–8

VARIATIONS

during the last 30 minutes of cooking, stir in any of the following:

½ cup raisins (dark or golden)

½ cup dried cherries, cranberries, or blueberries

½ cup toasted shredded coconut

Coconut Jasmine Rice Pudding

Jasmine rice has a delicate flavor, and this rice pudding not only takes advantage of that but also incorporates cinnamon and coconut to flavor the pudding. A delicious dessert or afternoon delight, this rice pudding is as scrumptious as it is delicious.

2 cups whole milk

1 cup sugar

2 cups heavy cream

4 large eggs, beaten

1 teaspoon ground cinnamon

1½ cups Jasmine rice, rinsed with cold water and drained

2 cups shredded coconut, toasted

Whipped cream, cinnamon sugar, or chopped mangoes and pinapple for garnishing

coat the insert of a 5- to 7-quart slow cooker with nonstick cooking spray. Heat the milk in a small saucepan until small bubbles form at the edges of the pan. Remove from the heat. Add the sugar and whisk until dissolved. Whisk together the sweetened milk, cream, eggs, and cinnamon in a mixing bowl. Stir in the rice. Transfer the mixture to the slow-cooker insert.

cover and cook on low for 2½ to 3 hours, until the pudding is set. Remove the cover, stir in the coconut, and cook covered for an additional 30 minutes. Allow the pudding to cool in the insert, then transfer it to a bowl. Cover with plastic wrap and refrigerate until cold.

scoop the pudding into bowls and garnish with whipped cream.

serves **8**

Chai Tea Rice Pudding

Flavored with spicy chai tea, this rice pudding has a delicious flavor and a sepia tint to it.

2 cups whole milk

4 chai tea bags

2 cup heavy cream

4 large eggs, beaten

¼ cup granulated sugar

⅔ cup packed light brown sugar

1 teaspoon vanilla bean paste

1½ cups medium-grain rice, such as Arborio, rinsed several times with cold water and drained

Whipped cream or cinnamon sugar for garnishing

coat the insert of a 5- to 7-quart slow cooker with nonstick cooking spray. Heat the milk in a small saucepan until small bubbles form at the edges of the pan. Add the tea bags to the milk and let stand for 10 minutes.

remove the tea bags and allow the milk to cool. Whisk together the chai milk, cream, eggs, both sugars, and vanilla bean paste in a mixing bowl, then stir in the rice. Transfer the mixture to the slow-cooker insert.

cover and cook on low for 2½ to 3 hours, until the pudding is set. Remove the cover and cook for an additional 30 minutes. Allow the pudding to cool in the insert, then transfer it to a bowl. Cover with plastic wrap and refrigerate until cold.

scoop the pudding into bowls and garnish with whipped cream.

serves 6–8

Old-Fashioned Tapioca Pudding

My local supermarket has a deli that sells tapioca pudding, and I have to say it's not very appealing. This tapioca, cooked to creamy richness with vanilla paste and heavy cream, will cure the worst day! I love to serve tapioca with fresh fruit or a fruit purée to cut its richness. The pudding will keep in the refrigerator for up to three days.

3 cups whole milk

1 cup heavy cream

1¼ cups sugar

½ cup pearl tapioca (not instant)

Grated zest of 1 orange

2 large eggs, beaten

1 teaspoon vanilla paste or vanilla extract

coat the insert of a 5- to 7-quart slow cooker with nonstick cooking spray. Whisk together the milk, cream, and sugar in a bowl. Pour into the slow-cooker insert, then sprinkle the tapioca evenly over the top.

cover and cook on low for 2 hours; the tapioca should be transparent. Stir the orange zest into the beaten eggs in a small bowl.

remove the cover from the slow cooker and stir the eggs and vanilla paste into the tapioca.

cover and cook for an additional 30 minutes, until the milk is absorbed. Remove the cover and let the pudding cool for 30 to 40 minutes.

serve warm or chilled.

serves **6–8**

Peach Melba Bread Pudding

Pêche Melba was created by iconic French chef Auguste Escoffier at the Savoy Hotel in London for Australian opera singer Nellie Melba. His creation of poached peaches and raspberry sauce over vanilla ice cream has become world famous, and this is my way of incorporating all the flavors into one simple dessert. The peaches and raspberries flavor the orange custard, and the resulting dessert is delicious served with berry sauce or whipped cream.

Two 16-ounce bags frozen unsweetened raspberries, defrosted and drained

1 cup superfine sugar

2 teaspoons fresh lemon juice

8 cups torn stale egg bread, challah, or croissants

12 medium peaches, peeled, pitted, and coarsely chopped, or three 16-ounce packages frozen peaches, defrosted, drained, and coarsely chopped

3 cups heavy cream

8 large eggs

Grated zest of 1 orange

¼ cup Grand Marnier or other orange-flavored liqueur or 1 teaspoon orange extract

1½ cups granulated sugar

coat the insert of a 5- to 7-quart slow cooker with nonstick cooking spray or line it with a slow-cooker liner according to the manufacturer's directions.

heat the berries, superfine sugar, and lemon juice in a small saucepan until the mixture comes to a boil. Taste the syrup and add more sugar is it is too tart. Strain the mixture through a fine-mesh; you should have ⅔ to ¾ cup of syrup. Put the bread in the slow-cooker insert and stir in the peaches. Pour the raspberry syrup over all.

whisk together the cream, eggs, orange zest, Grand Marnier, and granulated sugar in a large mixing bowl until blended. Pour over the bread in the slow-cooker insert and push the bread down to submerge it.

cover and cook on high for about 3 hours, until puffed and an instant-read meat thermometer inserted in the center registers 185°F. Uncover and allow to cool for 30 minutes.

serve from the cooker set on warm.

serves 6–8

Cappuccino Bread Pudding

A cappuccino from your favorite coffee bar is transformed into a jolt of a dessert in this simple slow-cooker preparation. Using leftover bread or croissants, this dessert can even be served as a wake-up call for breakfast!

8 cups torn stale egg bread, challah or croissants

2 cups chocolate chips or chopped chocolate

3 cups heavy cream

1 cup brewed espresso or strong coffee

8 large eggs

1 tablespoon vanilla extract

2 teaspoons ground cinnamon

1½ cups sugar

½ cup sugar mixed with 1 teaspoon ground cinnamon for garnishing (optional)

Hot fudge sauce for drizzling (optional)

spray the insert of a 5- to 7-quart slow cooker with nonstick cooking spray or line it with a slow-cooker liner according to the manufacturer's directions.

spread the torn bread evenly in the bottom of the slow-cooker insert and sprinkle with the chocolate chips. Whisk together the cream, espresso, eggs, vanilla, cinnamon, and sugar in a large bowl until blended. Pour over the bread and chocolate, pushing the bread down to submerge it.

sprinkle the pudding with the cinnamon sugar (if using). Cover the slow cooker and cook on high for about 3 hours, until puffed and an instant-read thermometer inserted in the center registers 185°F. Uncover and allow the pudding to cool for about 30 minutes.

serve from the cooker set on warm and accompany with hot fudge sauce for drizzling.

serves **8**

Double Chocolate Croissant Bread Pudding

Chocolate is one of those simple pleasures in life. Deep and rich, melting, gooey, and comforting, chocolate makes even the worst day a bit more bearable. This chocolate bread pudding embodies all I love best about chocolate. It is warm, and the chocolate is laced throughout the pudding and then found again in chunks melting into the bread. Make this on a day when you need to scream "I love chocolate" to the world. You won't be sorry!

8 cups torn stale croissants, egg bread, or challah

3 cups chopped bittersweet or semisweet chocolate

4 tablespoons (½ stick) unsalted butter, melted

3 cups heavy cream

8 large eggs

1 tablespoon vanilla bean paste or extract

1 cup sugar

coat the insert of a 5- to 7-quart slow cooker with nonstick cooking spray or line it with a slow-cooker liner according to the manufacturer's directions.

arrange the bread in the slow cooker and sprinkle with 1½ cups of the chocolate. Melt the remaining chocolate with the butter in a small saucepan over low heat. Remove from the heat and allow to cool.

whisk together the melted chocolate, cream, eggs, vanilla bean paste, and sugar in a large mixing bowl until blended; the mixture may look curdled. Pour over the bread and chocolate and push the bread down to submerge it.

cover and cook on high for about 3 hours, until puffed and an instant-read meat thermometer inserted in the center registers 185°F. Uncover and allow to cool for 30 minutes.

serve in the cooker set on warm.

serves 6–8

Piña Colada Bread Pudding

Each year my family spends Thanksgiving in Maui, not for the piña coladas but because we are college basketball fanatics and the season starts the week of Thanksgiving with an elite tournament in Maui. Our stay does include sitting by the pool and enjoying at least one or two piña coladas, those decadent frozen drinks flavored with coconut, pineapple, and rum. At home, dessert doesn't get much better than this tropical bread pudding, studded with pineapple, macadamia nuts, and coconut in the rum-flavored custard. You'll be singing "Tiny Bubbles" before you know it!

8 cups torn stale Hawaiian sweet egg bread, challah, or croissants

2 cups ½-inch chunks fresh pineapple

1 cup chopped macadamia nuts

1½ cups shredded sweetened coconut

3 cups heavy cream

8 large eggs

1 tablespoon vanilla extract or bean paste

¼ cup dark rum

1½ cups sugar

coat the insert of a 5- to 7-quart slow cooker with nonstick cooking spray or line it with a slow-cooker liner according to the manufacturer's directions.

put the bread in the slow-cooker insert, add the pineapple, nuts, and coconut, and toss to combine. Whisk together the cream, eggs, vanilla, rum, and sugar in a large mixing bowl until blended. Pour over the bread and push the bread down to submerge it.

cover and cook on high for about 3 hours, until puffed and an instant-read thermometer inserted in the center registers 185°F. Uncover and allow to cool for 30 minutes.

serve from the cooker set on warm.

serves 6–8

Coconutty Bread Pudding

Coconut is one of my favorite flavors, and in this bread pudding it not only flavors the egg custard but also sets the taste throughout the pudding. Add milk-chocolate chips and macadamia nuts, and this dessert is sure to make everyone at your table smile.

8 cups 1-inch cubes or torn stale sturdy white bread, such as Pepperidge Farm

1½ cups shredded sweetened coconut

1 cup chopped macadamia nuts

1½ cups milk-chocolate chips, such as Ghirardelli or Guittard

One 13- to 14-ounce can coconut milk

1 cup milk

1 cup heavy cream

8 large eggs

½ cup firmly packed light brown sugar

¼ cup dark rum (optional but, oh, so good)

Hot fudge, berry, or buttered rum sauce for serving

coat the insert of a 5- to 7-quart slow cooker with nonstick cooking spray. Put the bread, coconut, macadamia nuts, and chocolate chips in a large bowl. In another bowl, whisk together the coconut milk, milk, cream, eggs, sugar, and rum (if using).

pour the milk mixture over the bread and stir until the bread is soaked. Transfer the bread mixture to the slow-cooker insert. Cover and cook on low for 4 hours, until the pudding is cooked through and an instant-read thermometer inserted in the center reads 170°F. Uncover and cook for an additional 30 minutes.

serve the pudding with hot fudge sauce, berry sauce, or buttered rum sauce.

serves 8–10

Down East Indian Pudding

Legend has it that Indian pudding was served at the first Thanksgiving in Plymouth, Massachusetts. A steamed pudding similar to those served in England for holidays, Indian pudding is prepared using cornmeal and molasses and is flavored with cinnamon, ginger, and nutmeg. The warm pudding is served scooped into bowls and topped with maple-flavored whipped cream or ice cream.

½ cup yellow cornmeal

¾ cup water

4 cups milk

1 large egg

3 tablespoons sugar

½ cup dark molasses

2 tablespoons unsalted butter

1 teaspoon ground cinnamon

1 teaspoon ground ginger

½ teaspoon ground nutmeg

¼ teaspoon salt

½ cup raisins or other dried fruits, such as cranberries or blueberries

2½ cups heavy cream

¼ cup maple syrup

coat the insert of a 5- to 7-quart slow cooker with nonstick cooking spray. Stir together all the ingredients except the heavy cream and maple syrup in a large mixing bowl until well blended. Transfer the mixture to the slow-cooker insert.

cover and cook on high for 3 hours, until set. Carefully remove the slow-cooker insert and allow the pudding to cool for about 30 minutes.

whip the heavy cream in a mixing bowl to stiff peaks, then beat in the maple syrup.

serve the pudding from the cooker set on warm, and accompany with the maple-flavored whipped cream.

serves **8**

Grape-Nuts Custard Pudding

A staple on menus in New England, this comforting custard studded with crunchy Grape-Nuts cereal is comfort food of the first order. Serve the custard cold with unsweetened whipped cream.

1½ cups Grape-Nuts cereal (nuggets, not flakes)

6 large eggs

4 cups milk

1⅓ cups sugar

1 tablespoon vanilla bean paste

1 teaspoon ground cinnamon

2½ cups heavy cream

spray the insert of a 5- to 7-quart slow cooker with nonstick cooking spray. Sprinkle the cereal over the bottom of the slow-cooker insert. Whisk together the eggs, milk, sugar, vanilla bean paste, and cinnamon in a large mixing bowl. Gently pour over the cereal.

cover and cook on high for 2 hours, until the custard is just set. It may seem a little jiggly in the center but will firm while the custard cools. Carefully remove the insert from the liner and allow the pudding to cool to room temperature. Cover with plastic wrap and chill.

whip the cream in a mixing bowl until it forms stiff peaks.

scoop the pudding into bowls and top each serving with a dollop of the cream.

serves **8**

Chapter 12
Party in a Pot

Slow cookers are terrific for entertaining, especially if you are pressed for time and want to set the cooker in the morning and serve directly from it in the evening. These dishes are a little more upscale than weeknight fare, but don't rule them out for a family dinner or celebration during the week. In this chapter I include drinks for serving warm from the slow cooker, as well as warm dips that can be served from smaller cookers, sometimes called "little dippers." The slow cooker is also your friend at the barbecue on the patio, where your cooker will keep your side dish warm until you are ready to eat. Don't overlook the slow cooker at holiday times either; between drinks, gravies, sauces, mashed potatoes, and side dishes, the slow cooker keeps your dishes at a constant safe temperature for serving. So let's celebrate with our slow cookers, and enjoy the party!

How about a Drink?

Slow cookers are perfect for keeping your favorite hot cider or mulled wine warm, but not scalding hot, for serving all through the day. Keeping hot cocoa warm can be tricky, but the warm setting on the slow cooker helps to make a luxurious cocoa that will have your guests swooning with chocolate-mustached delight!

Mulled Red Wine

When I told an Italian friend who owns a wine bar in Umbria that I would be adding spices to red wine and heating it, he thought I'd gone over the edge, until he tasted this warming drink on a cold night. Serve this in glass mugs when people come for dinner; it's a great warm-up from the cold and helps get conversation going.

Three 750-ml bottles medium-bodied red wine, such as Zinfandel, Chianti, or Pinot Noir

¼ cup firmly packed dark brown sugar

1 teaspoon whole cloves

Three 4-inch cinnamon sticks

3 whole allspice berries

Zest from 2 lemons, cut into strips (see savvy)

add all the ingredients to the insert of a 5- to 7-quart slow cooker. Cover and cook on low for 3 to 4 hours. Remove the whole spices and zest.

keep the wine warm in the cooker for up to 8 hours.

serves **8**

zest savvy
It is important to cut only the zest (colored part of the peel) from the lemons and not the white pith, which is harsh and will give your drinks a tart and bitter taste. A serrated peeler works well to peel just the skin and not the pith.

Warm Mulled Cider

Warm cider is my magic elixir for curing the blues and facing down the cold during frigid winters. Fragrant with spices, the cider is liquid comfort for what ails you. Any leftover cider may be stored in the refrigerator.

8 cups apple cider

1 teaspoon whole allspice berries

Two 4-inch cinnamon sticks

6 whole cloves

¼ teaspoon ground ginger

1 cup brandy or rum (optional)

add all the ingredients except for the brandy to the insert of a 5- to 7-quart slow cooker.

cover and cook on low for 4 hours. Remove the whole spices and stir in the brandy (if using).

keep warm in the cooker for up to 8 hours.

serves about 12

Spiced Cranberry Cider

The combination of cider and cranberry juice makes perfect sense, and the result is a delicious ruby-colored, spicy drink flavored with orange zest.

One 48-ounce bottle cranberry juice cocktail

One 48-ounce bottle apple cider or apple juice

Two 4-inch cinnamon sticks

3 whole cloves

½ teaspoon ground ginger

Zest from 2 oranges, cut into julienne strips

combine all the ingredients in the insert of a 5- to 7-quart slow cooker. Cover and cook on low for 3 to 4 hours. Remove the whole spices (see savvy).

keep the cider warm in the cooker for up to 5 hours. Any remaining cider may be cooled to room temperature and refrigerated. Reheat the cider, a cup at a time, in the microwave.

serves 12

slow-cooker savvy
To remove the spices, I use a small strainer to catch the seasonings, which will float on top of the cider. Another gadget that works is a spider, used for scooping out deep-fried food from bubbling oil.

Hot Buttered Rum Cider

This buttered rum cider is a terrific way to warm up your family and friends after a day of skiing or playing in the snow. The buttered rum can be made ahead of time and frozen. The butter doesn't freeze rock solid because of the high alcohol content, so it can be easily measured for the recipe without any problem.

1½ cups (3 sticks) unsalted butter, at room temperature

1 cup firmly packed dark brown sugar

⅔ cup dark rum

2 teaspoons vanilla extract or vanilla bean paste

1 teaspoon ground cinnamon

½ teaspoon ground ginger

¼ teaspoon ground cloves

Two 48-ounce bottles apple cider or apple juice

beat together the butter, sugar, rum, vanilla, cinnamon, ginger, and cloves in a mixer bowl until smooth. Transfer the mixture to an airtight container and refrigerate for up to 2 weeks or freeze for up to 6 months.

place ½ cup of the butter mixture in the insert of a 5- to 7-quart slow cooker and add the cider. Cover and cook on low for 4 hours.

stir the cider before serving from the cooker set on warm.

serves 10–12

Warm Cranberry Punch

Warm cranberry and pineapple juices, spiced with fragrant cinnamon and cloves, make a terrific drink to serve during cold weather or at the holidays. The slow cooker will keep the punch at the perfect temperature for serving.

One 48-ounce bottle cranberry juice cocktail

4 cups pineapple juice

1 cup water

½ cup firmly packed light brown sugar

Three 4-inch cinnamon sticks

½ teaspoon whole allspice berries

1 teaspoon whole cloves

combine all the ingredients in the insert of a 5- to 7-quart slow cooker. Cover and cook on low for 2 hours. Remove the whole spices.

keep the punch warm in the cooker.

serves 12

Wassail

Sometimes when writing a book, you know when you've done too much research. I was always under the impression that *wassail* was a type of mulled wine, when in fact a *wassailing* was also singing in the Middle Ages to apple trees to ensure a good harvest. The wassail was a huge bowl of punch lugged into the orchard and the contents would vary, but apple cider or beer seemed to be the two winners here. So what's a girl to do? I'm sticking with the wine version because I like it—but it has a twist!

Three 750-ml bottles medium-bodied red wine, such as Zinfandel, Barolo, Pinot Noir

1 cup superfine sugar

3 whole star anise pods

3 cups dried apples

1 medium navel orange studded with about 20 whole cloves

1 medium lemon, thinly sliced

put all the ingredients in the insert of a 5- to 7-quart slow cooker. Cover and cook on low for 4 hours. Remove the spices, apples, and orange, leaving the lemon slices.

serve the wassail from the cooker set on warm.

serves 10

Luxurious Hot Cocoa

My friend Lora Brody is the goddess of chocolate; anyone who could write a book entitled *Growing Up on the Chocolate Diet* is someone you want to know! A dear friend and mentor, she has shared many recipes with me, but this one is my favorite, from her book *Chocolate American Style,* which I've adapted to the slow cooker. Lora says hot chocolate has to have more than big flavor, it also should be thick enough to soothe your insides, which is exactly what this does. Make sure to have plenty of garnishes on hand, such as whipped cream, marshmallows, peppermint candy canes, and shaved chocolate.

2 cups heavy cream

16 ounces semisweet chocolate, coarsely chopped

4 cups milk

1 teaspoon vanilla extract

combine all the ingredients in the insert of a 5- to 7-quart slow cooker. Cover and cook on low for 1 hour. Stir up the chocolate from the bottom of the pan with a whisk.

cover and cook on low for another 3 hours.

serve the hot chocolate in the cooker set on warm.

serves 10–12

White Chocolate Mocha

Although some people think that life is too short to eat or drink white chocolate, this coffee-flavored hot chocolate might change your mind. Use white bar chocolate instead of baking chips, because some baking chips don't melt, and your drinks may feel like they have pebbles in them!

2 cups whole milk

2 cups heavy cream

16 ounces white bar chocolate, such as Lindt or Perugina, finely grated

8 cups strong brewed coffee

2 teaspoons vanilla extract

combine the milk, cream, and chocolate in a saucepan and heat, whisking frequently, over medium-low heat until the chocolate is melted and smooth.

pour the mixture into the insert of a 5- to 7-quart slow cooker and add the remaining ingredients. Cover and cook on low for 3 to 4 hours.

serve the mocha from the cooker set on warm.

serves 10–12

Orange-Spiced Coffee

My husband, Chuck, is famous for his flaming dessert coffee, which he flavors with Cointreau, crème de cacao, and Kahlúa. Although the taste is incredible, we have to limit our guests to two! This slow-cooker recipe is an adult coffee with some of the same flavors, and it's a winner. Feel free to have a bottle of Kahlúa or crème de cacao on the side for pouring!

16 cups strong brewed coffee

1½ cups brandy

Three 4-inch cinnamon sticks

3 medium navel oranges, each studded with about 20 cloves

3 cups unsweetened whipped cream for garnishing

combine the coffee, brandy, cinnamon sticks, and oranges in the insert of a 5- to 7-quart slow cooker. Cover and cook on low for 3 hours. Remove the oranges and cinnamon sticks.

serve from the cooker set on warm, and accompany with whipped cream for garnishing.

serves 10–12

Appetizers

Appetizers are meant to be a little something to spur on your appetite for dinner without completely satisfying your hunger. They can accompany predinner drinks, or they can be part of what I call a "grazing party," where the entire party is appetizers and you go home full. I love the slow cooker for making warm dips and keeping them warm throughout the evening. The slow cooker also makes some terrific snack mixes and spicy nuts as well.

Everyone's Favorite Snack Mix

My children know it's holiday time when they smell snack mix. I've added some touches of my own to the original recipe over the years, like goldfish crackers and croutons, and it's still a winner. The good news is you don't have to heat up the oven, and you can freeze the snack mix for up to four months.

½ cup (2 sticks) unsalted butter, melted

2 tablespoons Lawry's seasoned salt

1 tablespoon garlic salt

¼ cup Worcestershire sauce

6 shakes Tabasco sauce

4 cups Crispix cereal

2 cups mixed nuts

One 8- to 10-ounce bag pretzel sticks

One 5-ounce bag plain or Parmesan goldfish crackers

Two 3-ounce bags herbed croutons

combine the butter, seasoned salt, garlic salt, Worcestershire, and Tabasco in the insert of a 5- to 7-quart slow cooker and stir to blend. Add the remaining ingredients and gently stir to coat each piece with the flavored butter.

cook uncovered on high for 2 hours, stirring occasionally. Reduce the heat to low and cook for an additional hour, stirring every 15 minutes, until the mix is dry and crisp.

transfer to baking sheets to cool completely before serving, or store in airtight containers.

serves 8–10

Spicy Crocked Nuts

These sweet and savory morsels are easy to make and keep on hand for nibbling when unexpected guests arrive. Once the nuts are "crocked," they are cooled to room temperature and may then be stored in airtight containers at room temperature for up to two days, or frozen for up to eight months. After a quick defrost, they are ready to serve either as a snack or tossed into salads or vegetable dishes.

4 tablespoons (½ stick) unsalted butter, melted

2 teaspoons Lawry's seasoned salt

1 teaspoon garlic salt

⅛ teaspoon cayenne pepper

4 tablespoons sugar

4 cups pecan halves, walnut halves, or whole almonds

combine the butter, seasoned salt, garlic salt, cayenne, and 2 tablespoons of the sugar in the insert of a 5- to 7-quart slow cooker. Cover and cook on high for 20 minutes.

add the nuts and stir to coat with the butter mixture. Cook uncovered for 2 to 2½ hours, stirring occasionally.

sprinkle the remaining 2 tablespoons sugar over the nuts, toss to coat, and remove the nuts to a baking sheet to cool completely before serving.

serves **8**

The Best Artichoke Spinach Dip on the Planet

Everyone has a recipe for this terrific dip, and my new favorite is this one, which includes bacon and white Cheddar cheese along with the usual suspects. Serve this with bagel chips, pita chips, or baguette slices.

6 strips bacon, cut into ½-inch pieces

1 medium onion, finely chopped

One 16-ounce package frozen chopped spinach, defrosted and drained thoroughly (see savvy)

One 16-ounce package frozen artichoke hearts, defrosted, drained, and coarsely chopped, or two 14- to 15-ounce cans artichoke hearts, drained and coarsely chopped

¼ teaspoon freshly ground black pepper

1½ cups mayonnaise

2 cups shredded sharp white Cheddar cheese

cook the bacon in a large skillet until crisp and remove it to paper towels to drain. Remove all but 2 tablespoons of the bacon drippings from the pan and heat over medium-high heat.

add the onion and sauté until it begins to soften, about 2 minutes. Add the spinach and artichoke hearts and sauté until the water in the pan has evaporated. Season the mixture with the pepper and turn it out into the insert of a 1½- to 3-quart slow cooker. Add the mayonnaise and cheese to the cooker and stir until blended. Cover and cook on low for 2 to 3 hours.

garnish the dip with the bacon bits and serve from the cooker set on warm.

serves **8**

spinach savvy
A potato ricer has a lot of uses, and squeezing spinach dry is just one of them. If you don't have a potato ricer, press the spinach in a sieve. The sauté will take the rest of the moisture out of the vegetables, ensuring that the dip isn't watery.

Hot Broccoli Dip

This dip gives new meaning to the phrase "eat your veggies." Filled with broccoli and mushrooms in a cheesy sauce, this dip is terrific served with pita chips.

4 tablespoons (½ stick) unsalted butter

1 medium onion, finely chopped

3 stalks celery, finely chopped

8 ounces white mushrooms, sliced

8 ounces broccoli florets (about 3 cups)

2 tablespoons all-purpose flour

1 cup chicken broth (or vegetable broth for a vegetarian dip)

2 tablespoons dry sherry

1 cup milk

1 teaspoon salt

6 drops hot sauce

3 cups finely shredded sharp Cheddar cheese

coat the insert of a 3- to 5-quart slow cooker with nonstick cooking spray. Heat 2 tablespoons of the butter in a large skillet over medium-high heat.

add the onion and celery and sauté until the onion begins to soften, about 3 minutes. Add the mushrooms and sauté until the mushrooms begin to color, 5 to 6 minutes. Transfer the contents of the skillet to the slow-cooker insert and add the broccoli. Melt the remaining 2 tablespoons butter in the same skillet over meduim heat.

add the flour to the skillet and cook, stirring, for 3 minutes. Stir in the broth, sherry, and milk and bring to a boil. Stir in the salt and hot sauce.

transfer the contents of the skillet to the slow-cooker insert and fold in the cheese. Cover and cook on low for 3 to 4 hours, until the broccoli is tender and the cheese is melted.

serve the dip from the cooker set on warm.

serves **8**

Refried Bean Dip

This simple dip is a real crowd pleaser; the smooth beans are balanced by chunky pieces of hot sausage, vegetables, and melting cheeses, giving the dip texture and personality. Serve this with sturdy tortilla chips for dipping.

8 ounces spicy sausages, such as chorizo, andouille, or Italian, removed from its casing

1 medium onion, chopped

2 Anaheim chiles, seeded and chopped

1 medium red or yellow bell pepper, seeded and chopped

Two 14- to 15-ounce cans refried beans (nonfat are fine here)

2 cups finely shredded mild Cheddar cheese, or 1 cup each finely shredded Monterey Jack and sharp Cheddar cheese

2 tablespoons finely chopped fresh cilantro

Tortilla chips for serving

spray the insert of a 1½- to 3-quart slow cooker with nonstick cooking spray. Cook the sausage in a medium skillet over high heat until it is no longer pink, breaking up any large pieces with the side of a spoon. Drain the sausage and put it in a mixing bowl to cool. Add the onion, chiles, and bell pepper to the same skillet and sauté until the bell pepper is softened, about 5 minutes. Add to the bowl with the sausage and allow to cool slightly. Add the refried beans to the bowl and stir to blend.

spoon half the bean mixture into the slow-cooker insert and sprinkle with half the cheese. Top with the remaining beans and cheese and sprinkle with the cilantro. Cover and cook on low for 2 to 3 hours.

serve from the cooker set at warm and accompany with sturdy tortilla chips.

serves **8**

Southwestern Chili con Queso

I discovered this dip shortly after I moved to San Diego in the early 1970s, and it quickly became one of my favorites. There are lots of variations on this theme, some using chorizo for added flavor and others using Velveeta, but I love this one with its smoky chipotle flavor.

One 8-ounce package cream cheese, cut into cubes

2 tablespoons unsalted butter

1 medium sweet onion, such as Vidalia, finely chopped

4 chipotle chiles in adobo, minced

1 medium red bell pepper, seeded and finely chopped

1 medium yellow bell pepper, seeded and finely chopped

2 teaspoons ground cumin

2 cups finely shredded sharp Cheddar cheese

2 cups finely shredded Monterey Jack cheese

Fresh vegetables for serving

Tortilla chips for serving

coat the insert of a 1½- to 3-quart slow cooker with nonstick cooking spray. Turn the machine on low and add the cream cheese. Cover and let stand while preparing the other ingredients.

melt the butter in a large sauté pan over medium-high heat. Add the onion, chipotles, bell peppers, and cumin and sauté until the bell peppers become softened, 4 to 5 minutes. Transfer the contents of the sauté pan into the slow-cooker insert and stir to blend with the cream cheese.

fold in the Cheddar and Jack cheeses. Cover and cook on low for 2 to 3 hours.

serve from the cooker set on warm with fresh vegetables and sturdy tortilla chips.

serves 8

Hot Dill and Swiss Dip

My friend and fellow cookbook author Phillis Carey made this terrific dip when we teamed up to do a fund-raiser for a local cancer center in San Diego. We decided to choose old favorite recipes and then prepared our spin on them. This was her favorite cheesy dip, and it's a winner, made with melting Havarti and Swiss cheeses. Serve with cold poached shrimp and crab claws or fresh vegetables for dipping.

2 medium sweet onions, such as Vidalia, finely chopped

2 tablespoons finely chopped fresh dill

1½ cups mayonnaise

2 cups finely shredded Havarti with dill

2 cups finely shredded Swiss cheese

coat the insert of a 1½- to 3-quart slow cooker with nonstick cooking spray. Combine all the ingredients in a bowl and transfer to the slow cooker. Cover and cook on low for 2 to 3 hours, until bubbling.

serve from the cooker set on warm.

serves **8**

Pizza Dip

This dip is really the basis for a pizza fondue. The delicious marinara, flavored with oregano and garlic, is warmed up and readied for dipping with mozzarella sticks, mini meatballs, bread sticks, crusty bread, fresh mushrooms, or cooked sausage rounds. This concept also makes a terrific casual dinner; just double the ingredients and serve from a larger slow cooker.

2 tablespoons extra-virgin olive oil

1 medium onion, finely chopped

2 teaspoons dried oregano

2 teaspoons dried basil

Pinch of red pepper flakes

3 cloves garlic, minced

Two 14- to 15-ounce cans crushed plum tomatoes, with their juice

2 tablespoons tomato paste

1 ½ teaspoons salt

½ teaspoon freshly ground black pepper

½ cup finely chopped fresh Italian parsley

heat the oil in a small saucepan over medium-high heat. Add the onion, oregano, basil, red pepper flakes, and garlic and sauté until the onion is softened, about 3 minutes.

transfer the contents of the skillet to the insert of a 1½- to 3-quart slow cooker. Add the remaining ingredients and stir to combine. Cover and cook on low for 3 to 4 hours.

serve from the cooker set on warm.

serves **8**

Seafood Dip

Filled with clams, shrimp, crab, and cheeses, this warm dip is scrumptious as well as luxurious. Serve with baguette slices or water crackers.

Two 8-ounce packages cream cheese at room temperature

½ cup mayonnaise

8 ounces lump crabmeat, picked over for shells and cartilage

4 ounces cooked shrimp, finely chopped

One 8-ounce can minced or chopped clams, drained

1 teaspoon Old Bay seasoning

1 tablespoon Worcestershire sauce

2 teaspoons prepared horseradish

2 cups finely shredded Gruyère cheese

1 cup freshly grated Parmigiano-Reggiano cheese

coat the insert of a 1½- to 3-quart slow cooker with nonstick cooking spray. In a large bowl, stir together all the ingredients until blended.

transfer the mixture to the slow-cooker insert. Cover and cook on low for 2 to 3 hours, until heated through.

serve from the cooker set on warm.

serves **8**

Warm Clam Dip

My mom's clam dip gets a warm-up here. It's terrific served with chips, pita crisps, or baguette slices.

Two 8-ounce packages cream cheese at room temperature and cut into cubes

½ cup mayonnaise

3 green onions, finely chopped, using the white and tender green parts

2 cloves garlic, minced

Three 8-ounce cans minced or chopped clams, drained with ¼ cup clam juice reserved

1 tablespoon Worcestershire sauce

2 teaspoons anchovy paste

¼ cup finely chopped fresh Italian parsley

coat the insert of a 1½- to 3-quart slow cooker with nonstick cooking spray. Combine all the ingredients in a large mixing bowl, adding the clam juice to thin the dip.

transfer the mixture to the slow cooker, cover, and cook on low for 2 to 3 hours, until bubbling.

serve from the cooker set on warm.

serves 6—8

Mornay Dip for Crab Claws and Shrimp

The days of formal cocktail parties at home seem to have given way to either catered affairs or the ubiquitous "get together" with less lavish food and drink. In many ways I miss the mountains of seafood and the chafing dishes filled with sauces for dipping. This is my ode to the good old days: a creamy sauce flavored with sherry and lobster stock that I serve with stone crab claws and colossal-size shrimp (see savvy).

2 tablespoons unsalted butter

2 medium shallots, finely chopped

2 teaspoons Old Bay seasoning

2 tablespoons all-purpose flour

2 cups lobster stock

¼ cup cream sherry

1 cup heavy cream

¼ cup finely chopped fresh Italian parsley

melt the butter in a small saucepan over medium-high heat. Add the shallots and seasoning and cook for 2 minutes, until the shallots are softened. Add the flour and cook for 3 minutes, whisking constantly. Gradually whisk in the stock and sherry and bring the mixture to a boil.

stir in the cream and parsley to combine. Transfer to the insert of a 1½- to 3-quart slow cooker. Cover and cook on low for 2 to 3 hours.

serve from the cooker set on warm.

serves **8**

party shrimp savvy
When serving shrimp at a party, plan on 4 jumbo shrimp per person, and then add a few extras just to make sure you don't run out of them. Jumbo shrimp number 21 to 25 per pound, so plan accordingly.

Hot Bloody Mary Dip for Shrimp

This warm dip for shrimp has all the flavors of that great cocktail, the bloody Mary, and a creamy texture from the addition of cream cheese. It's delicious for dipping with crab claws or sturdy tortilla chips.

Two 8-ounce packages cream cheese at room temperature, cut into cubes

1½ cups Clamato juice

2 cups spicy tomato juice or bloody Mary mix

2 tablespoons prepared horseradish

⅓ cup Worcestershire sauce

1 teaspoon Tabasco sauce

2 teaspoons celery salt

¼ teaspoon freshly ground black pepper

2 tablespoons fresh lemon juice

1 cup pepper vodka

4 green onions, finely chopped, using the white and tender green parts

4 stalks celery, finely chopped

coat the insert of a 3- to 5-quart slow cooker with nonstick cooking spray. Put the cream cheese in the insert, cover, and cook on low for 20 minutes, until the cream cheese begins to melt. Add the remaining ingredients and stir to combine.

cover and cook on low for 3 to 4 hours, stirring a few times during the cooking time.

serve from the cooker set on warm.

serves **8**

Maytag Blue and Walnut Dip with Apple Dippers

My favorite cheese, nuts, and fruit combine here for a sensational dip. Maytag blue cheese comes from The Maytag Dairy, which was founded by the son of the folks who gave us the Maytag appliances. The blue cheese is aged in caves in Iowa, and it's delicious, but you can use your favorite blue here. Many students ask me how to keep the apples from turning color, and a colleague here in San Diego shared with me that submerging the apples in Sprite will keep them perfectly colored for 4 hours. It does work, and I've used this trick lots of times. When you drain the apples for serving, make sure to pat them dry.

Two 8-ounce packages cream cheese at room temperature

½ cup mayonnaise

2 tablespoons Ruby Port

6 drops Tabasco sauce

1 cup chopped walnuts

2 cups crumbled Maytag blue cheese

4 to 6 Granny Smith Apples, cored and cut into 8 wedges each, for serving

Crackers for serving

coat the insert of a 1½- to 3-quart slow cooker with nonstick cooking spray. Put the cream cheese, mayonnaise, port, Tabasco, walnuts, and blue cheese in a mixing bowl and stir until blended.

transfer the mixture to the slow-cooker insert. Cover and cook on low for 2 to 3 hours, until heated through and bubbly.

serve from the cooker set on warm with the apple wedges and crackers.

serves **8**

Roasted Tomato and Mozzarella Bruschetta

Not only is this a terrific appetizer, but you can also serve these roasted tomatoes over pasta or as a sauce for a grilled entrée. The slow cooker roasts the tomatoes. When they cool, you stir in fresh mozzarella to make a terrific bruschetta topping to serve as part of an antipasto.

¼ cup extra-virgin olive oil

1 large red onion, coarsely chopped

2 teaspoons dried basil

1 teaspoon fresh rosemary leaves, finely chopped

4 cloves garlic, minced

Three 28- to 32-ounce cans whole plum tomatoes, drained

2 teaspoons salt

⅛ teaspoon red pepper flakes

8 ounces fresh mozzarella, cut into ½-inch dice

Lightly toasted baguette slices for serving

combine all the ingredients except the mozzarella and the baguette slices in the insert of a 5- to 7-quart slow cooker. Cover and cook on high for 2 hours. Uncover the cooker and cook on low, stirring occasionally, for 3 hours, until the tomato liquid has almost evaporated.

remove the tomato mixture to the bowl of a food processor and pulse on and off five times to chop the tomatoes and garlic. Transfer to a serving bowl to cool, then stir in the mozzarella.

serve with the toasted baguette slices.

serves **8**

Orange Chipotle Wings

Smoky chipotles, orange, and honey combine in this wing treatment to give you a sweet, smoky, and sticky chicken experience. Although there are six chipotles in this recipe, they provide more smoky flavor than heat, but if you would prefer to reduce the amount, that's fine.

3 pounds chicken wing drumettes

1 medium red onion, finely chopped

6 chipotle chiles in adobo, finely chopped

1 teaspoon ground cumin

2 cloves garlic, minced

1½ cups orange juice

½ cup honey

½ cup ketchup

½ cup finely chopped fresh cilantro

coat the insert of a 5- to 7-quart slow cooker with nonstick cooking spray.

arrange the wings on a rack in a baking sheet and broil until the wings are crispy on one side.

turn the wings and broil until crispy and browned, another 5 minutes.

remove the wings from the oven. If you would like to do this step ahead of time, cool the wings and refrigerate for up to 2 days; otherwise, place the wings in the prepared slow-cooker insert.

combine the remaining ingredients in a mixing bowl, pour over the wings, and turn the wings to coat with the sauce.

cover and cook the wings on high for 3 hours, until they are cooked through; turn them twice during the cooking process to ensure even cooking.

serve the wings from the cooker set on warm.

serves **8**

Spicy Rasta Wings

Jamaican jerk seasoning combines with a mango-flavored sauce for sweet and spicy wings with a deliciously different flavor. You can make your own jerk seasoning, or you can buy it in the supermarket.

3 pounds chicken wing drumettes

2 teaspoons jerk seasoning

1½ cups mango nectar

¼ cup firmly packed light brown sugar

coat the insert of a 5- to 7-quart slow cooker with nonstick cooking spray.

arrange the wings on a rack in a baking sheet and broil until the wings are crispy on one side.

turn the wings and broil until crispy and browned, another 5 minutes.

remove the wings from the oven. If you would like to do this step ahead of time, cool the wings and refrigerate for up to 2 days; otherwise, place the wings in the prepared slow-cooker insert.

combine the remaining ingredients in a mixing bowl, pour over the wings, and turn the wings to coat with the sauce.

cover and cook on high for 3 hours, turning the wings twice during the cooking time.

serve the wings from the cooker set on warm.

serves **8**

Kielbasa in Spicy Barbecue Sauce

This recipe falls into the category of a "no brainer" for me. A few ingredients are stirred together and cooked for a few hours, delivering a dynamite appetizer to serve friends and family. Serve this smoky, spicy, bourbon-flavored appetizer as part of a Super Bowl buffet.

2 cups ketchup

½ cup firmly packed light brown sugar

1 tablespoon Worcestershire sauce

1 teaspoon Creole mustard

1 teaspoon hot sauce

1 medium onion, finely chopped

½ cup bourbon

2 pounds kielbasa or other smoked sausages, cut into ½-inch rounds

combine all the ingredients in the insert of a 3- to 5-quart slow cooker. Cover and cook on low for 4 to 5 hours, until the sausage is heated through.

serve the kielbasa from the cooker set on warm, with 6-inch skewers.

serves **8**

Little Smokeys in Barbecue Sauce

Tiny smoked sausages bathed in a sweet and spicy barbecue sauce are a terrific starter for any party. Make sure to serve these little guys with six-inch skewers, so toothpicks won't get lost in the pot like they most assuredly do! Make sure also to have a plate on the side so used skewers can be deposited there. Better to find them on the plate than between your couch cushions!

Two 16-ounce packages mini smoked sausages (Hillshire Farms is a reliable brand)

2 tablespoons canola or vegetable oil

1 medium onion, finely chopped

2 teaspoons ancho chile powder

1½ cups ketchup

One 8-ounce can tomato sauce

¼ cup molasses

2 tablespoons Worcestershire sauce

¼ cup honey

arrange the sausages in the insert of a 1½- to 3-quart slow cooker. Heat the oil in a small skillet over medium-high heat. Add the onion and chili powder and sauté until the onion is softened, about 3 minutes.

transfer the contents of the skillet to the slow-cooker insert. Add the ketchup, tomato sauce, molasses, Worcestershire, and honey and stir to blend. Cover and cook over low heat 2 to 3 hours, until the sausages are heated through.

serve the sausages from the cooker set on warm.

serves **6–8**

Main-Course Entertaining

Main courses always shine in the slow cooker, and these are just a little more elegant than typical weeknight fare. Think of these as your go-to dishes when you want to impress someone without having to baby the dish along. Most of these dishes can be prepared the day before and reheated in the slow cooker for serving.

Curried Chicken with Coconut and Basil

This curry dish is made with boneless thighs, and they soak up the rich curry flavors and coconut milk. The basil adds a fresh touch at the end. Serve this curry with condiments on the side: chutney, toasted unsweetened coconut, banana chips, hard-cooked egg, crisp crumbled bacon, green onions, and/or toasted peanuts.

4 tablespoons (½ stick) unsalted butter

18 chicken thighs, boned and skinned

1 teaspoon garam masala

2 medium onions, finely chopped

1 teaspoon freshly grated ginger

2 cloves garlic, minced

1 large Granny Smith apple, cored and cut into ½-inch dice

¼ cup all-purpose flour

2 cups chicken broth

1½ teaspoons sweet curry powder

1 cup coconut milk

¼ cup finely chopped fresh basil

Steamed rice for serving

melt 2 tablespoons of the butter in a large skillet over high heat. Sprinkle the chicken thighs with the garam masala, add to the skillet in batches, and sauté until browned on all sides. Transfer the browned pieces to the insert of a 5- to 7-quart slow cooker. Add the onions, ginger, garlic, and apple to the same skillet and sauté over medium-high heat until the onions begin to soften, about 5 minutes. Transfer the contents of the skillet to the slow-cooker insert.

melt the remaining 2 tablespoons of butter in the skillet. Add the flour and cook, for 3 minutes, whisking constantly. Gradually whisk in the chicken broth and bring the mixture to a boil.

stir in the curry powder and coconut milk. Transfer the sauce to the insert of a slow-cooker. Cover and cook on low for 6 to 8 hours, until the chicken is tender. Sprinkle the basil over the curry and stir to blend.

serve over steamed rice.

serves 6–8

Prosciutto, Fig, and Fontina Stuffed Chicken Breasts

Sweet, salty, and cheesy, these delicious stuffed chicken breasts simmer in a delicious broth flavored with balsamic vinegar. Serve the chicken with a side of polenta, risotto, or pasta to soak up the sauce.

6 chicken breast halves, skinned and boned

1½ teaspoons salt

½ teaspoon freshly ground black pepper

6 thin slices prosciutto di Parma

6 dried figs, finely chopped

Six 6-inch-long and ½-inch-thick strips Fontina cheese

2 tablespoons unsalted butter

¼ cup finely chopped shallot

2 teaspoons dried sage leaves, crushed in the palm of your hand

⅓ cup balsamic vinegar

¼ cup Ruby Port

1½ cups chicken broth

½ cup heavy cream

place the chicken shiny-side down between sheets of plastic wrap and pound it until it is uniform in thickness.

sprinkle the chicken evenly with the salt and pepper. Lay a slice of prosciutto on each chicken breast, top with the chopped fig, and lay a strip of the cheese in the center of each breast. Roll each breast up from the top, tucking in the sides and securing with a 4-inch skewer, silicone loops, or kitchen string. Arrange the stuffed breasts in the insert of a 5- to 7-quart slow cooker, wedging the chicken to fit in one layer.

heat the butter in a small skillet over medium-high heat. Add the shallot and sage and sauté until the shallot is softened. Deglaze the skillet with the vinegar and Port, scraping up any browned bits from the bottom of the pan.

transfer the contents of the skillet to the slow-cooker insert. Pour in the broth. Cover and cook on high for 2½ to 3 hours, until the chicken is cooked through (170°F on an instant-read thermometer). Carefully transfer the chicken to a serving platter and cover with aluminum foil.

transfer the sauce to a saucepan and boil until the sauce is reduced by half. Stir in the cream and heat to serving temperature.

remove the skewers, silicone loops, or kitchen string. Using a serrated knife, cut each chicken breast crosswise into 4 pieces and serve in a pool of the sauce.

serves **6**

Stuffed Chicken Parmigiana

Traditional chicken Parmigiana with breaded chicken cutlets gets a makeover in the slow cooker. The chicken is stuffed with three cheeses and then set to simmer in an oregano-spiked tomato sauce. Mama Mia, don't forget the pasta!

2 tablespoons extra-virgin olive oil

1 large onion, finely chopped

Pinch of red pepper flakes

1½ teaspoons dried oregano

½ teaspoon dried basil

½ cup dry red wine

One 28-ounce can crushed tomatoes, with their juice

6 chicken breast halves, skinned and boned

1½ teaspoons salt

½ teaspoon freshly ground black pepper

1 large egg

1 cup fresh bread crumbs

½ cup finely shredded Parmigiano-Reggiano cheese, plus additional for garnishing

½ cup finely shredded Fontina cheese

½ cup finely shredded mozzarella cheese

½ cup finely chopped fresh Italian parsley

heat the oil in a large skillet over medium-high heat. Add the onion, red pepper flakes, oregano, and basil and sauté until the onion is softened, about 3 minutes. Add the wine and boil until reduced to about 2 tablespoons. Transfer the contents of the skillet to the insert of a 5- to 7-quart slow cooker. Add the tomatoes and stir to combine.

place the chicken breasts shiny-side up between sheets of plastic wrap and pound it to a uniform thickness. Sprinkle the chicken evenly with the salt and pepper. Combine the egg, bread crumbs, cheeses, and parsley in a small bowl.

spread the mixture over the chicken breasts and roll the chicken up. Carefully place the chicken in the tomato sauce. Cover and cook for 2½ to 3 hours, until the chicken is cooked through (170°F on an instant-read thermometer). Carefully transfer the chicken from the sauce to a serving platter and cover with aluminum foil.

slice the chicken with a serrated knife and serve each breast in a pool of sauce. Garnish with additional Parmigiano-Reggiano.

serves **6**

Chicken Breasts with Cornbread Stuffing

Cornbread stuffing with nuggets of corn, jalapeño, and bell pepper gives these chicken breasts a sweet and spicy Southwestern flavor. Topped with a cheesy cilantro cream sauce, this dish is terrific for a special dinner.

6 chicken breast halves, skinned and boned

1½ teaspoons salt

⅛ teaspoon cayenne pepper

2 tablespoons unsalted butter

½ cup finely chopped sweet onion, such as Vidalia (about ½ medium onion)

1 jalapeño pepper, seeded and finely chopped

½ cup finely chopped red bell pepper

1 cup frozen white corn, defrosted and drained

1 package Jiffy cornbread mix

¼ cup sour cream

½ cup mayonnaise

2 tablespoons olive oil

1 medium onion, chopped

1 teaspoon ground cumin

½ teaspoon dried oregano

2½ cups chicken broth

2 tablespoons cornstarch

1 cup heavy cream

1 cup finely shredded mild Cheddar cheese

½ cup finely chopped fresh cilantro

place the chicken shiny-side down between sheets of plastic wrap and pound it to a uniform thickness.

sprinkle the chicken evenly with the salt and cayenne. Melt the butter in a small skillet over medium-high heat. Add the sweet onion, jalapeño, and bell pepper and sauté until the onion is softened, about 4 minutes.

transfer the vegetables to a mixing bowl and allow to cool. Add in the corn, cornbread mix, sour cream, and mayonnaise, and stir to combine. The mixture should be stiff. Spread the mixture over the chicken breasts and roll up the chicken from the top of the breast, tucking in the sides and securing with 4-inch skewers, silicone loops, or kitchen string.

arrange the chicken in the insert of a 5- to 7-quart slow cooker, wedging the chicken to fit in one layer. Heat the oil in the same skillet over medium-high heat. Add the onion, cumin, and oregano and sauté until the onion is softened, about 3 minutes. Transfer the contents of the skillet to the slow-cooker insert and add the broth.

cover and cook on high for 2½ to 3 hours, until the chicken is cooked through (170°F on an instant-read thermometer). Carefully transfer the chicken to a serving platter and cover with aluminum foil. Transfer the sauce to a saucepan and boil until reduced by half.

dissolve the cornstarch in the cream in a small bowl and whisk into the sauce. Boil, whisking constantly, until thickened. Remove the pan from the heat, add the cheese and cilantro, and stir until the cheese is melted. Taste the sauce for seasoning and adjust.

remove the skewers, silicone loops, or kitchen string. Using a serrated knife, cut each chicken breast on the diagonal into 4 pieces, and serve the meat in a pool of the sauce, with any additional sauce on the side.

serves **6**

Chicken Breasts in Port Wine Smothered with Leeks

This extraordinary dish, made from the simplest of ingredients, is one from famed chef Fredy Girardet of the restaurant Girardet in Crissiér, Switzerland. I have made this dish as a braise on the stovetop for years, but it really does well in the slow cooker. I think the sauce is even more intense and flavorful. Girardet would serve this on a bed of potato and turnip gratin, but my family loves it with Potatoes Boulangerie (page 353).

4 tablespoons (½ stick) unsalted butter

4 large leeks, finely chopped, using the white and tender green parts

Salt and freshly ground black pepper

6 chicken breast halves, boned and skinned

1 cup Ruby Port

½ cup double-strength chicken broth

½ cup heavy cream

melt the butter in a large skillet over medium-high heat. Add the leeks and season with ½ teaspoon salt and ¼ teaspoon pepper. Sauté until the leeks are fragrant, 2 to 3 minutes. Transfer the leeks to the insert of a 5- to 7-quart slow cooker.

sprinkle the chicken with 1 teaspoon salt and ¼ teaspoon pepper and place atop the leeks in the slow-cooker insert. Pour in the port and broth. Cover and cook on low for 3 hours, until the chicken is cooked through.

transfer the chicken to a serving platter and cover with aluminum foil. Pour the leeks and liquid into a saucepan and boil for 5 minutes. Stir in the cream and season with salt and pepper if needed.

cut each chicken breast on the diagonal into 4 pieces. Ladle some of the leek sauce onto a plate and top with the chicken. Spoon over some of the remaining sauce.

serves **6**

The Best Thanksgiving Turkey Breast You'll Ever Eat

This turkey breast is for all those occasions when you want to serve only white meat turkey. I use this method to cook turkey breasts when I need meat for casseroles or salads as well. If you want a dark gravy, you will need to use demi-glace, because the drippings don't get very dark in the slow cooker.

2 medium onions, quartered

2 medium carrots, cut into 1-inch lengths

2 stalks celery, cut into 1-inch lengths

2 large sprigs thyme leaves

1½ teaspoons salt

½ teaspoon freshly ground black pepper

1 cup double-strength chicken broth

4 strips thick-cut bacon

One 3- to 4-pound bone-in turkey breast

2 teaspoons Wondra or other instant blending flour (optional)

arrange the vegetables and thyme in the insert of a 5- to 7-quart slow cooker. Sprinkle with the salt and pepper and pour in the broth.

arrange the bacon on top of the turkey breast and place in the slow-cooker insert on top of the vegetables. Cover and cook on high for 3½ to 4 hours, until the turkey registers 170°F on an instant-read thermometer. Carefully transfer the turkey breast to a serving platter and discard the bacon.

cover the turkey breast with aluminum foil and allow to rest for 15 minutes. Strain the sauce through a fine-mesh sieve into a saucepan and bring to a boil. Whisk in the flour (if using) and bring back to a boil. Taste and adjust the seasoning.

slice the turkey breast and serve with the gravy.

serves **8**

Stuffed Turkey Breast Braised in Pinot Grigio

Turkey breast is a great dish for a company dinner, but all too often it comes out of the oven dried out. The slow cooker braises the turkey to perfection and ensures that it is tender and juicy. This turkey breast is boned (your butcher can do this for you, but boneless breasts are also available at the supermarket), braised in white wine, and has a sensational cornbread and prosciutto stuffing. When the breast is sliced for serving, it has a spiral of the stuffing in the middle, a perfect complement to the delicious wine sauce.

CORNBREAD AND PROSCIUTTO STUFFING

2 tablespoons unsalted butter

1 medium onion, finely chopped

6 thin slices prosciutto, cut into julienne strips

1 teaspoon dried thyme

1 teaspoon dried sage

3 cups crumbled cornbread or packaged unseasoned cornbread crumbs

½ cup golden raisins

1 cup chicken broth, plus additional if needed

1 large egg, beaten

melt the butter in a small sauté pan over medium-high heat. Add the onion, prosciutto, thyme, and sage and sauté until the onion is softened and the prosciutto begins to curl in the pan, about 3 minutes.

transfer to a mixing bowl. Add the cornbread, raisins, 1 cup broth, and egg and stir to combine. If the stuffing appears dry, add more broth until it is the consistency you like. Set aside.

One 3- to 4-pound boneless turkey breast

2 teaspoons salt

1 teaspoon freshly ground black pepper

2 medium onions, quartered

2 medium carrots, cut into 1-inch pieces

3 stalks celery, cut into 1-inch pieces

1 cup Pinot Grigio wine

1 cup double-strength chicken broth

2 tablespoons unsalted butter

2 tablespoons all-purpose flour

lay the turkey breast, skin-side down, on a flat surface. Lay a piece of plastic wrap over the turkey and pound until the meat is an even thickness, ½ to ¾ inch. Sprinkle with the salt and pepper.

spread the stuffing over the turkey breast in a ½-inch layer. Roll up the breast from the narrower end and secure using kitchen string or silicone bands. Put the vegetables in the insert of a 5- to 7-quart slow cooker and pour in the wine and broth. Top with the turkey breast.

cover and cook on high for 3½ to 4 hours, until the turkey registers 170°F on an instant-read thermometer.

transfer the turkey to a serving platter, cover with aluminum foil, and allow to rest for 15 minutes. Strain the sauce through a fine-mesh sieve into a saucepan and boil for 5 minutes to reduce the liquid slightly. Mix the butter and flour to a paste, whisk it into the sauce, and return to a boil. Taste and adjust the seasoning.

remove the string or silicone loops from the turkey breast and cut into ½-inch slices. Serve with the sauce on the side.

serves **8**

Pork Chops Smothered in Figs and Sweet Onions

Thick-cut boneless pork chops simmer here in a sweet and savory broth of onions, dried figs, Dijon mustard, and Marsala until they are fork tender. The sauce is thickened and poured over the pork chops and is served with buttered noodles for a delicious meal.

2 tablespoons unsalted butter

2 tablespoons canola or vegetable oil

Eight 1-inch-thick boneless pork loin chops

1½ teaspoons salt

½ teaspoon freshly ground black pepper

4 medium sweet onions, such as Vidalia, cut into half rounds

1 cup Marsala wine (see savvy)

½ cup Dijon mustard

24 dried figs

½ cup beef broth

¼ cup water

2 tablespoons cornstarch

heat the butter and oil in a large skillet over high heat. Sprinkle the pork with the salt and pepper and add as many as will fit in a single layer to the skillet.

brown the chops on both sides in batches and transfer to the insert of a 5- to 7-quart slow cooker. Add the onions to the skillet and sauté until they become translucent, about 10 minutes. Add the Marsala and mustard to the skillet and bring to a boil, scraping up any browned bits from the bottom of the pan. Transfer the contents of the skillet to the slow-cooker insert and add the figs and broth. Cover and cook on high for 2½ to 3 hours or on low for 5 to 6 hours.

remove the chops from the sauce and pour the sauce into a saucepan. Skim off any fat from the sauce and bring to the sauce to a boil. Mix the water and cornstarch and whisk into the sauce. Bring to a boil, whisking constantly. Taste and adjust the seasoning.

serve the chops smothered with the sauce. The chops may be returned to the slow cooker with the thickened sauce and served from the cooker set on warm.

serves 6–8

marsala savvy
Using dry or sweet fortified wines like sherry or Marsala is really the choice of the cook. I like the sweeter versions because I think they have a bit more complexity. That said, there are many people who prefer the dry versions of these wines. It's really a matter of personal choice—just make sure not to buy the "Marsala cooking wine" that is found in the vinegar/sauce section of your grocers. It's filled with salt and other flavorings.

Cranberry Cinnamon Glazed Pork Loin

This beautifully colored pork loin braises to tender perfection in a port, cranberry, and cinnamon sauce. The sauce is then thickened after cooking and served over the pork. Serve this world-class entrée on a bed of wild rice with dried apricots and almonds.

One 4-pound boneless pork loin, rolled and tied with kitchen string or silicone bands

1½ teaspoons salt

½ teaspoon freshly ground black pepper

Two 14- to 15-ounce cans of whole berry cranberry sauce

½ cup Ruby Port

2 tablespoons balsamic vinegar

Two 4-inch cinnamon sticks

1 whole clove

¼ cup water

2 tablespoons cornstarch

season the pork with the salt and pepper and put it in the insert of a 5- to 7-quart slow cooker. Mix the cranberry sauce, port, and vinegar in a bowl and pour over the pork. Add the cinnamon sticks and clove. Cover and cook on low for 5 to 6 hours, until the pork registers 165°F on an instant-read thermometer and the meat is tender.

remove the meat from the slow-cooker insert, cover with aluminum foil, and allow to rest for 15 minutes. Strain the sauce through a fine-mesh sieve into a saucepan, and bring it to a boil.

stir the water and cornstarch together, whisk into the sauce, and bring back to a boil. Taste and adjust the seasoning.

remove the string or silicone bands from the pork and cut into ½-inch-thick slices. Serve with the sauce on the side.

serves **8**

Ham with Spicy Mustard Glaze

Fully cooked smoked hams can be served directly from the refrigerator, but they are so much more delicious when they are heated in the slow cooker and the juices of the ham mingle with a glaze or flavored sauce. You will need a large five- to seven-quart slow cooker for a bone-in ham. The results are tender and full of flavor no matter which glaze you decide to use.

One year for a holiday brunch, I was in charge of the ham, and my friends were bringing the sides. I had been traveling and had gotten home the night before the brunch. Fortunately I'd purchased the ham before I left, but now what to flavor it with? I checked the fridge and found apple cider and pub mustard and thought the two would make a fine combination. I added some cinnamon, cloves, and allspice to the pot and came up with a winner.

1½ cups apple cider

One 4-ounce jar Stonewall Kitchen pub mustard or other whole-grain mustard

½ cup firmly packed light brown sugar

Two 4-inch cinnamon sticks

3 whole cloves

4 whole allspice berries

½ cup Ruby Port

Two 15-ounce cans whole berry cranberry sauce

Grated zest of 2 oranges

½ cup orange juice

One 5-pound smoked ham

combine the cider, mustard, sugar, and spices in the insert of a 5- to 7-quart slow cooker. Add the port, cranberry sauce, and orange zest and juice and stir to combine. Put the ham on top of the glaze and spoon the glaze over the top of the ham.

cover the slow cooker and cook on high for 3½ to 4 hours or on low for 8 to 9 hours, spooning the glaze over the ham a few times during the cooking process.

remove the ham from the cooker, cover with aluminum foil, and allow it to rest for 15 minutes. If you would like to thicken the glaze, skim off any excess fat, strain it through a fine-mesh sieve into a saucepan and boil, stirring frequently, until reduced to about 2 cups. (You will have a lot of liquid from the ham that has diluted the glaze.)

slice the ham and spoon the glaze over the slices.

serves 10–12

Coca-Cola Ham

Southern cooks swear by their Coca-Cola hams, which are basted with cola throughout the baking time. I decided to have some fun with this one and made a slurry pasle out of cola, brown sugar, rum, and lime juice and zest. The paste gives the ham a sweet and tart flavor, and the juices from the ham make a terrific glaze to serve with the ham.

½ cup Coca-Cola

1 cup firmly packed light brown sugar

¼ cup dark rum

2 tablespoons fresh lime juice

Grated zest of 1 lime

One 5-pound smoked ham

mix the cola, sugar, rum, and lime juice and zest in the insert of a 5- to 7-quart slow cooker. Set the ham on top of the mixture and spoon some of the glaze over the top. Cover and cook on low for 8 to 10 hours, spooning glaze over the ham a few times as it cooks.

remove the ham from the slow-cooker insert, cover with aluminum foil, and allow it to rest for 15 minutes. If you would like to reduce the glaze, spoon off any fat from the top and pour the glaze into a saucepan. Bring to a boil and continue to boil, stirring frequently, until reduced to about 2 cups. (You will have a lot of liquid from the ham that has diluted the glaze.)

slice the ham and spoon the glaze over the slices.

serves 6–8

Stuffed Lamb in Ratatouille Sauce

Boneless leg of lamb gets dressed up with a stuffing flavored with dill and feta, and then is braised in a ratatouille mixture of eggplant, bell peppers, and tomatoes. The succulent meat absorbs the flavors from Provence in the sauce. Serve this meal with mashed potatoes or cooked orzo to soak up the delicious sauce.

RATATOUILLE SAUCE

2 Japanese eggplants, ends trimmed, cut into ½-inch dice

2 teaspoons salt

½ cup extra-virgin olive oil

3 medium onions, cut into half rounds

3 cloves garlic, minced

2 medium red bell peppers, seeded, and cut into ½-inch-thick slices

2 medium yellow peppers, seeded and cut into ½-inch-thick slices

2 teaspoons herbes de Provence

Pinch of red pepper flakes

½ cup full-bodied red wine

One 14- to 15-ounce can crushed tomatoes, with their juices

1 teaspoon freshly ground black pepper

put the eggplant in a colander in the sink and sprinkle with 1 teaspoon of the salt. Shake the colander and set aside for 30 minutes. Press down to remove any excess water and pat dry with paper towels.

heat the oil in a large skillet over medium-high heat. Add the onions, garlic, eggplant, bell peppers, herbs, and red pepper flakes and sauté until the vegetables have softened, 10 to 15 minutes. Deglaze the skillet with the wine, scraping up any browned bits from the bottom of the pan. Transfer the contents of the skillet to the insert of a 5- to 7-quart slow cooker.

stir in the tomatoes, remaining 1 teaspoon salt, and the pepper. Turn the cooker on high and cover.

One 4½- to 5-pound boneless leg of lamb, fat trimmed

1½ teaspoons salt

½ teaspoon freshly ground black pepper

2 tablespoons extra-virgin olive oil

Two 10-ounce packages baby spinach

¼ cup finely chopped fresh dill

8 ounces feta cheese, crumbled

lay the leg of lamb on a cutting board, place a piece of plastic wrap over it, and pound the lamb to an even thickness of about 1 inch. Sprinkle the lamb on both sides with the salt and pepper. Heat the oil in a large skillet over high heat. Add the spinach and cook, stirring, until the spinach is wilted.

transfer the spinach to a mixing bowl and let cool slightly. Add the dill and feta and stir to combine. Spread the mixture over the boned side of the lamb and roll up the lamb from the short side. Tie the lamb with kitchen string or silicone loops and add to the slow-cooker insert.

spoon some of the sauce over the top of the meat. Cover and cook on high for 4 hours or on low for 8 to 10 hours, until the lamb is tender. Remove the lamb from the cooker, cover with aluminum foil, and allow to rest for 20 minutes. Skim off any fat from the top of the sauce. Remove the strings or loop from the meat and cut into ½-inch slices.

serve the lamb in a pool of the sauce and pass the remaining sauce in a serving dish.

serves **6–8**

Beef Stroganoff

Stroganoff was popular in the 1950s when mushrooms and sour cream were considered exotic, but today most cooks have to dust off an old cookbook to find a recipe for this classic Russian dish. The original recipes called for beef to be quickly sautéed and then cooked with mushrooms, onions, and sour cream. This recipe uses lean round steak, tenderizes it with low slow cooking, and flavors it with meaty cremini mushrooms and dried porcini. At the last minute, add the cream and serve over rice or noodles.

1½ teaspoons salt

½ teaspoon freshly ground black pepper

1 teaspoon sweet paprika

1 cup all-purpose flour

2 to 2½ pounds round steak, cut into 1-inch pieces, fat removed

4 tablespoons (½ stick) unsalted butter

1 tablespoon canola or vegetable oil

2 medium onions, cut into half rounds

1 pound cremini mushrooms, sliced

¼ cup dry red wine

2 tablespoons tomato paste

2 tablespoons Worcestershire sauce

1 cup beef broth

¼ cup dried porcini mushrooms, crumbled

1 cup heavy cream or crème fraîche

Noodles or long-grain rice for serving

mix the salt, pepper, paprika, and flour in a large plastic zipper-top bag. Add the meat, toss to coat, and shake off the excess flour. Heat the butter and oil in a large skillet over high heat. Add the meat a few pieces at a time and brown on all sides.

transfer the browned meat to the insert of a 5- to 7-quart slow cooker. Add the onions and cremini mushrooms to the skillet and sauté over medium-high heat until the vegetables are softened and the mushrooms and onions begin to color, 7 to 8 minutes.

transfer the contents of the skillet to the slow-cooker insert. Deglaze the skillet with the wine, scraping up any browned bits from the bottom of the pan. Add the tomato paste, Worcestershire, and broth and heat. Transfer the liquid to the slow-cooker insert and stir in the porcini mushrooms.

cover and cook on high for 3 hours. Stir in the cream, cover, and cook on low for an additional hour.

serve with noodles or steamed long-grain rice.

serves **8**

Breakfast or Brunch

The slow cooker makes an ideal "butler" to prepare overnight oatmeal. It's best to use nonstick cooking spray to coat the inside of the cooker when making oatmeal or egg dishes, or you can fit the insert with a liner to help with cleanup.

Overnight Oatmeal

Waking up to a steaming bowl of oatmeal from the slow cooker is as easy as just adding water and salt. The oats cook to creamy goodness, and your only job the next morning is to pour on warm cream or milk and sprinkle with cinnamon sugar. Check out the variations that follow as well.

3¾ cups old-fashioned rolled oats

8 cups water

½ teaspoon salt

4 tablespoons (½ stick) unsalted butter, cut into small pieces

2 cups milk or cream, warmed, for serving

¼ cup cinnamon sugar for serving

coat the insert of a 5- to 7-quart slow cooker with nonstick cooking spray or line the insert with a slow-cooker liner according to manufacturer's directions.

combine the oatmeal, water, and salt in the cooker. Cover and cook on low for 8 to 10 hours or on high for 3 to 4 hours, until the oats are creamy. Stir in the butter.

serve with warmed milk and cinnamon sugar.

serves **8**

GRANOLA OATMEAL

reduce the amount of oats to 3 cups and add 1 cup granola to the slow cooker. Proceed as directed.

APPLE CINNAMON OATMEAL

add 1 cup dried apples, ½ cup firmly packed brown sugar, and ½ cup apple juice or apple cider to the slow cooker. Proceed as directed.

LOADED OATMEAL

when the oatmeal is done, serve it with a condiment bar of dried fruits such as cranberries, chopped nuts, granola, wheat germ, brown sugar, and fresh fruit such as berries and bananas.

Huevos Rancheros

A savory ranchero sauce, flavored with sausage nuggets, chipotles, onion, bell peppers, and tequila, bubbles away in the slow cooker and waits for eggs to poach on top before being served for breakfast, brunch, or dinner. Don't forget the requisite margaritas and tortillas!

1 pound bulk pork breakfast sausage

2 tablespoons canola oil

2 medium onions, coarsely chopped

3 chipotle chiles in adobo, minced

1 medium red bell pepper, seeded and coarsely chopped

1 medium orange bell pepper, seeded and coarsely chopped

1 medium yellow bell pepper, seeded and coarsely chopped

1½ teaspoons ground cumin

1½ teaspoons dried oregano

¼ cup tequila

Two 28-ounce cans crushed tomatoes

Eight 6-inch corn tortillas, cut into thin strips

½ cup finely chopped fresh cilantro (see savvy)

8 large eggs

2 cups finely shredded mild Cheddar, Monterey Jack, or pepper Jack cheese, or crumbled *queso fresco*

8 warm flour or corn tortillas for serving

cook the sausage in a large skillet over high heat until it is no longer pink. Drain it and transfer it to the insert of a 5- to 7-quart slow cooker. Wipe out all the fat in the skillet, add the oil, and heat over medium-high heat. Add the onions and chipotles and sauté until the onions begin to soften, 2 to 3 minutes.

add the contents of the skillet to the slow-cooker insert. Add the bell peppers, cumin, and oregano to the skillet and sauté until the bell peppers begin to soften, 4 to 5 minutes. Add the tequila to the skillet and scrape up any browned bits from the bottom of the pan.

transfer the contents of the skillet to the slow-cooker insert. Add the tomatoes and tortilla strips and stir to combine. Cover and cook on high for 3 hours, until the sauce is thickened. Stir in the cilantro. Crack the eggs one at a time in a small bowl and place on top of the sauce, arranging the eggs so that they all fit.

sprinkle the cheese over all the eggs. Cover and cook on high for 10 to 15 minutes, until the eggs are set.

put a tortilla on each plate and gently lift an egg out of the cooker onto the tortilla. Spoon the sauce over the eggs and around the tortillas.

serves **8**

slow-cooker savvy
If you have a round slow cooker, you may only be able to poach six eggs; larger oval cookers will poach all eight.

cilantro savvy
Don't like the taste of cilantro? If it tastes like soap to you, you are not alone, for many people with an acidic pH in their systems don't enjoy cilantro. Feel free to leave it out or substitute Italian parsley.

Egg Casseroles

A *strata* is a dish of layered bread, cheese, and flavorings, covered with an egg custard and baked to golden perfection. The slow cooker makes these dishes perfectly, and they are always moist and delicious, where the oven may dry them out a bit. Your choices for flavorings can be almost anything, from leftover vegetables from last night's dinner to leftover grilled salmon. Feel free to play with the flavors here and make them your own. The only "have to" is the proportion of bread and egg custard; after that it's your palette to paint.

Frittatas are Italian dishes using eggs stirred into leftovers and cooked on the stovetop. The slow-cooker frittatas use the strata formula to help you use up leftover veggies and bread, making a terrific meal for your family or friends.

Basic Strata

Strata are layers of bread, soaked with an egg and milk mixture and baked with cheese. This is the basic formula. Feel free to add your own flavors to the basic recipe.

8 cups torn or cubed (1-inch) stale bread, tough crusts removed

3½ to 4 cups shredded cheese

10 large eggs

3 cups milk

1½ teaspoons salt

½ teaspoon hot sauce

coat the insert of a 5- to 7-quart slow cooker with nonstick cooking spray or line it with a slow-cooker liner according to the manufacturer's directions.

spread a layer of the bread into the slow cooker and sprinkle with some of the cheese. Continue layering the bread and cheese until it has all been used, saving some cheese for the top.

whisk together the eggs, milk, salt, and hot sauce in a large bowl. Pour the mixture over the cheese and bread and push it down to make sure the bread becomes saturated. Sprinkle the remaining cheese over the top.

cover and cook on low for 4 hours, until the strata is cooked through (170°F on an instant-read thermometer). Remove the lid and cook for an additional 30 minutes.

serve the strata from the cooker set on warm.

serves 8–10

Croque Monsieur Strata

A toasted ham and cheese sandwich in France is called a *Croque Monsieur*. Generally made with Gruyère cheese and high-quality French ham on delicious bread, it is one of my favorites for lunch. This strata takes the combination and makes it into a delicious brunch dish. It is terrific served with a green salad; a vinaigrette on the salad will cut the richness of the ingredients, making this a wonderful way to start your weekend.

8 large eggs

2 cups whole or low-fat milk

6 shakes Tabasco sauce

1 tablespoon Dijon mustard

8 cups torn soft-crusted French bread, (if the crust is crispy, remove it and use the center of the bread)

8 ounces sliced Black Forest ham, cut into matchsticks

3 cups shredded Gruyère cheese

4 tablespoons (½ stick) unsalted butter, melted

coat the insert of a 5- to 7-quart slow cooker with nonstick cooking spray or line the insert with a slow-cooker liner according the manufacturer's directions.

whisk together the eggs, milk, Tabasco, and mustard in a large bowl until blended. Add the bread and ham to the bowl and stir to saturate the bread and distribute the ham.

spoon half the bread mixture into the slow cooker and sprinkle with half the cheese. Repeat the layers and drizzle with the melted butter.

cover and cook on low for 4 hours, until the strata is cooked through (170°F on an instant-read thermometer). Remove the lid and cook for an additional 30 minutes.

serve the strata from the cooker set on warm.

serves **8**

Salmon and Dill Strata

Not quite bagels with lox, this strata uses leftover grilled or poached salmon, and bagels as the bread. If you have no bagels on hand, egg bread or a white bread with some structure, like Pepperidge Farm, would be fine.

6 large eggs

1 cup whole or low-fat milk

1 cup sour cream (low fat is okay), plus additional for serving

3 cups cooked salmon in chunks

¼ cup chopped fresh dill

¼ cup finely chopped red onion

2 teaspoons grated lemon zest

½ teaspoon freshly ground white pepper

6 plain or egg bagels, cut into ½-inch pieces

One 8-ounce package cream cheese, cut into ½-inch cubes

½ cup drained and chopped capers for serving

Lemon wedges for serving

coat the insert of a 5- to 7-quart slow cooker with nonstick cooking spray or line the insert with a slow-cooker liner according the manufacturer's directions.

whisk together the eggs, milk, and sour cream in a large mixing bowl until smooth. Fold in the salmon, dill, onion, lemon zest, and pepper. Add the bagel pieces and mix, saturating the bread.

transfer half the mixture to the slow cooker and dot with half the cream cheese cubes. Repeat the layers. Cover and cook on low for 4 hours, until the strata is cooked through (170°F on an instant-read thermometer). Remove the lid and cook for an additional 30 minutes.

serve the strata from the cooker set on warm with the additional sour cream, capers, and the lemon wedges on the side.

serves 6–8

Sausage and Hash-Brown Casserole

This south-of-the-border dish is filled with nuggets of sausage, cheese, and green chiles. A great wake-up call any day of the week, it also makes a fine light dinner along with a fruit salad and corn muffins.

1½ pounds bulk pork sausage

2 medium onions, finely chopped

1 Anaheim chile, cored, seeded and finely chopped

1 medium red bell pepper, seeded and finely chopped

1 teaspoon ground cumin

½ teaspoon dried oregano

One 16-ounce package frozen shredded hash brown potatoes, defrosted, or 2 cups fresh shredded hash browns

6 large eggs, beaten

1 cup milk

1 cup mayonnaise

1 cup prepared salsa (your choice of heat)

2 cups shredded mild Cheddar cheese, or 1 cup shredded mild Cheddar mixed with 1 cup shredded pepper Jack cheese.

coat the insert of a 5- to 7-quart slow cooker with nonstick cooking spray or line the insert with a slow-cooker liner according the manufacturer's directions.

cook the sausage in a large skillet over high heat until it is no longer pink, breaking up any large pieces with the side of a spoon.

remove all but 1 tablespoon of fat from the pan and heat over medium-high heat. Add the onions, chile, bell pepper, cumin, and oregano and sauté until the onions are softened and translucent, 5 to 6 minutes. Transfer the mixture to a bowl and allow to cool.

add the potatoes to the bowl and stir to blend. In a smaller bowl, whisk together the eggs, milk, and mayonnaise. Pour over the sausage and potato mixture and stir to combine.

transfer half the mixture to the slow-cooker insert, then cover with half the salsa and half the cheese. Repeat the layers with the remaining ingredients. Cover and cook on high for 2½ to 3 hours, until the casserole is puffed, and cooked through (170°F on an instant-read thermometer). Remove the cover and allow the frittata to rest for 30 minutes.

serve from the cooker set on warm.

serves **8**

Zucchini and Leek Frittata

Delicate leeks and shredded zucchini flavor this delicate frittata, with tangy goat cheese and basil.

4 tablespoons (½ stick) unsalted butter

2 leeks, finely chopped, using the white and some of the tender green parts

3 cups grated zucchini, coarsely shredded

¼ cup finely chopped fresh basil

1½ teaspoons salt

½ teaspoon hot sauce

8 cups torn stale firm bread cubes

12 ounces goat cheese, crumbled

10 large eggs

3 cups milk

¼ cup finely chopped fresh chives for garnishing

coat the insert of a 5- to 7-quart slow cooker with nonstick cooking spray or line the insert with a slow-cooker liner according the manufacturer's directions.

melt the butter in a medium skillet over medium-high heat. Add the leeks, zucchini, and basil and sauté until the moisture in the pan has evaporated. Season with the salt and hot sauce and let cool to room temperature.

place half the bread in the slow-cooker insert and spread half the zucchini mixture over the bread. Top with half the goat cheese. Repeat the layers with the remaining bread, zucchini mixture, and goat cheese. Whisk together the eggs and milk in a large bowl. Pour into the slow-cooker insert and press down on the ingredients to saturate the bread. Cover and cook on low for 4 hours, until cooked through (170°F on an instant-read thermometer). Remove the lid and cook for an additional 30 minutes.

garnish with the chives and serve from the cooker set on warm. (The warm setting will keep this at a constant temperature without drying it out, making it a great dish for a brunch.)

serves 8–10

Side Dishes for Entertaining

Side dishes make the meal. If your stovetop and oven are taken up with other chores, the slow cooker comes to the rescue with some delicious options that can be served directly from the pot.

Green Beans with Cippolini Onions and Cremini Mushrooms

Tiny cippolini onions and meaty cremini mushrooms slowly simmer in this dish along with green beans in a soy and garlic butter sauce. This makes a great side dish to serve at the holidays or for a family get-together. Cold leftover beans may be made into a salad by tossing them with oil and rice vinegar.

½ cup (1 stick) unsalted butter, melted

¼ cup soy sauce

2 tablespoons rice wine (mirin) or dry sherry

2 cloves garlic, minced

24 cippolini onions, peeled

8 ounces cremini mushrooms, quartered

2 pounds green beans, ends trimmed, cut into 1-inch lengths

combine the butter, soy sauce, rice wine, and garlic into the insert of a 5- to 7-quart slow cooker and stir to blend.

add the remaining ingredients and toss to coat with the butter mixture. Cover and cook on low for 4 to 5 hours, until the beans and onions are tender.

drain the liquid from the vegetables and serve the vegetables immediately.

serves 6–8

Stuffed Artichokes

This recipe is from my childhood. My mom would stuff artichokes and braise them on the stovetop; the smells at my house were nothing like the tuna noodle smells at my friends' homes. The garlicky, cheesy bread stuffing would stick to the leaves of the artichokes, and the best part was finally getting to eat those delicious hearts. The slow cooker makes this recipe even simpler since you don't have to watch them as they cook. The artichokes are terrific either hot or at room temperature and make a great starter or side dish.

½ cup extra-virgin olive oil

1½ cups dry white wine or vermouth

2 cloves garlic, peeled

6 black peppercorns

Juice of 1 lemon

6 large globe artichokes, tough outer leaves peeled away, stems trimmed flush with the bottom

4 cups fresh bread crumbs

½ cup grated Parmesan cheese

1½ cups grated Romano cheese

4 cloves garlic, minced

Grated zest of 1 lemon

¼ cup finely chopped fresh basil

¼ cup finely chopped fresh Italian parsley

1 teaspoon freshly ground black pepper

combine ¼ cup of the oil, the wine, garlic, peppercorns, and lemon juice in the insert of a 5- to 7-quart slow cooker. Using your fingers, loosen the artichoke leaves so there are spaces for the stuffing between them. Combine the bread crumbs, cheeses, garlic, lemon zest, basil, parsley, and pepper in a small bowl.

push the stuffing, using a spoon, into the spaces between the leaves; the artichokes will begin to get fatter the more stuffing you put in. Arrange the artichokes in the slow-cooker insert and drizzle with the remaining ¼ cup oil. Cover and cook on low for 5 hours, until a leaf can be easily released and the artichoke heart is tender when pierced with the tip of a sharp knife.

serve the artichokes warm or at room temperature as a first course or a side dish.

serves **6**

Wine-Braised Artichokes

When it's artichoke season in the Salinas valley, I rev up the slow cooker for braised globe artichokes. Lemon, thyme, bay leaves, white wine, peppercorns, and garlic infuse the artichokes with a delicious flavor. Serve the whole artichokes as a starter or as a side dish with grilled meats, poultry, or seafood, accompanied by a garlic mayonnaise or lemon butter. Leftover artichokes may be refrigerated for up to two days.

2 large lemons, cut into quarters

2 bay leaves

1 teaspoon dried thyme

2 cups dry white wine or vermouth

10 black peppercorns

6 cloves garlic, peeled

6 large globe artichokes, tough outer leaves peeled away, stems trimmed flush with the bottom

squeeze the lemons into the insert of a 5- to 7-quart slow cooker. Add the lemon rinds, bay leaves, thyme, wine, peppercorns, and garlic.

arrange the artichokes stem-side down in the slow-cooker insert. Cover and cook on low for 4½ to 5 hours, until the leaves release easily and the heart is tender when pierced with the tip of a sharp knife.

remove the artichoke hearts from the cooker and serve hot or at room temperature.

serves **6**

artichoke savvy
To remove the choke from the artichoke, gently separate the middle leaves with your fingers until the tiny leaves that cover the choke are exposed. Pull the tiny leaves off to expose the choke. Using a teaspoon, gently scrape the choke off the artichoke bottom.

Shaved Brussels Sprouts with Pancetta

I have to admit, as a child Brussels sprouts were not a favorite, even though my mother would lovingly slow-sauté them in garlic-infused olive oil. It wasn't until I discovered the difference made by separating the leaves that I become a fan. Adding crispy pancetta, an Italian salt-cured pork, sealed the deal! The sprouts are delicious hot, warm, or at room temperature.

½ cup extra-virgin olive oil

3 ounces pancetta, finely chopped
(see savvy)

3 cloves garlic, sliced

2 pounds Brussels sprouts, ends trimmed,
cut into quarters, and leaves separated

1½ teaspoons salt

½ teaspoon freshly ground black pepper

heat the oil in a medium sauté pan over high heat. Add the pancetta and cook until crispy. Remove it to paper towels to drain. Add the garlic to the pan and cook over low heat until it begins to turn golden, being careful not to let it get brown.

pour the oil and garlic into the insert of a 5- to 7-quart slow cooker. Stir in the sprouts, salt, and pepper. cover and cook on high for 1 hour, until the leaves are tender. Stir in the pancetta and cook for another 30 minutes.

serve hot or at room temperature.

serves **6**

pancetta savvy
If pancetta isn't available, finely diced prosciutto may be substituted.

Diva Mashed Potatoes

When do ordinary mashed potatoes become "diva" mashed potatoes? When you can make them ahead of time and then heat them in a slow cooker. These mashed potatoes are similar to the ultimate mashed potatoes (page 351) in their preparation, but they have all the delicious additions of a loaded baked potato.

8 large russet potatoes, peeled and cut into 1-inch chunks

4 tablespoons (½ stick) unsalted butter

1 cup finely shredded mild Cheddar cheese

One 8-ounce package cream cheese at room temperature

1 cup sour cream

4 green onions, finely chopped, using the white and tender green parts

8 strips bacon, cooked crisp, drained, and crumbled

Salt and freshly ground black pepper

coat the insert of a 5- to 7-quart slow cooker with nonstick cooking spray or line with a slow-cooker liner according to the manufacturer's directions.

cook the potatoes in salted water to cover until tender when pierced with the tip of a sharp knife. Drain the potatoes thoroughly and place in the bowl of an electric mixer.

add 2 tablespoons of the butter, ½ cup of the Cheddar, the cream cheese, and sour cream and beat until fluffy and light. Stir in the green onions and bacon and season with salt and pepper. Transfer the potato mixture to the slow-cooker insert and top with the remaining butter and cheese.

cover and cook on low for 3 to 4 hours, until the butter is melted and the potatoes are heated through.

serve the potatoes from the cooker set on warm.

serves **8**

Grown-Up Mac and Cheese

Although there are mac and cheese recipes elsewhere in this book, this one is so special that you should serve it only to your very closest friends. Filled with gourmet cheeses and a sauce flavored with brandy, this dish is special as a side or light dinner entrée.

1 pound elbow pasta, cooked in salted water till al dente and drained

¼ cup (½ stick) unsalted butter

4 medium shallots, finely chopped

3 tablespoons all-purpose flour

1 tablespoon Dijon mustard

1½ cups milk

1 cup heavy cream

¼ cup brandy

2½ cups shredded Gruyère cheese

¾ cup shredded Comté cheese

¾ cup shredded Manchego cheese

½ teaspoon Tabasco sauce

coat the insert of a 5- to 7-quart slow cooker with nonstick cooking spray. Put a layer of the pasta in the insert. Melt the butter in a medium sauce panover medium-high heat. Add the shallots and sauté until they begin to soften, about 3 minutes. Add the flour and cook, whisking constantly, for 3 minutes. Whisk in the mustard, milk, cream, and brandy and bring the sauce to a boil while continuing to whisk.

remove the sauce from the heat, add 1½ cups of the Gruyère and ¼ cup each of the Comté and Manchego cheeses and the Tabasco, and stir until the cheeses melt. Spoon some of the sauce over the pasta in the insert, then sprinkle with some of the remaining cheeses, reserving some of the Gruyère for the top. Continue to layer the pasta, sauce, and cheese, ending with the Gruyère.

cover and cook on high for 2 hours, until the mac and cheese is heated through and bubbling. Remove the cover and cook for another 30 minutes. If you would like a crunchy top, fire up your crème brûlée torch and brown the cheese on the surface.

serve the mac and cheese from the cooker set on warm.

serves **8**

Entertaining Desserts

The end of the meal is what your guests will probably remember long after your party, so make sure to serve something that is show-stopping, whether it's a decadent hot fudge cake topped with caramel ice cream, fruits slow cooked in syrup, or a bread pudding filled with delicious flavors. These desserts all fit into the category of simple-but-delicious, and the best news is that the slow cooker will do all the work, leaving you more time to tend to the other parts of the meal.

Hot Fudge Sundae Sauce

There is nothing better than a decadent hot fudge sauce to serve over ice cream, cake, or bread pudding. This recipe is simple, and the results are spectacular. The sauce can be made in a 1½- to 3-quart slow cooker and any leftover hot fudge sauce may be refrigerated for up to two weeks or frozen for up to six months.

1 cup (2 sticks) unsalted butter, melted

8 ounces unsweetened chocolate, grated

3 cups sugar

2 cups evaporated milk

put all the ingredients in the insert of a 1½- to 3-quart slow cooker and whisk to blend the sugar into the butter and milk. Cover and cook on low for 2 hours, stirring once during the cooking time to distribute the melted chocolate.

serve from the cooker set on warm.

Makes about **6** cups

Bananas Foster Bread Pudding

Bananas Foster was made famous at Brennan's Restaurant in New Orleans. There are many versions of this flambéed dessert, but I love to make it into a bread pudding filled with bananas, brown sugar, and dark rum. Serve the bread pudding with a dollop of unsweetened whipped cream.

½ cup (1 stick) unsalted butter

2 cups firmly packed light brown sugar

4 medium bananas, cut into ½-inch rounds

8 large eggs

3 cups heavy cream

¼ cup dark rum

1 teaspoon ground cinnamon

1 tablespoon vanilla extract or vanilla bean paste

8 cups 1-inch cubes stale challah, egg bread, or Hawaiian sweet egg bread

¼ cup cinnamon sugar

Whipped cream for serving

coat the insert of a 5- to 7-quart slow cooker with nonstick cooking spray or line the insert with a slow-cooker liner according to the manufacturer's directions.

melt the butter in a large skillet over medium-high heat. Add 1 cup of the sugar and heat, stirring, until the sugar melts. Add the bananas and stir to coat. Remove the skillet from the heat and allow the bananas to cool slightly.

whisk together the eggs, cream, remaining 1 cup sugar, rum, cinnamon, and vanilla in a large bowl. Add the bread to the custard and stir to blend, making sure to saturate the bread. Spoon half of the custard-soaked bread into the cooker and top with half the bananas. Repeat the layers, ending with the bananas.

sprinkle the top with the cinnamon sugar. Cover and cook on high for about 3 hours, until puffed and an instant-read thermometer registers 185°F. Allow the pudding to cool for about 30 minutes.

serve with whipped cream.

serves 8

Ginger Cheesecake

Although I don't use the slow cooker often to bake cakes that could go into the oven, this cheesecake is not only incredibly smooth, but the steam from the cooker gives it an enhanced texture. Infusing the batter with the crystallized ginger will require an extra step, but the results are worth the time. You will need to use a rack for the inside your slow cooker and a six-inch springform pan that is three inches deep.

CRUST

1 cup crushed gingersnaps

4 tablespoons (½ stick) unsalted butter, melted

2 tablespoons light brown sugar

coat the inside of a 6-inch-wide and 3-inch-deep springform pan with nonstick cooking spray. Put the cookie crumbs, butter, and sugar in a mixing bowl and stir until well combined.

pat the mixture over the bottom and up the sides of the prepared pan.

BATTER

½ cup heavy cream

2 teaspoons crystallized ginger, finely chopped (see savvy)

Two 8-ounce packages cream cheese at room temperature

¾ cup sugar

2 large eggs

2 tablespoons all-purpose flour

½ cup sour cream

1 teaspoon orange extract

Orange slices for garnishing

put the cream and ginger in a small saucepan and bring to a boil. Turn off the heat and let the ginger steep in the cream.

cream the cream cheese and sugar in the bowl of an electric mixer until smooth. Add the eggs, one at a time, and beat until smooth. Add the flour and beat to incorporate. Strain the ginger cream through a fine-mesh sieve and add it to the batter along with the sour cream and orange extract. Beat until the mixture is light and fluffy. Pour the batter into the crust and smooth the top with an offset spatula.

pour ½ inch of water in the insert of a 5- to 7-quart slow cooker and arrange a rack in the bottom. Place the cheese-cake on the rack, cover, and cook on high for 2 to 2½ hours. Remove the cover, turn off the slow cooker, and allow the cheesecake to cool for 2 hours. Remove from the slow cooker, then cover and refrigerate overnight.

remove the cheesecake from the refrigerator 1 hour before serving. Release the sides of the springform pan and remove the cake from the bottom, using a long offset spatula.

transfer the cake to a serving platter or a cutting board. Dip a chef's knife into hot water, wipe dry, and cut the cheesecake into wedges, dipping the knife into hot water after each cut.

serve each piece of cheesecake garnished with orange slices.

serves 8–10

ginger savvy
To keep the ginger from sticking to your knife, coat the knife with nonstick cooking spray.

Pumpkin Maple Bread Pudding

Pumpkin and maple are two of my favorite flavors during the fall, and this bread pudding is a terrific dessert to serve during the holidays. The slow cooker will keep it warm for you until it's time for dessert. Serve this with whipped cream flavored with maple syrup.

1½ cups heavy cream

One 16-ounce can pumpkin purée (2 cups)

4 large eggs

½ cup maple syrup

½ cup firmly packed light brown sugar

2 teaspoons ground cinnamon

¼ teaspoon ground cloves

¼ teaspoon freshly grated nutmeg

⅛ teaspoon ground ginger

9 cups torn egg bread or leftover croissants

coat the insert of a 5- to 7-quart slow cooker with nonstick cooking spray or line with a slow-cooker liner according to the manufacturer's directions.

whisk all the ingredients except the bread in a large mixing bowl until smooth. Add the bread to the bowl and stir to soak the bread. Transfer the mixture to the slow-cooker insert. Cover and cook on high for about 3½ hours, until puffed and an instant-read thermometer registers 185°F. Allow the pudding to rest for about 30 minutes.

serve from the cooker set on warm.

serves **8**

Stewed Figs in Port Wine with Point Reyes Blue Cheese

Fresh figs are a luxury, but if you live in an area where you can find them, I urge you to try this delicious recipe. Bathed in a port wine syrup, the figs are plump and caramelized when they emerge from the slow cooker. A bit of Point Reyes or your favorite blue cheese and some toasted walnuts make the perfect accompaniment.

1½ cups Ruby Port

1 cup firmly packed light brown sugar

2 whole cloves

12 fresh figs

1½ cups crumbled Point Reyes blue cheese

1 cup chopped toasted walnuts

combine the port, sugar, and cloves in the insert of a 5- to 7-quart slow cooker. Add the figs stem-end up to the slow-cooker insert and spoon some of the syrup over the figs. Cover and cook on low for 1½ to 2 hours. Allow the figs to cool in the syrup for 1 hour.

remove the figs to a serving platter. Strain the syrup through a fine-mesh sieve into a saucepan and boil for 5 to 10 minutes until it is thickened. Allow the syrup to cool slightly.

arrange 2 figs in a pool of the syrup on each plate. Sprinkle with the crumbled blue cheese and toasted walnuts before serving.

serves 6

NOLA Bread Pudding with Whiskey Sauce

New Orleans is famous for its bread pudding, and each restaurant has its spin on this classic dessert. The famed bread pudding soufflé from Commander's Palace is a guilty pleasure, but any bread pudding is comfort food for the soul. This bread pudding is made with a rich custard flavored with cinnamon, vanilla, and nutmeg, but remember that this is just a template for you to follow. Have fun and add your own personal touches. Don't forget the whiskey sauce!

8 cups torn stale bread (a soft-crusted baguette works well as does sturdy white bread, such as Pepperidge Farm)

2½ cups heavy cream

6 large egg yolks

1 cup sugar

½ cup bourbon

½ cup milk

2 teaspoons vanilla extract or vanilla bean paste

1 teaspoon ground cinnamon

½ teaspoon freshly ground nutmeg

2 tablespoons unsalted butter, melted

Whiskey Sauce (recipe follows) for serving

coat the inside of a 5- to 7-quart slow cooker with nonstick cooking spray or line the insert with a slow-cooker liner according to the manufacturers directions.

put the bread in a large mixing bowl. In another bowl, whisk together the cream, egg yolks, sugar, bourbon, milk, vanilla, cinnamon, and nutmeg. Pour the mixture over the bread and stir to saturate the bread. Transfer the bread mixture to the slow-cooker insert and drizzle with the butter. Cover and cook on high for 4 hours, then remove the cover and cook for another 30 minutes.

serve with the whiskey sauce.

serves 8–10

WHISKEY SAUCE

½ cup (1 stick) unsalted butter

1½ cups firmly packed light brown sugar

2 cups heavy cream

¼ cup whiskey or bourbon

melt the butter in a saucepan over medium-high heat. Add the sugar and heat, stirring, until the sugar begins to bubble. Stir in the heavy cream and bring to a boil. Turn off the heat and stir in the bourbon.

serve the sauce warm over bread pudding, or let cool completely and refrigerate for up to 1 week.

makes about 3 cups

Cherries Jubilee Lava Cake

As a child, sitting in a fancy restaurant, when I saw the waiter pulling up to the table with a chafing dish on a cart, I knew one of two desserts was coming my way: crepes suzette or cherries jubilee. The brandy-flamed cherries, bathed in a spiked buttery sauce and served over vanilla ice cream, were my reward for not asking "Are we done yet?" I've taken that delicious dessert one step further by adding chocolate cake and sauce. The cherries bake underneath the hot fudge cake. Make sure to serve this with good-quality vanilla ice cream.

CHERRIES

Two 16-ounce bags frozen unsweetened pitted sweet cherries, defrosted and drained

¼ cup sugar

2 tablespoons cornstarch

2 tablespoons brandy or Grand Marnier

CHOCOLATE CAKE

½ cup milk

3 tablespoons unsalted butter, melted

1 teaspoon vanilla bean paste

1 cup granulated sugar

1 cup all-purpose flour

½ cup cocoa powder (make sure to use natural cocoa powder, not Dutch process)

2 teaspoons baking powder

¾ cup firmly packed light brown sugar

1¼ cups boiling water

coat the insert for a 3½- to 4-quart slow cooker with nonstick cooking spray. Add all the cherries, sugar, cornstarch, and brandy to the slow-cooker insert and stir to combine.

stir together the milk, butter, and vanilla bean paste in a mixing bowl. Gradually stir in the granulated sugar, flour, ¼ cup of the cocoa powder, and the baking powder.

spread the batter evenly over the cherries in the slow-cooker insert. Mix together the brown sugar and remaining ¼ cup cocoa powder in a small bowl and sprinkle evenly over the batter. Pour in the boiling water (do not stir).

cover and cook on high for 2 hours, until a skewer inserted into the center comes out clean. Uncover and allow to cool for about 20 minutes.

serve spooned from the slow cooker, so the cherries are a surprise resting on top of the cake.

serves 4–6

Acknowledgments

No one writes a book by themselves, and writing this book was much like the recipes in it; a long slow simmer, with lots of ingredients to add salt and spice to the dish. I would be remiss if I didn't recognize my amazing agent Susan Ginsburg, who not only leaps tall buildings in a single bound, but she's also a great girl friend, listening and giving good advice on all subjects; thank you, Susan, I am so grateful for all that you do for me. Susan's assistant Bethany Strout has kept me sane with the details and answering myriad random questions.

At Chronicle, a huge thanks you to Bill LeBlond for taking me into the family and steering this book on its path. Thanks also to my editors Amy Treadwell who guided me through the first half and Sarah Billingsley who has ably shaped and continued provide great suggestions for the finalized manuscript. Great thanks also to Barbara Otterhoff for copyediting, and Randy Mon for the terrific food styling, and James Baigrie for the beautiful photographs. Thanks also to David Hawk and Peter Perez for their terrific marketing and publicity suggestions; it's a pleasure to work with you two! To Doug Ogan, Beth Steiner, Michael Morris, Rachel Pedersen and all the other hard-working people at Chronicle, a toast for your terrific work!

I would like to thank the manufacturers' who sent me their machines to test the recipes. Lisa Callaghan at All-Clad was nothing but supportive when she heard about my project and provided me opportunities to demonstrate the All-Clad slow cooker, for which I am grateful. Thanks to Cuisinart and the team at Rachel Litner Associates who provided the Cuisinart machine for testing and were gracious in sending me supplemental materials, and thank you to Kim Roman at Digitas, and KitchenAid for the use of their machine in testing.

My family and extended family have been such a support, and all those test recipes don't get critiqued without the presence of my stalwart and delightful husband who has eaten more disasters than I'd care to count—thanks Dr. Chuck you won't have to eat anymore braised dinners for a while, but I know that another pot roast is only eight hours away! Our children, Carrie, Ryan, and Eric, have been such great cheerleaders no matter what I've been up to in the kitchen and I love that they still enjoy whatever Mom is cooking when they return home. Thanks also to my girl friend Lora Brody for blessing this project and being a great friend, who shares my passion for sports, great food, and wine. Big bear-hug for my friend Rick Rodgers who supported my efforts in writing this book—thanks Rick, you are one of the most generous people in this industry. My trusted recipe tester Robin Cox was always available to give feedback and honest evaluations for each recipe; watch out when she graduates from culinary school! My extended family of cooking-school owners, their managers, staff, and students make what I do a pleasure and although space doesn't allow me to name them all, I am privileged to come into their kitchens and do something that I love—life doesn't get much better than that! I toast each and every one who has welcomed me into their school and made me feel at home on the road.

Lastly, dear reader, I want to thank you for buying this book, and for trusting me in your kitchen. If you have problems, or want to chat, please visit my Web site, www.dianephillips.com. Now, let's eat!

A

B

Table of Equivalents

The exact equivalents in the following tables have been rounded for convenience.

LIQUID/DRY MEASURES

U.S.	Metric
¼ teaspoon	1.25 milliliters
½ teaspoon	2.5 milliliters
1 teaspoon	5 milliliters
1 tablespoon (3 teaspoons)	15 milliliters
1 fluid ounce (2 tablespoons)	30 milliliters
¼ cup	60 milliliters
⅓ cup	80 milliliters
½ cup	120 milliliters
1 cup	240 milliliters
1 pint (2 cups)	480 milliliters
1 quart (4 cups, 32 ounces)	960 milliliters
1 gallon (4 quarts)	3.84 liters
1 ounce (by weight)	28 grams
1 pound	454 grams
2.2 pounds	1 kilogram

LENGTH

U.S.	Metric
⅛ inch	3 millimeters
¼ inch	6 millimeters
½ inch	12 millimeters
1 inch	2.5 centimeters

OVEN TEMPERATURE

Fahrenheit	Celsius	Gas
250	120	½
275	140	1
300	150	2
325	160	3
350	180	4
375	190	5
400	200	6
425	220	7
450	230	8
475	240	9
500	260	10